WORDS, IDEAS, WORLDS

Photo courtesy of Ram Amit

WORDS, IDEAS, WORLDS

BIBLICAL ESSAYS IN HONOUR OF YAIRAH AMIT

Edited by

Athalya Brenner and Frank H. Polak

SHEFFIELD PHOENIX PRESS

2012

Copyright © 2012 Sheffield Phoenix Press

Published by Sheffield Phoenix Press
Department of Biblical Studies, University of Sheffield
45 Victoria Street
Sheffield S3 7QB

www.sheffieldphoenix.com

A CIP catalogue record for this book
is available from the British Library

Typeset by Forthcoming Publications
Printed by Lightning Source

ISBN 978-1-907534-50-8
ISSN 1747-9614

CONTENTS

ABBREVIATIONS

AASF	Annales Academiae scientiarum fennicae
AASOR	Annual of the American Schools of Oriental Research
AB	Anchor Bible
ABRL	Anchor Bible Reference Library
ADPV	Abhandlungen des Deutschen Palästina-Vereins
AnOr	Analecta Orientalia
AOAT	Alter Orient und Altes Testament
BA	*Biblical Archaeologist*
BASOR	*Bulletin of the American Schools of Oriental Research*
BEAJT	Beiträge zur Erforschung des Alten Testaments und des antiken Judentums
BETL	Bibliotheca ephemeridum theologicarum lovaniensium
BibInt	*Biblical Interpretation*
BM	*Beit Mikra*
BN	*Biblische Notizen*
BWANT	Beiträge zur Wissenschaft vom Alten und Neuen Testament
BWAT	Beiträge zur Wissenschaft vom Alten Testament
BZAW	Beihefte zur Zeitschrift für die alttestamentliche Wissenschaft
CAD	Ignace I. Gelb et al. (eds.), *The Assyrian Dictionary of the Oriental Institute of the University of Chicago* (Chicago: Oriental Institute, 1964–)
CANE	J. Sasson (ed.), *Civilizations of the Ancient Near East* (4 vols. New York: Scribners, 1995)
CAT	Manfred Dietrich, Oswald Loretz, Joaquin Sanmartín (eds.), *The Cuneiform Alphabetic texts from Ugarit, Ras Ibn Hani and Other Places* (Abhandlungen zur Literatur Alt-Syrien-Palästinas 8; Munster: Ugarit-Verlag, 1995)
CBQ	*Catholic Biblical Quarterly*
DJD	Discoveries in the Judaean Desert
DSD	*Dead Sea Discoveries*
ETL	*Ephemerides theologicae lovanienses*
FAT	Forschungen zum Alten Testament
FOTL	Forms of the Old Testament Literature
HAT	Handbuch zum Alten Testament
HKAT	Handkommentar zum Alten Testament
HSM	Harvard Semitic Monographs

HTR	*Harvard Theological Review*
HUCA	*Hebrew Union College Annual*
ICC	International Critical Commentary
ITL	International Theological Library
JAB	*Journal for the Aramaic Bible*
JANER	*Journal of Ancient Near Eastern Religions*
JANES	*Journal of the Ancient Near Eastern Society*
JAOS	*Journal of the American Oriental Society*
JBL	*Journal of Biblical Literature*
JJS	*Journal of Jewish Studies*
JNES	*Journal of Near Eastern Studies*
JQR	*Jewish Quarterly Review*
JSOT	*Journal for the Study of the Old Testament*
JSOTSup	Journal for the Study of the Old Testament, Supplement Series
JSS	*Journal of Semitic Studies*
KAI	H. Donner and W. Röllig, *Kanaanäische und aramäische Inschriften* (3 vols.; Wiesbaden: Harrassowitz, 1962–64)
KHAT	Kurzer Hand-commentar zum Alten Testament
KTU	Manfred Dietrich, Oswald Loretz, Joaquin Sanmartín (eds.), *Die Keilalphabetischen Texte aus Ugarit: einschliesslich der Keil-alphabetischen Texte ausserhalb Ugarits* (Alter Orient und Altes Testament 24; Kevelaer: Butzon und Bercker; Neukirchen–Vluyn: Neukirchener Verlag, 1976)
LHBOTS	Library of Hebrew Bible/Old Testament Studies
NICOT	New International Commentary on the Old Testament
OBO	Orbis biblicus et orientalis
OTL	Old Testament Library
OTS	Old Testament Studies
RBL	*Review of Biblical Literature*
SAAS	State Archives of Assyria Studies
SBLSCS	Society of Biblical Literature Septuagint and Cognate Studies
SBLSemSt	Society of Biblical Literature Semeia Studies
SBLWAW	Society of Biblical Literature Writings from the Ancient World
STDJ	*Studies on the Texts of the Desert of Judah*
TSK	*Theologische Studien und Kritiken*
UF	*Ugarit-Forschungen*
VT	*Vetus Testamentum*
VTSup	Vetus Testamentum, Supplements
WBC	Word Biblical Commentary
WMANT	Wissenschaftliche Monographien zum Alten und Neuen Testament
ZA	*Zeitschrift für Assyriologie*
ZAW	*Zeitschrift für die alttestamentliche Wissenschaft*
ZDPV	*Zeitschrift des deutschen Palästina-Vereins*

LIST OF CONTRIBUTORS

Ehud Ben Zvi, University of Alberta

Athalya Brenner, Tel Aviv University/University of Amsterdam

Diana Edelman, University of Sheffield

Cynthia Edenburg, Open University of Israel

J. Cheryl Exum, University of Sheffield

Yael S. Feldman, New York University

Edward L. Greenstein, Bar Ilan University

Lillian Klein Abensohn, American University, Washington

Israel Knohl, Hebrew University, Jerusalem

Nadav Na'aman, Tel Aviv University

Frank H. Polak, Tel Aviv University

Meira Polliack, Tel Aviv University

Dalit Rom-Shiloni, Tel Aviv University

Shulamit Valler, Haifa University

LIST OF PUBLICATIONS BY YAIRAH AMIT

Collated by Dana Torres

1978   *A Guide to the Hebrew Bible Bibliography Tutorial Exercise* (Tel Aviv University: The Faculty of Humanities [Hebrew]; 2nd edn 1984; 3rd edn 1986).

1981   Ed., *Aims and Methods of Teaching the Hebrew Bible in Junior High and High Schools: A Reader* (Tel Aviv: Tel Aviv University, the School of Education [Hebrew]; 2nd edn 1984; 3rd edn 1988]).

1981–82   '"And Joshua stretched out the Javelin that was in his hand…" (Joshua 8:18, 26)', *Shnaton: An Annual for Biblical and Ancient Near Eastern Studies* 5-6: 11-18 (Hebrew); English version in *In Praise of Editing in the Hebrew Bible: Collected Essays in Retrospect* (Sheffield: Sheffield Phoenix Press, 2012): 94-104.

1982   'The Position of the Exodus Tradition in the Book of Chronicles', in *Bible Studies: Y.M. Grintz in Memoriam* (ed. B. Uffenheimer; Te'uda, 2; Tel Aviv: Tel Aviv University, Hakibbutz Hameuchad Publishing House [Hebrew]): 139-55; English version in *In Praise of Editing in the Hebrew Bible: Collected Essays in Retrospect* (Sheffield: Sheffield Phoenix Press, 2012): 249-66.

1982   '"He is Lent to the Lord"—Tightening Hinting: A Literary Editorial Tool', *BM* 27: 238-43 (Hebrew); also in *Reflections on the Bible: Selected Studies of the Bible Circle in Memory of Yishai Ron*, IV (ed. E. Hamenahem; Tel Aviv: Am Oved Publishers, 1983 [Hebrew]): 27-33; English version in *In Praise of Editing in the Hebrew Bible: Collected Essays in Retrospect* (Sheffield: Sheffield Phoenix Press, 2012): 173-79.

1982   Ed. (with Ronit Shoshany), *Jeremiah: Annotated Bibliography and Hebrew Literature Items on the Book and on Teaching it—for the Teacher, the Student, and the Educated Reader* (Tel Aviv: Tel Aviv University, The School of Education [Hebrew]).

1983   'The Role of Prophecy and Prophets in the Book of Chronicles', *BM* 28: 113-33 (Hebrew); English version published 2006.

1983   'The Story of Amnon and Tamar: Reservoir of Sympathy for Absalom', *Hasifrut/Literature* 32: 80-87 (Hebrew); English version in *In Praise of Editing in the Hebrew Bible: Collected Essays in Retrospect* (Sheffield: Sheffield Phoenix Press, 2012): 181-88.

1984   'The Art of Composition in the Book of Judges' (PhD dissertation, Tel Aviv University [Hebrew]).

1985   'The Function of Topographical Indications in the Biblical Story', *Shnaton: An Annual for Biblical and Ancient Near Eastern Studies* 9: 15-30 (Hebrew).

1985   Ed. (with Ronit Shoshany), *Jeremiah: An Annotated Bibliography According to the 1985 Hebrew Bible Curriculum* (Tel Aviv: Tel Aviv University, The School of Education, The Unit of Research and Curriculum Development, supported by the Ministry of Education and Culture, experimental edn [Hebrew]).

1985   '"There was a Certain Man…, Whose Name Was…": An Editorial Variation and its Purposes', *BM* 30: 388-99 (Hebrew); English version in *In Praise of Editing in the Hebrew Bible: Collected Essays in Retrospect* (Sheffield: Sheffield Phoenix Press, 2012): 160-71.

1985   'Three Variations on the Death of Saul: Studies in the Fashioning of the World, in Reliability and in the Tendentiousness of Biblical Narrative', *BM* 30: 92-102 (Hebrew); English version in *In Praise of Editing in the Hebrew Bible: Collected Essays in Retrospect* (Sheffield: Sheffield Phoenix Press, 2012): 190-201.

1986   'The Ending of the Book of Judges', in *Proceedings of the Ninth World Congress of Jewish Studies, Division A: the Period of the Bible* (Jerusalem: World Union of Jewish Studies [Hebrew]): 73-80; English version in *In Praise of Editing in the Hebrew Bible: Collected Essays in Retrospect* (Sheffield: Sheffield Phoenix Press, 2012): 149-58.

1986   Ed. (with Ronit Shoshany), *Judges: An Annotated Bibliography According to the 1985 Hebrew Bible Curriculum* (Tel Aviv: Tel Aviv University, The School of Education, The Unit of Research and Curriculum Development, supported by the Ministry of Education and Culture, experimental edn [Hebrew]).

1986   'Lifelong Nazirism: The Evolution of a Motif', in *Studies in Judaica* (Teʿuda, 4; ed. M.A. Friedman and M. Gil; Tel Aviv: Tel Aviv University, University Publishing Projects [Hebrew]): 23-36; English version in *In Praise of Editing in the Hebrew Bible: Collected Essays in Retrospect* (Sheffield: Sheffield Phoenix Press, 2012): 132-46.

1986   'Some Thoughts on the Work and Method of Nehama Leibowitz', *Immanuel* 20: 7-13.

1986   'Teaching the Book of Joshua and its Problems', *ʿAl Hapereq* 2: 16-22 (Hebrew); slightly revised version published as 'Excursus D' in *The Rise and Fall of the Bible's Empire in Israeli Education: The 2003 Syllabus: Retrospect and Prospect* (Even Yehuda: Reches Educational Projects, 2010 [Hebrew]: 144-52.

1987   'The Dual Causality Principle and its Effects on Biblical Literature', *VT* 37: 385-400.

1987   'Judges 4: Its Contents and Form', *JSOT* 39: 89-111.

1987   Ed. (with Ronit Shoshany), *Kings: An Annotated Bibliography According to the 1985 Hebrew Bible Curriculum* (Tel Aviv: Tel Aviv University, The School of Education, The Unit of Research and Curriculum Development, supported by the Ministry of Education and Culture [Hebrew]).

1987   'The Story of Samuel's Initiation into Prophecy in Light of Prophetic Thought', in *Studies in Bible and Jewish Thought in Honour of Moshe*

Goldstein (ed. B.Z. Luria; Tel Aviv-Jerusalem: The Society for Bible Research in Israel [Hebrew]): 29-36; English version forthcoming in *In Praise of Editing in the Hebrew Bible: Collected Essays in Retrospect* (Sheffield: Sheffield Phoenix Press).

1987 Ed., *The Book of the Kings of Judah and Israel: A Reader* (experimental edition; Tel Aviv: Tel Aviv University, The School of Education, The Unit of Research and Curriculum Development, supported by the Ministry of Education and Culture [Hebrew; also published in Hebrew in 1989]).

1987 Ed. (with Ronit Shoshany), *Ezra and Nehemiah: An Annotated Bibliography According to the 1985 Hebrew Bible Curriculum* (Tel Aviv: Tel Aviv University, The School of Education, The Unit of Research and Curriculum Development, supported by the Ministry of Education and Culture [Hebrew]).

1988 'Biblical Utopianism', in *A Selection of Studies in Memory of Ishay Ron*, V (Tel Aviv: Am Oved Publishers [Hebrew]): 52-57; English version in *In Praise of Editing in the Hebrew Bible: Collected Essays in Retrospect* (Sheffield: Sheffield Phoenix Press, 2012): 26-32.

1988 Ed., *Law and Justice: Studies on the Biblical Law: A Reader* (Tel Aviv: Tel Aviv University, The School of Education, The Unit of Research and Curriculum Development, supported by the Ministry of Education and Culture [Hebrew]).

1988 'The Use of Analogy in the Study of the Book of Judges', in *Wünschet Jerusalem Frieden–Collected communications to the XIIth congress of the International Organization for the Study of the Old Testament, Jerusalem 1986* (ed. M. Augustin and K.D. Schunk; Frankfurt am Main; Bern/New York/Paris: Peter Lang): 387-94.

1989 (with others), *The Book of Samuel II* (ed. G. Galil; Olam Hatanach: A Commentary on the Bible; Jerusalem-Ramat Gan: Revivim Publishing House [Hebrew; republished by Davidson-Atai and thereafter by Divrey Hayamim Publishing]).

1989 Ed., The *Book of the Kings of Judah and Israel: A Reader* (Tel Aviv: Ramot–Tel Aviv University [Hebrew; experimental edn published 1987]).

1989 'The Multi-purpose "Leading Word" and the Problems of its Usage', *Prooftexts* 9: 99-114 (Hebrew version published 1994).

1989 'The Story of Ehud (Judges 3: 12-30): The Form and the Message', in *Signs and Wonders: Biblical Texts in Literary Focus* (ed. J.C. Exum; Atlanta: Scholars Press): 97-123.

1989 'Studies in the Poetics of the Book of Chronicles': *Studies in Bible and Jewish Thought in Honour of H.M.Y. Gevaryahu, A Tribute When he Reached the Age of 80* (ed. B.Z. Luria; Jerusalem: Kiryat Sefer [Hebrew]): 280-89; English version forthcoming in *In Praise of Editing in the Hebrew Bible: Collected Essays in Retrospect* (Sheffield: Sheffield Phoenix Press).

1990 'Biblical Utopianism: A Mapmaker's Guide to Eden', *Union Seminary Quarterly Review* 44: 11-17.

1990 (with Yair Hoffman), *Exile and Salvation: A Study Book on the Period of the Return to Zion* (Even Yehuda: Reches Educational Projects [Hebrew]).

1990 'Hidden Polemic in the Conquest of Dan: Judges XVII–XVIII', *VT* 60: 4-20 (Hebrew version published 1991).

1991 'Hidden Polemic in the Conquest of Dan: Judges XVII–XVIII', *BM* 36: 267-78 (Hebrew; English version published 1990).

1991 'The Repeated Situation: A Poetic Principle in the Modeling of the Joseph Narrative', in *Studies in Judaica* (ed. M.A. Friedman; Te'uda, 7; Tel Aviv: Tel Aviv University, University Publishing Projects [Hebrew]): 55-66; English version forthcoming in *In Praise of Editing in the Hebrew Bible: Collected Essays in Retrospect* (Sheffield: Sheffield Phoenix Press).

1992 *The Book of Judges: The Art of Editing* (The Biblical Encyclopaedia Library, 6; Jerusalem: Bialik Institute [Hebrew; English version published 1999]).

1992 'Dual Causality: An Additional Aspect', *BM* 38: 41-55 (Hebrew); English version in *In Praise of Editing in the Hebrew Bible: Collected Essays in Retrospect* (Sheffield: Sheffield Phoenix Press, 2012): 106-21.

1992 '"The Glory of Israel does not Deceive or Change his Mind": On the Reliability of Narrator and Speakers in Biblical Narrative', *Prooftexts* 12: 201-12; revised Hebrew version published 1997.

1992 'The Jubilee Law: an Attempt at Instituting Social Justice', in *Justice and Righteousness: Biblical Themes and their Influence* (ed. H.G. Reventlow and Y. Hoffman; JSOTSup, 137; Sheffield: JSOT Press): 47-59.

1992 'The Story of the Concubine in Gibeah as a Hidden Polemic against the Kingdom of Saul and Later (Judg. 19-21)', *BM* 37: 109-18 (Hebrew; English version published 1994).

1993 (with others), *The Book of Kings I* (ed. G. Galil; Olam Hatanach: A Commentary on the Bible; Jerusalem-Ramat Gan: Davidson-Atai [Hebrew; republished thereafter by Divrey Hayamim Publishing]).

1993 '"But With Us, the Living, Every One of Us Here Today": On Multi Voices in the Writings', *BM* 38: 313-19 (Hebrew); English version in *In Praise of Editing in the Hebrew Bible: Collected Essays in Retrospect* (Sheffield: Sheffield Phoenix Press, 2012): 85-92.

1993 'Jacob Licht and Exegesis as Designation and Mission', *Jewish Studies: Forum of the World Union of Jewish Studies* 33: 41-46 (Hebrew).

1993 '"Manoah promptly followed his wife" (Judges 13.11): On the Place of the Woman in Birth Narratives', in *A Feminist Companion to Judges* (ed. A. Brenner; Feminist Companion to the Bible, 4; Sheffield: JSOT Press): 146-56.

1994 (with others), *The Book of Judges* (ed. G. Galil; Olam Hatanach: A Commentary on the Bible; Jerusalem-Ramat Gan: Davidson-Atai [Hebrew; thereafter by Divrey Hayamim/Yediot Acharonot]).

1994 'Implicit Redaction and Latent Polemic in the Story of the Rape of Dinah', in *Proceedings of the Eleventh World Congress of Jewish Studies Division A: The Bible and its World* (Jerusalem: The Publications of the World Union of Jewish Studies; Magnes Press [Hebrew]): 1-8; rev. and expanded Hebrew version published 1996; English version in *In Praise of Editing in the Hebrew Bible: Collected Essays in Retrospect* (Sheffield: Sheffield Phoenix Press, 2012): 47-69.

1994 'Literature in the Service of Politics: Studies in Judges 19-21', in *Politics and Theopolitics in the Bible and Post Biblical Literature* (ed. H.G.

Reventlow and Y. Hoffman; JSOTSup, 171; Sheffield: Sheffield Academic Press): 44-59; Hebrew version published 1992.

1994 '"Am I Not More Devoted to You than Ten Sons"? (1 Samuel 1:8): Male and Female Interpretations', in *A Feminist Companion to Samuel and Kings* (ed. A. Brenner; Sheffield: Sheffield Academic Press): 68-76.

1994 'The Multi-Purpose "Leading Word" and the Problems of its Usage', *Sadan: Studies in Hebrew Literature* 1: 35-47 (Hebrew; English version published 1989).

1995 'Human Dignity in the Hebrew Bible', in *Human Dignity and Freedom in the Jewish Heritage* (The President's Study Group on the Bible and Sources of Judaism; Jerusalem: The Presidential Residence [Hebrew]): 32-46; republished 1999 in *'Al Hapereq* 16: 7-18 (Hebrew); and 2006 in *Questioning Dignity: On Human Dignity as Supreme Moral Value in Modern Society* (ed. J.E. David; Jerusalem: The Israel Democracy Institute and Magnes Press [Hebrew]): 13-25.

1995 'The Part and the Whole in Teaching the Hebrew Bible', *Journal of Educational Topics* 4: 18-34 (Hebrew); republished 1997 in *'Al Hapereq* 13: 129-40 (Hebrew); slightly revised version published as 'Excursus B' in *The Rise and Fall of the Bible's Empire in Israeli Education: The 2003 Syllabus—Retrospect and Prospect* (Even Yehuda: Reches Educational Projects, 2010 [Hebrew]), pp. 117-29.

1996 (with others), *The Book of Chronicles I* (ed. G. Galil; Olam Hatanach: A Commentary on the Bible; Jerusalem-Ramat Gan: Davidson-Atai [Hebrew; republished thereafter by Divrey Hayamim Publishing]).

1996 'Implicit Redaction and Latent Polemic in the Story of the Rape of Dinah', in *Texts, Temples, and Traditions—A Tribute to Menahem Haran* (ed. M.V. Fox, V.A. Hurowitz, A. Hurvitz, M.L. Klein, B.J. Schwartz and N. Shupak; Winona Lake, IN: Eisenbrauns [Hebrew]): 11*-28*; first short Hebrew version published 1994; English version in *In Praise of Editing in the Hebrew Bible: Collected Essays in Retrospect* (Sheffield: Sheffield Phoenix Press, 2012): 47-69.

1997 'Creation and the Calendar of Holiness', in *Tehillah le-Moshe: Biblical and Judaic Studies in Honor of Moshe Greenberg* (ed. M. Cogan, B.L. Eichler and J.H. Tigay; Winona Lake, IN: Eisenbrauns [Hebrew]): 13*-29*; English version in *In Praise of Editing in the Hebrew Bible: Collected Essays in Retrospect* (Sheffield: Sheffield Phoenix Press, 2012): 3-23.

1997 '"The Glory of Israel Does Not Deceive or Change his Mind": On the Reliability of Narrator and Speakers in Biblical Narrative', in *A Light for Jacob: Studies in the Bible and the Dead Sea Scrolls in Memory of Jacob Shalom Licht* (ed. Y. Hoffman and F.H. Polak; Jerusalem: Bialik Institute [Hebrew]): 45-56; English version published 1992.

1997 *History and Ideology in the Bible* (The Broadcasting University; Tel Aviv: The Ministry of Defense Publishing [Hebrew; rev. and annotated English version published 1999).

1997 '"The Men of Israel" and Gideon's Refusal to Reign', *Shnaton: An Annual for Biblical and Ancient Near Eastern Studies* 11: 25-31 (Hebrew);

English version in *In Praise of Editing in the Hebrew Bible: Collected Essays in Retrospect* (Sheffield: Sheffield Phoenix Press, 2012): 124-30.

1999   *The Book of Judges: The Art of Editing* (trans. J. Chipman; Leiden: E.J. Brill [Hebrew version published 1992]).

1999   *History and Ideology: Introduction to Historiography in the Hebrew Bible* (rev. and annotated edn of the Hebrew version from 1997; Sheffield: Sheffield Academic Press).

1999   *Judges: Introduction and Commentary* (Mikra Leyisra'el; Jerusalem: Magnes Press, The Hebrew University; Tel Aviv: Am Oved Publishers [Hebrew]).

1999   'Why Were the Mothers Barren?', in *Reading from Genesis: Creative Israeli Women Write on the Women of Genesis* (ed. R. Ravitzky; Tel Aviv: Yediot Acharonot-Sifrei Hemed [Hebrew]): 127-37; English version in *In Praise of Editing in the Hebrew Bible: Collected Essays in Retrospect* (Sheffield: Sheffield Phoenix Press, 2012): 34-44.

2000   'Bochim, Bethel, and the Hidden Polemic (Judg. 2.1-5)', in *Studies in Historical Geography and Biblical Historiography: Presented to Zecharia Kallai* (ed. G. Galil and M. Weinfeld; Leiden: E.J. Brill): 121-31.

2000   *Hidden Polemics in Biblical Narrative* (trans. J. Chipman; Leiden: E.J. Brill [abridged and rev. Hebrew version published 2003]).

2000   *Reading Biblical Stories* (The Broadcasting University; Tel Aviv: The Ministry of Defense Publishing [Hebrew; rev. and annotated English version published 2001]).

2000   'The Place of Jerusalem in the Pentateuch', in *Studies in Bible and Exegesis, 5: Presented to Uriel Simon* (ed. M. Garsiel, S. Vargon, A. Frisch and J. Kugel; Ramat Gan: Bar-Ilan University Press [Hebrew]): 41-57.

2000   'The Sunammite, the Shulamite and the Professor: Between Midrash and Midrash', *'Al Hapereq* 17: 74-87 (Hebrew; English version published 2001).

2001   'The Sunammite, the Shulamite and the Professor: Between Midrash and Midrash', *JSOT* 93: 77-91 (Hebrew version published 2000).

2001   *Reading Biblical Narratives: Literary Criticism and the Hebrew Bible* (trans. Y. Lotan; Minneapolis: Fortress Press, rev. and annotated edn; [Hebrew version published 2000]).

2001   'Progression as a Rhetorical Device in Biblical Literature', in *Homage to Shmuel: Studies in the World of the Bible* (ed. Z. Talshir, S. Yona and D. Sivan; Jerusalem: Bialik Institute; Beer Sheva: Ben-Gurion University of the Negev Press [Hebrew]): 21-48; English version published 2003.

2001–   'Elisha and the Great Woman of Shunem: A Prophet Tested', *Zmanim: A*
2002   *Historical Quarterly* 77: 4-11 (Hebrew).

2002   'I, Delilah—A Victim of Interpretation', in *first Person: Essays in Biblical Autobiography* (ed. P.R. Davies; London: Sheffifield Academic Press): 59-76; Hebrew version published 2004.

2002   'Teaching the Hebrew Bible in Public Education: A Study on the Curriculum', in *Values and Goals in Israeli School Curricula* (ed. A. Hofman and I. Schnell; Even Yehuda: Reches Educational Projects [Hebrew]): 239-64; rev. version published as 'Chapter One' in *The Rise and Fall of the Bible's*

Empire in Israeli Education: The 2003 Syllabus—Retrospect and Prospect (Even Yehuda: Reches Educational Projects, 2010 [Hebrew]): 33-54.

2003 'Biblical Criticism in the Teaching of the Hebrew Bible', in *Understanding the Bible in Our Times: Implications for Education* (ed. M.L. Frankel and H. Deitcher; Studies in Jewish Education, 9; The Melton Centre for Jewish Education; Jerusalem: The Hebrew University Magnes Press [Hebrew]): 101-13; revised version published as 'Excursus C', in *The Rise and Fall of the Bible's Empire in Israeli Education: The 2003 Syllabus— Retrospect and Prospect* (Even Yehuda: Reches Educational Projects, 2010 [Hebrew]): 130-43.

2003 'Epoch and Genre: The Sixth Century and the Growth of Hidden Polemics', in *Judah and the Judeans in the Neo-Babylonian Period* (ed. O. Lipschits and J. Blenkinsopp; Winona Lake, IN: Eisenbrauns): 135-51.

2003 *Hebrew Bible Curriculum for the Education System: From Kindergarten to the Twelfth Grade*[1] (Jerusalem: Ma'alot Publishing [Hebrew]); republished in *The Rise and Fall of the Bible's Empire in Israeli Education: The 2003 Syllabus—Retrospect and Prospect* (Even Yehuda: Reches Educational Projects, 2010 [Hebrew]): 165-242.

2003 *Hidden Polemics in Biblical Narrative* (Tel Aviv: Miskal—Yediot Acharonot Books and Chemed Books, abridged and rev. edn [Hebrew; English version published 2000]).

2003 'Progression as a Rhetorical Device in Biblical Literature', *JSOT* 28: 3-32 (Hebrew version published 2001).

2003 'A Prophet Tested: Elisha, the Great Woman of Shunem, and the Story's Double Message', *Biblical Interpretation* 11: 279-94; first short Hebrew version published 2001–2002.

2003 'When Did Jerusalem Become a Subject of Polemic?', in *Jerusalem in Bible and Archaeology: The First Temple Period* (ed. A.G. Vaughn and A.E. Killebrew; SBL Symposium Series, 18; Atlanta: Society of Biblical Literature): 365-74.

2004 'Endings: Especially Reversal Endings', *Scriptura* 87: 213-26; Hebrew version published 2009.

2004 'I, Delilah—A Victim of Interpretation', *BM* 49: 1-18 (Hebrew; English version published 2002).

2004 'Judges: Introduction and Annotations by Yairah Amit', in *The Jewish Study Bible: Jewish Publication Society Tanakh Translation* (ed. A. Berlin and M.Z. Brettler, consulting ed. M. Fishbane; New York: Oxford University Press): 508-57.

2005 'Knowledge before Love: On problems in Bible Teaching in Israeli Schools', in *The Heart of the Matter: Redefining Social and National Issues—A Tribute to Yair Tzaban on Reaching the Age of 75* (ed. R. Rosenthal; Jerusalem: Keter [Hebrew]): 287-96; short Hebrew version published in *Ha'aretz* newspaper on 24 January 2004; rev. English version published 2007; new rev. version published as 'Introduction', in *The Rise and Fall of the Bible's Empire in Israeli Education: The 2003 Syllabus—*

---

1. Responsible for the program as chairperson of the Committee

Retrospect and Prospect (Even Yehuda: Reches Educational Projects, 2010 [Hebrew]): 16-29.

2006 'The Delicate Balance in the Image of Saul and its place in the Deuteronomistic History', in *Saul in Story and Tradition* (ed. C. Ehrlich; Tübingen: Mohr Siebeck): 71-79.

2006 'Emor: The Establishment of the Sabbath According to Biblical Research', *Likrat Shabbat: Personal Insights on Parashat HaShavua* (ed. H. Achituv and A. Picard; Ein Tzurim: Merkaz Herzog [Hebrew]): 192-96.

2006 Ed. (with Ehud Ben Zvi, Israel Finkelstein and Oded Lipschits), *Essays on Ancient Israel in its Near Eastern Context: A Tribute to Nadav Na'aman* (Winona Lake, IN: Eisenbrauns).

2006 'Looking at History through Literary Glasses Too', in *Essays on Ancient Israel in its Near Eastern Context: A Tribute to Nadav Na'aman* (ed. Y. Amit, E. Ben Zvi, I. Finkelstein and O. Lipschits; Winona Lake, IN: Eisenbrauns): 1-15.

2006 'The Role of Prophecy and Prophets in the Chronicler's World', in *Prophets, Prophecy, and Prophetic Texts in Second Temple Judaism* (ed. M.H. Floyd and R.D. Haak; New York and London: T&T Clark): 80-101; Hebrew version published 1983.

2006 'The Saul Polemic in the Persian Period', in *Judah and the Judeans in the Persian Period* (ed. O. Lipschits and M. Oeming; Winona Lake, IN: Eisenbrauns): 647-61.

2006 'Simson: een superman of een held op non-actief? (= Samson: A Hero or a Non-Active Superman?)', *Schrift* 228: 177-80 (Dutch).

2007 'Het boek Rechters: meer dan een ketting? (= The Book of Judges: More than a Chain?)', *Schrift* 234: 209-12 (Dutch).

2007 'The Place of Genres in the Hebrew Bible Curricula', in *The Book of Michael: Between Now and Then* (Jerusalem: Keter; Even Yehuda: Reches Educational Projects [Hebrew]): 13-29; English version published 2008; rev. version published as 'Excursus A', in *The Rise and Fall of the Bible's Empire in Israeli Education: The 2003 Syllabus—Retrospect and Prospect* (Even Yehuda: Reches Educational Projects, 2010 [Hebrew]): 101-16.

2007 'Preface to M. Frankel, *Teaching the Bible: The Philosophy of Nechama Leibowitz* (Tel Aviv: Miskal—Yediot Acharonot Books and Chemed Books): 11-13.

2007 'Saul in the Book of Chronicles', in *Shai le-Sara Japhet: Studies in the Bible, its Exegesis and its Language* (ed. M. Bar-Asher, D. Rom-Shiloni, E. Tov and N. Wazana; Jerusalem: The Bialik Institute [Hebrew]): 3-15; English version in *In Praise of Editing in the Hebrew Bible: Collected Essays in Retrospect* (Sheffield: Sheffield Phoenix Press, 2012): 233-47.

2007 'The Study of the Hebrew Bible in Israel: Between Love and Knowledge', *Jewish History* 21: 199-208; short Hebrew version published in *Ha'aretz* newspaper on 24 January 2004; also published in Hebrew in 2005; rev. English version published 2007; new rev. version published as 'Introduction', in *The Rise and Fall of the Bible's Empire in Israeli Education: The 2003 Syllabus—Retrospect and Prospect* (Even Yehuda: Reches Educational Projects, 2010 [Hebrew]): 16-29.

Book Reviews

1994   Review of Sh. Ahituv, *Handbook of Ancient Hebrew Inscriptions From the Period of the First Commonwealth and the Beginning of the Second Commonwealth (Hebrew, Philistine, Edomite, Moabite, Ammonite and the Bileam Inscription)*, *'Al Hapereq* 8: 98-99 (Hebrew).

1994   'Love for Biblical Narratives: Book Review on F.H. Polak, *Biblical Narrative: Aspects of Art and Design*', *BM* 40: 109-13 (Hebrew).

1998   Review of I. Eph'al, *Siege and its Ancient Near Eastern Manifestations*, *'Al Hapereq* 14: 189-91 (Hebrew).

1998   Review of S.A. Geller, *Sacred Enigmas: Literary Religion in the Hebrew Bible*, *JQR* 89: 171-74.

1998   Review of R.H. O'Connell, *The Rhetoric of the Book of Judges*, *JQR* 88: 275-79.

1999   Review of M. Anbar, *Shechem or Sinai?*, *Cathedra* 94: 173-76 (Hebrew).

2000   Review of M.Z. Brettler, *The Creation of History in Ancient Israel*, *RBL* (http://www.bookreviews.org/pdf/2077_1262.pdf).

2005   Review of W.G. Dever, *Did God Have a Wife?: Archaeology and Folk Religion in Ancient Israel*, *RBL* (http://www.bookreviews.org/pdf/4910_5127.pdf).

2005   Review of W.M. Schniedewind, *How the Bible Became a Book: The Textualization of Ancient Israel*, *RBL* (http://www.bookreviews.org/pdf/4234_4174.pdf).

2005   Review of N. MacDonald, *Deuteronomy and the Meaning of Monotheism*, *RBL* (http://www.bookreviews.org/pdf/4297_4272.pdf).

2006   Review of A.D. Freedman, *God as an Absent Character in Biblical Hebrew Narrative: A Literary Theoretical Study*, *RBL* (http://www.bookreviews.org/pdf/4907_5129.pdf).

2006   Review of A. Shapira, *The Bible and Israeli Identity*, *Zmanim: A Historical Quarterly* 95:111-15 (Hebrew).

2006   Review of S. Niditch, *Judges: A Commentary*, *RBL* (http://www.bookreviews.org/pdf/6393_6881.pdf).

2007   Review of E. Assis, *Self-Interest or Communal Interest: An Ideology of Leadership in the Gideon, Abimelech and Jephthah Narratives (Judg 6–12)*, *RBL* (http://www.bookreviews.org/pdf/5078_5352.pdf).

2008   Y. Shimoni, *Dust, Katharsis: A Critical Review in the Humanities and Social Sciences* 10: 111-25 (Hebrew).

2009   'In Conversation with Thomas Römer, The So-Called Deuteronomistic History: The Book of Judges: Fruit of 100 Years of Creativity', *Journal of Hebrew Scriptures* 9: 28-35.

Encyclopedia and Dictionary Entries: A Selection

1988   57 Encyclopedia entries published in *The Israeli Encyclopedia of the Bible* (ed. Y. Hoffman; 3 vols.; Ramat-Gan: Masada). Only several entries from each volume will be listed below.

From vol. I: 'אדם וחוה' (= 'Adam and Eve'): 32-34; 'אסתר' (= 'Esther'): 80-82; 'דניאל' (= 'Daniel'): 199-201.

From vol. II: 'יונה' (= 'Jonah'): 311-13; 'מכות מצרים' (= 'Plagues of Egypt'): 458-60; 'מלכים, ספר' (= 'Kings, the book of'): 479-82.

From vol. III: 'עזרא ונחמיה' (= 'Ezra and Nehemiah'): 623-29; 'שטן' (= 'Satan'): 783-85;
'שיר השירים' (= 'The Song of Songs'): 790-93.

1997   'Teaching the Hebrew Bible', in *Teaching and Education: An Israeli Lexicon* (ed. Y. Kashti, M. Arieli and S. Shilasky; Tel Aviv: Ramot-Tel Aviv University [Hebrew]): 134-35.

2005   'Narrative Art of Israel's Historians', in *Dictionary of the Old Testament Historical Books* (ed. B.T. Arnold and H.G.M. Williamson; Downer's Grove, IL/Leicester: InterVarsity Press): 708-15.

2007   'The Hebrew Bible in the Israeli Education System', in *New Jewish Time: Jewish Culture in a Secular Age, An Encyclopedic View*, IV (ed. Y. Yovel, Y. Tzaban and D. Shaham; Jerusalem: Keter Publishing House [Hebrew]): 290-98.

2009   'Narrative Literature', in *The New Interpreter's Dictionary of the Bible, 4 (Me-R)* (ed. K.D. Sakenfeld *et al.*; Nashville, TN: Abingdon Press): 223-25.

Book Reviews and Articles in Hebrew Newspapers: A Selection

1991   *Ha'aretz* (January 25), 'Secular Archeology': on N. Na'aman and I. Finkelstein, *From Nomadism to Monarchy: Archaeological and Historical Aspects of Early Israel'*.

1992   *Ha'aretz* (April 23), 'Written Wisdom': on A. Hurvitz, *Wisdom Language in Biblical Psalmody.*

1992   *Ha'aretz* (October 11), On M. Weinfeld, *From Joshua to Josiah: Turning Points in the History of Israel from the Conquest of the Land until the Fall of Judah.*

1993   *Ha'aretz* (July 2), 'A Good Name is Better than a Good Ointment': on I. Knohl, *The Sanctuary of Silence: The Priestly Torah and the Holiness School.*

1995   *Ha'aretz* (August 2): on R.E. Friedman, *Who Wrote the Bible?*

1995   *Ha'aretz* (October 25), 'Holy Statistics': on Y. Liebermann, *Biblical Statistics.*

1996   *Ha'aretz* (June 5), 'In the Day you Eat from it your Eyes will be Open', *Da'at Mikra Encyclopedia of the Bible Software* (CD-ROM).

1997   *Ha'aretz* (March 5), '"Saul Reigned One Year and when he had Reigned Two Years Over Israel"': on Sh. Bar-Efrat's *Commentary and Introduction: Samuel I, Samuel II* (Mikra Leyisra'el).

1998   'On the Critical Exegesis of the Bible', *Hed Hachinuch* (= *Educational Echoes*) 72: 12-15.

2001   'The Force of a Story', *Hed Hachinuch* (= *Educational Echoes*) 75: 24-27.

2002   *Jerusalem Post* (October 18), 'Country Girl Makes Good': on J. Lotan, *Abishag.*

INTRODUCTION

Athalya Brenner and Frank H. Polak

This volume is for Yairah Amit, a modest tribute to her scholarly and public contributions over many decades, on the occasion of her retirement from teaching regularly at Tel Aviv University although not, as we hope, from research activities.

Yairah has been active in bible studies for decades. A principal place in her interest was her research. As a true patriot of Hebrew and of Israel (which, to her credit, she certainly is), she published first and foremost in Hebrew. On the other hand, her approach to research—as to life—has never been insular. Therefore, for the benefit and perusal of non-Hebrew speakers, she consistently republished her original Hebrew work also in English, often after serious revisions. This can be seen by consulting her 'List of Publications', which opens this volume. In addition, a selection of Hebrew articles previously unpublished in English has now been translated and is published concurrently with this volume, with personal reflections, under the title *In Praise of Editing in the Hebrew Bible: Collected Essays in Retrospect* (Sheffield: Sheffield Phoenix Press, 2012).

Yairah's engagement with things biblical has never been confined to academic research alone. She was and still is a dedicated, lively and attractive teacher, an educator who believes in certain principles, a talented administrator, and an influential cultural critic in the Israeli scene. Her many students, among them numerous former MA students and successful PhD candidates, belong to the elite of bible teachers and researchers in Israel. She was twice the chairperson of the Biblical Studies department at Tel Aviv University, before the department was made into a section in the department of Hebrew Culture Studies. She also combined her talents for teaching and for administration in directing, for many years, the Teachers Training Program in Bible, a two-year program mandatory for future high school teachers, also at Tel Aviv University but under the auspices of the Teachers' Training unit, not the department.

Indeed, Yairah's keen interest in education, in the bible and in its weight in public affairs—which is highly pronounced in Israel, even within 'secular' communities—were combined in her years-long involvement in the Israeli Ministry of Education committee for bible study. This committee has an advisory mandate and works together with the subject supervisor, in this case for bible, shaping policy and study from kindergarten up to university level. It determines texts, topics, curricula and syllabi—in short, it determines how the bible will be studied in all levels of state education. The committee is traditionally headed by an academic and includes both academics and teachers. Yairah was member of the committee, then its chairperson, for many years. In that capacity too she was engaged in bible study and teaching, not only in Academia but also outside it, as an agent of pedagogy and change. Her experiences in the committee were not always happy ones, since various Israeli religious, Zionist and post-Zionist attitudes to the bible cannot always be reconciled—and how can they be, in a young state trying to be Jewish as well as a modern democracy? The bible in Israel is political, and heated debates ensue because of it, in education and in society at large. Yairah wrote about that important part of her activities in her book, *The Rise and Fall of the Bible's Empire in Israeli Education: The 2003 Syllabus: Retrospect and Prospect* (Even Yehuda: Reches Educational Projects [Hebrew]).

As her 'List of Publications' shows, Yairah wrote academic book reviews as well as reviews for the popular daily and weekly Press, again pursuing her habit of social involvement and contribution, always from a scholarly perspective but also that of an interested citizen. As a scholarly book lover, and an interested scholar-citizen, she served and still serves on many committees whose task lies in between these two realms, such as the (Israeli) National Library committee. In those capacities, again, she is in a position to influence the reception, use and application of the bible not only academically but also socially.

Yairah is married. She has four children, two daughters and two sons, and thirteen grandchildren. She is extremely curious and an avid consumer of culture, over and beyond books—be it theatre, music, dance, film and more. The energy she applies to all that she undertakes is famous among all her friends and acquaintances. We are glad to have such a colleague and pleased that we can offer this volume to her.

* * *

By and large, Yairah's academic contribution to biblical studies can be divided into three main categories, two of which are general categories and one textual.

1. Literary analysis or the bible's poetics. Stepping from and beyond the first level of textual analysis and a biblical text's history, her work then turns to the text-as-is (the MT) and thereby encompasses what she considers significant poetic modes, or devices, with special emphasis on *editing* as a major factor fashioning the meanings of texts.

2. Ideologies embodied in the Hebrew bible and their link with writing (and reading) biblical literature, editing, and history. Her preoccupation with literary analysis, and in particular modes of editing, coupled with the recognition of place- and time-bound ideologies operating in biblical texts, lead Yairah to formulate her well-known ideas about the polemical nature of many biblical passages, be the polemics overt, covert or hidden in nature and expression, and to the tentative placing of polemics within viable historical circumstances.

3. These two directions are combined and enhanced in her numerous studies on the book of Judges, although she also discussed—among other texts—Genesis, 1–2 Samuel, and recently Chronicles. As can be gleaned from her 'List of Publications', the studies on Judges are especially prominent. They include an extended treatment of editing in Judges, as well as commentaries and essays on specific texts or issues.

In this volume we, the contributors, paid homage to Yairah and to her work by picking on these three directions, or categories, and their implications in an attempt to follow in her footsteps and take the inquiry further, within bible scholarship and beyond it into relevant areas of ancient and contemporary culture. The three categories have implications for each other, to the extent that they may partly overlap, as Yairah's own work shows. Therefore, as editors we have decided not to divide the essays here collected into categories but to present them in an alphabetical order, according to the authors' surname. Our readers will probably be aware of the connections of individual articles with facets of Yairah's work, and also of the interconnections between several of the essays themselves.

We end this short introduction by expressing our appreciation of Yairah and her work once again, and by asking her to continue her various activities with the curiosity, energy and zeal that are her hallmarks.

OBSERVATIONS ON LINES OF THOUGHT CONCERNING THE CONCEPTS OF PROPHECY AND PROPHETS IN YEHUD, WITH AN EMPHASIS ON DEUTERONOMY–2 KINGS AND CHRONICLES*

Ehud Ben Zvi

I have come to know Yairah as a friend and as a colleague. It is a pleasure and a privilege to offer her this contribution as a token of my deep appreciation for her and her scholarship. The topic for my contribution follows Yairah's interest in prophecy and historiography.

1. *Introduction*

Concepts of prophecy and prophets played central ideological and discursive roles at least from the early Second Temple period to the late Second Temple period and beyond in Jewish and early Christian thought. No essay can track their long trajectory of continuity and transformation throughout these periods, or the myriad of aspects associated with these concepts even in one period alone (e.g. the Achaemenid period, the late Second Temple period).

This essay thus brings forwards only *some* observations about these concepts within the intellectual discourse of Yehud in the Achaemenid period, that is during a *particular* period and in the main *only* from the perspective of *some* of the authoritative texts that existed within the Yehudite repertoire. The observations, however, are not a kind of random aggregate of considerations about some aspects of these concepts in Yehud. Although such aggregates may contain important 'nuggets' of information, they are unhelpful from a heuristic perspective, since they do not indicate a path for future research, fail to point to the interrelation among the observed attributes and characterizations, and consequently are unable to advance knowledge of

---

*   An oral version of this essay was delivered as the opening talk in a set of thematic sessions on 'Concepts in Ancient Jewish Discourse: Continuity and Transformation (6th c. BCE–3rd c. CE)', at the 2008 annual meeting of the Canadian Society of Biblical Studies held in Vancouver, BC, June 2008. The theme for the 2008 sessions was 'Concept/s of Prophecy (6th c. BCE–3rd c. CE)'. I wish to express my thanks to the participants in these sessions for their feedback and for illuminating my own research.

the discursive system within which the relevant concepts and their multiple aspects convey their significance. In addition and as a consequence, aggregates are not helpful for comparative purposes.

A central aim of the present essay is to show the potential of a heuristic approach that focuses on the intrinsic logic of particular lines of thought or ways of thinking about prophets and prophecy in Yehud, and above all, on their generative role within the ideological, intellectual discourse of the literati of the period.

This essay shows that these lines of thought and implied perspectives carried strong implications and generated multiple, partial but connective images of prophet and prophecy within the discourse of Persian period literati. These partial images often stood in creative tension with one another, generated other images and all of them together contributed to the shaping of a semantic/ideological field of meanings associated with the concepts 'prophets' and 'prophecy'. Moreover, many of these lines of thought provided an early basis for threads that eventually played important roles in discourses about prophets and prophecy in the late Second Temple period, early Judaism, and early Christianity.[1] The structuring role of these lines of thought and the ways in which they help to trace trajectories of concepts or comparative studies of them across cultures are due to the fact that many of them are related to systemic features of communities that are, at least in their discourses, centered around authoritative, written texts. Of course, this essay can deal only with the Achaemenid period in Yehud, but some of its general heuristic potential becomes clear through the discussion.

The point of departure for these observations is the book of Deuteronomy, or to be more precise, the explicit and implicit messages about prophets and prophecy conveyed by the book of Deuteronomy to its primary and intended (re)readership. This choice is not arbitrary. It is grounded in the fact that the general, ideological discourse reflected in Deuteronomy is clearly at work in Joshua–Kings and Chronicles and, to a large extent, is a commonplace in Yehud and in later periods. Moreover, it is relatively easy to track ways of thinking about prophets and prophecy, shaped by and reflected in Deuteronomy, that are at the same time deeply connected to images reflected in and shaped by other books within the authoritative repertoire of Yehud's literati. The emphasis will be on general images, implied perspectives, and minor or anonymous prophetic figures rather on the very individualized, direct portrayals of particular personages who are characterized as prophets, or also

---

1. One may approach these 'lines of thought' from the perspective or metaphor of 'cultural genes', ready to be activated in response to appropriate socio-cultural stimuli and whose expression (i.e. manifestation in the form of images, ideas and the like) by necessity influences (e.g. tends to partially or fully activate, repress, control) other cultural genes, whose own expression or lack thereof in turn influences the other genes.

as prophets, in either the deuteronomistic historical collection (hereafter, DHC) or Chronicles, e.g. Samuel, Elijah, Micaiah, the son of Imlah, Isaiah. The reason is simple: Much of the characterization of the latter personages reflects individual rather than generic traits. In other words, even if these personages were prophets or also prophets (e.g. Samuel is also a priest), prophets were not necessarily construed in terms of new Samuels or Isaiahs.[2]

Since these observations involve the book of Chronicles, which is later than DHC, and the prophetic books,[3] the discussion here provides also some glimpse at an early stage of lasting threads concerning the concept of prophet and prophets that eventually reached into early Judaism and Christianity.[4]

Finally, it must be stressed that this essay is about concepts of prophecy and prophets, and not about a very particular literary genre, 'the prophetic book' or its conceptual prototype.[5]

2. The Absence of a Presence and some of its Historiographic Implications

The main approach of Deuteronomy to prophets and prophecy may be characterized as one of social and ideological containment.[6] As is well-known, references to prophets or prophecy are not many in Deuteronomy. Both the presence and the absence of references convey meanings.

Turning to the evidence of the absence, it is easy to recognize that prophets play no role in Deut. 17.14-20, a pericope that construes a model for the leadership of the polity. Given the text-centered worldview of Deuteronomy and its implied and primary rereaderships, it is particularly significant that this pericope does not associate prophets with the writing or explaining of the book of Yhwh's teaching mentioned there. Deuteronomy's approach to the matter influenced, among others, the world portrayed in Chronicles. Thus, for

2. At the same time, it would be foolish to assume that social memories and texts about characters such as Elijah did not play an important role in the range of images evoked by the term 'prophet' in ancient Yehud. I wrote elsewhere about the importance of the 'generic prophets' to reconstruct the general concept of prophets of old among the intended and primary readership of the book of Kings (Ben Zvi 2004).

3. By 'prophetic books' I mean here Isaiah–Malachi, i.e., the 'latter prophets'.

4. Threads involving possible but necessarily hypothetical sources of the DHC and the present books in the DHC, however, will not be discussed in this essay.

5. I have written about the latter elsewhere (Ben Zvi 2003a, 2009).

6. The presence of a similar approach towards the king is widely acknowledged. Of course, this may not hold true if the book is approached from a mode of reading that focuses on taking up particular, 'detached' expressions and phrases, and that completely resignifies them in a way that is deeply associated with new ideological/literary settings, but which pays no attention to their meanings in their original *Sitz im Buch*. See, for instance, the interpretation of Deut. 18.15 in Acts 3.18-26. The *Pesharim* provide an excellent example of this mode of reading.

instance, the delegation sent to the cities of Judah with the book of Yhwh's teachings for the people includes priests, officials and even, by proxy, the king, but not prophets (see 2 Chron. 17.7-9).[7] Similarly, prophets play no role in Neh. 8.1-10. A similar tendency seems to be at work in Kings as well. To be sure, 2 Kgs 17.13 represents a balancing voice that might be seen as an early precursor of a way of constructing the past and its prophets that eventually found its 'classical' expression in *m. Abot* 1.1—which, interestingly enough, does not mention the priests.[8]

Continuing with our exploration of the evidence of absence in Deuteronomy, it is clear that prophets per se are not construed as playing an essential role in the administration or the even the day to day life of the polity.[9] Moreover, Deuteronomy does not state that prophets are necessary to mediate divine legitimacy to kings or to take it away from them—contrary to some prominent images of prophets in Samuel and sections of Kings.[10] Prophets also play no role in war in Deuteronomy. The priest and the officers are those who address the people before battle (Deut. 20.1-9).

Of course, there is more about prophecy in Deuteronomy, but these considerations already bear implications for historiography and for the ways in which it shapes social memory. The counterpart to a general attitude to prophets and prophecy that considers them as relatively marginal players in

---

7.   Even in 2 Chron. 34.21 the king inquires of Yhwh through Hulda, but she is not described as a learned interpreter of the book. In fact, the book does not come to her. This is to be balanced with the fact that in Chronicles prophets/prophetic voices are often portrayed as 'preachers' who communicate godly teachings, which in turn were not and within the discourse of the period could not have been construed as *not* grounded on authoritative texts; after all, the literati of the period imagined Israel as a 'text-centered' community. On Jehoshaphat's judicial reform and the ways in which the contents of the scroll of Yhwh's *Torah* are imagined in the Chronicler's account of the reign of this king see Knoppers 1994. On the text-centered concept of the community in Yehud see, for instance, Römer 2000. On the construction of memories of monarchic prophets in Chronicles and its significance, see Ben Zvi, forthcoming a.

8.   See Dan. 9.10 and the portrayal of Jeremiah, who is explicitly referred to as prophet in 2 Macc. 2, and cf. Josephus, *Apion* 1.41 and *Ant.* 4.165. On *Apion* 1.41 see Barclay 2007: 30-31. On the image of Moses as a prophet see below and Lierman 2004: 32-64 and Ben Zvi, forthcoming b.

9.   Unlike, for instance, the שׂרים (e.g. Deut. 1.15; 20.9), the כהנים (e.g. Deut. 18.3; 19.17), הכהנים הלוים (e.g. Deut. 17.9, 18; 24.8), or the elders (Deut. 19.12; 21.1-9, 19-20; 22.17-18).

10.   It might be claimed that the Mosaic character of the prophets mentioned in Deut. 18.5 includes an ability to legitimize the proper leader of Israel, but the matter is dubious. Certainly, to be 'like Moses' does not mean that the prophets were in charge of anointing the priests; and see Exod. 28.41; 29.7; Lev. 8.12. Other aspects of Deut. 18.5 will be discussed below.

the polity and its ideological/symbolic foundations[11] is the construction of historical periods in which those explicitly designated as prophets (i.e. prophets in a narrow way) did not play any significant role as prophets per se.

The DHC constructs two such periods: those of Joshua and of the Judges.[12] On the surface, the book of Kings seems very different, but one can easily note that most of the references to named prophets are associated with either Solomon's reign and its beginning and immediate aftermath, or with the northern kingdom of Israel. Prophetic activity is not prominent in the reports about the post-Rehoboam kingdom of Judah, references to Isaiah being the exception.[13] Even references to the role of prophets as anointing kings are restricted within these boundaries.[14]

One may be tempted to explain the difference away in terms of the reported stability of the House of David, and dwell on the importance of prophets in the period leading to the establishment of the dynasty in the book of Samuel. But one cannot but notice also that when the Davidic dynasty is re-established under Joash, it is the priest rather than the prophet who takes the initiative to restore the Davidide and it is the *people* who anoint him (2 Kgs 11.12). This concept of the people (rather than a prophet) anointing the king is taken up by Chronicles as it reshapes the description of the anointing of Solomon (see 1 Chron. 29.22). By doing so, Chronicles not only resolves tensions on this matter,[15] but also moves forward by having the people anointing not only

---

11. Unlike, for instance, *Torah* and its readers, Israel as a whole, or the temple and the priests.

12. There is a reference to an unnamed איש נביא ('prophet man') in Judg. 6.8-10. Deborah is referred to as אשה נביאה in Judg. 4.4, but acts more like a judge, within certain gender constraints imposed by the discourse of the time. The איש האלהים in Judg. 13.3, 6-8 is not a real 'prophet' but reflects the perception of Manoah's wife of a מלאך. On this passage and its interpretation in later traditions see Syrén 2000: 250-51; and below.

13. The exceptional case of Isaiah may be explained in terms of the centrality of the memory of deliverance of Judah in the days of Hezekiah in the postmonarchic period. This memory contributed much to the lionization of both Isaiah and Hezekiah in Persian period Yehud. Of course, when the historical narrative about the kingdom of Judah was deeply interwoven with that of the northern kingdom, prophets reappear (e.g. 1 Kgs 22.1-18; 2 Kgs 3.4-27).

14. See 1 Sam. 9.16; 10.1; 15.1, 23; 16.1-13; 1 Kgs 11.29-39; 19. 15-16; 2 Kgs 9.1-10.

15. Cf. and contrast 1 Kgs 1.34, 39, 45. Cf. also ancient versions. For a summary of the evidence and a discussion see Mulder 1998: 66-67. The case of the installation of Joash in 2 Kgs 11.12 is, however, clear and points at anointment by the people, though with the support of the priest.

In general terms, the question of whether the DHC constructs even a portion of the past in which anointment by priest and by prophet were equally normative is highly debatable. Samuel is both a priest and a prophet. Elisha is only a prophet, but events in the Elijah/Elisha narratives cannot be taken to represent necessarily regular, normative procedures (see 1 Kgs 18.30-37). The tension on the matter is clear in 1 Kgs 1.34, 39, 45. See also the voice of 2 Kgs 11.12.

the king, but also the priest. Thus, the people, not the prophets, become a consecrating agent and, as it were, Mosaic (cf. Exod. 28.41; 29.7; Lev. 8.12), or at least, within a reading that assumes that prophets anoint kings, the people become prophet-like.[16] This is consistent with the general 'democratization' tendencies in Chronicles. To be sure, these tendencies are at the core of Deuteronomy and play important roles in other Pentateuchal books,[17] though far less in the book of Kings.[18]

A tendency to construe images of the past in which prophets, as such, do not play a substantial role can easily be discerned also when one takes into account the world of knowledge about the past held by the literati in Yehud. Of course, they were aware of the representations of the past communicated by the prophetic books which were fully shaped around prophetic figures. Yet these central prophetic characters in the memory of the community are given no role in the DHC, with the exception of Isaiah, and not much in Chronicles either.

3. *Ways of Dealing with and Re-Shaping Images of a Past in which Prophets Play No Significant Role and their Historiographic Implications*

A world without prophets is highly problematic within the discourses of ancient Yehud.[19] The tendencies mentioned above had to be balanced. Some re-imagining of the construed past had to take place so as to make the social memories associated with this past fit better the existing ideological discourse.

---

16. Cf. Num. 11.29, but note the difference in the image of the prophet they evoke.

17. The idea of a covenant between the people and Yhwh instead of the king and Yhwh is at the core of Deuteronomy and Exodus–Numbers, and serves as the most salient example of this tendency. Another example involves the 'democratization' of royal myths of origin; see, for instance, Van Seters 1989. Within Chronicles there is a clear trend to reshape the narratives of Samuel–Kings in a way consonant with these 'democratization' tendencies; see Japhet 1997: 416-28.

18. One might argue that these observations about the role that prophets as such played or did not play according to constructions of various periods in the past of the literati may be explained in terms of tendencies in the sources underlying the DHC. It has often been proposed that the latter come from different groups, areas and periods. Although these sources were re-signified, by necessity, when they were embedded in the DHC, they may have still carried enough of their distinctive ideological flavor on these and other matters. Cf. Rofé 1991. Likewise, one may argue that limits on the malleability of collective memory played an important role (e.g. social memories agreed upon about Elijah or Elisha). Whatever the case, the observations advanced above *cannot be explained away*, since they reflect the message these books conveyed to the literati in the Persian period.

19. Because of its implications in relation to divine–human communication. See below.

Thus the book of Joshua prominently assigns prophetic roles to a personage who is not identified as a נביא in this book, that is, Joshua.[20] Deuteronomy plays with the characterization of Moses as a prophet (see below). Characters referred to as מלאך יהוה fulfill prophetic roles in Judges. Other prophetic roles are taken up by judges (see Judg. 2.17; cf. 9.7-20).[21] Whether redactional or not, Judg. 6.8-10 explicitly refers to a character as איש נביא. Moreover, the reference here may be a very early instance of re-imagining מלאך יהוה (see Judg. 6.11) as a prophet.[22] The reverse, namely the characterization of a prophet as מלאך יהוה is attested in Hag. 1.13 and 2 Chron. 36.15-16.[23]

Chronicles does not retell the period of the Judges or Joshua but clearly recognizes and corrects the relative lack of prophets in monarchic Judah. Its new prophets, however, are certainly neither in the mold of those in the book of Samuel nor like the northern prophets of Kings. Instead, Chronicles turns for inspiration to the basic portrayals associated with the 'anonymous, generic prophets' of Kings (e.g. 2 Kgs 9.7; 17.13-15; 21.10-15; 24.2).[24] Moreover, Chronicles assigns once again prophetic roles to non-prophetic figures, often temporarily, including in one case to a foreign king.[25]

To summarize the results up to now, there was a line of thought according to which prophets as prophets played no central role in the Israelite polities. This line of thought led to and was reflected in historical narratives in which they play either no role or only a marginal one. Such constructions of the past, however, were systemically untenable within the existing discourse and, accordingly, balanced by the association of prophetic roles with main personages (e.g. Moses, Joshua, some judges, and holders of several offices in Chronicles), or with some characters (e.g. מלאך יהוה in Judges), or simply

20. See Josh. 23.3-16; 24.1-2, and cf. Josh. 1.8.

21. Cf. also Judg. 6.36-39. Cf. Levin 2002.

22. One notes the characterization of מלאך יהוה as איש האלהים in Judg. 13.3, 6, 8 (10-11).

23. As is well-known, some early rabbinic sources understood several figures referred to as מלאך יהוה in the HB as prophets. See *Tg. Judg.* 2.1; 13.3.8; cf. *Lev. R.* 1.1. On these matters, see Syrén 2000; Smelik 1995: 350, 563-64, 639-40, and bibliography there.

24. This is not by chance, since the latter contributed much to the mental and ideological images that the general category of 'former prophets of Israel in the monarchic period' evoked among the authorship and intended and primary readerships of the book of Kings. See Ben Zvi 2004:

25. See Amit 2006: 80-101. Contrast with Schniedewind 1995, 1997. On Necho as a foreign monarch who communicates the voice of God and its context in Chronicles see Ben Zvi 2006: 270-88. The idea of a foreign individual communicating Yhwh's word to an Israelite leader seems to have conflicted with some later discourses; cf. 2 Chron. 35.22 with 1 Esd. 1.26b (Eng. 1.28); and see Josephus' recounting of the story in *Ant.* 10.75-76. On the latter, see Begg 1988: 161-63; and Feldman 1998: 429. For later treatments of the event see Wieder 1975: 65.

by the addition of new prophets to the narrative as in Chronicles. But why would there be a tendency to marginalize the prophet at all within this discourse? Deuteronomy serves again as an excellent starting point for addressing this question.

4. *Prophets/Prophecy and Torah: The Potentially Dangerous Character of Prophets/Prophecies and their Historiographical Implications*

The few references to נביא or נביאים that do appear in Deuteronomy deal directly or indirectly, and not unexpectedly, with Moses and *Torah*. As a whole, at least from the perspective of the primary and intended readership of the book, these references strongly suggest a tendency aimed also at containment and control, along with a related appropriation of (actual and imagined) prophets and prophecy.

Deuteronomy 13.2-6 is concerned with prophets (and dreamers) who may lead the people away from the path that Yhwh has commanded, that is, from the divine teaching as understood by the readers of the book. The underlying and generic argument is that people might believe the message of a prophet whose אות או מופת, that is, signs and wonders are fulfilled. Thus this text communicates the viewpoint that whereas 'miracles' may reflect Yhwh's will, they do not count at all, for Yhwh may be testing Israel to know whether it would follow the deity's instruction or fall for wonders. The logical conclusion of this approach is that true prophets would not perform miracles, for miracles serve no purpose. Chronicles, unlike Kings, develops an image of the past that is consistent with this line of thought.[26]

Deuteronomy 13.2-6 clearly asks its primary and intended readers to compare future prophets with Moses (see Exod. 4.28-31), and its logic implies that their teachings could deal with similar kinds of matters, and therefore it issues its warning about prophetic teachings that may differ from Moses'. This line of thought leads directly to two conclusions. First, there cannot be a prophet like Moses, because either (a) prophets reaffirm the already known Mosaic message and therefore are at best secondary to him, or (b) they are sent by Yhwh to test Israel and should/may be killed.[27] The second conclusion is that prophets are potentially dangerous. Deuteronomy communicates to its

---

26.   See, for instance, Amit 2006: 90. On Chronicles as following Deuteronomy closer than Kings, at least in some ways, see Knoppers 2001: and centuries later the attitude that miracles prove nothing played an important role in rabbinic thought. See *b. B. Metzi'a* 59b; *y. Mo'ed Qatan* 3, 1, 81c-d.

27.   Yhwh is construed as testing Israelites also in Deut. 8.2. The concept of the testing deity is common in the discourse of Persian period Israel and plays important roles in Chronicles and Job. That prophets are excellent testing 'agents' according to Deuteronomy is noteworthy. Significantly, these prophets are among the only divinely sent, testing agents that may/should be killed.

intended and primary rereaders that the contents of prophecies must be dealt with cautiously and pass the test of consistency with the Mosaic divine teachings. In other words, what the prophet says must be approved of by others as consistent with the commandments, as understood by the literati on the basis of their readings of the authoritative texts they have.

There is nothing strange about this attitude. In fact, it is typical of text-centered (religious) communities. 'Priests' of the revealed text/corpus that stands at the center of the community would tend to delegitimize those who proclaim newly revealed texts that purportedly serve as an alternative, a correction or even necessary addition, to the existing central text/corpus.

A corollary of the concept of the everlasting value of the existing divine instruction and commandments (see Deut. 13.5) associated with Moses is that no one in the community is able to change or add anything of substance to the existing divine instruction. It is not by accident that this stance is brought explicitly and emphatically to the forefront in Deut. 13.1, a verse that serves as an introduction and interpretive key to Deut. 13.2-6.[28] The fact that prophets—unlike priests, or kings, for instance—are singled out in this pericope reflects and communicates an image of prophets as among the most potentially dangerous in this regard. After all, they may perform miracles and claim to convey Yhwh's word.

If (non-testing) godly prophets cannot proclaim anything really new, what can and should they do? Within this line of thought the answer is obvious: They can and should encourage Israel to follow Yhwh, the commandments, Yhwh's teaching.[29] This way of thinking generates an image of prophets as preachers/teachers of *Torah*.[30] They encourage people to follow Yhwh's commandments/*Torah*, warn of the consequences of forsaking them, talk about calamities that followed past instances of abandoning them, and provide hope, without which following Yhwh's teaching would have been hardly possible.[31]

28. For an important discussion of the concept underlying Deut. 13.1 and its implications see Levinson 2003.

29. The idea that the prophetic books do not provide 'new' knowledge but rather comment on, and help Israel understand, *Torah* and therefore under ideal circumstances would have been superfluous occurs in rabbinic Judaism (see *b. Ned.* 22b) and later literature (e.g. Rambam, *Mishne Torah*; see in particular *Sefer haMadda'—Hilkhot Yesodei haTorah* [ספר המדע – הלכות יסודי התורה] 9.1). Cf. Halivni 1993: 32.

30. It is worth stressing that the idea that prophets may explain past events, communicate a sense of causality in history and urge people, and particularly leaders, to follow a godly path existed also outside ancient Israel, and in much earlier periods than the Achaemenid. See, for instance, the letters of Nur-Sîn to Zimri-Lim (cf. Nissinen *et al.* 2003: 17-22).

31. This message of hope serves also to resolve cognitive dissonances that emerged because of tensions between their ideological discourse and the circumstances in the worldly world. Cf. Carroll 1979.

This image of the prophet as a teacher/preacher occupies a central role in Chronicles and is at the very core of the prophetic books, but appears also in Kings (e.g. 2 Kgs 17.13). Often, this image leads to that of a failed preacher/ teacher, because—from the perspective of literati in Yehud—monarchic Judah and Israel suffered a just judgment and therefore they must have not listened to the voice of the preacher/teacher prophets.[32] Since at the center of the monarchic polities stood kings and royal elites, this image generates (literary and ideological) portrayals of prophets confronting, attempting to teach, warning and proclaiming just judgment against, often, recalcitrant monarchs and high officers.[33] Moreover, images of rejecting the prophetic message easily lead to those of rejecting the messenger. Thus this line of thought is conducive to the development of portrayals of prophets of old who were persecuted, and eventually leads to prophetic martyrology. The book of Jeremiah contains salient images of prophetic persecution, and so does Kings (especially within the stories of Elijah and Elisha—including references to the execution of prophets, and see also the case of Micaiah). Similar images— including one of murder—appear in Chronicles (e.g. 2 Chron. 16.7-10; 24.20-21). This way of thinking and its related images has, as is well-known, an important 'afterlife' in the late Second Temple period.[34]

Within the discourse of the literati in Yehud, to imagine the prophets preaching was to imagine them explaining past and future events and incul- cating a sense of causality in history to their audiences. The resulting image of the prophet as interpreter of historical events generates that of prophets as 'historians', and eventually even as authors of written books of 'historical' content. This image is clearly attested in Chronicles (e.g. 2 Chron. 12.15; 13.22; 20.34; 26.22),[35] and has an afterlife in Josephus and rabbinic litera- ture.[36]

---

32. See, for instance, 2 Kgs 17.13-17; Jer. 7.25-26, 25.4; 35.15; 44.4-5; Zech. 1.3-6; 2 Chron. 36.15-16.

33. These are legion in the DHC, Chronicles and prophetic literature.

34. On prophetic martyrology see Rofé 1988: 197-213. This way of thinking is manifested in later works such as the *Martyrdom of Isaiah* and impacted both early Christian and rabbinic literatures.

35. For a discussion on prophets as historians in Chronicles, see Schniedewind 1995: 208-30.

36. On the prophet as historian in Josephus see Feldman 2006: 219-21. On Josephus as either a prophet or as a person fulfilling some prophetic roles, see Feldman 2006 and Grabbe 2006: 245. According to *b. B. Bat.* 14b-15a, Jeremiah wrote the book of Kings, Samuel wrote Judges and Samuel, Gad and Nathan wrote the book of Samuel. Prophets, however, are not imagined as writing historiographical works in the Second Temple period and thus Chronicles was thought to be written by Ezra (the genealogies up to his own time) and Nehemiah (all the rest). This is consistent with the well-known trend in rabbinic literature to construe a marked caesura between First and Second Temple periods.

There is also a clear link between the image of prophets as teachers and the concept that Yhwh's word, that is, prophecy, becomes a didactic book, which underlies the entire production of the prophetic books. Even as prophecy is Yhwh's necessary word, and even when the prophetic role as preacher/teacher of Israel is conceived of as absolutely indispensable to a sustainable future, both are imagined as subordinate to the Mosaic *Torah*. The conclusion of Mal. 3.22-24 is an emphatic and emphatically placed example of this understanding of prophets and prophecy.[37]

5. *The Image of Prophets as Foreseers and Some of its Implications*

An important component of images of prophets in Israel and the ancient Near East was that of foreseeing the future. Within the discourse in Yehud, foreseeing the future was seen, as a matter of course, in terms of a gift of Yhwh (e.g. 1 Sam. 3.19; 9.6). Again Deuteronomy is a helpful starting point to discuss some of the ways in which the (partial) image of a prophet as a foreseer contributed to the re-imagination of the prophet and prophecy within the discourse of Yehud literati. The relevant text is Deut. 18.9-22. It begins in vv. 9-13 by forbidding Israel to seek information through a common list of means of divination, and from anyone except Yhwh. Prophecy, however, is not included in the list of forbidden activities, and implicitly excluded by the following verses, which refer to prophets who are supposed to speak in the name of Yhwh about things to come. Thus the text connotes to the rereaders that prophecy is the only legitimate way to achieve knowledge about the future. The reasoning is clear: The Israelites can turn to none but Yhwh about the future. So they should ask for and listen to the voice of Yhwh. But there is a problem: the Israelites are not able to do so directly (v. 16), thus they require an intermediary, the prophet. The question is, to be sure, whether the intermediary or his/her message would be trustworthy.

For an explicit construction of Jeremiah as the last prophet in rabbinic literature, see *Pesiq. Rab. Kah.* 13.14. See also Wieder 1975.

37.   The question of whether Mal. 3.22-24 was originally written as a conclusion to the book of Malachi, or as a conclusion to a collection of the twelve prophetic books of which Malachi was the last, does not have a clear answer. Either way, even if fortuitously, Mal. 3.22-24 ended up communicating in a very explicit way a crucial interpretative key for the entire corpus of biblical prophetic books, implicit in the discourses of Yehud and later in rabbinical, medieval, and classical Judaisms. One may notice, for instance, that Rambam quoted this text of Malachi as proof that prophets are not supposed to bring a new *Torah*, but warns people not to trespass the *Torah* (i.e. the *Torah* of Moses). See Rambam, *Mishne Torah, Sefer haMadda'* - *Hilkhot Yesodei haTorah* [הלכות יסודי התורה – ספר המדע] 9.1).

The relevant criteria are given in v. 22 which states, 'if the prophet speaks in the name of Yhwh and the oracle does not come true, that oracle was not spoken by Yhwh; the prophet has uttered it presumptuously: do not stand in dread of him' (NRSV).[38] Since no one can know for sure which prophecy will come true in the future, the adoption of this as the only criterion—as demanded by Yhwh—removes the possibility of relying on divination/ proclamation by prophets in the present as a way to know the future.[39] Given that no other ways of divination are allowed in Deuteronomy, this way of thinking leads the intended and primary readers to the conclusion that people cannot access sure knowledge about the future. The only thing they can know for sure is that they should follow Yhwh's commandments (cf. Job, Qoheleth and Chronicles).[40]

But this is a conclusion that had to be balanced by other perspectives in the discourse of Yehud. For instance, the very same concept—that whatever a true prophet says is fulfilled—encourages the development of portrayals of highly reliable historical prophets whose words were fulfilled in the past, and even a kind of conceptualization of the past in terms of a series of prophecies and their fulfillment. This mode of thinking about prophets and prophecy is clearly present in numerous pericopes in the book of Kings (e.g. 1 Kgs 12.15; 14.18; 15.29; 16.12; 17.16; 2 Kgs 9.36; 10.10; 14.25; 17.23; 24.2; cf. von Rad 1953).

Moreover, the more important the event is considered to be within this discourse, the more likely that it be construed as a fulfillment of some prophecy, which is another way of saying that crucial events were not left to chance, but directly and explicitly reflected Yhwh's will as manifestly made known to Israel.[41] This being so, this way of thinking tends to create an image of Yhwh as a deity who would not do anything of importance for Israel without letting Yhwh's prophets know (see Amos 3.7).[42]

---

38.   To be sure, on the surface, there is nothing new in the idea expressed there. Prophets in the ancient Near East—including, of course, Israel—were supposed to provide true knowledge concerning the future, and certainly not to mislead. Nevertheless, the readers cannot but notice that in Deut. 18.21-22, this widely accepted concept becomes the *only* test of prophetic legitimacy and authority (see v. 21) for those seeking knowledge of the future.

39.   This non-comprehensive essay focuses on the lines of thought that emerge from this criterion. Within the discourse of ancient Israel there existed other ways of dealing with the matter (Crenshaw 1971: 49-61).

40.   In Chronicles events are presented as explicable but not predictable (Ben Zvi 2006: 4, 25, and *passim*).

41.   E.g. 2 Kgs 24.2; 2 Chron. 10.15.

42.   The concept of a divine assembly imagined in terms akin to a royal court (with Yhwh as king and prophets as his servants) is at work in Amos 3.7. As mentioned in the introductory section, this essay does not and cannot deal with all the concepts of prophecy

Conceptualizations of prophecy as statements about the future that must be fulfilled are commonplace in the prophetic books.[43] They contributed not only to the construction of highly didactic memories of the past, but also and above all they granted much hope to the literati in Yehud. Without them all the divine promises to bring Israel to a utopian situation would be of no value.

As important as these considerations are, the conceptualization of prophecy mentioned had to be placed in proportion within the discourse of the Yehudite literati. First, as already discussed, the fact that something that was prophesied did happen does not necessarily mean that the relevant prophecy represents ideologically acceptable thought, or that the prophets who uttered it were good prophets. The prophecy had to be consistent with the Mosaic *Torah*, as understood in the relevant circles.

For example, first and beyond the obvious, the image of the pious northern prophets anointing non-Davidic kings over Israel that is so common in the book of Kings cannot be upheld by Chronicles. After all, a prophet calling anyone who is not a Davidide to reign over Israel is calling him to depart from Yhwh's ways as understood by the Chronicler. This situation calls for a reshaping of northern prophets in Chronicles. Nothing drastic has to be done to the image of a prophet like Micaiah, the son of Imlah, but a central figure in terms of memory of the past and hope for the future such as Elijah has to be reshaped and re-appropriated (2 Chron. 21.12-15). Whereas Oded (previously unknown)—a pious, successful northern prophet—is made to appear as soon as the northern kingship vanishes (2 Chron. 28.9-15), most of the other northern prophets are made to disappear from the historical narrative. However, as usual in Chronicles, there is also a voice balancing and informing this approach, and see 2 Chron. 10.15.[44]

Secondly, the partial image of prophets announcing a future that must be fulfilled is also balanced and informed by constructions of a deity who may change his mind, whether in response to human reaction to a previous divine announcement (cf. Jonah 3) or otherwise, therefore making it impossible to

---

that existed in Israel, but only with some of them and particularly some 'lines of thought'. The image of prophets as Yhwh's servants in a royal/divine court is not analyzed here, though somewhat adumbrated in the discussion on מלאך יהוה. For a study on the issue of divine secrecy and communication in the ancient Near East, including a good discussion on Amos 3.7, see Lenzi 2008: 250-55 and *passim*.

43.   For the most part, this conceptualization is simply assumed as self-evident, but there are cases in which explicit statements are made for rhetorical purposes (e.g. Isa. 40.8).

44.   It should be stressed that the reference to the prophecy of Ahijah the Shilonite in Chronicles serves, in the main, ideological and narrative purposes that are different from those in DHC (Ben Zvi 2006: 117-43).

know which of the deity's words will actually be fulfilled (cf. Ezek. 33.12-20).[45]

Thirdly, the partial image of prophets announcing a future that must be fulfilled is also informed and balanced by the position that the efficacy of prophecy is to be understood in terms of serving its social role as intended by Yhwh (for instance, it may effect a change in attitudes in a particular population) rather than in terms of literal fulfillment (see Rofé 1988: 167-70). Certainly, an approach that sees prophets as mere individuals who proclaim precisely what will happen stands in tension with understandings of prophecy as a 'warning voice calling for repentance' (e.g. Zech. 1.3-6; cf. Jer. 18.7-11), in which case prophecy would be conditional. Not incidentally, these approaches to prophecy and prophets confront each other and inform each other in a very salient way in Jonah, which is the only meta-prophetic book in the Hebrew Bible (Ben Zvi 2003b).

6. Prophets as Moses-Figures, Moses as a Prophet, and Ways of Thinking about Prophets and Prophecy

Deuteronomy 18.9-22 serves also as a good starting point for exploring another influential line of thought concerning prophecy and prophets. According to the text, Yhwh will raise prophets in Israel, because divine messages require intermediaries/messengers. These pious prophets will follow the mold of the archetypical intermediary/messenger, Moses (v. 15). Turning the prophets into Mosaic figures, directly and indirectly, strongly impacts the images they evoke. Within a discourse in which Moses and *Torah* are deeply intertwined, a Mosaic figure cannot be imagined as anything but someone who is a *Torah* follower, who follows Yhwh's commandments. In practical terms, this means these prophets must be imagined as following the agreed upon readings of existing authoritative texts.

Thus Deut. 13.2-6 and Deut. 18.9-22 both convey to the intended and primary rereaders of Deuteronomy that by being Mosaic, prophets cannot actually be a second or alternative Moses, for there was only one Moses. The same point in a slightly different, but explicit way is made in Deut. 34.10-12, at the rhetorically most significant slot of the book's, and the Pentateuchal collection's, conclusion.[46] The precise language of Deut. 34.11 is meant to evoke that of Deut. 18.15, and by so doing it shuts the door—as it were—on, while ironically drawing attention to, a potential decontextualized understanding of Deut. 18.15. Decontextualized readings became more popular

---

45. On this and related matters, see Ben Zvi 2010.

46. For a study of similar incomparability formulas in Kings see Knoppers 1992; and note his final comment on Deut. 34.10-12 (Knoppers 1992: 431); on Deut. 34.10-12 in particular, see Chapman 2000: 113-31 and bibliography there.

among some groups in the late Second Temple period, including a particular reading of this very verse.[47]

The characterization of prophets as Mosaic characters is directly involved in the association of additional attributes with prophets and prophecy. To begin with, prophets who are created on the model of Moses are not necessarily a good fit for diviners interested only or mainly in finding someone's donkeys, or in providing information on mundane, personal matters that may interest an individual. Moses is construed as someone who prophesied about Israel as a whole, about national matters and events in the far future. A Mosaic prophet is one who deals with the general issues of the nation. Significantly, this is the general image of prophets and prophecy that appears in the prophetic books as well as in Chronicles and to some substantial extent in Samuel–Kings.

Moses is also the human teacher par excellence. A Mosaic character is likely to be imagined as a teacher of godly teachings. Conversely prophecy, that is, divine communication, is imagined to deliver didactic, divine messages aimed at leading Israel to follow the ways of the already known *Torah* as expressed in the authoritative texts of the community. Since Yhwh is a teacher, too, it is difficult to imagine that Yhwh will not try to teach Israel, that is, to send messages and messengers that would allow Israel to turn towards Yhwh to understand its situation properly. This line of thought thus converges with and reinforces the one discussed in Section 3.

To be sure, the ideological *topos* of Mosaic prophets cannot but evoke the image of a prophetic Moses.[48] But if Moses is a prophet (see Deut. 34.10; Hos. 12.14), in fact the greatest of all, then one may anticipate a line of thought according to which *Torah* and all the Mosaic commandments are prophecies. This approach opens the door to the characterization of non-Mosaic, but fully authoritative commandments thought to originate in Yhwh as prophecy, and of those who announce them as prophets. This is particularly relevant to Chronicles, in which the cult has two founders: Moses and David (de Vries 1988).[49] Moreover, as I have shown elsewhere, the readers of

47.   See, for instance, the interpretation of Deut. 18.15 in Acts 3.20-26. The *Pesharim* provide an excellent example of this mode of decontextualized readings. This type of reading is very common in rabbinic literature.

48.   The identification of Moses as a prophet is commonplace in rabbinic literature and later Jewish literature, and so is his incomparability (e.g. *Num. R.* 14.20; *Deut. R.* 11.10; and cf. later Rambam's *Thirteen Principles*. See also Lierman 2004: 32-64.

49.   See 2 Chron. 8.14 and esp. 29.25:

ויעמד את־הלוים בית יהוה במצלתים בכנרות

במצות דויד וגד חזה־המלך ונתן הנביא כי ביד־יהוה המצוה ביד־נביאיו

"He stationed the Levites in the house of the LORD with cymbals, harps, and lyres, according to the commandment of David and of Gad the king's seer and of the prophet Nathan, for the commandment was from the LORD through his prophets" (NRSV).

1 Chron. 16.35 most likely imagined David as one who knows the future (even the far future, just like Moses: Deut. 4.25-28; 31.16-18). Furthermore, although David makes the reference to the future exile, the matter is not presented as new knowledge, or as knowledge not widely shared by the community, or that needs to be repeated as a warning. The people are also imagined as knowing the far future, which is as much a prophetic feature as is knowledge of the past—which is what the readers of Chronicles acquire through reading the book, or reading the prophetic books for that matter (Ben Zvi 2007). Prophecy is thus conceived of as being among Israel, even if they are not all prophets. Finally, if godly words are prophecy, would it be possible for other personages, including pious, Davidic singers, to bear some prophetic traits? 1 Chron. 25.1-5 opens the door for the development of such images.[50]

7. *In Sum*

The present discussion has shown that (a) multiple, deeply interconnected, yet partial images of prophecy and prophets were generated by some common lines of thought, and (b) these images and their implications gave rise to additional, image-generating lines of thought that created new threads in an already dense tapestry. The resulting vast 'sea' of partial, at times overlapping and at times contradictory, multiple images allowed Yehudite literati to configure and reconfigure continuously their understanding of what today we may refer to as the semantic (and ideological) field of prophecy and prophets that existed in their discourse.[51] Although this study is about the intellectual discourse in Achaemenid Yehud, the lines of thought continue to be at work and influence the concepts of prophet and prophecy in the late Second Temple period and early Christianity and Judaism.[52] In fact, one may say that some fundamentals of these concepts were adumbrated in this period, and particularly, but not only, in Deuteronomy and Chronicles. The question of how they did develop, and against which historical backgrounds, requires a separate discussion.[53]

---

50. On this issue see also Ben Zvi, forthcoming a.

51. For this reason, narrow definitions of 'prophecy' or 'prophet' cannot but fail to reflect the actual concepts at work within this discourse, or for that matter, in the discourses of the late Second Temple period and its aftermath.

52. For perceptions of prophecy in the late Second Temple period, see Barton 1986; Floyd and Haak 2006.

53. The same holds true for comparative studies on the ways in which the mentioned, implied ways of thinking may or may not have played roles in the discourses of other text-centered communities in history (e.g. some Muslim, Medieval Jewish, Baha'i and Sikh communities), even if their responses to potentially comparable issues would certainly vary.

Bibliography

Amit, Y.
  2006   'The Role of Prophecy and Prophets in the Chronicler's World', in Floyd
          and Haak 2006: 80-101.
Barclay, J.M.G.
  2007   *Against Apion* (*Flavius Josephus: Translation and Commentary*, vol. 10;
          ed. S. Mason; Leiden/Boston: E.J. Brill).
Barton, J.
  1986   *Oracles of God: Perceptions of Ancient Prophecy in Israel after the Exile*
          (London: Darton, Longman & Todd).
Begg, C.T.
  1988   'The Death of Josiah: Josephus and the Bible', *ETL* 64: 157-63.
Ben Zvi, Ehud
  2003a   'The Prophetic Book: A Key Form of Prophetic Literature', in M.A.
          Sweeney and E. Ben Zvi (eds.), *The Changing Face of Form Criticism for
          the Twenty-First Century* (Grand Rapids: Eerdmans): 276-97.
  2003b   *Signs of Jonah: Reading and Rereading in Ancient Yehud* (JSOTSup, 367;
          Sheffield: Sheffield Academic Press/Continuum).
  2004   '"The Prophets"—Generic Prophets and their Role in the Construction of
          the Image of the "Prophets of Old" within the Postmonarchic Readership
          of the Book of Kings', *ZAW* 116: 555-67.
  2006   *History, Literature and Theology in the Book of Chronicles* (London:
          Equinox).
  2007   'Who Knew What? The Construction of the Monarchic Past in Chronicles
          and Implications for the Intellectual Setting of Chronicles', in O. Lipschits,
          G.N. Knoppers and R. Albertz (eds.), *Judah and the Judeans in the Fourth
          Century B.C.E.* (Winona Lake: Eisenbrauns): 349-60.
  2009   'The Concept of Prophetic Books and Its Historical Setting', in D.
          Edelman and E. Ben Zvi (eds.), *The Production of Prophecy: Constructing
          Prophecy and Prophets in Yehud* (London: Equinox): 73-95.
  2010   'A Contribution to the Intellectual History of Yehud: The Story of Micaiah
          and its Function within the Discourse of Persian-Period Literati', in P.R.
          Davies and D. V. Edelman (eds.), *The Historian and the Bible: Essays in
          Honour of Lester L. Grabbe* (LHBOTS, 530; London and New York:
          T&T Clark): 89-102.
forthcoming a 'Chronicles and its Reshaping of Memories of Monarchic Period Prophets:
          Some Observations', in M. Boda and L. Beale (eds.), *Prophets and Proph-
          ecy in Ancient Israelite Historiography* (Winona Lake: Eisenbrauns).
forthcoming b 'Exploring The Memory of Moses The Prophet in Late Persian/Early
          Hellenistic Period Yehud/Judah', in E. Ben Zvi and D.V. Edelman (eds.),
          *Remembering Biblical Figures in the Late Persian and Early Hellenistic
          Periods: Social Memory and Imagination* (Oxford: Oxford University
          Press).
Carroll, R.P.
  1979   *When Prophecy Failed: Cognitive Dissonance in the Prophetic Traditions
          of the Old Testament* (New York: Seabury Press).

Chapman, S.B.
    2000   *The Law and the Prophets: A Study in Old Testament Canon Formation*
            (FAT, 27; Tübingen: Mohr Siebeck).
Crenshaw, J.L.
    1971   *Prophetic Conflict: Its Effect Upon Israelite Religion* (BZAW, 124; Berlin:
            W. de Gruyter).
Feldman, L.H.
    1998   *Studies in Josephus' Rewritten Bible* (Journal for the Study of Judaism
            Supplement Series, 58; Leiden: E.J. Brill).
    2006   'Prophets and Prophecy in Josephus', in Floyd and Haak 2006: 210-39.
Floyd, M.H., and R.D. Haak (eds.)
    2006   *Prophets, Prophecy and Prophetic Texts in the Second Temple Period*
            (LHBOTS, 427; London and New York: T&T Clark).
Grabbe, L.L.
    2006   'Thus Spake the Prophet Josephus…: The Jewish Historian on Prophets
            and Prophecy', in Floyd and Haak 2006: 240-49.
Halivni, D. Weiss
    1993   'From Midrash to Mishnah: Theological Repercussions and Further
            Clarifications of "Chate'u Yisrael"', in M. Fishbane (ed.), *The Midrashic
            Imagination: Jewish Exegesis, Thought, and History* (Albany: SUNY
            Press, 1993): 23-44.
Japhet, S.
    1997   *The Ideology of Chronicles and Its Place in Biblical Thought* (BEAJT, 9;
            Frankfurt am Main: Peter Lang, 2nd edn).
Knoppers, G.N.
    1992   '"There Was None Like Him": Incomparability in the Books of Kings',
            CBQ 54: 411-31.
    1994   'Jehoshaphat's Judiciary and the "Scroll of Yhwh's Torah"', *JBL* 113:
            59-80.
    2001   'Rethinking the Relationship between Deuteronomy and the Deuterono-
            mistic History: The Case of Kings', *CBQ* 63: 393-415.
Lenzi, A.
    2008   *Secrecy and the Gods: Secret Knowledge in Ancient Mesopotamia and
            Biblical Israel* (SAAS, 19; Helsinki: The Neo-Assyrian Text Corpus
            Project, University of Helsinki).
Levin, C.
    2002   'Prophecy in the Book of Judges', paper presented at the annual meeting
            of the Society of Biblical Literature, Toronto, November 23–26.
Levinson, B.M.
    2003   'Your Must Add Nothing to What I Command You: Paradoxes of Canon
            and Authorship in Ancient Israel', *Numen* 50: 1-51.
Lierman, J.
    2004   *The New Testament Moses: Christian Perceptions of Moses and Israel in
            the Setting of the Jewish Religion* (Tübingen: Mohr Siebeck).
Mulder, M.J.
    1998   *1 Kings. I. 1 Kings 1–11* (Historical Commentary on the Old Testament;
            Leuven: Peeters).

Nissinen, M., with C.L. Seow and R.K. Ritner
2003 *Prophets and Prophecy in the Ancient Near East* (SBLWAW, 12; Atlanta: Society of Biblical Literature).

Rad, G. von
1953 'The Deuteronomistic Theology of History in the Books of Kings', in *Studies in Deuteronomy* (trans. D. Stalker; London: SCM Press): 74-91.

Rofé, A.
1988 *The Prophetical Stories* (Jerusalem: Magnes Press).
1991 'Ephramite Versus Deuteronomistic History', in D. Garrone and F. Israel (eds.), *Storia e tradizioni di Israel: Scritti in onore de J. Alberto Soggin* (Brescia: Paideia): 221-35.

Römer, T.
2000 'Du Temple au Livre: L'idéologie de la centralization dans l'historiographie deutéronomiste', in T. Römer and S.L. McKenzie (eds.), *Rethinking the Foundations: Historiography in the Ancient World and in the Bible. Essays in Honour of John Van Seters* (BZAW, 294; Berlin/New York: W. de Gruyter): 207-25.

Schniedewind, W.
1995 *The Word of God in Transition: From Prophet to Exegete in the Second Temple Period* (JSOTSup, 197; Sheffield: Sheffield Academic Press).
1997 'Prophets and Prophecy in the Books of Chronicles', in M.P. Graham, K.G. Hoglund and S.L. McKenzie (eds.), *The Chronicler as Historian* (JSOTSup, 238; Sheffield: Sheffield Academic Press): 132-49.

Smelik, W.F.
1995 *The Targum of Judges* (OTS, 36; Leiden: E.J. Brill).

Syrén, R.
2000 'The Targum as a Bible Reread, or How Does God Communicate with Humans', *JAB* 2: 247-64.

Van Seters, J.
1989 'The Creation of Man and the Creation of the King', *ZAW* 101: 333-42.

Vries, S. de
1988 'Moses and David as Cult Founders in Chronicles', *JBL* 107: 619-39.

Wieder, A.A.
1975 'Josiah and Jeremiah: Their Relationship According to Aggadic Sources', in M.A. Fishbane and P.R. Mendes-Flohr (eds.), *Texts and Responses: Studies Presented to Nahum N. Glatzer on the Occasion of his Seventieth Birthday by his Students* (Leiden: E.J. Brill): 60-72.

WOMEN AND MEN HE CREATED THEM:
GENDER AND IDEOLOGIES IN THE BOOK OF JUDGES

Athalya Brenner

Ostensibly, the book of Judges is about 'judges'. These 'judges', שופטים, as is widely demonstrated in the book, are persons who effect collective deliverance from [military] danger[1] more than, as more usual for the verb שפט Qal and its nominal derivatives, they engage in legislative and juridical activities.[2] Mostly the stories and short[er] notes about 'judges' in this book, apart from one, are about male judges and their escapades. However, as has been noticed by many scholars, it begins and ends with stories about women.[3] From Achsah (Judg. 1.12-15) and a reference to the Kenites (1.16), Jael's group, which will come to fruition in chs. 4–5, to the abducted Shiloh women in ch. 21, woman figures are depicted again and again as major lynch pins in

---

1. So also in e.g. 1 Sam. 8.5-6, when the Israelite elders ask Samuel to 'Give us a king to govern us', according to the JPS and the NSRV, while the KJV has 'to judge us'.

2. The juridical and the military functions are at times coupled in biblical literature, viewed as required, complementary attributes of a leader's ability to fulfill the leading role, notably as in 1 Sam. 8.20b: 'Let our king rule over us and go out at our head and fight our battle' (JPS), 'and that our king may govern us and go out before us and fight our battle' (NSRV), 'and that our king may judge us, and go out before us, and fight our battles' (KJV). Here too the term translated 'govern' more recently and 'judge' earlier is the Heb. שפט Qal. And see *inter alia* BDB for the term (where both 'judge' and 'govern' are given unproblematically as head meanings, 1071). For this article this is a minor point, worth referring to briefly simply because for decades now a shift judge→govern, rule or a certain contextual synonymity has been taken for granted in Judges research. It is perhaps worth noting that the only 'judge' in the book of Judges to actually engage in juridical activity is Deborah: 'She used to sit under the palm of Deborah between Ramah and Bethel in the hill country of Ephraim; and the Israelites came up to her for judgment' (Judg. 4.5, NSRV), 'And she dwelt under the palm tree of Deborah between Ramah and Bethel in mount Ephraim: and the children of Israel came up to her for judgment' (KJV); and somewhat obscured in the JPS: 'She used to sit under the Palm of Deborah, between Ramah and Bethel in the hill country of Ephraim, and the Israelites would come to her for decisions', and the NIV: 'She held court under the Palm of Deborah between Ramah and Bethel in the hill country of Ephraim, and the Israelites came to her to have their disputes decided'

3. See, for example, Lillian Klein Abensohn in this volume.

the evolving drama of local stories made national: the drama of attempts to move from local leadership and its overriding discontents, in spite of occasional success, to a more central government that would generate a greater success rate and greater security for its subjects, or partners.

The roles woman figures fulfill in the individual sections (such as the Achsah story) or in larger units (Samson's biography, chs. 13–16), as well as in the overriding plan of the book, the ideological 'national' framework, vary. They may be defined in traditional terms, i.e. as daughters, wives or mothers, that is, as male-relational figures. Achsah, Jephthah's daughter and the young women of Shiloh/Jabesh Gilead are introduced as daughters, as are Samson's Timnite wife and her sister and the Levi's runaway wife (ch. 19). The latter is primarily a wife, albeit a secondary one (*pileges̆*); and wives are also Achsah, Jael, Gideon's Shechemite wife (also defined as a *pileges̆*, 8.31), the wife of Jephthah's father, Manoah's wife; and according to many interpreters, ancient and modern, Deborah too—the only female 'judge' in this book—is wife of Lappidoth, her absent husband—or of Barak.[4] Let us not forget the mothers: Sisera's mother, Abimelech's mother (= Gideon's Shechemite wife), Jephthah's Mother, Samson's mother (wife of Manoah), Micah's mother; and last but not least, the metaphorical mother, the 'mother in Israel', Deborah again. Woman figures can also appear as independent agents, for better or for worse, with no male filiation. Such are the wise women in the court of Sisera's mother, the woman from Thebez who kills Abimelech, the whore from Gaza and Delilah. Most of these female figures are nameless as well as male-relational: they are important for the plot and message, may even assume male knowledge, functions or roles (Deborah and Jael, Samson's mother), but are depicted as socially marginal because of their social dependency on males or their namelessness. Whatever the individual story or case may be, all these descriptions are enveloped in two rubrics, both repeated several times, both editorial. The first repeated comment covers chs. 2–16 (end of Samson's biography): 'And the sons of Israel [*sic*: בני ישראל] did/ continued to do what was bad in Yhwh's eyes' (2.11; 3.7, 12; 4.1; 6.1; 10.6; 13.1). The second comment frames the last five chapters of the book, appearing at the beginning of the last section and at its very end: 'In those days there was no king in Israel, each man [*sic*: איש] would do what was right in his eyes' (17.6; 21.25).[5]

In this article I shall attempt to assess the ways female figures and typecasts are used in Judges for the purpose of either supporting or else negating the alleged need for central leadership, or kingship, so as to uphold a thriving social order. In this I wish to go beyond the basic recognition that woman figures indeed feature largely in Judges and in an evaluative manner, for

4. Cf. Shulamit Valler's article in this volume.
5. Both translations are mine, AB.

instance as phrased by Tammi Schneider in her 'Introduction' to her Commentary on Judges (1999: xiv):

> One of the major components affecting the evaluation of the judges is the role of women in their lives. With the exception of Ehud, Tola, Jair, Elon, and Abdon, the stories of the individual judges contain some reference to a woman, either by name or description of relationship to them, who heavily affect the judge's character and actions.

Or in her 'Conclusion' (pp. 288-89):

> Men in Judges often receive a negative evaluation because of the women in their lives, and the roles those women take, though the characters of the women themselves are not always seen negatively... Achsa could be considered a vehicle for a slightly negative evaluation of Othniel... In Judges the focus is not on the women as characters evaluated in their own right but as foils through whom the men, especially the judges, are tested... Women also serve to reveal the impact of Israel's actions on the nation of Israel at large... The Shiloh women's tragic plight demonstrates how Israelite society strayed so that women were institutionally raped and the system of protection was intentionally destroyed.

I find Schneider's position absolutely correct and balanced, in as far as it goes, in that she de-marginalizes woman figures by pointing out clearly some of their functions as a literary device, while simultaneously emphasizing their marginal status—as indicators for assessing males and their behavior—in the biblical text itself. However, I would like to take this further, especially because, crucially, woman figures open and close the book of Judges, framing it on both ends.

That the book of Judges almost begins and certainly ends with woman figures is a given fact and an indication of their importance to it. They appear as individuals and in groups, in various roles, as agents and as objects, as autochtones and as allochtones, in stories as well as in short notes. Let us look again at the list of female figures earlier categorized into daughters, mothers and wives, but this time from another perspective: that of the order they appear to our view within the book. Achsah stars already in ch. 1, at least in the fragment about Judah, a rare reference in Judges (vv. 12-15). Then come Deborah and Jael as 'national' saviours, as against the unnamed mother of Sisera and the group of her companions (chs. 4–5). Gideon has many wives, among them a secondary wife from Shechem, Abimelech's unnamed mother (8.31). This wife and mother from Shechem is not an actor or an agent in the stories depicting her husband and son. However, her community of origin is instrumental in Abimelech's attempt to secure dominance and eventually his downfall and death—at the hand of a woman (9.50-55). Remember Dinah and Shechem (Genesis 34)? If you do, you know already at the beginning of Judges 9 that it will end in tragedy. Abimelech is killed by an unnamed woman and his attempt to institute kingship is thus aborted.

Jephthah's mother is an unnamed *zōnāh*, 'harlot'—which is difficult to understand, since it is implied that Jephthah's paternity is recognized by his hostile half-brothers (11.1-3); his daughter is nameless too (11.30-40). The daughter is sacrificed to Yhwh after Jephthah's vow, willingly on her part— believe it or not. In Samson's saga (chs. 13–16) women seem as important as Yhwh's spirit and the Nazirite condition, even more so perhaps, as motivation and cause for the stories to unfold: from his mother, so much more proper and intelligent than her bumbling husband (ch. 13); to his first Philistine wife the Timnite and her barely mentioned sister (14.1–15.6); to the Gaza whore [all of them unnamed] (16.1-3), then to Delilah who delivers him to his fate and glory in death (the rest of ch. 16). Micah's mother, of the Ephraim hills, uses her money, stolen then returned to her by her son, to establish a local temple round a statue and an ephod; these are eventually taken, together with the appointed Levite priest, by the Danites on their migration to the northern Laish/Dan (chs. 17–18). The secondary wife of the Levite, again unnamed (as is her husband, apart from his tribal tag), is raped by the men of Gibeah, perhaps ultimately murdered by her husband when she returns in the morning (ch. 19).[6] In the ensuing civil strife the Benjaminites are nearly extinguished (ch. 20). To circumvent the decision not to allow exogamic wives to Benjamin men, two solutions are found: four hundred virgins are imported from Jabesh Gilead, after all other locals have been killed; and the other Benjaminites are encouraged to kidnap Shiloh girls dancing in the vineyards and to marry them. These last two groups are unnamed as well and there is no doubt that the young women are illegally taken by the Benjaminites (the root גזל, *gzl* Qal, 'to rob'[7] is used in 21.23 for this action). This is the end of the civil war and of the book: 'In those days there was no king in Israel; every man did what was right in his eyes'. Thus, we begin by reading about a well-established daughter in Judah, newly married and working for the success of her marriage (see Klein in this volume), outside the natural habitat—so to speak—of the 'judges'; and we end our reading with two groups of daughters = young women, coerced this

6. It is not at all clear whether the woman was dead in the morning, or died thereafter. The text is somewhat opaque: 'Toward morning the woman came back; and as it was growing light, she collapsed at the entrance of the man's house where her husband was. When her husband arose in the morning, he opened the doors of the house and went out to continue his journey; and there was the woman, his concubine, lying at the entrance of the house, with her hands on the threshold. "Get up," he said to her, "let us go". But there was no reply. So the man placed her on the donkey and set out for home' (vv. 26-28, JPS; emphasis mine, AB).

7. גזל Qal and Nif. and derivative nouns such as גזלה ('robbery' or 'something robbed', BDB: 159-60) appear in the Hebrew Bible over forty times. The English translations seem to have shied away from the strong definition of the Benjaminites' action. Thus the translations of this term are softer: 'carried off' (JPS, NIV), 'caught' (KJV), 'abducted' (NSRV).

way or the other to marry the corrupt Benjaminites, with neither their fathers nor they themselves having a say in this matter.

A quick analysis of this list will show that:

1. Most of the woman figures, be they individuals or groups, are unnamed. The only named female figures are Achsah, Deborah, Jael, and Delilah.
2. Most figures fulfill traditional male-relational roles: mothers, wives, secondary wives, daughters, or a combination thereof. There are two categories of exceptions: saviours and sexual objects. Abimelech's killer, Deborah and Jael are saviours—although, in the case of the last two, they boast absent husbands in the biblical text and/or in its interpretation [Deborah]; Delilah is a temptress, another of Samson's women is a *zōnāh*, 'prostitute', and others are sexual objects in addition to being wives and/or daughters (in the Gibeah story and in its aftermath).
3. A fair number are allochtones in some degree: so are Jael, Sisera's mother and her companions, Abimelech's mother and Abimelech's killer, Samson's women apart from his mother, and the Jabesh Gilead women.
4. All female figures are involved in events presented as of inter-tribal or national import. And, finally,
5. Only a minority—the 'saviour' category together with Samson's mother, perhaps also Achsah, perhaps also Jephthah's daughter—are depicted as wholly or mostly positive characters. The others are painted either negatively or indifferently, or else as nameless victims.

On this occasion I happily exempt myself from asking, or answering, questions about the historical *truth* content of such stories. The narrated time is indeed that of the last quarter of the second millennium BCE; but this has no bearing whatever on the historicity or veracity of the narrated tales. The narrating time is what counts: and this is unknown although much investigated and much speculated upon. To the connection between woman figures as framers and meaning bearers of this biblical text, and the narrating or editing or composition time, we can now turn.

In what follows I shall use as guides, or hermeneutical keys, two sets of studies. The first is the work done by Yairah Amit on biblical literature in general and in particular on Judges, and especially on the book's editing, important work in Hebrew and in English that features largely in this volume (1999a [Hebrew 1992], 2000 [2001]); and her work on biblical literature, polemics and ideology (1999b, 2001, 2009). The second is work in progress of my PhD student Ingeborg Löwisch, first in Amsterdam and now in Utrecht, on female genealogies in the Hebrew Bible, especially in 1 Chronicles 1–9 (Löwisch 2009).

Amit ultimately views Judges as the end product that is a unified editorial composition displaying a method, a frame, a purpose, and a plan. She shows us that attributing parts of the book to Deuteronomistic editorial activities is not enough to explain the book as a whole. Without going into her arguments or conclusions in detail, let me just state her position: she views *Judges 'as extant'*, in her repeated phrase, as anchored in the Assyrian conquest of the Northern Kingdom and the existential crisis it produced; that is, she attributes the book as edited principally to the last quarter of the eighth century BCE, and posits it as inspiration to the Deuteronomic school rather than a derivative of the latter (Amit 1999: 358-83, especially pp. 367-75; Amit 2009).

For my purpose here, leaving the date of composition/editing aside for the duration, accepting that Judges is a more or less unified editorial entity highlights the fact that it not only abounds in female stories but also that such stories frame it at its beginning and at its end and this, in turn, highlights the editorial status. Looked at from the other side of the same prism, that Judges begins and ends with female stories—let us be more precise, with daughters' stories (Achsa and the daughter of Jabesh-Gilead and Shiloh)—supports the idea of its compositional/editorial unity.[8] This framing, in a highly—even deliberately—organized and artistic composition, can hardly be incidental.

By way of illustration, let me compare this phenomenon of framing a biblical book by female figures to another biblical book, of another genre, where the situation is similar. In Proverbs, the first section (chs. 1–9) is indicated as such by its own title (Prov. 1.2) and by the title of the next section (10.1), among other things. This section has female figures—personified Wisdom in her various guises (Prov. 1.20-33; 2.1-15; 3.13-18; 4.5-13; 8.1-21, 22-36; 9.1-12), the זרה (*zārāh* [other? Strange? foreign?]) woman (2.16-19; 5.3-20; 6.24-perhaps to v. 35]; ch. 7), and Woman Folly (9.13-18)—at their centre. The last section of Proverbs (chs. 30–31) also has various female figures and figurations: there are sayings about female matters or in which females play a prominent although not a positive role (30.15-28); instruction from the otherwise unknown Lemuel's mother to her son-king concerning women and wine (31.1-9); and this last collection of Proverbs, as well as the whole book, culminates in the acrostic poem about the אשת חיל, 'woman of valour', that ends it.

Proverbs, beyond any scholarly doubt, is an edited work constructed of shorter and longer components, of various dates and provenances. Editing, as Amit has shown us, has ideologies to promote. An act of editing shapes a text, especially when the text harks back to variable sources, styles and beliefs. Departures and accidents may occur in editing, but would not be expected in major points, such as the all-important beginning or end.

---

8. This of course does not imply a denial of the probable history, perhaps a long one, oral and/or written, of individual sections, or even a proto-Judges composition.

Therefore, neglecting to view the arrangement of female-figure frames as meaningful in some way, perhaps time- and place-related, may be an ideo-logically motivated mistake made by critics and readers, for their own ends. This must be true for Proverbs, where the 'female' content of its beginning and end and the significance thereof have been analyzed at great length (for instance Camp 2000). Having examined the 'cosmic qualities assigned to both Woman Wisdom and the Strange Woman', Camp suggests that:

> ...more than moral pedagogy is at stake. In these two figures lies a fundamen-tal and multidimensional expression of religious self-understanding...a paradigm through which other literature may be read (p. 324).

The same applies to Judges, again a many-layered composition eventually edited into a whole according to a plan. Why does such an editorial plan require a framing by female figures, some of which are not simply reflections or refractions of bad, bad male behavior, even when the female figures are depicted as relational? At least Achsah, Jael, and Delilah are tricksters: they trick men. Is this only a reflection on men that is attributed to woman trick-sters and to their actions, in view of trickster mythology (Tannen 2007; Landay 1998) out of and in the bible (Jackson 2002[9]) and in Proverbs? Tricksters have elements of godliness in them, apart from being liminal; this is common to many cultures. A female trickster, like a male trickster in this respect, is more than a reflection: she plays a transformative role in being an agent for social change.

Furthermore, with a little bit of creative arithmetic, we can also arrive at twelve major individuals or groups of females in Judges, discounting for the time being marginal figures such as Abimelech and Jephthah's mothers, and Samson's Gaza whore. Somehow and perhaps unconsciously, twelve woman figures over and against twelve judges? Or, perhaps consciously? At any rate, interesting.

So far there are three factors that point to a more prominent role, beyond reflections of male behavior, for female characters in Judges as an edited whole: the beginning and end framing, the trickster and saviour roles, and the quantity of female figures. Let us move on with the investigation by discuss-ing the implied editorial envelope of Judges not only in connection with, but also beyond, the woman issue.

Is the edited Judges a propaganda manifest for the kingship, covertly for Davidic kingship to be more precise, assessing pre-monarchic modes of government as inadequate and leading to anarchy, to individual rather than collective-motivated behaviour which destroys the fabric of society? This is a possibility, and such propaganda would be more apparent in chs. 1 and 19–21

---

9. Jackson meanwhile completed her PhD in Oxford about female tricksters in the Hebrew Bible (degree awarded 2008), with a chapter on the topic of the 2002 article. Although I have seen the dissertation, I was unable to consult it at the time of writing.

because of the Judah story and pre-monarchical anarchy, respectively. (another framing device?). With such a possibility, with such an ideology, women will be foregrounded as a mostly negative example, in the sense that where women run society, or are allowed too much freedom, or motivate, or provoke male action, chaos follows; and the women, ironically, are among the first to get hurt. Or, put differently: where men are weak, when women get a chance to prevail, catastrophe will not be late in coming and often will first affect the women themselves. Thus the proper social order is transgressed almost beyond repair. A reading such as this will be in keeping with general notions of morality and gender norms in the Hebrew bible. It will explain why most of the female figures in Judges are nameless—they are not in fact important enough to have names, even fictive ones (and see Schneider 1999: 289). Almost all of the Judges female figures are traditionally male-related anyhow, or victims, or both; and the large amount of 'negative' or victim figures would support such a view. In that case, feminist scholars have argued, that female figures frame Judges is no reason for feminist celebration: it is just one more proof that women, in biblical times, were socially inferior and that their judgment in sociopolitical matters was considered suspect. Just by the way, the framing of Proverbs by female figures can be similarly explained as non-complimentary to women, by attributing the framing to the editorial claim of the book to be addressed to 'a son' or 'sons' who are the learning targets: what is better than positing sexual figures, or mother figures, as metaphors for learning or acquiring learning, for at least capturing the attention of the young, privileged, metrosexual 'students'?

And this reference to Proverbs may lead to yet another conjecture. Is perhaps the book of Judges, according to Amit a 'history book' (1999a: 382-83), designed to teach 'boys' such as those of Proverbs, again using woman figures to attract those presumably heterosexual privileged boys to the task of learning? That the composition was later, at some time, posited as part of Israel's first 'history' *cycle* (Joshua to the end of 2 Kings), or 'saving history' according to some, is a moot point. This too is worthy of consideration; which, according to my knowledge, has not been done in biblical scholarship thus far.

And there are other possibilities still. Can Judges, or Proverbs for that matter, be read as female-authored literature, because of the emphasis on woman figures and the framing by such figures on both ends? Such a reading will be important, even empowering, for female readers but, because of the reasons listed—relationality to males, namelessness, victimization, negative portrayal, ensuing social chaos more than positive portraits—such a possibility does not seem to this reader feasible, not to mention the difficulty of defining female authorship in the bible in general, including the most 'natural' candidate for female authorship in the bible, the Song of Songs. So let us move further.

Ingeborg Löwisch reads genealogies in 1 Chronicles 1–9 and elsewhere for traces of female active participation in such genealogies, for stories as well as for fragments. In her understanding, genealogical narration about women—as wives, mothers, sisters, daughters, ancestors, leaders, builders of cities and so on—signifies an act of memory, an archival effort (Löwisch 2009: 228-56). This conscious act of memory dialogically supports the exclusive social order, a regular patriarchy, while also revealing its weaknesses and actual inclusivity. Furthermore, Löwisch assigns the composition or insertion of female material, an effective act of commemoration and memory creation, to times of social or political crisis, post-trauma times, when old orders are endangered and new ones need to be reformulated. Such is the situation, in her view, for 1 Chronicles 1–9, once again a collection of various materials carefully edited into a unified whole. In the later Persian period, say from the late fifth the early fourth century BCE, a period of uncertainty politically and culturally and economically for the small, reformulated Jerusalem/Judah/Benjamin community, new memories must be found and recorded, all weapons must be enlisted for this effort. Women—even foreign women—may be considered more elevated community members in such emergencies; and information about them, authentic or invented, is included and recorded. Such is the situation in 1 Chronicles, as Löwisch shows, specifically in the case of past, long-ago Judah genealogies, where women play a relatively prominent role, because of the apparent need to [re]create Judah memory for the present and future (and see the story about Achsah in Judges 1, again a Judah story).

Applying Löwisch's insights to woman figures in Judges will lead to the following tentative conclusions. The *narrated*, and edited, Judges collection is about crisis events as told, to be sure—political, military, ethnic, religious and social crises. Women are always more visible in (narrated) times of crisis, then and now, whenever 'then' might have been. Crises, local or otherwise, bring women to the foreground of social activity and even politics, then and now; and this will account for the presence of female figures in individual stories, or in cycles. But: Who and when would have been interested in centering women to the point of framing the entire composition by woman figures? While assessing women's contributions as largely motivational for men or secondary in themselves, this framing nevertheless constitutes an act of de-marginalizing women, of recall, of inclusion as much of or perhaps more than exclusion. Clearly, a composition date of crisis, a *narrating/editorial* date of crisis, is to be sought here, a time for memory, when the northern tribes that feature largely in Judges and the royal order ostensibly introduced to solve the problems of that era, were no longer in existence.

Traditional bible scholarship points to a Deuteronomistic or Dtr editorial frame for Judges, that is, in a time when the northern kingdom was no more and the memory of northern groups and locals would have already been necessary and subjected to Judahite purposes. This is certainly, once again, a possibility, with the Babylonian conquest of Jerusalem serving later as initializing a further crisis point. When both the territory (the North and Judah) and the monarchy are gone, it is urgent to memorize, recall and manufacture their essence as imagined, or idealized.

And yet, there is also one more option. Even Amit, who advocates the 'art of editing' as the cohesive element that holds Judges together, admits to the possibility that the book's editorial frame could have been created in 'waves' so to speak, that parts of it might have been younger than the tentative date she assigns to its main part. I would like to suggest that the final, last editorial effort for Judges, the one that posited chs. 17–21, or at least 19–21, at the end of the book, be considered alongside the similar frame of Proverbs, and alongside the inserted women's stories in the 1 Chronicles 1–9 genealogies. Here too we should read Amit's assessment of Judges and its last chapters. For her, chs. 19–21 are not the proper editorial ending to the book but a departure, an 'artificial' ending. She states the reasons for this analysis, then concludes:

> …the editorial tendency, that appended Chapters 19–21, is not consistent with the implied editing of Judges. Hence the book is to be seen within the boundaries of Chapters 1–18, while Chapters 19–21 are an editorial deviation, whose purpose is to relate to the needs of the broader context. On the other hand, one should note that this appended editing used various sophisticated techniques in order to obscure the fact of its appending and to create the impression of a natural continuation (Amit 1999a: 357).

And, a little earlier on the same page—

> Their appearance is the result of editorial reworking that had an interest in connecting our story to the composition of the book, as if Chapters 19–21 serve a compositional function of closing the circle of the entire book.

From the perspective that I have been attempting here, excising stories in whose centre stand female figures, albeit victims in the case of the last chapters, would detract from the book's structure, in the same way that taking away chs. 30–31 in Proverbs would. Furthermore, judging three chapters (or five) out of twenty-one as an appendage that is somehow alien to an overall editing envelop makes the implied editing irrelevant to a large chunk of text; and if we add the number of verses that can be labeled Deuteronomistic, the implied editing part will become even smaller.

It therefore seems to me that, if 'editing'/'implied editing' is to be retained as a cohesive factor for the book of Judges, it must be assigned to at least two 'waves'. Amit is perhaps correct in assigning the first 'wave' to the last quarter of the eighth century BCE, a time of grave crisis; or, maybe, the proponents of the Deuteronomic provenance are in essence correct. At any rate, the hallmark of this editing is the assessment of a period as the period of 'judges', and of theological disloyalty to Yhwh (chs. 2–16, perhaps also 17–18 with no 'judge' in them but the associative connection with Samson's tribe, Dan). Be that as it may, a second editing 'wave' that includes the factors concerning women figures—framing it at beginning and end, tricksterism, relationality, large-scale namelessness, negative as well as positive social roles (chs. 1, 17–21 or 19–21)—is implied not only from reading Judges on its own but also by reading it in parallel with Proverbs. And the principle of crisis as a push for memory composition, also as apparent in 1 Chronicles 1–9, is probably valid for Judges as much as it is valid for Proverbs and Chronicles—perhaps in the same Early Second Temple period?

Quite a number of allochtonous women are mentioned in Judges, not always kindly. This may be in parallel to the exogamy/endogamy battles featuring in Ezra/Nehemiah, among other things. And creating a memory of what is no more, is a third room, in Homi Bhabha's idiom, where women are allowed, in whatever capacity, whether or not they were ever in actuality allowed opportunities and influence in times past.

To summarize. In this short article I tried to understand why in the book of Judges woman figures feature so largely; moreover, why they actually frame the book front to back, as it is ultimately transmitted to us. It is almost customary to view chs. 17–21 or at least 19–21 as 'additions' to the 'original' book, since no 'judges' are mentioned in them. Excluding those chapters from the as-is composition would not undermine its framing by woman figures (Delilah in ch. 16, and the cheated and idolatrous mother in ch. 17!), but is hardly justified. First, no known version of Judges exists without those chapters. Second, much material in this collection is indeed woman-focused. Third, the book's name, together with the name's influence on interpretation, is late-editorial. That names eventually given to biblical books were at times arbitrary or non-descriptive, derived from their opening words, then changed in translation according to contents, is borne out by שמות = Exodus, ויקרא = Leviticus, and so on and so on—who knows what the original name of Judges was, or its name in any stage of its edited coming-into-being? 'Women and men in God's Service' is a possibility, one of many. Fourth, the book's placing between Joshua and Kings makes it a 'historical' book, whereas its original purpose, or context, might have been completely different, not to mention the purpose and content of its individual components, short or long.

Basically, I used four hermeneutical keys, two biblical and two biblio-graphical. The biblical ones where the textual facts that woman figures abound in Judges and Proverbs, both complex and heavily edited collections, to the point of framing these two biblical books, and varied roles they per-form in them. The bibliographical keys were studies by Amit on Judges and Löwisch on 1 Chronicles 1–9, considering editorial framework in the case of the former; issues of female inclusion in the latter; and crisis, ideology and memory in the work of both. Possibilities of interpretation were offered as reflections, the only rejected interpretation being—and regrettably so—that of female authorship/editorship of Judges (or Proverbs, for that matter).

'Judges', women, framing, editorial activities, ideologies, memory manufactured or (re)produced, times of composition. I rest my case, certainly to be continued.

Bibliography

Amit, Yairah
    1999a   *The Book of Judges: The Art of Editing* (trans. Jonathan Chipman; Biblical Interpretation Series, 38; Leiden: E.J. Brill).
    1999b   *History and Ideology: Introduction to Historiography in the Hebrew Bible* (rev. and annotated from the Hebrew version, 1997; Sheffield: Sheffield Academic Press).
    2000   *Hidden Polemics in Biblical Narrative* (trans. Jonathan Chipman; Biblical Interpretation Series, 25; Leiden: E.J. Brill).
    2001   *Reading Biblical Narratives: Literary Criticism and the Hebrew Bible* (trans. Jael Lotan; Minneapolis: Fortress Press).
    2009   'The Book of Judges: Dating and Meaning', in G. Galil, M. Geller and A.R. Millard (eds.), *Homeland and Exile: Biblical and Ancient Near Eastern Studies in Homeland in Honour of Bustenay Oded* (Leiden: E.J. Brill): 297-322.
Camp, Claudia V.
    2000   *Wise, Strange and Holy: The Strange Woman and the Making of the Bible* (JSOTSup, 320; Sheffield: Sheffield Academic Press).
Jackson, Melissa
    2002   'Lot's Daughters and Tamar as Tricksters and the Patriarchal Narratives as Feminist Theology', *JSOT* 26: 29-46.
Landay, Lori
    1998   *Madcaps, Screwballs and Con Women: The Female Trickster in American Culture* (Philadelphia: University of Pennsylvania Press).
Löwisch, Ingeborg
    2009   'Genealogies, Gender, and the Politics of Memory: 1 Chronicles 1–9 and the Documentary Film *Mein Leben Teil 2*', in Athalya Brenner and Frank Polak (eds.), *Performing Memory in Biblical Narrative and Beyond* (Sheffield: Sheffield Phoenix Press): 228-56.
Schneider, Tammi J.
    1999   *Judges* (Berit Olam; Collegeville, MN: Liturgical Press).
Tannen, R.S.
    2007   *The Female Trickster: Post Modern and Post-Jungian Perspectives on Women in Contemporary Culture* (London: Routledge, 2007).

Hidden Ancestral Polemics in the Book of Genesis?

Diana Edelman

Yairah has devoted much of her career to identifying polemics in biblical stories, highlighting the importance of this task in helping understand one type of literary genre used by implied authors to convey views and beliefs they considered correct and to critique those they considered incorrect. I felt it would be appropriate to deal with the most elusive type of polemic she has identified, the hidden polemic, in this piece that is meant to honour her and her contributions to biblical scholarship on the occasion of her retirement. I dedicate this piece to Yairah, my long-time colleague and friend.

Introduction

The divine promise of the land to Abraham and his descendants is an integral, necessary component of an origin story. Since the patriarchal stories ostensibly function as an origin story for Israel (e.g. Van Seters 1992: 78-103; Davies 1992: 89, 124-27; Mullen 1997: 11-12, 67-71, 156),[1] Yhwh's calling of Abraham and his leading him to a new home, where he is to settle down peacefully amongst the locals and grow over time into a mighty nation that will rightfully occupy and control the land in the future, is logically associated with Genesis' function as an origin story. But is this the only function of the land promise in the book? After all, in most origin stories, the promise becomes a reality before the tale has ended.[2] In addition, I would like to

---

1.   As argued by J. Van Seters, their plotline reflects one of the two standard ways of explaining a nation's origin that were used in Greek tradition: they tell how a deity led a single ancestor, Abraham, to a new homeland, where he settled peaceably and grew into a mighty nation over time (1992: 212). Unfortunately, none of these early works has survived; we only have secondary citations of bits in the work of later writers, so their specific format, contents, and use of various motifs is uncertain. The suggested story lines may or may not be correct, therefore.

2.   In addition, the origin-story template presumed both a divine pantheon and ancestral gods (the *penates* and an occasional *lar*) that travelled with the people to their new land, where they were established as the guarantors of ongoing ownership after

suggest that Yhwh's insistence that he controls the land and its distribution might simultaneously function as a thematic hidden polemic against ancestor worship. An important theme in Genesis is the modelling of correct views about the nature and functions of Yhwh, the sole deity, for the early Jewish community. A polemic against ongoing ancestor worship in 'the promised land' would be consistent with this larger theme, since the dead were considered in some biblical texts to be 'divine ones' (e.g. 1 Sam. 28.13; Isa. 8.19) who had knowledge and could be sought out for help by their living descendants.

Yairah's work on polemics has focused on their constituting a genre that appears primarily in a narrative format (2000), but she also notes that 'literary polemic' appears in various biblical genres: stories, psalms, law, prophetic literature, and wisdom. She points out the presence of polemical topics, many of which revolve around the concept of deity and related issues like divine control over the human world, appropriate ways to worship God, membership in Israel, the nature of Israel's bond to the land, and what the proper function and rights of acceptable forms of leadership are (Amit 2000: 4; 2003: 137). I will suggest that the theme of Yhwh's control over the promised land in Genesis, which spans the patriarchal stories in chs. 12–36, plays a dual role; overtly, it is part of the plot of the origin story found in these chapters but, at the same time, drives home a hidden polemic against ancestor consultation/worship. Here, I will be suggesting the presence of a polemical topic that addresses primarily Yhwh's existence as the sole divinity and the controller of earth, of communication between the two realms, and of entitlement to land. The suggested polemic is explored more 'directly', however, in two narrative units within the book: Abraham's purchase of a burial cave for Sarah (Gen. 23) and the burying of the foreign gods by Jacob and his group under an oak near Shechem upon re-entering the land, before going to build an altar for Yhwh at Bethel, following a divine command (Gen. 35.1-4).

Hidden polemics are the most elusive type in the Hebrew Bible (HB) because they are implicit, not explicit, or introduced in an unexpected manner or wording (Amit 2000: 93-98, 221-23; 2003: 138-39). The reader senses the presence of a polemic through textual clues that direct his/her attention during the reading process to a hidden polemical issue. With this type of polemic there is a danger of eisegesis; more than a single clue must be present; the topic of the polemic must appear in other HB texts, and its presence should have been noted before in the tradition of interpretation (2000: 96-97; 2003: 142-43). A rhetorical reason for the need to conceal the polemic should be given, though all hidden polemics arguably could arise

---

successful settlement. This is clearly seen in the later, yet complete Roman version of the story template in the Aeneid. For a discussion, see Bailey 1935: 30-34, 88, 92-98.

from 'the special sensitivity of the subject and fear of hostile response' that drove the issue 'underground' (2000: 97-98; 2003: 139).

Fortunately, I am not alone in suggesting that the elimination of ancestor worship is a hidden polemic in Genesis. O. Loretz (1978) and T. Römer (1992) have argued that the patriarchal narratives are intended to create common national heroes for all Jews in the place of more localized divinized ancestors venerated by clans and extended lineages. Both argue this transformation took place with the development of theoretical monotheism, where Yhwh assumed functions formerly associated with the local ancestors, especially the guarantee of progeny to perpetuate a family and land ownership (Loretz 1978: 178-89, 192; Römer 1992: 218, 220-21).[3] Citing a range of biblical texts, H.C. Brichto has argued that ancestral ownership of the land and worship by their descendants was an integral feature of 'pre-biblical' religion that had to be accommodated to and integrated into the later normative view expressed in 'biblical' religion that Yhwh, not the ancestors, is the ultimate owner of all property (1973: 11).

In many cultures, past and present, an important function of the ancestors was and is the lineal transmission of property and family authority. A particularly revealing example of the former function is the recent change in burial patterns among the Mbeere in Kenya. Once the government introduced freehold tenure and registered land titles in the late 1960s, divesting extended kin groups of corporate rights in land, the graves of lineal forebears came to be used to support the claims of their descendants to ownership of land based on founders' rights to particular territories (Glazier 1984). In 1930, the traditional practice of corpse exposure in the bush had been outlawed and burial was mandated. The physical presence of an ancestral tomb on the periphery of gardens or in adjoining bush, combined with the extension of the oral genealogical lineage past the normal four generations to as many as ten and in one case, twenty-two generations, became the basis of land ownership claims in litigation cases that were adjudicated by local committees of men and overseen by an outsider. Prior to this time, the availability of unexploited wilderness had meant that little use had been made of the ancestors of the three- or four-generation lineage to assert rights to part of a larger, lineage-controlled estate, and there had been no ancestral tombs within the occupied land (Glazier 1984).

---

3.   However, I am unclear whether Yhwh was replacing an ongoing veneration of royal ancestors as a way to lay claim to lands that had been part of the former kingdoms of Israel and Judah, on the one hand (for royal ancestor worship, see, for example, Hallo 1992), or whether he was replacing more localized ancestors, who were seen to oversee the passing on of lands within a clan or extended lineage, as argued by Loretz (1978: 191-92). Regardless, the Genesis narratives assert in no uncertain terms that it is Yhwh and Yhwh alone who will give Israel its land in perpetuity.

In China, there are public rituals that revolve around the ancestral tomb of the founder of the lineage, domestic rituals that centre on the commemoration of three to four prior generations of ancestors who are represented by tablets, and ancestral halls in which ancestral tablets of great genealogical depth are preserved (Ahern 1973). The ancestral tablets, in contrast to ancestral tombs, were the means of lineal transmission of property and family authority. Only ancestors who passed on properties to their descendants were commemorated by a tablet.

A. Porter emphasizes how the individual vs. corporate nature of ancestors varies according to the sedentary or pastoral nature of a society. In social systems based on fixed-plot cultivation, like ancient Israel and Judah, genealogies and genealogical depth are important and ancestors will be individually recognized and named. By contrast, in pastoral societies, where territory associations are fluid, the ancestors often are a generalized, undifferentiated group that perpetuates a communal identity and territorial association (2002: 8).

According to K. van der Toorn, in the Emar texts dating from the mid-second millennium BCE, references to domestic 'gods' are to ancestors who are 'named', 'invoked', and 'honoured' (1994: 47; 1996a: 74-75). Ancestors are supernatural beings that must be attended ritually by the main heir, and such actions guarantee the inheritance of family property (1994: 49). The ancestors are represented by statuettes, which are transmitted over the generations in a family; at Nuzi, they are called *ilānu*, 'gods' (Draffkorn 1957; van der Toorn 1994: 38, 54; 1996a: 73) and in the Old Babylonian period, they represent the 'gods of the house' that transmit inheritable property and are to be associated with cultic installations in houses and tombs at Nippur and Ur (van der Toorn 1996a: 70). Van der Toorn points out that Hebrew personal names provide evidence that important dead male relatives could be deified and argues that the *teraphim* in the Bible represent the same use of statuettes to represent deified ancestors (1990; 1996b: 11).

Psalm 16.2-4 refers to the practice of making blood libations to, and invoking the names of, the ancestors, called the 'holy ones', who are in the underworld ('the ground'). It has been suggested by various scholars that vv. 2-3 have been altered over time and that, originally, they read something like, 'I said to YHWH, "You are my Lord! My God is not 'Al; not the holy ones who are in the ground"' (Nyberg 1935: 120); or, 'I said, "You are my Lord, my God! Not 'Aliy [nor] all the saints in the ground"' (Pope in Cooper 1981: 457; Smith 1993: 107). 'Aliy is used as an epithet of Ba'al in the Ugaritic texts (e.g. *CTA* 16 III:5-9),[4] so its use in 16.2 in reference to a deity other

---

4.   The relationship of the epithet *'aliy* to the Hebrew epithet *'elyon*, used in the Bible of El or generically, of a god (*'el*), is unclear. Neither is to be associated with the epithet *'al 'iyn* (e.g. *KTU* 1.4 v:59; 1.5 v:17; 1.6 v:10; 1.101:17-18), used of Ba'al in the Ugaritic texts, which derives from another root (van Zijl 1972: 282-84, 341-45; Cooper 1981: 452).

than Yhwh is likely to allude to Ba'al. In addition, in the mythic cycle of texts relating to Ba'al uncovered at Ugarit, this deity is defeated by Mot, who enters his heavenly palace through the window, and Ba'al then spends part of the year in the underworld but always returns from there to rule in heaven for the remaining part of the year. The dead ancestors, especially of royalty and heroes (Spronk 1986: 161-96), were believed to have been able to participate in the feast of Ba'al's annual revivification, the autumnal New Year festival, when they were revivified by the god (*KTU* 1.21 II.5-6) or by El, with the god (*KTU* 1.22 I:6-8; Spronk 1986: 153, 155-58, 164, 171, 173-74). The end of v. 4 affirms the psalmist will not invoke either the name of 'Aliy [Ba'al] or the dead holy ones, which appear to be acceptable practices in some contemporary circles, since he recognizes that Yhwh alone is his Lord.

Verse 5 goes on to assert that 'the boundary lines have fallen for me in goodly places; I have a good heritage'. When this verse is seen in connection with the earlier discussion on vv. 2-4, a link between the dead ancestors and land rights becomes apparent. There seems to be a rejection in Ps. 16.2-5 of known practices of turning to ancestors or to the deity 'Aliy [Ba'al], as a basis for asserting land claims, in favour of recognizing Yhwh as the giver of the land and guarantor of its ongoing possession.

Psalm 49.12 condemns the rich, who invoke the names of their deceased ancestors (Smith 1993). It does not indicate why they might do this, but a logical inference would be to lay claim to ancestral holdings and inheritance. In vv. 18-19 it is asserted that any person who has been praised for doing well for himself during his lifetime will join the generation of his 'fathers' upon death, none of whom will ever see the light again. There is an assertion that no amount of wealth can be given to Elohim as a ransom for one's mortality and that, upon death, the wealthy end up in She'ol without their worldly accumulations, like everyone else. They do not become influential ancestors who continue to oversee family interests from beyond the grave.

Exodus 21.6 probably alludes to ancestral worship. The rule for making a slave who waives his right to manumission a permanent member of his master's household required that he be taken 'before the gods', where his ear was to be pierced by his master (Exod. 21.6). The gods have been considered a reference to the family ancestors, since the piercing takes place at the doorpost of the house (Draffkorn 1957: 219-20; van der Toorn 1996b: 8-9). The Deuteronomistic version of the law eliminates the reference to the gods, which is consistent with its views of exclusive monotheism, but does not substitute Yhwh in their place (Deut. 15.16-17). This may be due again to the implied context that the act/rite was to take place at home and not in a sanctuary.

The eight HB references to land being 'the inheritance of the fathers', נחלת אבות, may preserve this same idea that the ancestors influence the living and oversee the transfer of property (Num. 21.3-4; 27.7; 36.3, 8; 1 Kgs 21.3-4; Prov. 19.14). However, the five uses in Numbers might be intended in a 'neutralized' sense to represent a patrimony or property handed down within a family rather than property whose ongoing tenure was guaranteed by ancestors, who were regularly honoured with blood libations. If Numbers is the latest of the five books of the Pentateuch to be formulated (Römer 2007), its author would probably want to avoid practices that challenged the authority of Yhwh Elohim; its purpose seems to be to provide examples of specific applications of the newly emphasized set of laws that defined a Jew.

In a reversal of the former view that the ancestors gave inherited property, there are a number of passages that emphasize it is Yhwh who is the source of such land. Two expressions are found: נחלת יהוה (1 Sam. 26.19; 2 Sam. 20.19; 21.3; Ps. 127.3) and חלק יהוה (Pss. 16.5; 119.57; 142.6). The former is parallel to נחלת אבות but replaces the fathers/ancestors with Yhwh. The second uses the synonym 'portion' in place of 'inheritance'. Elsewhere, these two nouns are used as synonyms together in Deut. 10.9; 12.12; 14.27, 29; 18.1 and Job 20.29, while the verbal form of חלק is used to describe Yhwh's assigning of נחלות in Num. 2.58; Mic. 2.4, and Prov. 17.2. In contrast to the claims in Genesis that Abraham's descendants will own the land in perpetuity, all these passages emphasize the view that Yhwh alone is responsible for allotting land and guaranteeing its ownership. However, Mic. 2.4 expresses the view that Yhwh can revoke such ownership if he so chooses.

The existence of ancestor worship has been identified in texts from Ugarit and also from Mari although, in the latter case, cautionary remarks have been expressed by J. Sasson, who has shown that some of the deities presumed in the past to represent divinized ancestors were rather deities in their own right (2001). P. Matthiae argued that a funerary cult of royal ancestors was first introduced in Syria and Mesopotamia in the Middle Bronze II period, which involved the regular observance of ritual banquets in order to ensure the human fecundity of the dynasty and the fertility of nature (1979). Following the functions proposed by J. Healy (1978), Matthiae fails to include the granting of land rights among the roles of the ancestors. Both scholars appear to have overlooked the important role of guaranteeing land ownership as well as future offspring to possess that land. On the other hand, perhaps the funerary cult of royal ancestors had a slightly different emphasis than that practised within clans or extended families, where ongoing entitlement to land rights would have been a higher priority. Kings felt little threat of losing royal estates, whereas individuals were at the constant mercy of higher officials and the king.

Abraham's Purchase of a Family Tomb Site at Machpelah (Genesis 23)

In Genesis 23, the story of Abraham's purchase of a field with a cave at its edge that was to serve as the family burial site may contain a hidden polemic against ancestor worship and the belief that ancestors guaranteed the ongoing use of land within a family. This episode is part of the larger narrative about the life of the patriarch Abraham but also has been tied to the cycle of stories about Jacob by the report that Abraham, Isaac and Jacob were all buried in the family tomb site at Machpelah. At the same time, Abraham's status as a resident alien (גר ותושב) may be designed to address issues faced by the Israelite and Judean diaspora communities and to encourage them to go ahead and establish family tombs in their new places of residence. But did those who, after deportation, were forced to resettle in a new region on assigned plots of land bear the status of גר? The extended storyline emphasizes the need for the proper burial of the dead and models a multi-generational tomb in a space purchased for that purpose, in a situation where land rights are not otherwise held or hereditary.

I suspect that the securing of the agricultural field of Ephron in addition to the 'double portion' cave is an integral part of the Abrahamic cycle. It continues to develop the theme of faith, trust, and obedience in Yhwh and his capacity to deliver on his word. Throughout 12.1–25.11, the terms of the divine reward for Abram/Abraham's obedience to Yhwh change in accordance with the degree to which he complies or does not.

It is interesting to observe that in the opening command from Yhwh in 12.1, the land is part of the stipulation to be fulfilled, not part of the reward that will come with compliance. The latter is limited to becoming a great nation, a great name, and becoming the lightning rod for blessing for all families of the earth (12.2-3). Upon Abram's arrival in Canaan, Yhwh appears to him and promises to give the land to his descendants (12.7). It is only after he separates from his nephew Lot, who should not have left Haran with him according to the command in 12.1, that the land comes to be included as a form of reward to Abraham as well as his offspring (13.14-17).

The reward of land is reiterated in the formal covenant (ברית) Yhwh enters with Abram in 15.17-21, except the land will go to his descendants, not to Abram, after he has challenged God to make good on his promise to become a great nation (15.1-6). After Abram allows Sarah to cast out Hagar and Ishmael, the first-born son but not the intended father of the chosen line of blessed descent, Yhwh initiates a second covenant (ברית) in which he reconfirms that the land that currently is a place of sojourning (מגורים) will be given to Abram and his descendants as a perpetual holding (לאחזת עולם, 17.8).

The issue of land arises in a slightly different form after Abraham is willing to sacrifice Isaac in response to a divine command; here God promises
that Abraham's offspring, who will be as numerous as the stars of heaven and
the sand on the seashore, shall possess the gate of their enemies (22.17). For
the first time, the land promise implies that the land will have to be conquered
before it will become the inheritance of the people who will become Israel.
Yet, the conquest may already be hinted at in Gen. 15.12-16, where Yhwh
announces a forthcoming 400-year slavery, after which Abraham's descendants will return 'here' to Canaan in the fourth generation, 'for the iniquity
(עֲוֹן) of the Amorites is not yet complete'. This is a proleptic summary of the
plot line that extends from Exodus through Deuteronomy but probably also
through the end of the book of Joshua, including the military conquest of the
land once the iniquity (עֲוֹן) of the current occupiers of Canaan has run its
allotted time. In this way, the conquest is justified as Yhwh's use of the
Israelites to punish the Amorites, a view that seems to be consistent with the
ideology expressed in Judg. 2.1-5.

Thus, there is ongoing attention drawn through repetition and the shifting
of terms to Yhwh's power to give and take away the land of Canaan to
whomever he chooses. He alone controls its allocation, control over which
he will give as a reward for recognition that he is Israel's *'elohim* and for
obedience to his path (Gen. 22.18). It seems there is a bit too much protest
being made about this point, as if it were something that could be disputed;
other potential rivals for the role would be local regional gods and ancestors.

Abraham's purchase of the cave of Machpelah can be read in two ways. In
the first, Abraham insists on buying the cave at Machpelah, which lies at the
edge or end of the field of Ephron, so that when his negotiations are successful, he owns a piece of the promised land in addition to a burial plot. Rather
than trying to separate spatially from the natives by situating the grave at the
end of agricultural land as a boundary between two ethnic groups (*contra* e.g.
Sternberg 1991: 31; Cohn 2003: 152, 160; Stavrakopoulou 2009: 72), his
goal is to purchase workable land that he will pass on to his heirs, which also
contains a cave where the family will be buried for future generations. His
initial description of the cave 'at the end' of the field is designed rhetorically
to prompt an offer of sale for the larger field; in the remaining negotiations,
the cave is described to be 'in the field', no longer at its end or edge (23.11,
17), and it disappears from the negotiations in favour of the field, where
Abraham subsequently says he will bury his dead (23.13-14).

In this way, the patriarch has called Yhwh's bluff for not yet fulfilling the
remaining term of divine promise involving him personally, and as noted by
Sternberg (1991: 56), paying a price that represents a shekel per year for the
time his descendants will be in exile before they take possession of the land
(15.13-16; 23.15-16). His actions would parallel his taking matters into his

own hands in earlier episodes; twice he passed Sarah off as his sister and secured wealth/blessing as a result (12.10-20; 20.1-16) and twice he tried to get God to deliver on the promise of progeny (15.1-6; 16.1-4), so it would be consistent with his character for him to slip back into his old ways of mistrust concerning Yhwh's promise to give him as well as his descendants the land of Canaan as inheritable land. The name of the parcel of land in question, מכפלה (*machpelah*), means 'double portion', which also may hint at Abraham's securing for himself a 'double portion' of promised inheritance, which often went to the eldest male heir (Deut. 21.17).[5] The suggestion by S. Boorer that Ephron is portrayed as the human agent for the divine granting of the land as an eternal possession (אחזת עולם) is not convincing (2000: 180). Yhwh is not present in this narrative, directing the outcome, and the very steep price Abraham ended up paying would suggest no divine intervention or agency here.

In the second reading, the story anticipates the fulfilment of Yhwh's preceding promise in 22.17 that 'your descendants will possess the gate of their enemies'. Here, Abraham once again serves as a trickster, as in the four episodes mentioned in the preceding paragraph. Through skilful negotiations in the 'city gate' with the Hittites of the land, who are going to be dispossessed in the future according to Yhwh's plan (15.18-21), he manages to gain a permanent foothold in the form of a אחזת קבר, an 'owned gravesite', located in a field he bought that he will hand down to his descendants. In this way, he fulfils the divine promise in a small, personal way with one piece of Hittite land, but this time, without directly challenging God about the unfulfilled promise. The phrasing in 22.17 lacks enough specificity to allow his actions to be in compliance with the announcement, though there has been no reason for him to consider the Hittites as enemies. Even so, he has managed to secure a 'double portion' of the promised land that he can pass on to his divinely designated heir, Isaac.

Such a reading would be more or less consistent with G. von Rad's view that the Priestly writers would not have wanted the patriarchs to go unrewarded, having forsaken everything for the promise, so that 'in death they were heirs and no longer "strangers"', resting in the grave that belonged

---

5. I do not think M. Sternberg has made enough of the name of the site and Abraham's crafty triumph over the locals (1991). Is it likely that the biblical author would have portrayed him to be the victim of the Hittite Ephron, who threw the field into the bargain as a means of upping the price so high he figured Abraham would not have been able to pay? Does Abraham unwittingly end up with this field, which gives him an owned piece of the promised land so that he triumphs in the end in spite of the intentions of Ephron to deter or price-gouge him? Or, is it Abraham's intention all along to gain the field as well as the cave on it by suggesting Machpelah as the site to be purchased, which by definition included a cave within a field?

to them rather than in Hittite soil or a Hittite grave (1961: 245). Ibn Ezra made the same point without resorting to source criticism: 'It informs us that God's word to Abraham that he would possess the land as an inheritance was fulfilled' (1988: 232). However, both overlooked the emphasis on the field that comes with the grave and so did not fully appreciate all that is going on in this story.

In either case, Abraham's refusal of the Hittite offer to allow him to bury in any of their graves and the offer of Ephron to 'give' him the field and cave as a gift reflect his clear desire to own the tomb and accompanying land, in the latter case, in perpetuity. 'A gift of land would be valid for the lifetime of the donor only, after which the donor's heirs could reclaim it from the donee/recipient or his heirs' (Westbrook 1991: 15). Abraham's offer to give the full price and to pay it immediately signals to the audience his desire to transfer ownership immediately to himself and his descendants (Westbrook 1991: 27).

Having bought the field and the cave, a family tomb is established, which becomes the final resting place for the bones of Sarah (23.19), Abraham (25.9), Isaac, Rebekah and Leah (49.31), and Jacob (49.29-32; 50.1). All the patriarchs have existed in the land as semi-nomadic גרים, 'resident aliens', without a permanent residence.[6] Yet, they own a family tomb within the boundaries of the land that their descendants will possess and for which they will pass on rights of tenureship to later generations, in fulfilment of Yhwh's covenant with Abraham.

Why has the author of Genesis, or one or more subsequent editors, been sure to create a single family tomb for all the patriarchs and most of the matriarchs? To do so, (t)he(y) has/ve ignored other traditions about burial sites for Jacob at Shechem (Gen. 33.19; 50.5; Acts 7.15-16; e.g. Bruston 1887: 205-206; Skinner 1912: 538; von Rad 1961: 426; Loewenstamm 1992: 87-93) or possibly the 'threshing floor'/cultic site of Atad at Abel-mizraim (Gen. 50.7-11; Meyer 1906: 280-81; Skinner 1912: 538; Loewenstamm 1992: 89-90). One possible reason would be to point out their humanness, to emphasize that even heroes and heroines, once they die, are dead and cease to exist in any other form. The term מת, 'deceased', is used repeatedly in the story (23.3, 4, 6, 8, 11, 13, 15) rather than the name of the deceased or her relationship as wife; these appear in the narrator's summaries (23.1, 2, 19).[7]

---

6. The phrase גר ותושב is typically considered a verbal hendiadys referring to someone living outside the land of their birth as a resident alien. The second term, 'dweller', should not be taken literally here to mean that Abraham and his family had settled down permanently in Hebron. The patriarchs are depicted as semi-nomads, living in tents and moving frequently around the land of Canaan.

7. T. Römer (1992: 222) offers a similar explanation. He thinks the tomb at Machpelah is meant to demonstrate the profanation of tomb sites that otherwise had been the focus of the veneration of dead, divinized ancestors, while maintaining intact the function

The emphasis on a single tomb appears to be to create familial kinship among the patriarchs, who otherwise appear to have represented unrelated local legendary figures.

An alternate explanation that I have found less convincing is that the purchased cave and plot is a rhetorical device intended to demonstrate the proper ways by which the ancestors and their descendants might 'reclaim' their land (Blenkinsopp 1992: 102; Mullen 1997: 145 n. 64).[8] As only one of two parcels bought in a legal transaction by the ancestors (cf. Gen. 33.19-20), it does not represent the fulfilment of the promise of the land, which was not to be acquired through purchase but deeded as a gift. Thus, the proposal by J. Blenkinsopp that the land theme in the Genesis stories would more naturally refer to the re-appropriation of the land after the return from exile is not likely (1992: 102, 120). On the other hand, the expectation that the land would be 'given' or granted by a superior would be in keeping with the land grants made under the Neo-Babylonian rulers and those that likely were made to settle in both Yehud and Samaria (Samerina) by Persian kings.

Having arisen 'from before his dead' (מעל פני מתו), Abraham twice refers to the need 'to bury my dead מלפני, "out of my sight"', in the negotiations with the Hittites (23.4, 8). There is clearly a play on words introduced here in the use of a similar phrase within the same sentence. The first phrase has been seen to express the idea that the dead person is unclean, though no rationale is provided (Westermann 1981: 373), and the apparently self-explanatory logic eludes me. Rabbinic proposals for the meaning do not help much either: Abraham had been lying on Sarah's face, face to face, weeping bitterly at her departure (Abravanel); he had been watching his dead (*Ahavath Jonathan*); he had been kissing the dead, which was permitted in those days (*Ts'ror Hamor*); or he had been standing near her body to win sympathy from his Hittite audience for his request for a burial place (*Hak'tav v'Hakabalah*; Kasher 1957: 172, 250). The second phrase, 'out of my sight',

---

of a tomb to legitimate the life of a group in a territory, as demonstrated by H. Gese (1977: 33-34).

8.   The account of how Jacob purchased a plot of land near Shechem and erected an altar there to El-elohey Israel in 33.20 has a different function. It is not concerned with eliminating the ancestors as guarantors of the land but rather emphasizes the antiquity and legitimacy of this sanctuary site on land owned directly by Israel's ancestor. The tying of Joseph to the tomb of Jacob and to inheriting Shechem in 48.21-22; 50.50 reflects an attempt to link a portion of Egyptian Jews back to this early sanctuary. When placed within the larger context of the patriarchal narratives, however, especially those dealing with Abraham, it can no longer count as a sanctuary within the land of promise, since it has been obtained by purchase and, by implication, was not the continuation of the legitimate altar that had been established by Abraham at the Oak of Moreh in the same vicinity (12.6).

seems redundant; a statement he needed land to bury his dead would have sufficed. This phrase may then serve to introduce a hidden polemic in the story, to which the repetition of the two similar phrases is designed to draw attention; to what might it allude?

Two options for the meaning of 'out of my sight/from before me' come to mind. It could refer to an alternate burial practice, like exposing the dead above ground or cremating the dead (the latter option is noted also by Hertz [Kasher 1957: 173, 250]) rather than immediate bodily interment. The first was the eventual practice in Zoroastrianism and the second was a Greek custom also found in Neo-Hittite kingdoms like Hamath. Or, it might be an allusion to the use of ancestral statuettes or representations of the dead (*teraphim*?), which Abraham is eschewing: the dead are dead and need to be removed from any secondary earthly presence or visible representation.[9]

A second clue pointing toward a likely hidden polemic here is the phrase that the Hittites use to characterize Abraham in v. 6: נשיא אלהים אתה, 'you are a mighty prince' or 'you are one brought along by God'.[10] The root נשא also has the legal meaning 'to confiscate property' (Greenfield 1977; Westbrook 1991: 13). Thus, the semantic range allows the presence of a pun or a polemic, depending how one construes the alternate reading, in addition to the double meaning normally associated with אלהים. Not only are the Hittites using expected hyperbole during the formal proceedings, which the Judean/Jewish audience is to recognize as an unwitting recognition that Abraham is, indeed, favoured and protected by God (so e.g. von Rad 1961: 243; Wenham 1994: 127), but in addition, Abraham is a 'confiscator of the gods'. He is depriving the Hittite ancestors of their land by buying it and making it part of the permanent inheritance of his family. Or, he is preventing Sarah from being viewed as a minor deity after her death by placing her out of sight without any earthly representation in statuette form, teaching the audience that all such representations that they may possess of deified dead should be confiscated.[11]

9. I am drawn to the possibility that the repetition of the two similar phrases in this verse, מעל פני and מלפני, might be intended to call to mind in the audience the First Commandment: you shall have no other gods על פני (Exod. 20.1; Deut. 5.6). It did so for me. In addition, there may be a deliberate allusion here to the 'hiding' of the foreign gods later on in Gen. 35.2-4, which relocates likely deified ancestors 'out of sight'—like Sarah, who is not to become one but who is properly buried. In this way, the two hidden polemics might be rhetorically linked.

10. The second rendering has been suggested by Gottstein 1953. He never considered the possibility that אלהים was being used as a superlative, to be rendered into idiomatic English as an adjective.

11. It is usually thought that only males were made deified ancestors but that would need to be verified. Even if it were the case, the author may have used a female specifically

It is curious that the HB favours the underdog and trickster form of hero
(Niditch 2000: xv-xvi, 149-50) rather than the royal type (Edelman 2011:
161-70), the military berserker type (Mobley 2005), or one that is too closely
associated with divinity. There are no tales of half-human, half divine heroes
as in the Greek world,[12] whose fame during their lifetime could lead to the
creation of sites for hero worship after their death. It is probably significant
that no burial site is given for Moses or for Elijah, both of whom might have
become foci of cults of veneration and had suspiciously divine traits associated with them. The willingness to point out the tomb site of the patriarchs
and matriarchs at Machpelah may be meant to shift the perception of one's
dead relatives from 'knowing ones' who have become minor divinities (e.g.
1 Sam. 28.7-14; Isa. 8.19-20) to dead forefathers and mothers (so previously
Loretz 1978: 191-92; Römer 1992: 222) while maintaining the integrity of
the favoured form of monarchic-era burial—multi-generational bench tombs
(Bloch-Smith 1992: 55, 58-59)—and the idea that the dead continue an
altered form of existence in Sheol and need to be tended to by their living
descendants. It is all right to 'honour your (dead) mother and father' by feed-
ing them periodically (Exod. 20.12; Deut. 5.16); it is not all right to worship
them (e.g. Deut. 26.14; Ps. 16.3-4) and consider them to have become minor
deities who can be petitioned to help you with problems (1 Sam. 28.7-14; Isa.
9.19-20; Ps. 49.12).

Jacob's Burying of the 'Foreign Gods' (Genesis 35.1-4)

These four verses form a very small unit within the larger cycle of Jacob
stories, referring the audience back to earlier narrative episodes to clarify their
current function. Specifically, in v. 1 we are taken back to Jacob' theophany
and vow at Bethel (28.19-22) as well as the story of his flight to his uncle
Laban after stealing Esau's birthright (Genesis 27), his marrying of his two
cousins, his servitude to pay the bride-price, the prosperity he gained from
working amongst Laban's herds (Genesis 29–31), his subsequent flight from
Laban, the unsuccessful search for Laban's family gods, the covenant made
between the two kinsmen in Mizpah/Galed, and his return to Cisjordan after
meeting his brother Esau at the Jabbok (Genesis 32–33). In order to understand the command in v. 2 for the family and household to 'put away the
foreign gods (אלהי הנכר)[13] that are among you' before moving south and

---

to make the point, as part of the signalling of a hidden polemic in the incident being
narrated.

12. Except perhaps for Samson.

13. As noted by J.A. Soggin (1992: 197), this expression is found predominantly in
Deuteronomic/Deuteronomistic texts: Deut. 31.16, Josh. 24.20; Judg. 10.16; 1 Sam. 7.3;
Jer. 5.19.

east to Bethel[14] and his reported hiding of these gods under the oak that was near Shechem in v. 4, we are sent to search the earlier episodes for examples of 'foreign gods'. While the rabbis suggested the gods in question were gods worshipped by foreign tribes (Hertz in Kasher 1959: 187, 279) or those taken as spoil from Shechem (Targum Jonathan [Amit 2000: 199]; Rashi *et al.* Kasher 1959: 187-88, 279]), the specific gods we find are the household gods, also called the *teraphim*, of Laban,[15] which were stolen by his daughter Rachel (31.19, 30, 34).[16] The only information we are given to help understand the motivation for the theft is the prior claim made by Rachel and Leah jointly that their father Laban regarded them as נכריות, 'foreigners'; he had sold them to Jacob and had not protected their dowries but, instead, was using the wealth personally, and they had no portion or inheritance left in their father's house. All the property Elohim has taken away from Laban (and bestowed upon Jacob) rightly belongs to them and their children (31.14-16). This justifies their decision to encourage Jacob to leave Paddan-Aram and return to the land of 'his fathers/ancestors' and his kindred (31.3).

The comment that this group of Aramaean descent had brought with them 'foreign gods' from Paddan Aram that needed to be hidden after entering the 'promised land' seems to convey a hidden polemic against ancestral consultation/worship within a more overt polemic against worshipping any gods other than Yhwh (for the latter, see e.g. von Rad 1961: 331; Westermann 1986: 551). The deified dead would qualify as 'other gods' and so be covered in that general category. The fact that the only gods mentioned earlier in the story were ancestral ones, *teraphim*, however, leaves a strong clue that the reader is supposed to narrow the meaning of 'foreign gods' in this case specifically to ancestors (e.g. von Rad 1961: 331; contra e.g. Skinner 1912: 423).[17]

14. A. Alt proposed that these verses recalled the custom of an ancient pilgrimage from Shechem to Bethel, preceded by purification (1938). His proposal has been widely adopted; see, for example, its acceptance by appeal to the use of the verb עלה in a number of psalms in such a context in von Rad (1961: 331) and Westermann (1986: 550). Soggin proposed that it alludes instead to Josiah's 'elimination of Canaanite polytheism from Judah's faith and ritual in favour of monotheism' (1992: 198). I prefer to view this as a hidden polemic against ancestor worship, in the context of a more explicit polemic against the worship of gods other than Yhwh, based on the regular burial of superfluous cultic paraphernalia in favissae and not on a specific historical incident. For a good survey of buried cultic images, see Keel 1973: 315-26.

15. For this meaning see, for example, Draffkorn 1957: 222-23.

16. According to *Sechel Tob, T.S.* 35, 9, the *yod* is omitted from *hasiru* (הסרו) to indicate that only Rachel was suspected of possessing strange gods, i.e. Laban's *teraphim* (Kasher 1959: 187). Ibn Ezra says this verse implies that both wives had strange gods (*Va-yishlach* 35.2; 1988: 332).

17. In addition, the location of the favissa under an oak near Shechem may point to another possible polemic against a particular cultic site located in or near Shechem, which is to be seen as unorthodox, tainted with 'foreignness'. See, for example, Amit 2000: 199.

The suggestion that Jacob's command to remove the foreign gods is secondary in Gen. 35.2bβα, 4, created under the inspiration of Josh. 24.23, is possible[18] but does not preclude the presence of the proposed hidden polemic against ancestor worship.[19] Amit sees an anti-Samarian polemic at work in each case and points out that the failure to destroy the foreign gods by burning or smashing them before their (ritual) burial alludes to an ongoing 'paganism' that continued to permeate Shechem (2000: 199). The LXX (Gen. 35.4) specifies Jacob 'destroyed them [the gods] until this day' but this reading is often seen to be a later expansion. For Amit, the MT wording reflects a later attempt to strip the site of the holiness it was afforded else-where in Genesis by having both Abram (Gen. 12.6-7) and Jacob (33.18-20) build altars there and also in Deuteronomistic tradition, where Shechem was viewed to have been particularly holy (Deut. 11.29-30; Josh. 8.30-35; Anbar 1992: 119; Amit 2000: 199-200). The likely presence of an anti-Shechemite/ anti-Samarian polemic does not overturn the simultaneous presence of the explicit polemic against the worship of foreign gods/gods other than Yhwh or the hidden polemic against the worship of ancestors as minor deities.

Genesis 35.1-4 seems at first glance to condemn any attempt to give power to non-native ancestors in the 'promised land' of Canaan, but this may be an explicit polemic pointing to an underlying hidden polemic advocating the elimination of all ancestor worship in the land among those identifying them-selves as members of the religious community of Israel. One could propose that this passage reflects an underlying debate about how to deal with brides who originate from a distant region: are they to abandon their family gods and turn to those of their husband's family in their new home, or can they continue to petition their family's ancestors in their new home? In any case, it is likely that this problem had been encountered already for centuries and that a solution was already in place as part of accepted cultural practice. Do ancestors have limited territorial jurisdiction, even where kinship ties exist to descendants no longer locally resident?

The suggestion by E. Nielsen (1955: 107-108, 122) that the תרפים represent Aramaean gods buried in an act of sympathetic magic to subdue his enemy, on analogy with the Egyptian execration texts and figurines, would make better sense had that action taken place at the boundary established between him and Laban at the end of ch. 31.

18.   For a number of factors pointing to the text being Deuteronomistic and exilic or post-exilic in its vocabulary, see Soggin 1992: 197. Keel had already discussed a number of these (1973: 327-29, 331-32). His suggestion that an old E-text about the hiding/burial of obsolete cultic objects at Shechem was present in ch. 35 and was subsequently expanded overlooks the possibility that the entire tradition in vv. 1-4 is late in origin, either a late insertion in the book or deliberately framed by the author of Genesis to link with the Deuteronomistic texts.

19.   Amit 2000: 199, building on the arguments of Zakovitch 1980 and Anbar 1992. The latter argues that Joshua 24 is already a post-exilic addition.

It seems more likely that the burial of the 'foreign' gods in v. 4 is meant to model behaviour that even 'native' Israelites should emulate in connection with their own deified ancestors in the 'promised land'. The narrative makes clear that it is Yhwh who protected Jacob when he was outside the land in Paddan-Aram, showing he has no territorial limitations. Within the plot-line of Genesis, Yhwh also brought Jacob back 'home' to the land he had promised to his 'grandfather' Abraham, so that the promise to Abraham concerning progeny and land would be fulfilled. Neither Rachel's family gods nor Jacob's dead ancestors Abraham or Isaac, had he chosen to consult them, could have done this. By implication, Yhwh controls the land and is the source of divine communication via dreams and other forms of appearance (28.12; 35.9) to his followers, whether they are in the land or not.[20]

Yhwh is 'the god of the fathers' (32.9), a phrase that subtly instructs the audience not to confuse the dead with a real god.[21] The phrase is used once in the Isaac stories to describe 'the god of Abraham, your father' (26.24), by which Yhwh's status as the deity worshipped by the head of the family, who now has died, is emphasized. It appears in varying formats in the Jacob stories, always with אלהי as the element in the construct state used to designate the divine, not אל: 'the god of Abraham your father and the God of Isaac (28.13), 'the god of my father', spoken by Jacob in reference to Isaac (31.5), 'the god of your father' spoken by Laban to Jacob (31.29, adopting the better attested singular form of 'father' in various Greek MSS and the Palestinian Targum), 'the god of my father, the god of Abraham and the fear of Isaac', 31.42), and 'the god of my father Abraham and the god of my father Isaac' (32.9), with the use of 'the god of their fathers' in 31.53 being a late addition not found in the LXX. All these instances artificially create lineal descent

---

20. In his argument that Jacob and Laban concluded their boundary covenant by swearing by their divinized ancestors and sacrificing to them in Gen. 31.52-54, B. Halevi (1975: 109) misunderstands the polemical correction made in the text. While this might well have been what the audience would have expected to happen, the writer has corrected that view to say that they both sacrificed to the God who had been worshipped by their common ancestors, not by the deified common ancestors themselves. Halevi's argument has been adopted by E. Bloch-Smith (1992: 123).

21. Here I differ with T. Römer, who has suggested that in Genesis the expression אלהי אב is meant to identify the former deified dead, made into ancestral gods, with Yhwh (1992: 223-24). Had that been the intent, I would have expected the generic term אל to have been used, as it has in the Genesis narratives with the epithets Shaddai, Roi, 'Olam and 'Elyon. I think these uses are attempts to identify generic types of deities being alluded to under the four epithets with the monotheistic deity, Yhwh Elohim. The single occurrence of אל אב in Gen. 49.25 in 'Jacob's Blessing' should be understood similarly. Otherwise, however, the term *'elohim* is already being used to allude to Yhwh Elohim, the only deity. We both reject the long- normative view of A. Alt that the 'god of the fathers' was a non-territorial deity worshipped by a nomadic group (1929).

among the three patriarchs while asserting that each of them worshipped the same divine entity, *'elohim*, who, by implication, is the only god among the living or the dead.

The ancestors were not the only former deified or divine beings on the hit list of the author of Genesis: Asherah, the former consort of Yhwh Sebaot during the time of the monarchy, was also actively eliminated in order to make Yhwh Elohim the sole deity in heaven. As a result, her former function as the giver of human life, attested by the thousands of female fertility figures found predominantly in Judah, whose production dramatically declined in Yehud during the Persian period, needed to be transferred to Yhwh. Genesis has a number of stories that emphasize that it is Yhwh, and Yhwh alone, who opens and closes human wombs (18.14; 20.17-18; 21.1-2; 29.31; 30.2, 22). The emphasis on Yhwh's controlling crop and animal fertility, evidenced indirectly in the theme of blessing and directly in the stories of excellent grain yields (Gen. 26.12-13) and herd increases (Gen. 30. 29-30), may be a similar move to attribute to Yhwh the functions otherwise associated with Ba'al.

Conclusion

In the book of Genesis, the land theme appears to function on two levels simultaneously. A decision to create an origin story for the community dedicated to the worship of Yhwh Elohim led to the use of a standard origin story, in spite of its theology being at odds with that espoused by the writer. It was necessary to replace the divine pantheon and ancestral gods (the equivalent of the Roman *penates* and an occasional *lar*) that normally travelled with a people to their new land and, after successful settlement, were established as the guarantors of ongoing ownership, with Yhwh Elohim alone.[22]

Once Yhwh was conceived of as the sole deity in heaven, any obstacles that might arise to prohibit execution of his plan would, by default, have to result from human failing or error or from his divine whim.[23] As a result, Yhwh now had to accompany Abraham in his journey, rather than the ancestral gods, and guarantee ongoing possession of the new land. To drive home this point, the author needed to emphasize that the ancestors were mere humans who ceased to have any influence upon their death. They were not

22. According to C. Bailey, in the *Aeneid* these function on the level of both house-deities and state-gods transplanted from Troy, which reflected the historical process whereby the state cult took over the gods of the household and fields and established them as official state cults with temple and priests (1935: 30-34, 88, 92-98).

23. The reference to 'us' in Gen. 1.26 could be construed to refer to other created orders in heaven, like angels, rather than deities, leaving 6.2, 4 as the only problematic passage from a monotheistic perspective. Yet, even here, a clear distinction is being made that this situation belonged to 'prehistory' rather than historical time as the ancients knew it—'in those days'.

divinized ancestors who guaranteed their descendants' ongoing possession of family lands. The very premise of the book of Genesis includes a polemic against divinized ancestors and ancestor worship as part of the larger explicit and implicit polemics against views that make room for the existence of deities other than Yhwh.

Two specific texts have been examined where the rejection of the cult and power of the ancestors seems to be expressed via the mechanism of a hidden polemic, hidden because of the sensitivity of the issue among early Jewish populations resident in 'the homeland' and in the diaspora. Abraham's purchase of the burial cave of Machpelah in Genesis 23 has not generally been acknowledged to address the issue of ancestral divinization and worship. I have argued that there is a rhetorical emphasis on 'the dead' (23.3, 4, 6, 8, 11, 13, 15) who need to be buried out of sight (vv. 4, 8), without the creation of subsequent *teraphim* images, in a tomb that becomes a multi-generational family burial site for descendants of the 'promised' blood-line, male and female (23.19; 25.9; 49.29-32; 50.1). The three male heads of the family worship Yhwh as their god or the god of their father or forefathers in turn (26.24; 28.13; 31.5, 29, 42; 32.9 and secondarily, 31.53), leaving no room for the forefathers to be considered gods themselves. Jacob's burial of the foreign gods under the oak near Shechem in Gen. 35.1-4 has been linked explicitly but not uniquely with Laban's stolen *teraphim* (images of family gods) in the history of scholarship. I have added an overlooked rhetorical strategy as part of that linkage: Rachel and Leah claim in 31.16 that their father has treated them as 'foreigners', which anticipates and so reinforces the connection of the 'foreign gods' in 35.2 and 4 with the images of the dead family ancestors.

Bibliography

Ahern, E.M.
>   1973   *The Cult of the Dead in a Chinese Village* (Stanford: Stanford University Press).

Alt, A.
>   1938   'Die Wallfahrt von Sichem nach Bethel', in R. Abramowski (ed.), *In piam memoriam Alexander von Bulmerincq: Gedenkenschrift dargebracht von einem Kreise von Freunden und Kollegen* (Riga: n. i.): 218-30.
>   1929   *Der Gott der Väter. Ein Beitrag zur Vorgeschichte der israelitisichen Religion* (BWANT, 48/dritte Folge, 12; Stuttgart: Kohlhammer).

Amit, Y.
>   2000   *Hidden Polemics in Biblical Narrative* (trans. from Hebrew by J. Chipman; Biblical Interpretation Series, 25; Leiden: E.J. Brill).
>   2003   'Epoch and Genre: The Sixth Century and the Growth of Hidden Polemics', in O. Lipschits and J. Blenkinsopp (eds.), *Judah and the Judeans in the Neo-Babylonian Period* (Winona Lake: Eisenbrauns): 135-51.

Anbar, M.
   1992   *Josue et l'alliance de Sichem (Josue 24:1-28)* (Beiträge zur biblischen
              Exegese und Theologie, 25; Frankfurt am Main: Peter Lang).
Bailey, C.
   1935   *Religion in Virgil* (Oxford: Clarendon Press).
Blenkinsopp, J.
   1992   *The Pentateuch: An Introduction to the First Five Books of the Bible* (New
              York: Doubleday).
Bloch-Smith, E.
   1992   *Judahite Burial Practices and Beliefs about the Dead* (JSOTSup, 123;
              JSOT/ASOR Monograph Series, 7; Sheffield: Sheffield Academic Press).
Boorer, S.
   2000   'The Priestly Promise of the Land: Genesis 17.8 in the Context of P as a
              Whole', in N.C. Habel and S. Wurst (eds.), *The Earth Story in Genesis*
              (Sheffield: Sheffield Academic Press): 175-86.
Brichto, H.C.
   1973   'Kin, Cult, Land and Afterlife—A Biblical Complex', *HUCA* 44: 1-54.
Bruston, C.
   1887   'La mort et la sépulture de Jacob', *ZAW* 7: 202-10.
Cohn, R.L.
   2003   'Negotiating (with) the Natives: Ancestors and Identity in Genesis', *HTR*
              96.2: 147-66.
Cooper, A.
   1981   'Divine Names and Epithets in the Ugaritic Texts', in S. Rummel (ed.),
              Ras Shamra Parallels: The Texts from Ugarit and the Hebrew Bible, III
              (AnOr, 51; Rome: Pontificium Istitutum Biblicum): 333-469.
Davies, P.R.
   1992   *In Search of 'Ancient Israel'* (JSOTSup, 148; Sheffield: JSOT Press).
Draffkorn, A.E.
   1957   '*Ilani/Elohim*', *JBL* 76: 216-24.
Edelman, D.
   2011   'Saul as a Young Hero', in J.-M. Durand and T. Römer (eds.), *Le jeune
              héros* (OBO, 250; Fribourg: Academic Press Fribourg; Göttingen:
              Vandenhoeck & Ruprecht): 161-83.
Gese, H.
   1977   'Der Tod im Alten Testament', in *Zur biblischen Theologie: Alttestament-
              liche Vorträge* (Beiträge zur evangelischen Theologie, 78; Munich:
              Kaiser): 31-54.
Glazier, J.
   1984   'Mbeere Ancestors and the Domestication of Death', *Man* NS 19: 133-47.
Gottstein, M.H.
   1953   'נשיא אלהים (Gen. XXIII 6)', *VT* 3: 298-99.
Greenfield, J.C.
   1977   '*Našû-nadānu* and its Congeners', in M. de Jong Ellis (ed.), *Essays on the
              Ancient Near East in Memory of Jacob Joel Finkelstein* (Memoirs of the
              Connecticut Academy of Arts and Sciences, 19; Hamden: Archon Books):
              87-91.

Halevi, B.
    1975   'עקבות נוספים לפולחן אבות' ('New Traces of Ancestor Worship'), *BM* 64:
            101-17 (Hebrew).

Hallo, W.M.
    1992   'Royal Ancestor Worship in the Biblical World', in *'Sha'arei Talmon':
            Studies in the Bible, Qumran, and the Ancient Near East Presented to
            Shemaryahu Talmon* (Winona Lake, IN: Eisenbrauns): 381-401.

Healy, J.F.
    1978   '*Mlkm/rp'um* and the *kispum*', *UF* 10:87-91.

Ibn Ezra
    1988   *Ibn Ezra's Commentary on the Pentateuch: Genesis (Bereshit)* (trans. and
            annotated by H.N. Strickman and A.M. Silver; New York: Menorah
            Publishing).

Kasher, M.M.
    1957   *Encyclopedia of Biblical Interpretation: A Millennial Anthology. Genesis.*
            III (trans. H. Klein; New York: American Biblical Encyclopedia Society).
    1959   *Encyclopedia of Biblical Interpretation: A Millennial Anthology. Genesis,*
            IV (trans. H. Klein; New York: American Biblical Encyclopedia Society).

Keel, O.
    1973   'Das Vergraben der "fremden Götter" in Genesis XXXV 4b', *VT* 23:
            305-33.

Loewenstamm, S.E.
    1992   'The Death of the Patriarchs in Genesis', in *From Babylon to Canaan:
            Studies in the Bible and Its Oriental Background* (Jerusalem: Magnes
            Press): 78-108.

Loretz, O.
    1978   'Vom kanaanäischen Totenkult zur jüdischen Patriarchen—und
            Elternehrung', *Jahrbuch für Anthropologie und Religionsgeschichte* 3:
            149-201.

Matthiae, P.
    1979   'Princely Cemetery and Ancestors Cult at Ebla During the Middle Bronze
            II', *UF* 11: 563-69.

Meyer, E.
    1906   *Die Israeliten und ihrer Nachbarstämme: alttestamentliche Unter-
            suchungen* (Halle a. S.: M. Niemeyer).

Mobley, G.
    2005   *The Empty Men: The Heroic Tradition of Ancient Israel* (ABRL; New
            York: Doubleday, 2005).

Mullen, E.T., Jr
    1997   *Ethnic Myths and Pentateuchal Foundations: A New Approach to the For-
            mation of the Pentateuch* (SBL Semeia Studies; Atlanta: Scholars Press).

Niditch, S.
    2000   *A Prelude to Biblical Folklore: Underdogs and Tricksters* (Chicago/
            Urbana: University of Illinois Press).

Nielsen, E.
    1955   'The Burial of the Foreign Gods', *Studia Theologica* 8: 103-22.

Nyberg, H. S.
  1935   *Studien zum Hoseabuche: Zugleich ein Beitrag zur Klärung des Problems der alttestamentlichen Textkritik* (Uppsala Universitets Årsskrift, 1935: VI; Uppsala: A.B. Lundequistska).

Porter, A.
  2002   'The Dynamics of Death: Ancestors, Pastoralism, and the Origins of a Third-Millennium City in Syria', *BASOR* 325: 1-36.

Rad, G. von
  1961   *Genesis: A Commentary* (trans. from German 1956 original by J.H. Marks; OTL; London: SCM Press).

Römer, T. C.
  1992   'Les récits patriarchaux contre la vénération des ancêtres', in O. Abel and F. Smyth (eds.), *Le livre de traverse: de l'exégèse biblique à l'anthropologie* (Paris: Editions du Cerf): 213-25.
  2007   'Israel's Sojourn in the Wilderness and the Construction of the Book of Numbers', in R. Rezetko, T.H. Lim, and W.B. Aucker (eds.), *Reflection and Refraction: Studies in Biblical Historiography in Honour of A. Graeme Auld* (VTSup, 113; Leiden: E.J. Brill): 419-45.

Sasson, J.M.
  2001   'Ancestors Divine?', in W.H. van Soldt (ed.), *Veenhof Anniversary Volume: Studies Presented to Klaas R. Veenhof on the Occasion of his Sixty-Fifth Birthday* (Uitgaven van het Nederlands Historisch-Archaeologisch Instituut te Istanbul, 89; Leiden: Nederlands Instituut voor het Nabije Oosten): 413-28.

Skinner, J.
  1912   *A Critical and Exegetical Commentary on Genesis* (ICC, 1; Edinburgh: T. & T. Clark).

Smith, M.S.
  1993   'The Invocation of the Deceased Ancestors in Psalm 49:12c', *JBL* 112: 105-107.

Soggin, J.A.
  1992   'Jacob in Shechem and in Bethel', in M. Fishbane, E. Tov and W. Fields (eds.), *'Sha'arei Talmon': Studies in the Bible, Qumran, and the Ancient Near East Presented to Shemaryahu Talmon* (Winona Lake: Eisenbrauns): 195-98.

Spronk, K.
  1986   *Beatific Afterlife in Ancient Israel and in the Ancient Near East* (AOAT, 219; Kevelaer: Butzon & Bercker; Neukirchen–Vluyn: Neukirchener Verlag).

Stavrakopoulou, F.
  2009   'Ancestor Ideologies and the Territoriality of the Dead in Genesis', in E. Ben Zvi, D. Edelman and F. Polak (eds.), *A Palimpsest: Rhetoric, Ideology, Stylistics and Language Relating to Persian Israel* (Piscataway, NJ: Gorgias Press): 61-80.

Sternberg, M.
  1991   'Double Cave, Double Talk: The Indirections of Biblical Dialogue', in J.P. Rosenblatt and J.C. Sitterson Jr (eds.), *'Not in Heaven': Coherence and Complexity in Biblical Narrative* (Bloomington, IN: Indiana University Press): 28-57.

Toorn, K. van der
1990   'The Nature of the Biblical Teraphim in the Light of the Cuneiform Evidence', *CBQ* 52: 203-22.
1994   'Gods and Ancestors in Emar and Nuzi', *Zeitschrift für Assyriologie* 84: 38-59.
1996a   'Domestic Religion in Ancient Mesopotamia', in K. Veenhof (ed.), *Houses and Households in Ancient Mesopotamia* (Leiden: Nederlands Historisch-Archaeologisch Instituut te Istanbul): 69-78.
1996b   'Ancestors and Anthroponyms: Kinship Terms as Theophoric Elements in Hebrew Names', *ZAW* 108: 1-11.
Van Seters, J.
1992   *Prologue to History: The Yahwist as Historian in Genesis* (Louisville, KY: Westminster/John Knox Press).
Wenham. G.J.
1994   *Genesis 16–50* (WBC, 2; Dallas: Word Books).
Westbrook, R.
1991   *Property and the Family in Biblical Law* (JSOTSup, 113; Sheffield: JSOT Press).
Westermann, C.
1986   *Genesis 12–36: A Commentary* (trans. from German 1981 original by J.J. Scullion; London: SPCK).
Zakovitch, Y.
1980   'The Tendency of the Story about the Burial of the Alien Gods in Shechem (Gen 35:2, 4)', *BM* 25: 30-37 (Hebrew).
Zijl, P.J. van
1972   *Baal: A Study of Texts in Connexion with Baal in the Ugaritic Epics* (AOAT, 10; Kevelaer: Butzon & Bercker).

REWRITING, OVERWRITING, AND OVERRIDING: TECHNIQUES OF EDITORIAL REVISION IN THE DEUTERONOMISTIC HISTORY[*]

Cynthia Edenburg

In her book, *The Book of Judges: The Art of Editing* (1999), Yairah Amit has shown that biblical editors are not just redactors who arbitrarily snip, paste and combine texts, but purposeful authors and masters of literary artistry who play a key role in the formation of biblical compositions. The following essay was written in appreciation of Yairah's scholarly work, her tutelage and her warm and collegial encouragement.

Noth's hypothesis regarding the unity and coherence of the Deuteronomistic History (DtrH) was based upon his view of the Deuteronomist (Dtr) as a historian who made use of source material. According to the classic formulation of the DtrH hypothesis, the hallmarks of deuteronomistic composition are use of comprehensive structuring devices (such as the chronological framework, as well as proleptic and retrospective discourses); and a peculiar style of discourse marked by characteristic phraseology, and a penchant for motive clauses.[1] Such stylistic and structural markers have highlighted themes and concepts that were subsequently associated with deuteronomistic ideology, all of which provided a basis for distinguishing between deuteronomistic composition and redaction on the one hand, and non-deuteronomistic materials on the other hand. Materials that deviate from deuteronomistic outlook and style either derived directly from the Dtr's sources, or were added at a late stage to the completed DtrH by scribes who were not partner to the Dtr's work. Noth held that it was possible to distinguish between the Dtr's sources and late additions whose secondary character was evident, since they severed the narrative continuity and disrupted the literary and

   [*]   An early version of this essay was presented with the financial assistance of the Open University of Israel research authority at the 2006 annual meeting of the Society of Biblical Literature.
   1.   One should also note the complex syntax characteristics of deuteronomistic discourse. Surprisingly, deuteronomistic syntax has not been studied until recently; see Polak 2010, and cf. Gross 1987, de Regt 1991.

chronological framework which imparted unity upon the Dtr's composition (Noth 1962: 68-85; 1991: 23, 66-67, 77 n. 2, 86 n. 3). Most of the secondary material was easily identified as 'appendices' that accreted in blocks and provided the basis for the subsequent division of the composition into the separate 'books' of the Former Prophets.

Nevertheless, Noth's view of the inherent unity of the DtrH has been challenged. On the one side, advocates of the multiple redaction approach attribute to different deuteronomistic editions increasingly more material, previously considered non-deuteronomistic or even post-deuteronomistic in origin.[2] However, the multiple redaction approach obscures the contribution made by post-deuteronomistic scribes who wished to revise the DtrH without resorting to whole-scale rewriting. Although these scribes occasionally employed deuteronomistic idiom, the texts they composed challenge the deuteronomistic narrative as well as its basic concepts and ideals. On the other side are scholars who employ final-form readings of Deuteronomy–Kings to argue for editorial unity (e.g. Sweeney 2001: 33-176; Peckham 1985). However, it should be evident that this approach confuses canonical interpretation with redaction criticism, and neglects the role revision plays in producing the text's final form.

Indeed, redaction analysis must provide an adequate explanation of the considerations that led later scribes to change the shape of the text they received. Competent editors and revisers are motivated by literary concerns, or historical and ideological considerations that necessitated updating or revising texts to reflect changing realities and outlooks, and certainly the same holds true for biblical scribes. Thus, although final-form reading strategies do not prove compositional unity, they may help us understand the editorial considerations that motivated later redactors to revise the form and message of previous texts.

How, then, did Biblical authors work to revise source material? Although they left us no formal statement of method or intent, there is *empirical evidence* available in the texts themselves, and close examination of the texts reveals three main models: rewriting, overwriting, and overriding. In the *rewriting* model the author/editor rewrites the source material according to his own outlook, while omitting or harmonizing conflicting views (cf. van der Toorn 2007: 133-37). The outstanding example of this method in the Hebrew Bible is provided by Chronicles, which is still best understood as a thorough revision of the Deuteronomistic History (McKenzie 1999; Van Seters 2007). The method of rewriting as a means of revision was already practiced by Assyrian scribes who dealt with changing historical circumstances by producing new recensions of royal annals, which occasionally

---

2.   For a survey see Römer and de Pury 2000: 67-74.

conflicted with previous narratives of the events (cf. Olmstead 1916: 7-9, 21-27, 53-59; Tadmor 1981: 18-21; Levine 1981: 62-63; Liverani 1981: 252-57). Thus, there is no reason to suppose that Judean scribes were not familiar with this method of editorial revision already in the late Iron Age. And yet, the existence of conflicting accounts within the biblical narratives indicates that the authors did not find it necessary to rewrite their sources and eliminate narrative, editorial and ideological inconsistencies.

Instead, scribes more often chose to revise the narratives they received by *overwriting* them with new material reflecting their tendencies. These revisions frequently take the form of expansions set directly into the received narratives with little or no attempt at easing the transitions between the host narrative and the insertion (van der Toorn 2007: 125-32). It is often assumed that scribes preferred to revise by expansion and refrained from rewriting, out of antiquarian interests or respect for the text before them which had attained the status of authoritative or sanctified scripture. This, I think, is doubtful, for the very act of inserting an expansion is an overwriting of the previous text and causes a shift in the reader's perception of the text's purpose and significance (cf. van der Toorn 2007: 126). Instead, we should entertain the possibility that the tactic of expansion or overwriting was initially adopted as a simple means for revision in an age when 'scratch paper' was not readily available for drafting a formal rewriting.

This method may be illustrated by both deuteronomistic and post-deuteronomistic overwritings. Thus, for example, the confusion that stems from the narrative breaks and repetitions in Josh. 8.3-13 is best explained as the result of overwriting, in which a revision is inserted directly into the narrative by means of parataxis. The opening of this section in Josh. 8.3a conveys the impression that Joshua intends to deploy all of his forces immediately against Ai, but this is deferred until the following day according to 8.10. In the interim, according to 8.3b-9, a select group is sent ahead to lie in ambush behind the town. However, any attempt to read 8.3-13 as a unified account must break down when confronted with the contradictory figures regarding the size of the ambush (30,000 vs. 5000 men, cf. 8.3, 12; and see, e.g., Noth 1971: 50-51; Fritz 1994: 87, 91-92; van der Meer 2004: 420-23, 442-52). The most satisfactory solution is to view 8.3-9 as a secondary expansion that breaks the original continuity in vv. 1-2, 10-14 (e.g. Rösel 1975: 161; Butler 1983: 84; Fritz 1994: 87-88; van der Meer 2004: 442-48).[3] The question that concerns us here is what motivated a subsequent scribe to overwrite the original narrative with new material, by which the mobilization for battle occurred in two separate stages?

---

3. Cf. Mazor 1994 and Nelson 1997: 109-12 who argue that the original narrative is represented by the shorter text of the LXX, which lacks Josh 8.11b-13. However, Nelson admits that vv. 11b-13 might have dropped out of the LXX *Vorlage* due to homoioteleuton.

It is evident that the later scribe was not concerned with improving the tactical sense of the story, for his ambushers must now conceal themselves in the field for a full day before moving into action. Instead, a likely motivation for the overwriting in vv. 3-9 was to enhance the figure of Joshua. The ambush tactic was dictated at the outset by Yhwh (v. 2b), which might detract from the image of Joshua as military commander. However, the scribe overwrote the account so that Joshua could convey the instructions and fully expound the tactics that were only intimated by Yhwh's directive (vv. 4-8; cf. also 6.6-7 and see Römer 2005: 87). The overwriting further holds that the ambush force was sent a day ahead (vv. 3-9), thereby alleviating the original hiatus between receiving Yhwh's orders and acting upon them (cf. v. 10). Consequently, the overwriting highlights Joshua's alacrity in executing his commission.

A similar motivation for overwriting is evident in the Priestly revision of the Gibeonites' deception. In the core story (Josh. 9.3-17, 22-27), Joshua made peace with the Gibeonites after they convinced him that they come from afar, as mandated by Deut. 20.10-15. When the deception is discovered, Joshua confronts the Gibeonites and curses them, binding them to menial service at an Israelite sanctuary. Early readers of this story in its larger context might have understood it as a tendentious account of the origins of the sanctuary at Gibeon, which was subsequently superseded by the royal sanctuary in Jerusalem (cf. 1 Kgs 3.4; Na'aman 2009: 112-17). Although there is no evidence of the later history of the sanctuary at Gibeon, it might have enjoyed renewed prestige during the Neo-Babylonian period, when the Jerusalem temple lay in ruins. Within this larger context, early Persian period readers might have viewed the story as an exemplar that undermines the status of alternate cult sites north of Jerusalem, and consequently, they might have read it as a programmatic call for support for the rehabilitation of the Jerusalem temple. At the same time, it was difficult to gloss over the inherent tension between the story of the Gibeonite ruse and aspects of late deuteronomistic ideology. On the one hand, the late deuteronomic revision of the rules for warfare justifies the injunction to proscribe the indigenous population so that their practices would not infiltrate the Israelite cult (Deut. 20.15-18; cf. Nelson 2002: 246-47). On the other hand, the exilic revision of the conquest account depicts Joshua as the faithful follower of Moses who annihilated the Canaanites 'as commanded by Moses, the servant of Yhwh' (Josh. 11.12, 15, 20, 23, cf. 1.5, 17; 3.7; 4.10, 14; 8.35; Deut. 34.9; cf. Römer 2005: 133-34). After the story of the Gibeonites was placed within its context, readers must have been surprised that Joshua was 'credited' with introducing into the sanctuary workers who supposedly derived from the indigenous, non-Israelite population of Canaan.[4] How could Joshua's treatment of the Gibeonites be reconciled with the deuteronomistic ideology regarding the peoples of the land (e.g. Van Seters 1983: 328-29; Nelson 1997: 124-25)? To this end a later, Priestly scribe utilized the tactic of overwriting in order to redirect the reader's attention away from Joshua's culpability for appointing this supposedly foreign group to the cult personnel at Yhwh's sanctuary. This scribe salvaged Joshua's reputation by ascribing to the leaders of the congregation (נשׂיאי העדה) the initiative to spare the Gibeonites and make them a subservient group.[5] The final-form reading shows how this editorial strategy revises the reader's perception of the Gibeonite alliance. The Priestly scribe inserted the solution proposed by leaders of the congregation *before* that offered by Joshua; thus, Joshua may now be viewed as making the best of a bad thing, by turning the oath sworn by the leaders to spare the Gibeonites and dedicate them to the service of the congregation into a curse that they be forever bound as menials to the staff of the sanctuary.

One more example will suffice to illustrate how the overwriting technique not only revises narrative structure, but also shapes readers' attitude towards the narrative and its subject. The narrative of the war at Gibeah begins by reporting that all the Israelites convened at Mizpeh, where they assembled a force of 400,000 men (Judg. 20.1-2), and that the Benjaminites *heard* about this assembly (v. 3a). Readers might expect that Benjamin would directly respond to hearing about the muster of armed troops at Mizpah, since Mizpah itself lies within the territory of Benjamin (cf. Mizpeh in Josh. 18.26-28), and is only about a two hours' march away along the main north-south road from Gibeah (*Tel el-Ful*),[6] but this expectation is not fulfilled until v. 14. In the interim, the narrator returns to the assembly at Mizpah, where the Israelites investigate the circumstances behind the dismembering of the concubine's corpse and deliberate how to react (vv. 3b-10). Immediately afterwards the narrator relates that the tribes gathered against *the city*, namely, Gibeah (v. 11), but do not open battle, instead demanding to receive the culprits from Gibeah (vv. 12-13).

The narrative break following 20.3a undoubtedly indicates that new material has been inserted into the account, thereby disrupting the flow of the narrative. In my opinion, the original account comprised *1-*2, 3a, and

---

4. Most recently I argued that the story of the Gibeonite deception is a post-deuteronomistic composition, and see Edenburg, forthcoming.

5. Moreover, the revision pictures the Gibeonites as serving the congregation ('hewers of wood [...] *for the whole community*', Josh. 9.21) rather than the sanctuary ('hewers of wood [...] *for the House of my God*', v. 23).

6. Elsewhere, rallying of troops follows upon *hearing* that the opposing side has assembled, e.g., 1 Sam. 7.7; 2 Sam. 10.7; 2 Kgs 3.21; cf. Josh. 9.1-2; 10.1-5; 11.1-4; Judg. 4.12-13; 1 Sam. 13.3-5; 2 Sam. 5.17-18.

12-14.[7] In this account the Israelites sent from Mizpah their demand that the Benjaminites hand over the men of Gibeah. Although the Benjaminites had heard about the gathering of troops at Mizpah (v. 3a), they assembled for war only when faced with the Israelites' demands. The original narrative seems to have assumed that report of the incident at Gibeah circulated prior to the Mizpah assembly, and that the main purpose of the assembly was to muster troops to enforce the demand for extradition. This account is not overly concerned with justifying the Israelites' course of action since, after all, justice was on their side (vv. 12-13). And yet, a reader sympathetic with Benjamin might find that the Israelites initiated the hostilities by invading Benjaminite territory, while the Benjaminites responded only when faced with an ultimatum which the Israelites backed up with a force of 400,000!

A later scribe retarded the flow of events by overwriting the narrative, in order to resolve ambiguities and to more fully justify the action of the Israelites. This scribe employed Priestly style in a novel fashion, which may indicate his distance from the traditional priestly circles (Burney 1918: 457-58; Becker 1990: 266-69; Edenburg 2003: 57, 165-69). The added material bridges the gap between the visual message of the dismembered concubine (19.29-30) and the ultimatum issued to Benjamin (20.12-13). According to the overwritten version of events, the tribes assembled at Mizpah in order to *investigate* the circumstances behind the grisly message (20.3b), and they decided how to respond only after hearing the Levite's testimony (vv. 4-7). In reaction, the Israelites swore not to return to their homes until dealing with the men of Gibeah in accordance with their *just* deserts (v. 8, 10b) and then mobilized forces at Gibeah (v. 11), thereby showing that they undertook to execute their oath without delay.

Although the action of the Benjaminites in v. 14 does not differ from that already ascribed to Israel in vv. 1 and 11, the overwritten narrative refrains from attributing to Israel any warlike intentions, laying instead the whole burden for the outbreak of hostilities on the side of Benjamin. The overwriting of the narrative in 20.1-13 creates the impression that the Israelites attempted to postpone the war even if it could not be adverted. Thus, the disruption of the reader's expectations in 20.3b helps pass the onus for the war from Israel to the side of Benjamin. War does not break out because the Benjaminites *heard* (וישמעו) about the massive force assembled at Mizpah (v. 3a), but because they would not *listen to* (לא אבו לשמוע) the reasonable demands of Israel (v. 13).

The examples of overwriting examined above demonstrate that the strategy was employed at various stages in the revision of the DtrH (exilic and Priestly revisions of the Josianic Josh. 8 and 9, and a Priestly influenced

_____

7. See Edenburg 2003: 51-60. Alternately, the interpolation includes 20.3b-13, and see, e.g., Budde 1897: 133-34; Gray 1986. 228.

revision of post-deuteronomistic Judges 20). In each of the three cases, the overwriting was inserted into the narrative *before* the section it was intended to revise. This strategy *predisposes* the reader towards a final-form reading of the text.

This strategy was also employed on a larger scale in a fashion which I call 'overriding''. Authors who utilize this method refrain from reworking or otherwise emending the material they receive, but 'override' its message by appending new blocks of narrative that challenge the reader to question the concepts and ideals embodied in the previous meta-narrative.[8] The scribes who employed the tactic of 'overriding' did not integrate their texts into the narrative strand of the host composition, but simply placed them alongside the previous narrative, generally at strategic junctures; for example, preceding introductions, as with the alternate account of the conquest (Judg. 1.1–2.5), the stories of Micah's image and the outrage at Gibeah (Judg. 17–18, 19–21), or following summations, as with the lists following the summary of the conquest (Josh. 13.1–19.51), and the report about life under Babylonian rule (2 Kgs 25.22-30; cf. Römer 2005: 179-83).

The overriding purpose of these texts has been largely overlooked. Since the nineteenth century, these blocks have been considered editorial accidents or appendices that were added in order to update the main narrative or to supplement it with antiquarian information derived from alternate sources, for which no proper context was found within the stream of the main narrative (e.g. Auberlen 1860: 536-68; Noth 1991: 66-69, 77 n. 2, 86 n. 3). The view of these materials as incidental leftovers obscures the editorial intentions that might have led to their inclusion in the historiographic composition.

The strategy of overriding can be illustrated by Joshua 13–19 and Judges 1, both of which override the deuteronomistic account of the conquest. However we might explain the fact, the deuteronomistic conquest account in Joshua 6–11 displays a strong Benjaminite and Ephraimite orientation (e.g. Alt 1953: 178-84; Noth 1971: 11-13; Römer 2005: 82-90; cf. Schunck 1963: 25-39). The major conquest narratives are located in the territory of Benjamin and Ephraim; and Joshua, the national leader, is supplied with an Ephraimite lineage. Within the stream of the narrative, the conquest of representative towns in Judah appears to be an afterthought tacked on to the account of the victory at Gibeon, which takes place in Benjaminite territory. The post-deuteronomistic scribe who added the diverse lists and other materials (Joshua 13–19) to the deuteronomistic account of the conquest, may have tried to revise this Benjaminite–Ephraimite orientation by granting Judah privilege of place at the head of the tribal allotments, while providing alternate accounts in which Judean heroes, rather than Joshua, are credited

8.   This method was already employed by second millennium cuneiform scribes, and see Otto 1994: 163-82; van der Toorn 2007: 150-51.

with conquering Hebron and Debir. The narrative framework provided for these lists and alternate accounts reinterpret the conquest of Canaan as a two-part process: pan-Israelite conquest, followed by tribal possession of the land.[9] Thus, the added tribal lists and accounts appear to augment the pan-Israelite conquest narrative, even though their basic premises and motivation run counter to one another.

At a later stage the author of Judges 1 reacted to the revised version of the conquest and possession of Canaan with a concise and tendentious rewriting which emphasizes Judah's exploits. The conflict between the accounts in Judges 1 and Joshua is well known; therefore I will proceed to the rationale that guided the author who added this conflicting material (see, e.g., Weinfeld 1993: 388-400; Auld 1975: 261-85; Younger 1995: 75-92). This alternate account, placed *after* the story of the complete conquest under Joshua, can only be understood as an attempt to override the authority of the previous narrative. The competing account in Judges 1 does away with the figure of a national leader, and demolishes the ideal of 'all Israel', by highlighting the failure of all the tribes—apart from Judah—in driving out the Canaanites from the tribes' allotments. The rationale of the injunction to dispossess and expel the Canaanites from the land Yhwh gives to Israel holds that the native peoples would lead the Israelites to stray from their pact with Yhwh and worship the gods of Canaan, becoming in effect Canaanites themselves (Exod. 34.11-16; Deut. 7.2-4, 16; 20.18; Judg. 2.1-5). Thus, the alternate account of the conquest in Judges 1 implies that only Judah actually inherited the land, while all the other tribes are suspect of Canaanization. The force of such an accusation in the context of the conflicting claims to represent the 'real' Israel in the post-exilic period should be apparent. This alternate conquest account in Judges 1 displays an anti-Benjaminite tendency; all this account can say about Benjamin is to fault them for not dispossessing the Jebusites of Jerusalem, when previously, in v. 8, Judah had already been credited with conquering the city. Instead, Benjamin remains to dwell among the foreign Jebusites who have established themselves in Jerusalem. We may well surmise how this charge might have resounded in ears familiar with the situation in the land of Benjamin following the Babylonian conquest. I suggest, then, that Judges 1 overrides the deuteronomistic story of the conquest, not only to imbue it with a Judean, rather than Ephraimite orientation, but in order to reflect concerns relevant to new political realities.

The editorial strategy of 'overriding' also helps explain why the story of the Outrage at Gibeah was placed precisely at the juncture between the story

9. Cf. Noth 1971: 10-11. Despite the Judean orientation of this complex, the editor added that Judah was unable to dispossess the Jebusites in Jerusalem (Josh. 15.63). Given the post-deuteronomistic origin of this material, the comment may reflect the depopulation of Jerusalem following the Babylonian conquest.

of Micah's image and Samuel's birth narrative. On the one hand, the Gibeah story is an independent and self-contained narrative that could have easily been placed at a number of different junctures, such as after Judges 1 (cf. Josephus, *Ant.* 5.136-74), or after the ark narrative (1 Sam. 4.1–7.1), or even in between any of the saviour stories in Judges. On the other hand, the text includes several catch-phrases that recur in the two narratives immediately preceding and following it. In, my view, these intertextual links indicate that the Gibeah story was composed for its present context (Edenburg 2003: 318-50; cf. Zakovitch 1983: 161-83). Thus, even though we may be justified in interpreting the aims of the narrative as an independent composition, we can achieve full appreciation of its purpose only by considering how it functions within the context for which it was composed. There can be no doubt that the Gibeah story was conceived as an anti-Benjaminite polemic, notwithstanding the story's end, which was necessitated by the context for which the narrative was intended. It is likely that the author wanted to kill off Benjamin, but was constrained by the fact that Benjamin, as both a lineage and a territory, is central to the story of the foundation of the monarchy. Thus, as a compromise, the final act of the story explains that Benjamin survived—although greatly reduced—only thanks to the concern of the other tribes for the ideal wholeness of Israel.

Many recent readings of the Former Prophets view the Gibeah story as an introduction to the story of the foundation of the monarchy, since it is thought to demonstrate the lawlessness and anarchy that prevail in a society with no central authority (e.g. Crüsemann 1978: 162; Jüngling 1981: 275-78, 292-92; Veijola 1977: 15-29; Mayes 2001: 256-58). Thus, it is supposed that the story argues for the necessity of kingship as a means to maintain social order. However, the details of the story do not support this view, for the tribes spontaneously act in perfect accord to avenge the wrong committed by the people of Gibeah, and it is doubtful that a king could either prevent the crime or act with greater efficacy to punish the wrongdoers. In fact, apart from the framing statements, 'In those days there was no king in Israel' (Judg. 19.1a; 21.25a), which imitate those of 17.6a and 18.1a, nothing in the story suggests that the implied subject is the monarchy, or any other institution of leadership.[10] If anything, the story seems to extol an ideal view of a leaderless society capable of acting to enforce the social norms and values (see, e.g., Bleek 1878: 199-200; Amit 1999: 337-41). Thus, the placement of the Gibeah story within its context does *not* supply a proper introduction to the story of the founding of the monarchy. The narrative's purpose is evident in its avowed subject, namely, the wrongdoings of Benjamin and its

---

10. For the dependence of Judg. 19.1a and 21.25a on 17.6a, 18.1a, see, e.g., Noth 1962: 79; Crüsemann 1978: 157; Amit 1999: 345-48; Edenburg 2003: 326-27.

unwarranted preservation from annihilation, based solely on the idea that no means be spared to prevent the violation of the wholeness of 'all Israel'. Accordingly, placement of an anti-Benjaminite polemic prior to the narrative block dealing with the establishment of the monarchy acts to counterbalance the positive attitude towards Benjamin that is apparent in the DtrH, and to predispose the reader to suspect all things associated with Benjamin and Gibeah. In this context, the story serves to *override* the portrayal of Benjamin as the instrument through which Yhwh manifests his favour in providing a divinely ordained king to rule Israel. This editorial tactic leads the reader to question not only the legitimacy of Benjamin, its towns and populace, but also to view as dubious any institution born on Benjaminite soil.

Finally, I would like to examine how 2 Kgs 25.22-30 does not merely update the DtrH, but also imposes upon it new structure and meaning, overriding the purpose previously implied by the whole composition.

I agree with those who find the proper conclusion to the DtrH in 2 Kgs 25.21b: *Thus Judah was exiled from its Land* (ויגל יהודה מעל אדמתו; and see, e.g., Jepsen 1956: 60-77; Lipschits 2005: 295-99; Römer 2005: 122-23, 140 n. 68). This conclusion stands in opposition to the statement closing the story of the conquest (Josh. 11.23): *Joshua took all the land that Yhwh had promised to Moses.* These antithetic summaries stamp the DtrH as the story of the total turnabout in relations between Yhwh and his people. Yhwh fulfilled his promise to grant the entire land to his people, but their actions finally caused him to renege upon his promise and turn them out from the land in punishment. This plot is indeed foreshadowed by the last section of threats in Deut. 28.64-65. No future renewal of the relationship is implied; since Yhwh's people continuously turned their backs on him, he in turn abandons them, and leaves them to serve other gods in foreign lands. Thus, the DtrH as a whole does not address future hopes, but focuses on the significance of the present for those who lived through the Babylonian conquest.

The notices in 2 Kgs 25.22-30 convey a different message, and anti-climactically deconstruct the antithetic symmetry of the historical composition that previously concluded in v. 21. Not all Judah had been exiled after all; following the assassination of Gedaliah, all the remaining people fled to Egypt, thus closing the history of Yhwh's people in the promised land with their return back to Egypt. A new structural frame for the history is hereby implied, in which the story beginning with deliverance from Egypt comes full circle and ends with return to Egypt. The message sounded in the overriding conclusion is that life goes on; not in Judah, but in the Diaspora. This point is elaborated in the closing account of the favour bestowed by Amel-Marduk upon Jehoiachin in exile. It is evident that this overriding account was composed for the Diaspora community, with the purpose of presenting the Babylonian king as protector (Murray 2001: 245-65; Becking 2007: 174-89). In opposition to the original closing of the DtrH, the overriding conclusion does anticipate a future, albeit in the Diaspora and under foreign rule.[11] Life indeed goes on in the Diaspora, but does the overriding account foresee an end to Yhwh's wrath? Does the author envision the people living there as Yhwh's people? Ironically, Yhwh is completely absent from the overriding conclusion, and whatever theological concerns this author wished to express are conveyed by means of human agents (Wolff 1975: 85-86; Murray 2001: 264-65; Becking 2007: 186-87). Despite the careful refrain from overt mention of Yhwh, there is perhaps some intimation that the people can remain the people of Yhwh even in the Diaspora. This is implied by Amel-Marduk's act of grace towards Jehoiachin. Even though the exiled king's elevation does not mean that the restoration of the Judahite monarchy is imminent, Yhwh may be viewed as acting again on behalf of his people, this time through the agency of the Babylonian king—his newly designated viceroy.

In summation, once we recognize the overriding intention of these materials, they can no longer be viewed as accidental appendices. Moreover, the overriding character of these texts indicates that they derive from non-deuteronomistic hands, and were inserted into the DtrH with the intention of significantly changing the outlook and inherent message of the work.

Finally, it remains to consider how these editorial techniques relate to the mechanics of scroll production. Emanuel Tov has recently assessed the technical limitations restricting scribal interference as observed in the scrolls from the Judean desert. Interlinear writing was employed sparingly for corrections and in only a few instances were full lines restored. The narrow margins (1.0–3.0 cm) of the majority of the scrolls did not provide adequate space for writing additional material (Tov 2002: 193-94). Moreover, although many scrolls were preserved along with cover or handle sheets attached at their beginning and ends, these sheets were left empty and not utilized for correction or revision (111-118). These findings led Tov to surmise that 'No rewriting, adding, or deleting could be executed in the form of corrections of existing scrolls... Instead, editors and scribes must have created fresh copies for expressing their novel thoughts' (342; cf. also van der Toorn 2007: 146-49).

The Qumran scrolls, however, derive from a post-redactional stage in the evolution of the biblical texts, and therefore do not falsify the proposition that biblical scribes might have revised existing copies of scrolls without recourse to extensive recopying. Instead, I propose that the editorial strategy of *overriding* circumvents the technical limitations inhibiting revision by adding

---

11.   Cf. Römer 2005: 177. Römer thinks the new conclusion reflects the interests of the Diaspora community of the Persian period. However, 2 Kgs 25.22-30 does not envision residing in the Diaspora by choice, contrary to the situation in the Persian period. Thus, I think it more likely that the designated audience lived under Babylonian rule.

the overriding content to the beginnings and ends of scrolls. For this purpose, scribes could either utilize the handle sheets or inscribe new sheets that they subsequently attached to the beginning or end of a scroll.

This proposal has significant implications for how we should understand the shape of the DtrH. It would appear that the scribes who employed the overriding technique did not split the DtrH into separate scrolls. Instead, it seems likely that the DtrH was from the outset conceived as a composition comprising several scrolls, and it was in this form that the authors of the overriding material knew the work. This, of course, does not imply that the idea of the DtrH as a unified composition is fallacious, but rather that the complete composition was broader in scope than was practical for one scroll (Haran 1985: 1-5). The concept of 'book' or composition is not equivalent to 'scroll', just as a 'book' or a composition is not the same as a 'volume'. By the same token, the fact that both the *Enuma Elish* and the Gilgamesh epic take up several tablets does not indicate that they were conceived as anthologies, but rather that the medium of the clay tablet imposed technical restrictions upon cuneiform scribes that had to be circumvented when writing long texts. The same is also true for the medium of papyrus or leather scrolls. Although papyrus rolls may have been used for preparing drafts of literary compositions, I think it likely that compositions that were intended for preservation would have been inscribed upon the thick but durable leather sheets (גויל) that were generally employed for the biblical scrolls found at Qumran (cf. Tov 2004: 34-35). The total length of the final form of the five books from Deuteronomy to Kings is only slightly shorter than the total length of the Pentateuch.[12] Accordingly, a scroll comprising Deuteronomy and the Former Prophets would be just as heavy and unwieldy as a Torah scroll. Even if we reduce the extent of the original composition of the DtrH by subtracting material thought to be late deuteronomistic or post-deutero-nomistic additions (e.g. Josh. 13–22, 24; Judg. 1.1–2.5; 17–21; 2 Sam. 21–24; 1 Kgs *17–22; 2 Kgs *1–8), the length of the postulated composition would result in a scroll that would still be awkward to manipulate. In actuality, there is no empiric evidence that lengthy compositions like the DtrH were originally written on a single scroll.

Accordingly, I conclude that the DtrH was not *subsequently* divided into scrolls along the borders of the overriding material that was inserted into the continuous narrative (Judg. 1.1–2.5; 17–21; 2 Sam 21–24). Instead, the opposite proposition holds, namely that the beginnings and ends of the scrolls provided convenient opportunities to add overriding materials. Therefore, it seems more likely that the DtrH was composed from the outset as a set of

---

12.   According to the Masoretic computations Deuteronomy, Joshua, Judges, Samuel and Kings contain 5269 verses, while the Pentateuch comprises 5845 verses.

five scrolls (Deuteronomy, Joshua, Judges, Samuel and Kings) that were meant to be read as a continuous narrative. Consequently, further studies of the DtrH should take into consideration the separate transmission and redaction history of each of its constituent scrolls.

Bibliography

Alt, A.
    1953   'Josua', in *Kleine Schriften zur Geschichte des Volkes Israel*, vol. 1 (Munich: C.H. Beck,): 176-92; repr. from *Werden und Wesen des Alten Testaments* (ed. P. Volz *et al.*; BZAW, 66; Berlin: A. Töpelmann, 1936): 13-29.

Amit, Y.
    1999   *The Book of Judges: The Art of Editing* (trans. Jonathan Chipman; Biblical Interpretation Series, 38; Leiden: E.J. Brill).

Auberlen, C.A.
    1860   'Die drei Anhänge des Buches der Richter in ihrer Bedeutung und Zusammengehörigkeit', *TSK* 33: 536-68.

Auld, A.G.
    1975   'Judges I and History: A Reconsideration', *VT* 25: 261-85.

Becker, U.
    1990   *Richterzeit und Königtum* (BZAW, 192; Berlin: W. de Gruyter)

Becking, B.
    2007   'Jehojachin's Amnesty, Salvation for Israel? Notes on 2 Kings 25,27-30', in *From David to Gedaliah: The Book of Kings as Story and History* (OBO, 228; Fribourg: Academic Press Fribourg; Göttingen: Vandenhoeck & Ruprecht): 174-89.

Bleek, F., and J. Wellhausen
    1878   *Einleitung in des Alte Testament* (4th edn, ed. and revised by J. Wellhausen; Berlin: G. Reimer).

Budde, K.
    1897   *Das Buch der Richter* (KHAT; Freiburg: Mohr/Siebeck).

Burney, C.F.
    1918   *The Book of Judges* (London: Rivingtons; repr., New York: Ktav, 1970).

Butler, T. C.
    1983   *Joshua* (WBC, 7; Waco, TX: Word Books).

Crüsemann, F.
    1978   *Der Widerstand gegen das Königtum; Die antiköniglichen Texte des Alten Testamentes und der Kampf um den frühen israelitischen Staat* (WMANT, 49; Neukirchen–Vluyn: Neukirchener Verlag).

Edenburg, C.
    2003   'The Story of the Outrage at Gibeah (Jdg. 19–21): Composition, Sources and Historical Context' (unpublished PhD dissertation, Tel Aviv University, 2003; Hebrew with summary in English).
    forthcoming   'Joshua 9 and Deuteronomy; an Intertextual Conundrum: The Chicken or the Egg?', in R. Person and K. Schmidt (eds.), *Deuteronomy in the Pentateuch, Hexateuch, and the Deuteronomistic History* (FAT, II; Tübingen: Mohr/Siebeck).

Fritz, V.
1994 *Das Buch Josua* (HAT; Tübingen: Mohr/Siebeck).

Gray, J.
1986 *Joshua, Judges and Ruth* (New Century Bible; Grand Rapids: Eerdmans, rev. edn).

Gross, W.
1987 'Zur Syntagmen-Folge im hebräischen Verbalsatz: die Stellung des Subjekts in Dtn 1-15', *BN* 40: 63-96.

Haran, M.
1985 'Book-size and the Device of Catch-lines in the Biblical Canon', *JJS* 36: 1-11.

Jüngling, H.-W.
1981 *Richter 19—Ein Plädoyer für das Königtum; Stilistische Analyse der Tendenzerzählung Ri 19,1-30a; 21,21* (Analecta Biblica, 84; Rome: Biblical Institute Press).

Jepsen, A.
1956 *Die Quellen des Königsbuches* (Halle a.S.: M. Niemeyer, 2nd edn).

Levine, L.D.
1981 'Manuscripts, Texts and the Study of the Neo-Assyrian Royal Inscriptions', in F.M. Fales (ed.), *Assyrian Royal Inscriptions: New Horizons* (Orientis Antiqui Collectio, 17; Rome: Istituto per l'Oriente): 49-70.

Lipschits, O.
2005 *The Rise and Fall of Jerusalem: Judah under Babylonian Rule* (Winona Lake, IN: Eisenbrauns).

Liverani, M.
1981 'Critique of Variants and the Titulary of Sennacherib', in F.M. Fales (ed.), *Assyrian Royal Inscriptions: New Horizons* (Orientis Antiqui Collectio, 17; Rome: Istituto per l'Oriente): 225-57.

Mayes, A.D.H.
2001 'Deuteronomistic Royal Ideology in Judges 17–21', *BibInt* 9: 256-58.

Mazor, L.
1994 'A Textual and Literary Study of the Fall of Ai in Joshua 8', in S. Japhet (ed.), *The Bible in the Light of its Interpreters* (Jerusalem: Magnes [Hebrew]): 73-108.

McKenzie, S.L.
1999 'The Chronicler as Redactor', in M.P. Graham and S.L. McKenzie (eds.), *The Chronicler as Author: Studies in Text and Texture* (JSOTSup, 263; Sheffield: Sheffield Academic Press): 70-90.

Meer, M.N. van der
2004 *Formation and Reformulation: the Redaction of the Book of Joshua in the Light of the Oldest Textual Witnesses* (VTSup, 102; Leiden: E.J. Brill).

Murray, D.F.
2001 'Of all the Years the Hopes—or Fears? Jehoiachin in Babylon (2 Kings 25:27-30)', *JBL* 120: 245-65.

Na'aman, N.
2009 'The Sanctuary of the Gibeonites Revisited', *JANER*: 101-24.

Nelson, R.D.
    1997   *Joshua: A Commentary* (OTL; Louisville, KY: Westminster/John Knox Press).
    2002   *Deuteronomy: A Commentary* (OTL; Louisville, KY: Westminster/John Knox Press)

Noth, M.
    1962   'The Background of Judges 17–18', in B.W. Anderson and W. Harrelson (eds.), *Israel's Prophetic Heritage: Essays in Honor of James Muilenburg* (London: SCM Press): 68-85.
    1971   *Das Buch Josua* (HAT; Tübingen: Mohr/Siebeck, 3rd edn).
    1991   *The Deuteronomistic History* (JSOTSup, 15; Sheffield: Sheffield Academic Press, 2nd edn; trans. of *Überlieferungsgeschichtliche Studien* (Darmstadt, 1967, 3rd edn).

Olmstead, A.T.E.
    1916   *Assyrian Historiography; a Source Study* (Columbia, MO: University of Missouri Press).

Otto, E.
    1994   'Aspects of Legal Reforms and Reformulations in Ancient Cuneiform and Israelite Law', in B.M. Levinson (ed.), *Theory and Method in Biblical and Cuneiform Law: Revision, Interpolation and Development* (JSOTSup, 181; Sheffield: Sheffield Academic Press): 160-96.

Peckham, B.
    1985   *The Composition of the Deuteronomistic History* (HSM, 35; Atlanta: Scholars Press).

Polak, F.H.
    2010   'The Book of Samuel and the Deuteronomist: A Syntactic-Stylistic Analysis', in Christa Schäfer-Lichtenberger (ed.), *Die Samuelbücher und die Deuteronomisten* (BWANT, 188; Stuttgart: Kohlhammer): 4-73.

Regt, L.J. de
    1991   'Word Order in Different Clause Types in Deuteronomy 1–30', in K. Jongeling *et al.* (eds.), *Studies in Hebrew and Aramaic Syntax, Presented to Professor J. Hoftijzer on the Occasion of his Sixty-fifth Birthday* (Studies in Semitic Languages and Linguistics, 17; Leiden: E.J. Brill): 152-72.

Römer, T.
    2005   *The So-Called Deuteronomistic History: A Sociological, Historical and Literary Introduction* (London: T. & T. Clark).

Römer, T.C., and A. de Pury
    2000   'Deuteronomistic Historiography (DH): History of Research and Debated Issues', in A. de Pury *et al.* (eds.), *Israel Constructs its History: Deuteronomistic Historiography in Recent Research* (JSOTSup, 306; Sheffield: Sheffield Academic Press): 24-141.

Rösel, H.N.
    1975   'Studien zur Topographie der Kriege in den Büchern Josua und Richter', *ZDPV* 91: 159-71.

Schunck, K.-D.
    1963   *Benjamin: Untersuchungen zur Entstehung und Geschichte eines Israelitischen Stammes* (BZAW, 86; Berlin: A. Töpelmann).

Sweeney, M.A.
2001   *King Josiah of Judah: The Lost Messiah of Israel* (Oxford: Oxford University Press).

Tadmor, H.
1981   'History and Ideology in the Assyrian Royal Inscriptions', in F.M. Fales (ed.), *Assyrian Royal Inscriptions: New Horizons* (Orientis Antiqui Collectio, 17; Rome: Istituto per l'Oriente): 13-33.

Toorn, K. van der
2007   *Scribal Culture and the Making of the Hebrew Bible* (Cambridge, MA: Harvard University Press).

Tov, E.
2002   'Copying of a Biblical Scroll', *Journal of Religious History* 26: 189-209.
2004   *Scribal Practices and Approaches Reflected in the Texts Found in the Judean Desert* (STDJ, 54; Boston: E.J. Brill).
2006   'The Writing of Early Scrolls: Implications for the Literary Analysis of Hebrew Scripture', *DSD* 13: 339-47.

Van Seters, J.
1983   *In Search of History: Historiography in the Ancient World and the Origins of Biblical History* (New Haven: Yale University Press).
2007   'The "Shared Text" of Samuel–Kings and Chronicles Re-examined', in R. Rezetko *et al.* (eds.) *Reflection and Refraction: Studies in Biblical Historiography in Honour of A. Graeme Auld* (VTSup, 113; Leiden: E.J. Brill): 503-15.

Veijola, T.
1977   *Das Königtum in der Beurteilung der deuteronomistischen Historio-graphie: eine redaktionsgeschichtliche Untersuchung* (AASF B., 198; Helsinki: Suomalainen Tiedeakatemia).

Weinfeld, M.
1993   'Judges 1.1–2.5: The Conquest under the Leadership of the House of Judah', in A.G. Auld (ed.), *Understanding Poets and Prophets; Essays in Honour of George Wishart Anderson* (Sheffield: JSOT Press): 388-400.

Wolff, H.W.
1975   'The Kerygma of the Deuteronomistic Historical Work', in W. Brueggemann and H.W. Wolff (eds.), *The Vitality of Old Testament Traditions* (Atlanta: John Knox Press): 83-100, 141-43.

Younger, K. Lawson
1995   'The Configuring of Judicial Preliminaries: Judges 1.1–2.5 and its Dependencies on the Book of Joshua', *JSOT* 68: 75-92.

Zakovitch, Y.
1983   'The Associative Principle in the Arrangement of the Book of Judges as a Tool for Uncovering its Compositional History', in A. Rofé and Y. Zakovitch (eds.), *Isac Leo Seeligmann Volume: Essays on the Bible and the Ancient World* (Jerusalem: Rubinstein [Hebrew]): 161-83.

SAMSON AND HIS GOD:
MODERN CULTURE READS THE BIBLE

J. Cheryl Exum

When I first met Yairah Amit in the 1980s, we were both working on the book of Judges, and we discovered that we shared interests and ideas, in particular about Judges as literature. Since then, this subject has often been for us a topic of lively conversation, most recently at a conference in the Netherlands on the theme 'Samson: Hero or Fool?' The fundamental issue in addressing that question, it seems to me, is the nature of Samson's relationship to his god, a topic on which both Yairah and I have spilled no little ink, for, despite appearances, the Samson story is far from a simple tale (Amit 1999: 266-308). This is the topic I want to address here, but, rather than rehearse familiar scholarly arguments, I want to broaden the scope by considering how the question of the nature of Samson's relationship to God has been resolved in modern times in selected examples from literature, music and film.[1] Characterization, point of view, modes of narration, gaps and ideology—topics to which Amit has made important contributions (e.g. Amit 1999, 2000, 2001)—are all issues that retellings of the story in different media have to address in one way or another. Retellings often reflect and draw attention to problems, gaps and ambiguities in the biblical text, and can thus shed light on the dynamics of the story. It is not just a question of how retellings portray Samson's relationship to God but also of how the characters of Samson and God need to be changed in order to establish a suitable, intelligible relationship for the intended audience.

In the interests of space, I limit my discussion to four retellings of the Samson story: John Milton's dramatic poem *Samson Agonistes*, a classic in English literature; George Frederic Handel's oratorio *Samson*, which is based

---

1. For reasons of space I am not including art, where one can find, e.g., paintings of Samson (as an instrument of God) pulling down the Philistine temple, paintings in which Delilah is held responsible for Samson's downfall (see Exum 1996: 189-96), and the occasional painting that suggests divine responsibility for Samson's plight (Exum 1998). For a fascinating overview of the reception of the Samson story from ancient to modern times, see Gunn 2005: 170-230.

on it; Vladimir (Ze'ev) Jabotinsky's *Samson*, an influential book in modern Hebrew; and Cecil B. DeMille's lavish Hollywood epic *Samson and Delilah*, which uses Jabotinsky's novel as one of its primary sources. This particular selection allows us to see not only how the biblical text is appropriated in retelling but also what happens to the Bible in a retelling of a retelling. Although they are only illustrative, not definitive for what happens to the story in later retellings, these works reveal how a poet, a novelist, a composer and a filmmaker, like biblical scholars and ordinary readers, struggle to come to terms with Samson's problematic relationship to his god.

The Biblical Evidence

To understand how the biblical text presents the relationship between Samson and God, we should look first at what the narrator specifically tells us (the more difficult question, of course, is not what the evidence is but how to evaluate it). Judges 13 is a miraculous birth account. It may be later than the stories of Samson's adventures in chs. 14–16, but in the present form of the narrative it sets the stage for what follows by marking Samson as an extraordinary individual and alerting the reader from the outset to his destiny. Samson's boisterous escapades in chs. 14–16 present a stark contrast to the heavily theological tone of the birth account, but divine activity is indicated in these chapters by means of four distinctive features, which they share with ch. 13: (1) statements about the role played by God that allow the reader to share the narrative point of view, 13.24; 14.4; 16.20; (2) references to the influence of the spirit of the Lord, 13.25; 14.6, 19; 15.14; (3) Samson's Nazirite status, 13.5, 7; 16.17; and (4) direct intervention by God in response to Samson's prayer, 15.18-19; 16.28-30 (Exum 1983).

Amit describes Samson as both a tool, an instrument used by God to wreak havoc upon the Philistines, and a fool, 'when he dares to act independently' and tells Delilah the secret of his strength (Amit 2008). Clearly Samson is an instrument in a divine plan, a deliverer who appears to have no control over the important events in his life. His destiny is determined before he is born: to 'begin to deliver Israel from the hand of the Philistines' (13.5), but, significantly, only to begin it. Although it may seem as though Samson has a mind of his own, when, against his parents' wishes, he insists upon marrying a Philistine, the reader learns that this, too, is part of God's plan, 'for he was seeking an occasion against the Philistines', who at that time had dominion over Israel (14.4). We might assume that Samson is unaware of God's involvement in his choice of a foreign wife, a choice that will have disastrous consequences, since we are told that his parents do not know about it. Later, just after his hair is cut, Samson lacks even more important knowledge: the awareness that God has left him (16.20).

From his youth Samson is animated by the spirit of the Lord. When he tears a lion asunder (14.6) and kills thirty men for their fine clothes (14.19), it is because the spirit takes possession of him. The spirit also causes Samson's bonds to melt and inspires him to kill a thousand Philistines with the jawbone of a donkey (15.14). Even when the spirit is not mentioned as inciting Samson to perform incredible feats, such as tying burning torches to the tails of jackals and sending them through the Philistine grain fields (15.4-5) or carrying the gates of Gaza to a hilltop near Hebron (16.3), the reader understands that Samson's superhuman strength is a gift of God, symbolized by his uncut hair and his Nazirite status. But Samson did not choose to be a Nazirite; that was determined before his birth. Nor does he choose to cut his hair; he is asleep when the fatal haircut takes place. He should, of course, have foreseen that Delilah would cut his hair, since she tried every other means he maintained would rob him of his strength.

I agree with Amit that the biblical tale takes an instrumental view of heroism (Amit 2008; Exum 2008). Its interest lies in Samson's deeds as God's agent with a god-given mission, not in his understanding of God's plan for him or in his character development (indeed, his character does not develop).[2] Nevertheless, he is aware of his uniqueness, if not necessarily his role: 'I have been a Nazirite to God from my mother's womb. If I be shaved, then my strength will leave me and I shall become weak and be like any other man' (16.17; translations throughout are mine). On the basis of the parallels between the two accounts (Exum 1981: 3-9), should we assume that Samson's fateful liaison with Delilah, like his doomed marriage to the Timnite, is from God, because he is seeking an occasion against the Philistines? Or is Samson responsible for his fate? Should we hold him accountable for 'wasted charisma', for not living up to his Nazirite calling (von Rad 1962: 333-34)? Does Samson betray his god by revealing the secret of his strength to a woman?

Narratively speaking, the revelation of the secret is unavoidable. The story of Samson and Delilah is a variation of a traditional folktale in which a woman discovers a man's secret and brings about his downfall by revealing it, a tale adapted by the biblical narrator for his own theological/ideological purpose.[3] For the story to work, Samson's strength must derive from

---

2.   Samson repeats his follies; he does not learn from his mistakes (as in *Samson Agonistes*, for example; see below). As I have argued elsewhere (Exum 1992: 37 *et passim*), this quality of repetition going nowhere is characteristic of comedy.

3.   Gunkel cites two Egyptian examples, among others: the tale of the man whose heart is hidden in a tree and who dies when his wife reveals his secret and the tree is cut down; and the myth of Re, who is tricked by Isis into revealing the secret of his name, thereby giving her magic power over him (1913: 54-55). Gaster cites, among others, the Greek legend about King Nisus of Megara, who had a purple or golden hair on the middle of his

something that can be taken away. Making Samson a Nazirite, who must not cut his hair, provides a means to connect the time-honoured motif of strength residing in the hair to the more important theme of the biblical story, that the strong man's power comes from God. The narrator, however, assiduously avoids making it a direct connection. Thus Samson says that his strength will leave him if his hair is cut (16.17), and this is what happens (v. 19); however, the crucial v. 20 follows to reveal that Samson's strength comes not from his hair but from God. In time, Samson's hair begins to grow (v. 22), which we could interpret as presaging the return of his strength, but not until after Samson has prayed to God for strength 'just this time' is he able to destroy the Philistine temple (vv. 28-30).

Regardless of whether or not we conclude that Samson has control over the events that lead to his blinding and death—and to the ideologically 'desired' outcome that he kills more Philistines at his death than he had killed in his lifetime (16.30)—there are two places in the story where he does something to affect the course of events. In 15.18-19, when it seems he will die of thirst, he calls upon God:

> He was very thirsty, and he called on the Lord and said, 'You have granted this great victory by the hand of your servant, and now I shall die of thirst and fall into the hands of the uncircumcised'.

Significantly, he reveals a degree of self-understanding in referring to himself as God's 'servant', and God responds to his servant's plight by miraculously providing water. Only once more does Samson call upon God for help, when the Philistines bring him to the temple for their amusement, and this time he is more direct: 'O Lord God, remember me, please, and strengthen me, please, only this once, O God, that I may be avenged upon the Philistines for one of my two eyes' (16.28), and, 'Let me die with the Philistines' (v. 30). God answers his prayer, granting him the strength to pull the temple down upon himself and all the people in it (v. 30). These two occasions when Samson calls upon God are acknowledgments of his dependence on God, acknowledgments that *he* has no control over what happens. Nevertheless, he does not have to pray, any more than he has to reveal his secret to Delilah.[4] We encounter here the familiar biblical paradox of divine causality and human freedom.

If, in the biblical account, Samson's actions suit perfectly the divine purpose, then both parties bear responsibility for what happens, though perhaps not equally. An instrumental view of the hero as a strategic, but dispensable

---

head. When the Cretans besieged Megara, his daughter Scylla fell in love with the enemy king and pulled out the hair from her father's head, so that he died (1981: 436-39).

4. Actually he has to do both to meet the requirements of the story, but that is not the same thing as having no freedom within the story.

tool in God's plan to inflict injury on the Philistines may not trouble the biblical narrator (and, after all, Samson fulfilled his destiny), but it has troubled readers.[5] One response, exemplified particularly well by David Gunn, is to challenge the instrumental view of the hero. Gunn argues that Samson is not simply a tool but rather is aware of his divinely appointed role and struggles against it (1992). In my view, the root of the problem lies not so much in the character of the hero as in the all-too-human God-character whose purpose the hero serves and whose 'occasion' against the Philistines serves his own limited self-interest. (And Gunn is not too impressed by the God-character either.) Only when God does not appear in the story as a character whose motives and acts are disclosed to the reader by an omniscient narrator, as happens in the modern examples we shall consider, does the problem of divine causality versus human freedom disappear.[6]

Ze'ev Jabotinsky's Samson *and Cecil B. DeMille's* Samson and Delilah

In his novel *Samson*, first published in 1927 as *Judge and Fool*, the Revisionist Zionist leader and political philosopher Ze'ev Jabotinsky secularizes the story, removing any suggestion that God, if there is a god, plays a role in Samson's life and death or that Samson enjoys any real relationship with his god. The mighty deeds Samson performs under the influence of the spirit of God in the biblical story are systematically downplayed and naturalized in order to make them appear more realistic. Samson kills a panther pretty much with his bare hands (cf. 14.6), but it takes time and great effort, and he wounds it first with a sword and then throws mustard into its eyes to distract and temporarily blind it (27-28). Samson's slaughter of thirty men from Ashkelon while under the influence of the spirit and his theft of their garments (14.19) are not recounted directly but rather conveyed to the reader in the form of a conclusion drawn by Samson's Philistine friend Ahtur, when he finds a bale of thirty cloaks at the door of his house:

> Ahtur had no doubt that they were Philistine cloaks, and that Samson had obtained them by robbery, but to the day of his death he never discovered where Samson had got them nor to whom they had belonged (94).

The absence of any reference to the slaughter of thirty innocent men makes Samson appear more moral and less Herculean, and even the theft cannot be proved.

---

5. See Exum 1992: 18-39 for a reading of the Samson story as embodying a comic, or classic, vision (which does not necessarily mean we like the way the story ends), and 1992: 42-44 for discussion of hostile transcendence in the story.

6. On the omniscience and reliability of the biblical narrator, cf. Sternberg 1985: 84-128, 153-72 *passim*; Amit 2001: 93-102.

Jabotinsky's treatment of Judg. 15.14, in which the spirit comes mightily upon Samson, causing his bonds to dissolve and enabling him to slaughter a thousand Philistines with a donkey's jawbone, not only challenges but potentially discredits the biblical account. The capture of Samson with the help of the Judahites is part of one Philistine leader's scheme to make money by selling Samson back to some of his own people. Angered when he discovers this, Samson throws a donkey's jawbone into the man's face, killing him. The event is witnessed by Machbonai, a Levite who has taken on the responsibility of recording the story of Samson's life for posterity. But he records a version 'after his own fashion, and his report, rather than what actually happened, [becomes the official record that] will remain in the memory of man [*sic*] for all time' (185). Similarly, although Jabotinsky retains the reference to the spirit beginning to inspire Samson in the camp of Dan (13.25), he doubly removes it from an authoritative source. The information is attributed to the meddlesome Machbonai, who heard of it from Samson's mother Hatzlelponi, who, as the novel makes clear, is hardly a reliable witness.

Like the reference to the spirit in Judg. 13.25, the statement in 13.24 about Samson being divinely blessed reaches Jabotinsky's reader through the character Machbonai rather than through the omniscient narrator (36). The novel ignores the biblical narrator's two other statements about divine activity, God's using Samson to further his cause against the Philistines (14.4) or leaving Samson when his hair is cut (16.20). Though Jabotinsky's narrator, like the biblical narrator, is omniscient, there is no place in this modern, secular novel for a deity whose motives and activities are accessible to the reader.

Not surprisingly, Samson does not pray in Jabotinsky's version of the story. Indeed, the reader learns early on that

> ...the Danites prayed only when they had to. Their daily lives were taken up with the rough work of the fields, with tending the cattle, with the struggle against poverty and against each other, and they seldom thought of the invisible (78).[7]

Since there are no prayers to be answered, there is no allusion to Samson's thirst and the miracle of water at Lehi (15.18-19). Nor does Samson pray to God for help before destroying the Philistine temple, as in the Bible; instead he utters the wish, 'May my soul perish with you!'

---

7. We also learn that Samson had never heard of Moses, though he had been told about Joshua (99), and that the Rechabites, with whom Samson spends one of the three joyful weeks of his life, never prayed: 'They had no altar; they never prayed. Even the little children knew that Jehovah was God, that he knew all things, that all things were subject to him, and consequently that there was no need to remind him of anything' (126). The other two happy weeks were with his Timnite bride Semadar and with Delilah in the valley of Sorek (152).

Some of Jabotinsky's most striking departures from the biblical story involve Samson's Nazirite status. Jabotinsky thoroughly dispenses with the miraculous element in the biblical birth account, giving us instead Samson's mother's story of a visit by a stranger whom she recognized as God himself, and who prophesied that 'her son would grow to be a great servant of God' (33).[8] But her version of the visit is suspect, and rumour has it that the mysterious stranger was a Philistine vagabond. The rumour is widely accepted, even by Samson, especially because it seems to explain his attraction to things Philistine (166). Only near the end of his life does Samson learn the truth, that the stranger was circumcised and thus not a Philistine.[9] But what is the 'truth'? Machbonai self-importantly declares:

> The truth is not what happened on any particular night. The truth is what will stand for ever in the memory of man [*sic*], and that is known only to one—to me... And what I have written will endure as the truth from generation to generation (170-71).

Whereas the reader of the biblical account may wonder to what extent Samson understands his role, in Jabotinsky's novel Samson is aware of his mission, having been told about it by his (less than trustworthy) mother; however, he never seems truly committed to it:

> I am a Nazarite. In the year of the earthquake a messenger came to my mother from Jehovah. A duty was laid upon me and strength was put into my shoulders, and I was given the power to govern men. Things go hard for our tribe without a protector and avenger. That is the task ordained for me, and it cannot be altered (51).

Indeed, Jabotinsky's Samson is no more faithful to the Nazirite vow than his biblical predecessor, who eats honey from the carcass of a lion (14.9) and takes part in a wedding feast where alcohol would have been served (14.10). When Machbonai the Levite first makes his acquaintance, Samson is eating, drinking and making merry with his Philistine friends at an inn in Timnath, where he is known by his Philistine nickname Tayish ('he-goat'). Samson explains,

> 'In Zorah I am a Nazarite, and in the land of Ephraim also, but here I am not. The olive prospers in the grove, the wheat in the field; everything has its own place.' And he drank his cup of wine (19).

---

8.   Hatzlelponi is not a little deranged and is thus held in awe by her neighbours. 'She has spent her whole life in a fever—even that night by the well. She does not know', explains Machbonai (170).

9.   When Hatzlelponi told Manoah about the man's visit, Manoah took a faithful servant with him, tracked down the man and killed him. The servant tells Samson about it, adding that the man was circumcised and thus one of Samson's people (213-15).

Nevertheless, like the biblical Samson, he does not cut his hair. On this crucial point too, however, Jabotinsky departs dramatically from the biblical account by severing completely the connection between Samson's strength and his hair. There is nothing in the novel about the Philistines trying to discover the secret of Samson's strength for the simple reason that there is no secret. When Samson is shaved by Delilah, he is shamed, and the laughter of the Philistines demoralizes him. His strength remains, but he simply gives up and does not defend himself. When, much later, he manages to destroy the temple of Dagon, killing more at his death than he killed in his life, he does not need God's help.

For Jabotinsky, Samson is not a tool nor is he a fool in the way he appears to be in the biblical story. He is not a tool because he is not the instrument of a god who uses him to further his goal. And he is not the fool of the biblical story, because he does not reveal a secret to Delilah.[10] There is no secret to his strength, and his Nazirite status is well known to all.

Removing any trace of divine activity from the story leaves Samson the master of his fate. Character development thus becomes all important for our understanding of what makes Samson tick, and Jabotinsky supplies Samson, as well as other characters, with motivation. The Philistines are portrayed sympathetically, and Samson is considerably more complex than the one-dimensional biblical character, though he is not introspective, which makes him seem rather shallow. Although at times Jabotinsky seems concerned to make Samson likable, or at least sympathetic, even noble,[11] none of his characters achieves any real depth. We learn interesting details about them, but they remain essentially static and do not develop or change. Samson, for example, is a man of two sides, two natures, a kind of split personality. He spends part of his time in Philistia, enjoying himself in the company of his Philistine friends, and part of his time among his own people, where he is a leader of a faithful band of followers and a judge who settles disputes but is not well liked. He has a reputation for being a wise judge, but 'there was almost always something provocative about his decisions' (132) and many were dissatisfied with them.[12] He loves the Philistines, dislikes his own people, and this continues to be the pattern throughout his life, even after his fatal capture.[13]

10. In what sense he *is* a fool, as the original title, *Judge and Fool*, suggests, is left for the reader to decide.

11. For example, Samson is an honourable man. At the wedding games in Timnath, his friends are insulted by the Philistines and he goes out of his way to keep the peace.

12. '[T]he more influential people were in the main dissatisfied with him. He did not judge in the traditional manner' (101).

13. In a lengthy speech to the Saran while he is in prison but before he is blinded, Samson declares, 'I love you [the Philistines]... And that is why I do not love Dan, and

Throughout his life Samson seems to wait for things to happen to him. Surprisingly, he does not mourn the loss of his sight (207), and when he is freed from prison, he eventually returns to the inns of Gaza, where his 'jokes and riddles had changed: they were no longer mere playful foolery, there was bitterness and mockery in them. But he was not aware of this himself, and his companions took no note of it' (210). He is bored. But his strength is as great as ever (211-12) and, when he does pull down the Philistine temple, it is because he has been goaded by Delilah, who tells him that she will raise their newborn child as an enemy of Israel.

By destroying the temple of the Philistine oppressors Samson does become an Israelite hero of sorts; however, by drawing attention to his divergences from the biblical account, as, for example, when Machbonai claims to be writing the story of Samson's life that will be remembered, and by offering contradictory versions of events (for example, competing claims about Samson's birth), Jabotinsky intimates that the biblical account has embellished the role of this Israelite Hercules. On more than one occasion Jabotinsky's Samson expresses the certainty that his people are destined to throw off the yoke of oppression and become great, but this theme is not well developed. What has Samson's time upon this evil earth taught him? That his people need strong weapons ('get iron') and a strong leader ('choose a king') if they are to succeed—and to 'learn to laugh' (220).

Jabotinsky's *Samson* was one of the main sources used by Cecil B. DeMille for his 1949 biblical blockbuster *Samson and Delilah*, starring Hedy Lamarr and Victor Mature.[14] Though the screenplay by Jesse Lasky, Jr, and Fredric Frank relies on Jabotinsky's novel for gap filling, it tells a very different story, one recognizably based on the biblical account, and this is nowhere clearer than in the film's religious dimension. Although the film revolves around Samson and Delilah's tempestuous love affair, the issue of Samson's relationship to his god is a crucial theme. The nature of that relationship is spelled out most clearly in a theological discussion between Samson and Delilah at the critical moment just before he entrusts her with the secret of his strength.

---

why I hate Dan's kinsmen... [But] I am not one of you! Invite me to your feasts, Philistine, and I will come and help you to pass the time pleasantly, even if the feast be held round the place of my execution. I will drink and jest with you gladly. But build up? You said "Build up?" With you? *On* you? I don't believe in you.'

14. Twentieth Century Fox, 1949; the other source acknowledged in the opening credits, besides the Bible, is Harold Lamb, whose original treatment, prepared in 1936, served as the basis of the screenplay (a presentation copy from DeMille, with the words, 'Harold—Here is your child grown to maturity' is among Lamb's papers in the UCLA Library, Department of Special Collections, Manuscripts Division). The film has a memorable musical score by Victor Young.

In this scene, Samson discloses to Delilah that his strength comes from his invisible god, whose power is everywhere. This power is a gift that makes men [*sic*] greater than themselves, he says, and he will have strength as long as he keeps faith with God. In an allusion to his Nazirite status in the Bible, Samson divulges that he has been dedicated to God and has broken many vows, but one he has kept: he has not cut his hair. As in the biblical account, it is not simply a case of his strength residing in his hair. His hair is the 'mark of his power', just as the mane of a lion is the symbol of its power and the mane of a stallion, the symbol of its power. The strongest ram has the heaviest wool; if you cut it, you deprive it of the shield of its strength. To Delilah's question, 'You believe that this great god of yours has given you your power through your hair? You do believe that, don't you?', he replies, in a line reminiscent of Jabotinsky, that this is what his mother taught him. So, subtly, the secret of Samson's strength has become a question both of his faithfulness to his vow and of what he believes. When Delilah deceives him, cuts his hair, and summons the Philistines to take him prisoner, she taunts, 'Call on your god, Samson!' He replies, 'I've betrayed him; he would not hear me'. Like Jabotinsky's Samson, he simply lets himself be taken without putting up any resistance.

DeMille cannot avoid naturalizing, for he cannot make God a character in a realistic film for a modern audience. As Jabotinsky had done, DeMille has Samson tear a lion apart with his bare hands, without indicating the specific role played by the spirit of the Lord in Judg. 14.6, so that it becomes simply a sign of his superhuman strength. Similarly there is no direct divine involvement when Samson fulfils his wager to the wedding guests who had answered his riddle (14.19). As in Jabotinsky's *Samson*, Samson steals the thirty festal garments, but he does not kill anyone. DeMille even makes the event humorous by having the men running around without their tunics and cloaks and complaining to the Philistine guards that they were overpowered by some giant or demon.

To set the proper reverent mood for his film, DeMille introduces the story with a voiceover, in which the audience is treated to a rather muddled speech about human superstition, idolatry, tyranny, oppression and the will for freedom. It is the unquenchable will for freedom, a divine spark, we are told, that drives Samson, in whom strength and folly are fused, but this will to freedom is not very much in evidence in the film. At the film's end, creating a kind of frame for the story, we see the young boy Saul, Israel's future king, and Miriam, the wholesome girl-next-door to whom Samson was never attracted,[15]

15. As Samson tells his 'little mother', 'Forbidden figs are sweeter'. Miriam is the uninteresting alternative to the femme fatale Delilah; for a more detailed discussion of the film, with special attention to Delilah, see Exum 1996: 175-237.

looking back on the destruction Samson has wrought among the Philistines. Miriam, who always loved Samson, sums up the significance of the Israelite hero's life with a simple comment: 'His strength will never die, Saul, men [*sic*] will tell his story for a thousand years'.

Within this framework, DeMille adopts the biblical narrator's use of answered prayer (15.18-19; 16.28-30) to show the behind-the-scenes activity of Samson's invisible God. This device effectively encourages the viewer to conclude that God is with Samson and to recognize that God has a purpose for Samson, without suggesting, as the biblical account could be seen to do, that Samson is simply a 'tool' in an overarching divine plan. The biblical Samson's call to God when he is thirsty, having slain a thousand men with a donkey's jawbone (Judg. 15.18-19), becomes, in DeMille's version, a prayer to God *before* the slaughter. At Lehi, the captured Samson prays for strength to destroy Israel's enemies and for God to show the Philistines his power. There is a clap of thunder, and a great dust storm arises, simultaneously serving as the sign of God's presence (the spirit of God coming mightily upon Samson in Judg. 15.14) and of God's response to Samson's prayer (thus there is prayer in this scene, as in 15.18-19, but its content has been changed). Samson slays the Philistine troops with the jawbone in a spectacular deliverance, which is only somewhat naturalized by having Samson fend them off from a position in a narrow gorge. 'Never did mortal man fight like this', reports a messenger who escaped. 'When he called upon his god, the thunder and the whirlwind and the lightning were in his blows.'[16]

Samson's prayer for strength to pull down the temple in Judg. 16.28-30 is echoed in the film when Samson prays, 'I pray thee, strengthen me, O God, strengthen me only this once' and 'My eyes have seen thy glory, O God, now let me die with my enemies'.[17] The prayer is granted and the audience is treated to a spectacular scene of destruction. Of the retellings discussed here,

---

16. It may be that the idea of a thunderstorm comes from Jabotinsky, but for Jabotinsky it is only a backdrop for this scene.

17. The prayers in the film that correspond to the biblical prayers are given a biblically authentic ring with their use, typical of sword-and-sandal films, of 'thee' and 'thou' to address God. This one is fairly literal in following the biblical version of Samson's appeal to God for strength 'only this once' and the prayer for death with the Philistines, but substitutes 'my eyes have seen thy glory, O God' for the vengeful 'let me be avenged upon the Philistines for one of my two eyes', which would not be appropriate for DeMille's properly pious hero. If we take *nqm* to refer to vindication, not vengeance (Mendenhall 1973: 76-77; Peels 1995: 265-66), then we could view the biblical Samson as aspiring to be the legitimate agent of God's punishment of the Philistines rather than simply concerned with retaliation. His other acts against the Philistines, however, are retaliatory.

only DeMille's *Samson and Delilah* shows Samson destroying the temple; the others have an eyewitness describe the events.[18]

To the two occasions in the biblical account when Samson appeals to God, DeMille adds four more: three prayers by Samson and one by none other than Delilah. Just before he is blinded, having said that God would not hear him if he called upon him, Samson prays not for deliverance but to praise God for teaching him a lesson: 'O Lord, my eyes did turn away from you to look upon the fleshpots of my enemies. Now you take away my sight that I may see again more clearly. Blessed be the name of the Lord.' DeMille thus gives us a Samson whose relationship to God is constant, at least from his point of view (cf. 'he did not know that the Lord had left him', Judg. 16.20), in spite of having broken his vow.

In a remarkable turn of events in the film, and an inspired instance of gap filling, Delilah, repentant and plagued with guilt for what she has done, prays to Samson's—that is, the 'real'—god:

> O God of Samson, help me! He said you are everywhere, that you are almighty. Hear me! Give back the light to his eyes; take my sight for his. O God of Samson, help me!

She goes to the granary to seek Samson's forgiveness and to beg him to come away with her to the valley of the Nile, where they can be together. When she arrives, Samson is praying, 'How long will you forget me, O Lord… Do not forsake me, O Lord… Send me your sign.' Delilah, it seems, is that sign, and both their prayers will be answered. When Samson realizes that, in spite of everything, he still loves Delilah, he asks God to show him the way. This prayer is answered too. Samson rejects Delilah's offer to go away with her and allows himself to be taken to the temple, where he will utter his final prayer.

DeMille turns the story of Samson and Delilah into a love story for all time. As the Saran, the leader of the Philistines, astutely observes, 'No man with eyes could resist you, Delilah, but only a fool would trust you'. Samson is a fool for trusting Delilah, but he is in love (cf. Judg. 16.4). When Delilah accuses him of not telling her the secret of his strength because 'you don't trust me enough', he replies, 'I love you enough' and tells her.

Milton's Samson Agonistes *and Handel's* Samson

Milton's *Samson Agonistes* is worlds apart from Jabotinsky's *Samson* and DeMille's *Samson and Delilah*. It is vastly different from the biblical account as well, for Milton transforms the rambunctious, impulsive biblical strong

---

18. In *Samson Agonistes* the messenger who describes the scene is an eyewitness; in Handel's *Samson* it appears that the messenger is giving an eyewitness account; in Jabotinsky's *Samson* the eyewitness describes the events in a letter.

man into a tragic hero who is neither fool nor tool.[19] In order to do this, he does not retell the biblical story following the course of Samson's life, as Jabotinsky and DeMille do, but rather begins with the blinded Samson in the prison-house in Gaza, where he is visited by Manoa, his father, Dalila, his wife, and a Philistine warrior, the giant Harapha of Gath (in keeping with Milton's Greek tragic models, the action takes place within the space of twenty-four hours). Dealing with a period of Samson's life of no interest to the biblical writer—the time between Samson's imprisonment and his destruction of the Philistine temple—gives Milton the freedom to show Samson's rehabilitation, so to speak, his self-recriminations and his renewed dedication to God.[20] The decision to tell the story as a dramatic poem means that everything reaches the reader through dialogue (there are not even any stage directions). Unlike the biblical account, where the reader is left wondering to what extent Samson understands his place in God's plan, in Milton's tragic poem Samson's speeches give us considerable insight into his self-understanding. God is beyond representation, offstage, and not, as in the biblical account, a participant in the events whose intentions and miraculous direct interventions are described by the reliable, omniscient narrator for the benefit of the reader. Samson's relationship to his god is therefore, unavoidably and predictably, very different from what we find in Judges 13–16.

In *Samson Agonistes*, the early events in Samson's life, both his mighty exploits against the Philistines and the betrayals by his Philistine wives,[21] are recalled in the dialogue, with major contributions from the Chorus of Danites. Whereas his incredible feats of killing the lion, slaughtering thirty men from Ashkelon for their garments, dispatching a thousand men with a donkey's jawbone, and pulling up the gates of Gaza are all acclaimed as signs of Samson's prodigious strength rather than, as in the biblical account, presented as God acting directly through him,[22] in *Samson Agonistes* Samson

19. Milton's protagonist is more like the blind poet himself, persecuted for his anti-royalist and anti-Catholic positions, who saw himself as the defender of the true faith and the victim of an unhappy marriage, than he is like the wild, libidinous biblical character.

20. According to Lieb (2007: 426-28), the book of Job served as a 'subtext' for both *Samson Agonistes* and *Paradise Regained*, both published in the same volume in 1671.

21. Milton makes Delilah Samson's wife, although she is not his wife in the biblical story, and a Philistine; although the biblical text never identifies Delilah as a Philistine, most readers assume she is one (see Exum 1993: 69-72).

22. The Chorus recounts Samson's killing of the lion (ll. 127-29), his slaughter of Philistines with the jawbone of an ass (ll. 142-45) and his pulling up the gates of Gaza (ll. 146-50); Harapha and Samson speak of the murder of the men from Ashkelon for their garments (ll. 1185-88, 1195-1205); Harapha also mentions the gates of Gaza (ll. 1094-95); and Samson also refers to the jawbone incident (ll. 262-64). The closest Milton ever comes to representing the effect of the spirit of the Lord on Samson is when the Chorus refers to the Spirit that rushed on Samson in the camp of Dan (l. 1435; cf. Judg. 13.25); in

is aware of his calling, and views his marriages to both the Timnite *and* Dalila as presenting the opportunity to fulfil his destiny.

> [My parents] knew not
> That what I motioned was of God; I knew
> From intimate impulse, and therefore urged
> The marriage on, that, by occasion hence,
> I might begin Israel's deliverance,
> The work to which I was divinely called.
> She proving false, the next I took to wife
> (O that I never had! fond wish too late)
> Was in the vale of Sorec, Dalila,
> That specious monster, my accomplished snare.
> I thought it lawful from my former act,
> And the same end, still watching to oppress
> Israel's oppressors… (ll. 222-33).

This presentation of Samson fills a gap created by Judg. 14.4, where the reader is informed that Samson's parents did not know that Samson's determination to wed a Philistine was part of a divine objective, and nothing is said about Samson's knowing it (leading me to posit above that Samson probably shared his parents' lack of knowledge).

Milton treats Samson's strength as a gift of God: 'For never was from Heaven imparted/ Measure of strength so great to mortal seed/ As in thy wondrous actions hath been seen' (ll. 1438-40). More than once, Samson, defeated and dejected, blames himself for being a fool for divulging his secret to a woman ('Fool! I have divulged the secret gift of God/ To a deceitful woman: tell me, friends,/ Am I not sung and proverbed for a fool/ In every street?'),[23] but, as a tragic hero, Samson rises above this pitiable state both through his introspective reflections on his failure to live up to his calling and by resisting Dalila's entreaties and her tears, when she tempts him a second time, thus proving beyond question that he has learned his lesson.[24]

reference to the incident at Lehi, Samson describes the fact that 'cords to me were threads/ Touched with the flame' as simply the state of things. A typical tragic protagonist, Samson is a lone hero; he blames his fellow Israelites for not supporting him when they could have (ll. 241-76, 1208-16). Hamilton, Handel's librettist, removed these references for political reasons; see Smith 1995: 292, and, on the historical background, 292-99.

23.   Lines 201-204; see also 46-52, 201-205, 233-36, 375-80, 497-99, 532-40. Milton makes a point about Samson abstaining from alcohol (ll. 541-57), but, Samson laments, 'But what availed this temperance, not complete/ Against another object more enticing?' (ll. 558-59).

24.   Dalila comes to the prison to beg Samson to let her take him home and care for him (cf. DeMille's Delilah, who acts similarly). She offers a series of plausible explanations for her betrayal, but Milton does not let her have the last word, and has the Chorus brand her as 'a manifest serpent by her sting' (see Exum 1996: 200-202).

Although he has a god-given mission to deliver his people, a mission he has
been well aware of since birth, Samson is no tool, for Milton, as noted above,
has changed the role of God from that of a character who is personally
involved in Samson's exploits (Judg. 13.25; 14.6, 19; 15.14-16, 19) and
whose intentions are known (14.4) to one who is rather more transcendent
and who works behind the scenes in mysterious ways, though these ways are
just and justifiable to humans (ll. 293-94).[25] Samson may know that he is
meant to deliver Israel from its oppressors and even feel God working
through him ('I knew from intimate impulse'), but the paradox of human
freedom and divine causality that we find in the biblical story is only a
shadowy subject in the background, for Milton has shifted the emphasis from
a divine agenda in which Samson has a predetermined role to the issue of
human trust in God's wisdom and purpose, as exemplified by Manoa, the
Chorus and Samson.

> ...why else this strength
> Miraculous yet remaining in those locks?
> His might continues in thee not for naught... (Manoa, ll. 586-588).

> ... God had not permitted
> His strength again to grow up with his hair
> ... were not his purpose
> To use him further yet in some great service... (Manoa, ll. 1495-99).

> Yet God hath wrought things as incredible
> For his people of old; what hinders now? (Chorus, ll. 1532-33).

> My trust is in the living God who gave me,
> At my nativity, this strength... (Samson, ll. 1139-40).[26]

> All these indignities...these evils I deserve and more,
> Acknowledge them from God inflicted on me
> Justly, yet despair not of his final pardon,
> Whose ear is ever open, and his eye
> Gracious to readmit the suppliant... (Samson, ll. 1168-73).

Theological discussion replaces biblical storytelling. Moreover, what was
in the Bible an account of God's use of Samson to achieve a desired end (to
'begin to deliver Israel' with the result that 'the dead that he slew at his death
were more than those he had slain during his life', 13.5; 16.30) becomes in
Samson Agonistes a contest between God and Dagon, between true religion
and idolatry, raising the stakes to a 'higher' plane.

---

25.   This theme is picked up in Handel's *Samson* in 'Just are the ways of God to man'
(Act II, Scene 1).
26.   Samson shows his trust in God by challenging Harapha to combat to prove whose
god is God.

...all the contest is now
'Twixt God and Dagon; Dagon hath presumed,
Me overthrown, to enter lists with God,
His deity comparing and preferring
Before the God of Abraham. He, be sure,
Will not connive, or linger, thus provoked,
But will arise, and his great name assert... (Samson, ll. 461-67).

To which Manoa responds with equal conviction:

With cause this hope relieves thee; and these words
I as a prophecy receive, for God,
Nothing more certain, will not long defer
To vindicate the glory of his name
Against all competition, nor will long
Endure it doubtful whether God be Lord,
Or Dagon (ll. 473-78).

Prayer plays a role in this hope and confidence in God, but, in keeping with Milton's portrayal of the deity, God's role in answering prayer is described indirectly. It is, for example, through Manoa that we hear of 'God, who caused a fountain at thy prayer/ From the dry ground to spring, thy thirst to allay/ After the brunt of battle' (ll. 581-83). Samson's final prayer for vengeance and death in Judg. 16.28, 30 is not reported by the messenger who describes Samson's destruction of the temple, which takes place offstage. At one point Samson reveals his (temporary) despair and hopelessness with a wish for death:

Nor am I in the list of them that hope;
Hopeless are all my evils, all remediless;
This one prayer yet remains, might I be heard,
No long petition—speedy death,
The close of all my miseries and the balm (ll. 647-51).

And, in the end, he is described by the messenger, who witnessed the events, as standing, head bowed, 'as one who prayed' (l. 1637). The theme of revenge (Judg. 16.28) is placed in the mouth of the Chorus, which describes Samson's death as not willed but necessary:

O dearly-bought revenge, yet glorious!
Living or dying thou hast fulfilled
The work for which thou wast foretold
To Israel, and now ly'st victorious
Among thy slain self-killed,
Not willingly, but tangled in the fold
Of dire Necessity, whose law in death conjoined
Thee with thy slaughtered foes, in number more
Than all thy life had slain before (ll. 1660-1668).

Prior to his death, as a sign of Samson's 'heroic magnitude of mind' (l. 1279) and dedication to God, Milton has Samson, whose strength is returning with his hair, refuse to abuse this 'consecrated gift' and commit a greater sin than his earlier one by performing before the Philistines in their temple, 'prostituting holy things to idols/ A Nazarite, in place abominable' (ll. 1354-59). He changes his mind, however, when he feels 'some rousing motions in me, which dispose/ To something extraordinary my thoughts' and has a presentiment that 'this day will be remarkable in my life/ By some great act, or of my days the last' (ll. 1382-89). In Judges, Samson achieves his purpose to *begin* to deliver Israel when he kills more at his death than in his life. In *Samson Agonistes* the Samson who does these things emerges as a heroic, noble figure, favoured by God. As Manoa eulogizes:

> Samson hath quit himself
> Like Samson, and heroicly hath finished
> A life heroic, on his enemies
> Fully revenged—hath left them years of mourning,
> ...To Israel
> Honour hath left and freedom...
> To himself and father's house eternal fame,
> And, which is best and happiest yet, all this
> With God not parted from him, as was feared,
> But favouring and assisting to the end.
> Nothing is here for tears, nothing to wail
> Or knock the breast; no weakness, no contempt,
> Dispraise, or blame; nothing but well and fair,
> And what may quiet us in a death so noble (ll. 1709-24).

Milton's great epic poem concludes with the Chorus's affirmation of the mystery and unfathomable wisdom of God and the lesson to be learned by all from the illustrious example of his 'faithful champion' Samson:

> All is best, though we oft doubt
> What the unsearchable dispose
> Of Highest Wisdom brings about,
> And ever best found in the close.
> Oft he seems to hide his face,
> But unexpectedly returns,
> And to his faithful champion hath in place
> Bore witness gloriously; whence Gaza mourns,
> And all that bind them to resist
> His uncontrollable intent:
> His servants he, with new acquist
> Of true experience from this great event,
> With peace and consolation hath dismissed
> And calm of mind all passion spent.[27]

27.   Milton's picture of God is far from simplistic; the issues of doubt and God's seeming to hide his face are addressed at length in the Job-like words of the Chorus, ll.

Milton's retelling of the biblical story receives a faithful retelling in Handel's *Samson*, and oratorio, as a musical drama, provides a fitting format for rendering musically the stirring, lofty sentiments of Milton's great opus. There are, of course, differences. The libretto, by Newburgh Hamilton, of necessity leaves out large sections of the dialogue, in addition to adding some new bits (some from other works by Milton) and introducing new characters.[28] But the plot line, in which Samson broods over his betrayal of his secret, is visited by Manoah, Dalila and Harapha and comes to see how he might nevertheless serve his god, follows closely *Samson Agonistes*. Like Milton's Samson, although he curses his folly for revealing his secret to a woman—'But had I sight, how could I heave my head /For shame? thus, for a word, or tear, divulge/ To a false woman God's most secret gift,/ And then be sung, or proverb'd for a fool!'—Samson is neither a fool[29] nor a tool, for the same reasons as in *Samson Agonistes*. He is aware of his dedication to God from birth but *Samson* devotes little space to Samson's mission to deliver Israel from Philistine oppression, speaking of it only in broad and grandiloquent terms:

> My strength is from the living God
> By Heav'n free-gifted at my birth
> To quell the mighty of the earth,
> And prove the brutal tyrant's rod
> But to the righteous peace and rest,
> With liberty to all opprest ('Put on your arms', Act II, Scene 4).

Although Handel and Hamilton do not follow Milton in having Samson see God at work in his marriage to Dalila, the relationship between Samson and God is essentially the same as in *Samson Agonistes*, though given less attention.[30]

667-709. Handel's picture is less complex, and little of this speech is retained ('God of our fathers', an air sung by an Israelite man in Act I, Scene 3).

28.   The significant difference is the introduction of the character Micah, who has a major part; minor parts for Israelites and Philistines are also included. *Samson* was begun in 1741, the same year in which Handel wrote *The Messiah*, and was completed in 1742. Handel's relationship with his librettists is a complex issue; see Hurley 2001: 168-70; cf. Smith 1995: 323-39. Performance will have an effect on the audience's interpretation of the piece; in many cases Handel made curtailments in the recitatives in performance, while in others they are a matter of custom. For discussion of differences between Hamilton's libretto and Milton's *Samson Agonistes*, and their significance for Handel's *Samson*, see Rooke 2012: 98-120.

29.   In fact, his weakness is described as understandable: 'Wisest men/ Have erred, and by bad women been deceived' (*Samson Agonistes*, ll. 210-11); 'The wisest men have error'd, and been deceiv'd/ By female arts' in Hamilton's libretto (*Samson*, Act I, Scene 2).

30.   Samson's marriage to the Timnite is not mentioned in the oratorio. As in *Samson Agonistes*, there is no reference to the spirit of the Lord as the force behind his killing of the lion (mentioned by Micah) or his victory with the ass's jawbone (mentioned by

As befits an oratorio on a biblical subject, *Samson* is more triumphant in tone than its Miltonic source.[31] This is due, in particular, to the foregrounding of God as the champion of Israel, especially as the climactic contest between God and Dagon approaches, the contest that proves 'whose God is God: Dagon, of mortal make/ Or that Great One whom Abram's sons adore'. These words, sung by Micah (an alto role created for the oratorio), are followed by the Chorus's affirmation of God as Israel's only hope and saviour:

> Hear, Jacob's God, Jehovah, hear!
> Oh save us, prostrate at thy throne!
> Israel depends on thee alone.
> Save us, and show that thou art near! (Act II, Scene 4).

The contest of the gods is anticipated at the oratorio's beginning, when the Chorus of Philistines and Dalila sing Dagon's praises ('Awake the trumpet's lofty sound!' [Chorus]; 'Ye men of Gaza' [Dalila]; material not in *Samson Agonistes*). At other key points as well, the Chorus of Israelites and Micah call on God as their salvation, and bid him come to Samson's aid. It is the Chorus that, on God's behalf, urges Samson to crush the Philistines.

> To fame immortal go
> Heav'n bids thee strike the blow
> The Holy One of Israel is thy guide (Act III, Scene 1).

Before he goes to the temple, Samson expresses the hope that God will use him to glorify his name:

> Let but that spirit (which first rush'd on me
> In the camp of Dan) inspire me at my need:
> Then shall I make Jehovah's glory known!
> Their idol gods shall from his presence fly.
> Scatter'd like sheep before the God of Hosts (Act III, Scene 1).

The messenger who describes what happened in the temple does not mention Samson's dying prayer (Judg. 16.28-30), and his death is not described as an unsought but necessary consequence of his pulling down the temple, as it is in *Samson Agonistes*.

At the end of Act II the challenge has been issued, and attention is forcefully drawn to the contest by the Chorus of Israelites, who appeal to

---

Harapha). Apart from these, Samson's glorious deeds are not specified; however, also as in *Samson Agonistes*, Samson refers to the 'spirit (which first rush'd on me/ In the camp of Dan)' ('Be of good courage', Act III, Scene 1).

31. Handel's *Samson* foregrounds Samson's role as a national hero, embodying the ideal of resistance to tyranny and false religion (Catholicism) of the eighteenth-century Protestant British public; see Rooke 2012: 111-20.

God with the rousing 'Hear Jacob's God' (in A minor) and by a Double Chorus of Israelites and Philistines singing, competitively, 'Fix'd in his everlasting seat' (D major):

> Fix'd in his everlasting seat, Jehovah rules the world in state.
> Fix'd in his everlasting seat, Great Dagon rules the world in state.

But all this emphasis on the demonstration of God's power and glory does not diminish Samson's role, and Handel's *Samson* ends with jubilant celebration of Samson's life. The source text, *Samson Agonistes*, concludes with an affirmation of trust in God ('All is best, though we oft doubt...'), *preceded* by praise of Samson, and culminating in 'calm of mind all passion spent', the response that tragedy intends to elicit. In contrast, Handel leaves the audience exultant and uplifted by an air sung by an Israelite woman, followed by a chorus, both in D major (neither text appears in *Samson Agonistes*):

> (Air) Let the bright Seraphim in burning row
> Their loud, uplifted angel trumpets blow.
> Let the Cherubic host, in tuneful choirs,
> Touch their immortal harps with golden wires.
>
> (Chorus) Let their celestial concerts all unite
> Ever to sound his praise in endless blaze of light.

Samson and his God

Jabotinsky's novel, with its account of Samson's exploits, trials and triumphs, is closest in tone and spirit to the rowdy adventure stories found in the Bible; Milton and, following him, Handel, for whom Samson displays a certain tragic grandeur, are the furthest removed from them. DeMille's retelling most faithfully represents the biblical story, but it takes itself more seriously than either Jabotinsky's *Samson* or Judges 13–16. None of these cultural reworkings of the Samson story has an omniscient narrator who tells us, authoritatively, what God intends to happen or what events are directly attributable to God, and so the paradox of divine causality and human free will—which is what makes the biblical story so much more than a simple tale—ceases to be a difficulty. Samson might see himself as the instrument of God, and other characters in a retelling might be convinced of it, but that is not the same as divine causality. In these modern retellings we are no longer faced with the thorny question of Samson's awareness of his place in the divine plan that the biblical story raises. In Jabotinsky's *Samson*, Milton's *Samson Agonistes*, Handel's *Samson* and, less emphatically, DeMille's *Samson and Delilah*, Samson believes he has a god-given mission to deliver his people. Whereas Jabotinsky, by creating a character destined to become the unreliable

'biblical' narrator, encourages his readers not to agree, Milton, Handel and
DeMille present Samson's relationship to his god in a way that disposes
audiences to accept the idea of Samson as an instrument of God's will (if not
in reality, then as an acceptable premise of their retellings).

The novel is the best medium for reproducing the biblical paradox of
divine causality and human freedom, but Jabotinsky chose instead to make
his novel about Samson a secular one. In his film, DeMille could have used a
voiceover to report God's miraculous interventions in the events of Samson's
life, but this would have been less realistic and thus less appealing to modern
audiences, as well as less effective than showing us Samson's glorious deeds,
having Samson and those around him recognize the hand of God in them and
letting the audience draw their own conclusions. Wisely, DeMille does not
propose to speak for God, and the voiceover at the beginning of the film does
not even mention God, only a 'divine spark' identified as the will for freedom. Although DeMille uses Jabotinsky's *Samson* to fill gaps, he basically
follows the biblical story, relying especially on the ostensible granting of
Samson's prayers and the ample testimony of other characters to establish a
relationship between Samson and God in which Samson is empowered by
God and chooses to do God's will.

Presenting God as a speaker in a dramatic poem would have been at odds
with Milton's view of a God whose ways are not the ways of humans but are
just and justifiable. Those who do not believe in God are fools, and there are
misguided souls who question God's justice (ll. 295-99); but believers, who
may be able to influence God by action and appeal, will recognize that God,
in his divine wisdom, has a purpose for his creation. In Milton's version,
Samson becomes a tragic hero who, having made a mistake and seen his
error, reaffirms his dedication to God, and whose decision it is to serve God's
purpose. Handel's oratorio, following *Samson Agonistes*, has Samson,
Manoah and the Israelites sing about God and proclaim his glory rather than
having God sing for himself, and Handel and his librettist Hamilton even
bring a new character, Micah, on stage to serve this reverential function.
Handel's Samson is not so tragic as Milton's, and his presentation of Samson
as hero could be seen as more instrumental than Milton's because of the
prominence given to God as saviour of Israel while Samson's role is that of
God's champion and servant—but faithfulness to God's laws and doing
God's will are Samson's choice.

Though naturalizing events by removing God from direct responsibility
for all that happens to Samson appears to be the preferred way to tell the
story for moderns, I find the biblical account more interesting—a more
challenging, provocative literary creation—because of the ambivalent
potential of the God-character, the unusual portrayal of the human hero as

one who pursues personal vendettas rather than some loftier purpose, and the abiding ambiguity of Samson's relationship with this god that results. No dialogue ever takes place between them. It remains uncertain, and debatable, whether or not Samson only unwittingly serves God's purpose and whether or not he is merely a tool dispensable in God's plan.

Bibliography

Amit, Yairah
> 1999   *The Book of Judges: The Art of Editing* (trans. Jonathan Chipman; Biblical Interpretation Series, 38; Leiden: E.J. Brill).
>
> 2000   *Hidden Polemics in Biblical Narrative* (trans. Jonathan Chipman; Biblical Interpretation Series, 25; Leiden: E.J. Brill).
>
> 2001   *Reading Biblical Narratives: Literary Criticism and the Hebrew Bible* (trans. Yael Lotan; Minneapolis: Fortress Press).
>
> 2008   'Samson: Both Tool and Fool' (unpublished paper presented at the conference 'Samson: Hero or Fool?', Radboud University Nijmegen, 9–11 April 2008).

Exum, J. Cheryl
> 1981   'Aspects of Symmetry and Balance in the Samson Saga', *JSOT* 19: 3-29 (errata in *JSOT* 20: 90).
>
> 1983   'The Theological Dimension of the Samson Saga', *VT* 33: 30-45.
>
> 1992   *Tragedy and Biblical Narrative: Arrows of the Almighty* (Cambridge: Cambridge University Press).
>
> 1993   *Fragmented Women: Feminist (Sub)versions of Biblical Narratives* (JSOTSup, 163; Sheffield: JSOT Press/Valley Forge, PA: Trinity Press International).
>
> 1996   *Plotted, Shot, and Painted: Cultural Representations of Biblical Women* (JSOTSup, 215; Gender, Culture, Theory, 3; Sheffield: Sheffield Academic Press).
>
> 1998   'Lovis Corinth's *Blinded Samson*', *BibInt* 6: 410-25.
>
> 2008   'The Many Faces of Samson' (unpublished paper presented at the conference 'Samson: Hero or Fool?', Radboud University Nijmegen, 9–11 April 2008).

Gaster, Theodor H.
> 1981   *Myth, Legend, and Custom in the Old Testament*, II (Gloucester, MA: Peter Smith).

Gunkel, Hermann
> 1913   'Simson', in *Reden und Aufsätze* (Göttingen: Vandenhoeck & Ruprecht): 38-64.

Gunn, David M.
> 1992   'Samson of Sorrows: An Isaianic Gloss on Judges 13–16', in Danna Nolan Fewell (ed.), *Reading between Texts: Intertextuality and the Hebrew Bible* (Louisville, KY: Westminster/John Knox Press): 225-53.
>
> 2005   *Judges* (Blackwell Bible Commentaries; Oxford: Basil Blackwell).

Hurley, David Ross
    2001   *Handel's Muse: Patterns of Creation in His Oratorios and Musical Dramas, 1743–1751* (Oxford: Oxford University Press).
Jabotinsky, Ze'ev
    1976 [1927] *Samson* (Johannesburg: Jewish Herald Pty).
Lieb, Michael
    2007   'John Milton', in Andrew Hass, David Jasper and Elisabeth Jay (eds.), *The Oxford Handbook of English Literature and Theology* (Oxford: Oxford University Press): 413-30.
Mendenhall, George E.
    1973   *The Tenth Generation: The Origins of the Biblical Tradition* (Baltimore: The Johns Hopkins University Press).
Peels, H.G.L.
    1995   *The Vengeance of God: The Meaning of the Root NQM and the Function of the NQM-Texts in the Context of Divine Revelation in the Old Testament* (Oudtestamentische Studiën, 31; Leiden: E.J. Brill).
Rad, Gerhard von
    1962   *Old Testament Theology*, I (trans. D.M.G. Stalker; New York: Harper & Row).
Rooke, Deborah W.
    2012   *Handel's Israelite Oratorio Libretti: Sacred Drama and Biblical Exegesis* (Oxford: Oxford University Press).
Smith, Ruth
    1995   *Handel's Oratorios and Eighteenth Century Thought* (Cambridge: Cambridge University Press).
Sternberg, Meir
    1985   *The Poetics of Biblical Narrative: Ideological Literature and the Drama of Reading* (Bloomington: Indiana University Press).

Mock Abrahams, Silent Gods, Nascent States: The Sacrifice of Isaac and Familicide in Early America

Yael S. Feldman

For Yairah,
May our mutual fascination
with biblical literature and ideology,
past and present,
continue to thrive…

> The Judeo-Christian scriptures should be regarded as the first complete revelation of the structuring power of victimage in pagan religions… The Bible was the first to replace the scapegoat structure of mythology with a scapegoat theme that reveals the lie of mythology (Girard 1987: 118).

René Girard's apotheosis of Scripture at the expense of mythology was his way of laying the foundation for nothing less than a debate on *the origins of human violence*, held in California in 1983. It goes without saying that his statement opened the door to 'a lot of questions', as Girard's primary challenger, Walter Burkert, was quick to observe. As a classicist, Burkert argued from—and in defense of—mythology. As a literary Hebraist I would argue from literature and from the Hebrew Bible, taking to task Girard's claim that while 'the Bible' invented the 'demythification' of myth, literature has continued the process by 'rehabilitating the victims and overturning the scapegoating on which mythology is founded' (Girard 1987: 115).

As my analysis will illustrate, it is not the violent foundations of mythology alone that are 'overturned' by literature, but often also those of the very biblical tradition that Girard so trustingly applauded. Moreover, at times literature also unravels the popular hyphenated concept, 'the Judeo-Christian scriptures', thereby revealing the lie of the ostensible seamlessness between its two components (Cohen 1970). By so doing, it may indirectly remind us that 'monotheism' is a similarly problematic compound concept, veiling historically significant differences, especially in the exercise of violence in God's name.

Before turning to my literary test case, however, let me point out that although this theme is even more pressing today than it was in the 1980s, when the conference to discuss the origin of violence was convened, for me, as a native Israeli, it is old hat. The question of violence, whether in the name of the Almighty or later secular 'gods', is commonplace in a country where the trauma of war and terrorism is never distant, and where the memory of the Holocaust still looms large, affecting both politics and psychology. In Israel this trauma has more often than not been symbolized by the archetypal biblical story, the aborted filicide for God narrated in Genesis 22. How and why the divinely prohibited sacrifice of Isaac became a trope for human violence and enacted homicide is an intricate tale I have told elsewhere (Feldman 2010). All I wish to stress here is that the sacrificial narrative, which was unique to Israel in the not too distant past, has become, since the trauma of 9/11 and in its wake, a global preoccupation. Affecting an ever growing circle of people, it arises from a reality of life lived too close to the altar; from one's confrontation with the tragic choice between being the sacrificer or the sacrificed; and from the excruciating realization that the line separating selfless heroism (self sacrifice) from fanaticism—of any kind— may be quite thin indeed, almost imperceptible.

Yet this tragic awareness is not new, even on a global scale. Nor is it the product of the twentieth century, bloody as this was. To illustrate this point, I turn now not to contemporary fiction, Israeli or other, but rather to early America. Here too we can discover authors who wrestled with the ethical implications of their own sacrificial narratives as well as with their biblical origin—the near-sacrifice of Isaac (Mizruchi 1998).

I begin with a quote:

> Fiction did not flourish in early America, where it was generally viewed as a useless or demoralizing pastime. Before Charles Brockden Brown, America had no professional man of letters. *Wieland,* his first novel, appeared in 1798; among the romances by anonymous young ladies [*sic*], it was a pioneering effort to create a serious American literature.

This is how the cover of my 1973 paperback edition re-introduces this early American Gothic tale, almost two centuries (!) after its original publication. By claiming *Wieland* as the first American novel, the publishers were evidently trying to overcome the historical breach between its outlandish trappings and its potential contemporary readers. And they seem to have succeeded. Scholarly interest in this precursor has grown by leaps and bounds, peaking in the establishment of a Brown society in 1998, and eventually in the publication of a volume named *Revising C.B. Brown* (Verhoeven 2004).

Initially, the interest in Brown and especially in *Wieland* stemmed from their position at an historical junction, at the rupture between an identifiable national American literature and its English mother/land and mother/letters. I suggest, however, that this novel should also arouse a more global concern, as a part of the debate over the origins of human violence mentioned above.

This debate can be traced back, in fact, to 1932, when the American Psychological Association decided by a vote of 346 to 10 that violence was the result of 'nurture' rather than 'nature'… Forty years later the bubble had burst, and in the 1970s the 'Science of Violence' was revived in both anthropology and cultural studies, featuring such major studies as *Homo Necans* [Killer Man]: *The Anthropology of Ancient Greek Sacrificial Ritual and Myth*, by the Swiss classicist Walter Burkert, and *Violence and the Sacred* by literary and cultural interpreter René Girard;[1] to these two we may add Derrida's discussion of Plato's 'Pharmakos' in *Dissemination*, and *The Dilemma of Zealous Nationalism* by New Testament scholar Robert Jewett. All four studies were published in 1972–73.

With the exception of Derrida, the divergent approaches of these scholars (and others) were presented in 1987 in the book *Violent Origins: Ritual Killing and Cultural Formation* (Burkert, Girard and Smith, 1987). Curiously, but perhaps predictably, their exchange only confirmed my Israeli perspective, for the debate over violence has been often filtered through the lens of ritual sacrifice, and especially *human* sacrifice, or scapegoating.

So the first question to ask is what bearing may the 'violence debate' have on 'the first American novel'? Well, the brief answer is that in this novel an affectionate father and husband, Theodore Wieland, murders his family in obedience to what he perceives to be a divine injunction…

Though classified as 'American Gothic' (Christophersen 1993), the novel is anchored in historical fact; actually, in several facts. As recognized already two centuries ago, that horrible plot was *not* the invention of Brown, himself a scion of a Philadelphia Quaker family and a student of law before becoming a professional author (and whose very first publication was, by the way, a dialogue on *The rights of women* [*Alcuin*, 1797])… Like Dostoyevsky after him, Brown must have known that life can be more sensational than art, and that the press is a good place for culling such sensations. As it happened, in 1796 reports were circulating in print about a gruesome ritual murder by one James Yates, reportedly a gentle and sober farmer in Tomhannock, New York who, on a nice Sunday evening in 1781, had been visited by apparitions—angels by his own confession—that commanded him to destroy all his idols, including his own Bible and…his whole family. Shockingly, he promptly obeyed (Axelrod 1983: 47-53).

---

1. Followed by his *The Scapegoat and Things Hidden since the Foundation of the World*.

It was this shocking homicidal conversion that was apparently indicated by Brown's subtitle for the novel, 'The Transformation'. The timing of this transformation, both in the real-life case and in its literary reworking, eerily raises the specter of Girard's claim that ritual killing is at the base of any cultural formation. Perhaps this is why Brown stresses, in his brief 'Advertisement' (Preface), that 'these events took place between the conclusion of the French and the beginning of the Revolutionary War'...[2]

It should come as no surprise that this is the direction that the critical literature seems to have taken. There is a scholarly consensus that 'the wilderness'—a fact of life of the Early Republic and the setting chosen by Brown for his 'American Tale' (the second subtitle of the novel)—is the culprit of the homicidal transformation: 'Yate's act, like Theodore Wieland's, was born', says Alan Axelrod, 'of that world, a wilderness isolated from the emotionally and intellectually tempering influence of city civilization and organized religion' (1983: 57).

The opposition between urban civilization and the yet unconquered, threatening wilderness is of course typical of the frontier construction of any nascent nation-state, as Hebrew fiction, for one, amply documents (e.g. S. Yizhar, Amos Oz, Shulamith Hareven). Brown's wilderness anticipates, in fact, the Israeli 'desert'; and the 'savage' North American Indians it harbors foreshadow the native Arab and other nomads that populate the 'wilderness' of Hebrew literature (Feldman 2010: 197-98, 304-305). Indeed, the anxiety over 'nation founding' is elaborated on in recent, more nuanced studies of *Wieland*. These studies focus on the enormous weight of the demand to fraternize one's fellow citizens and empathize with the enlarged national family (Stern 1997), while at the same time 'picking up the knife, as it were…against [one's] former self, that elder kinsman-turned-antagonist, Great Britain' (Christophersen 1993: 35). No wonder then that *Wieland*'s violent family romance is ultimately seen as a mirror image of the early American Republic, or better, as a warning against the ethical dangers it was facing (Samuels 1996). Needless to say, this construction is very popular in Israeli fiction as well, not excluding the anxiety over masculinity (Feldman 2010: 288-94), suggested too in recent interpretations of *Wieland,* Yates, and other cases of familicide reported in the post-Revolutionary era (Barnes 2002).

But there is more to *Wieland* than the crisis of the patriarchal family *qua* nation at a time of turbulence. Twentieth-century scholarship has followed an intertextual link signaled by the title of the novel. Ostensibly a scion of a Pennsylvania family of German descent, Theodore Wieland's fictional roots are traced to the highly influential eighteenth-century German poet Christoph

---

2.   Namely, between the 1760s and 1776.

Martin *Wieland* [1733–1813], whose little-known long epic verse poem in four cantos [and 125 pages!], *Die Prüfung Abrahams* (1753), was published in English in 1778 as *The Trial of Abraham* (Axelrod 1983: 61-65). Though faithful to the main outline of Genesis 22, the so-called 'Sacrifice of Isaac', the German epic is in fact an elaborated Christian 'midrash' (homily, exegesis). Among the rest, it fills in the gaps of the terse biblical text by dwelling at length on the contradictory emotions of pain and joy experienced by both father and son. Significantly, however, it does *not* deviate from the biblical counter-violent closure of the story (which, we may recall, replaces human sacrifice with animal sacrifice). On the contrary, just as the angel *Eloa* [in Hebrew אלוה, 'God'...] begins to speak to Abraham, Isaac's binding ropes melt as if by fire, and he recognizes his personal guardian angel...[3]

Bearing this conclusion in mind, I would like to propose that Brown's complex intertextual linkage with both Genesis and C.M. Wieland's poem complicates his rewriting of the sacrificial narrative, somewhat (though not quite) in the way theorized by Girard. To my mind, the eponymous title of the novel signals *difference from* rather than *resemblance to* its textual models. But to see this we need to begin at the beginning—not with the ritual killing by Theodore, but with the life and death of his father, Wieland the elder. For it is Wieland the elder who is the originary mock Abraham of our story. His is the story of an orphaned German lad who had been sent to London to be trained as a trader. Resenting his apprenticeship, he found solace in the teachings of different antinomian religious sects, and eventually in the Bible itself. However, because he was an undisciplined autodidact, 'his constructions of the text were hasty', suggests his daughter, 'and formed on a narrow scale', so that he became 'alternately agitated *by fear and by ecstasy*' (Brown 1973: 15; emphasis mine).[4]

Nevertheless, he had 'imbibed an opinion that it was his duty to disseminate the truth of the gospel to the unbelieving nations' (Brown 1973: 16). Since 'the North American Indians naturally presented themselves as the first objects for this species of benevolences', he had embarked for Philadelphia as soon as his apprenticeship was over (Brown 1973: 17). After fourteen years of 'thrifty and laborious manner' he was able to relinquish work and devote himself to the pursuit of his beliefs. On a top of a rock, a precipice sixty feet above the river, he built a temple to his Deity (a veritable 'City on the Hill', as critics have remarked; Samuels 1996: 45). There he used to go twice daily, praying and presumably *waiting for a revelation or sign of*

---

3. Thanks to my colleague Paul Fleming for his generous help in reading the German text.
4. Was Brown rewriting—though with a difference—Paul's 'fear and trembling'? (See Phil. 2.12-13: 'You must work out your salvation in fear and trembling'.) Since the Greek for 'in trembling' is *tromos* [= tremor], could it also be translated as 'ecstasy'?

*election.*⁵ But in vain. Unlike Abraham's God in both Genesis and the poem by his eponymous precursor, his Deity was silent. This Wieland, who had earlier seen himself as '*bound* (!) to mercantile service' (Brown 1973: 14), was now bound to an unresponsive deity and an unrealizable duty. Not only was he not elected; he soon began to feel—*pace* Kafka's antihero in 'Before the Law'—that 'he was no longer permitted to obey. The duty assigned for him was transferred, in consequence of his disobedience, to another, and all that remained was to endure the penalty' (Brown 1973: 20).

If we remember that Wieland's orphanhood is Brown's fictional construction, not to be found in his historical or intertextual models, its significance will come to the fore. Lacking any parental figure, and living a solitary, monadic life despite his formal matrimony, Wieland the elder has no real human contact, no collective with which he could exercise his 'mimetic desire', to use Girard's terms. His daily pilgrimage to his temple seems to be his way to address this lack, possibly working through his frustrated desire for the divine, and along the way competing with those anonymous, better others who will ultimately be elected for the duty and mission he craves but cannot act upon.

To a degree, Wieland's life story recapitulates that of the biblical Abraham, reflecting the puritan tradition that viewed America as the New Jerusalem (Bercovitch 1975). Unlike Abraham, however, his desire for the divine is not reciprocated. His god is silent. Not temporarily 'eclipsed', as in Buber's famous formulation in the wake of World War II (1952), but silent in the sense of that demonic/divine ambiguity soon to be caught by Johannes de Silentio, namely Kierkegaard: 'Silence is the *demon's* trap, and the more that is silenced, the more terrible the demon, but silence is also *divinity's* mutual understanding with the *single individual*' (Kierkegaard 2006: 97; emphasis mine). Ultimately, it is the lack of 'economy' (Derrida 1992) in Wieland's particular sacrificial contract that turns it demonically violent, thereby exposing its precariousness.

But why? What is the logic behind Wieland's strange death, recently termed 'spontaneous combustion'? What does he pay penalty for? Is there a cause and effect relationship between the solitariness of his being and the silence of his object of desire? Or is Wieland, as a fictional construction, the victim of a conflict between two systems of cultural formation? Unable—on his own—to activate the mythological mechanism of scapegoating (or sacrifice) that ostensibly purifies the community and allows for the formation of

---

5.   Over a century later, Sherwood Anderson, one of the forefathers of twentieth century American fiction (1876–1941) will bravely dramatize the disastrous results of the melding of the wish for divine election with the trope of sacrifice. His experiment has in turn affected the early fiction of Israeli author Amos Oz. See my forthcoming '"Give me a sign": Bible, Election, and Sacrifice in Sherwood Anderson and Amos Oz'.

culture, he is also excluded from Biblical election, from what Kierkegaard describes as the Divine's 'mutual understanding with the single individual'. Doubly frustrated, Wieland's desire-turned-rage is therefore directed back upon himself in a kind of self auto-da-fé.

This mock Abraham turned Isaac, or better Christ, is, however, a *failed* sacrifice. Ultimately, his self-immolating signals not the success of cultural formation but its violent ruin. For Wieland the elder's traumatic death is recapitulated by his progeny, and in a very cruel way. As mentioned above, it is his own son who begins hearing voices, ostensibly divine voices, that finally command him to murder/sacrifice all his loved ones. Significantly, the sacrificial death wish of the father is not transferred to the second generation verbatim, but rather takes on the more lethal form of sacrificing/murdering others.

Moreover, since the human source of the voices Wieland the younger hears is revealed only late in the novel, the veracity of an ancient Gnostic belief, 'God is man-eater' (*The Gospel of Philip*; cited by Burkert in Burkert, Girard, and Smith 1987: 175) is held in abeyance. Clearly, however, the protagonist himself, Wieland the son, does accept this possibility. He fully obeys the ostensibly divine voice despite its breach of the ethical (as Kierkegaard will later define it), thereby bringing about the demise of his whole family.

The narrative itself nevertheless vehemently denies this outrageous imagining of a Gnostic-like evil demiurge. Yet, this denial does not 'salvage' the image of the absent god drawn in the first part of this American tale. In the final analysis, the Almighty is silent here once again. At the same time, whereas if in the case of the father the source of his violent death remains opaque, here the demand for sacrifice/victimization/violence[6] clearly does not emanate from the divine but from the demonic—or rather from a demonical human.

Read this way, the devastating destiny of the Wieland family problematizes the 'national anxiety' interpretation of the novel. *Wieland* can be read not only as a comment on a particular project [the American early Republic] gone awry, but also as a critique of and warning against a universal malfunctioning. Brown constructs a universe in which Divine silence and humans' lack of proper communal bonding share the responsibility for violence. Moreover, his construction of the circulation of violence and trauma between the generations brings home the terrifying possibility that the distance between *self*-immolation (Wieland the elder) and immolation of the *other* (Wieland the younger) may be easily crossed. *Wieland* makes clear (as do other stories, Amos Oz's tale about the biblical Judge Jephthah, among

---

6.   On the potential semantic slippage between the concepts 'sacrifice' and 'victim' in several languages including Hebrew, see Feldman 2010: 34-36 and *passim*.

others; see Feldman 2010: 183-214) that there is a scarily easy 'logical' transition from one mental state to the other (and compare the shift from martyrs to suicide bombers). Moreover, it is perhaps no accident that the traumatic violence of these stories is expressed sexually as well—in the incestuous desire that governs the plot with disastrous results (see Stern 1997 and Feldman 2010, Chap. 4, respectively).

Above all, Brown's harsh verdict allows for *no* mechanism of redemptive sacrifice—mythological (scapegoat) *or* Christian (self-sacrifice) (see Bersani 1990; LaCapra 2001). From this perspective, this novel, a foundational text of American literature, challenges Girard's trusting apotheosis of Scripture at the expense of mythology. By blocking the path to redemption, of any kind, it rather reveals the lie not only of pagan mythology, but of Christian mythology as well (Verhoeven 2004).

Bibliography

Axelrod, Alan
    1983   *Charles Brockden Brown, an American Tale* (Austin: University of Texas
            Press).
Barnes, Elizabeth
    2002   'Love with a Vengeance: Wieland, Familicide and the Crisis of Mascu-
            linity in the Early Nation', in Millette Shamir and Jennifer Travis (eds.),
            *Boys Don't Cry?: Rethinking Narratives of Masculinity and Emotion in the
            U.S.* (New York: Columbia University Press): 44-63.
Bercovitch, Sacvan
    1975   *The Puritan Origins of the American Self* (New Haven: Yale University
            Press).
Bersani, Leo
    1990   *The Culture of Redemption* (Cambridge, MA: Harvard University Press).
Brown, C.B.
    1973 [1798]   *Wieland or The Transformation: An American Tale* (Harmondsworth:
            Penguin).
Buber, Martin
    1988 [1952]   *Eclipse of God: Studies in the Relation between Religion and Philosophy*
            (Atlantic Highlands, NJ: Humanity Books).
Burkert, Walter
    1983 [1972]   *Homo Necans [Killer Man]: The Anthropology of Ancient Greek Sacrifi-
            cial Ritual and Myth* (trans. Peter Bing; Berkeley: University of California
            Press).
Burkert, Walter, René Girard and Jonathan Z. Smith
    1987   *Violent Origins: Ritual Killing and Cultural Formation* (Stanford, CA:
            Stanford University Press).
Christophersen, Bill
    1993   *The Apparition in the Glass: Charles Brockden Brown's American Gothic*
            (Athens: University of Georgia Press).

Cohen, Arthur A.
1970   *The Myth of the Judeo-Christian Tradition* (New York: Harper & Row).
Derrida, Jacques
1981 [1968]   'Plato's Pharmacy', in *Dissemination* (trans. Barbara Johnson; Chicago: University of Chicago Press).
1995   *The Gift of Death* (trans. David Wills; Chicago: University of Chicago Press).
Feldman, Yael S.
2010   *Glory and Agony: Isaac's Sacrifice and National Narrative* (Stanford, CA: Stanford University Press).
forthcoming   '"Give me a sign": Bible, Election, and Sacrifice in Sherwood Anderson and Amos Oz'.
Girard, René
1977 [1972]   *Violence and the Sacred* (trans. Patrick Gregory; Baltimore: The Johns Hopkins University Press).
Jewett, Robert
1973   *The Captain America Complex: The Dilemma of Zealous Nationalism* (Philadelphia: Westminster Press).
Kierkegaard, Søren
2006 [1843]   *Fear and Trembling* (ed. C. Stephen Evans and Sylvia Walsh; Cambridge: Cambridge University Press).
LaCapra, Dominique
2001   *Writing History, Writing Trauma* (Baltimore: The Johns Hopkins University Press).
Mizruchi, Susan L.
1998   *The Science of Sacrifice* (Princeton, NJ: Princeton University Press).
Samuels, Shirley
1996   *Romances of the Republic: Women, the Family, and Violence in the Literature of the Early American Nation* (Oxford: Oxford University Press).
Stern, Julia
1997   *The Plight of Feeling: Sympathy and Dissent in the Early American Novel* (Chicago: University of Chicago Press).
Verhoeven, W. M.
2004   '"This blissful period of intellectual liberty": Transatlantic Radicalism and Enlightened Conservatism in Brown's Early Writings', in Philip Barnard, Mark Kamrath, and Stephen Shapiro (eds.), *Revising Charles Brockden Brown: Culture, Politics, and Sexuality in the Early Republic* (Knoxville: University of Tennessee Press): 7-40.
Wieland, Christoph Martin
1753   'Die Prüfung Abrahams', in *C.M. Wielands Poetische Werke, Dritter Band* (ed. J.G. Gruber; Leipzig: C.J. Göschen, 1818) (translated as *The Trial of Abraham*, 1778).

READING PRAGMATICALLY:
INTERPRETING THE BINDING OF ISAAC

Edward L. Greenstein

> In truth, there is but one state of mind from which you can 'set out', namely,
> the very state of mind in which you actually find yourself at the time you do
> 'set out'—a state in which you are laden with an immense mass of cognition
> already formed, of which you cannot divest yourself if you would... (C.S.
> Peirce 1966a: 188).[1]

> It is the very nature of an hypothesis, when once a man has conceived it, that it
> assimilates every thing to itself as proper nourishment; and, from the first
> moment of your begetting it, it generally grows the stronger by every thing
> you see, hear, read, or understand. This is its great use (Laurence Sterne,
> *Tristram Shandy*, II, ch. 19).

No narrative in the Hebrew Bible has evoked so many readings, and so many
passionate ones, as the 'masterpiece' (Gottwald 1959: 253) known to Christians as the Sacrifice of Isaac and to Jews as the Binding of Isaac or *Akedah*
(Genesis 22). Readings have ranged widely, from the religious existentialism
of Kierkegaard (1954: 21-132), who found in Abraham's trial an internal
conflict between a father's ethical love for his son and an amoral impulse to
fulfill the divine mandate; to the Freudian inclination to find a murderous
desire in Abraham (cf. Wellisch 1954);[2] to the feminism of Phyllis Trible
(1991), who, using a logic drawn from reading the story in context, argues
that the test between love of child and devotion to deity would have been
better applied to Sarah, who had previously displayed her dedication to Isaac,
than to Abraham, who had not (see Genesis 21; cf. Trible 1991). The story
has been taken by some to be tragedy (e.g. Kierkegaard 1954: 124-29; Wiesel
1976: 69-97; Mleynek 1994)[3] and by others—impressed by a certain ironic

---

1. A briefer version of this essay was presented as a lecture at the World Congress of
Jewish Studies in Jerusalem, summer 2001. The bibliography has been only a little
updated.
2. For a critique, see, e.g., Kaplan 1990.
3. Humphreys 1985: 81-83 argues that, although 'the situation...contains the elements
of tragedy,...the action of the hero denies them realization'.

humor and the happy ending—to be a comedy (e.g. Exum and Whedbee 1990; Kaminsky 2000).

Among the plethora of interpretations there is, however, a high degree of consensus. Exegetes may disagree about whether the narrative polemicizes against child sacrifice (e.g. Coats 1973; Amit 2000: 60-70),[4] or about whether the test is one of obedience (e.g. Coats 1973; Levenson 1993: 13 and passim; Wenham 1995: 102) or faith (e.g. Kierkegaard 1954; Moster 1988–1989). But what almost everyone agrees on is that, on the one hand, very little pathos is expressed, and, on the other, the story is suffused with feeling— 'fraught with background', in Erich Auerbach's (1953: 12) famous phrase.[5] The great Bible scholar Hermann Gunkel (1964: 11) wrote:

> Whoever possesses heart and feeling must perceive…in the case of the sacrifice of Isaac, that the important matter [of the story] is…to impart to the hearer the heartrending grief of the father, who is commanded to sacrifice his child with his own hand, and then his boundless gratitude and joy when God's mercy releases him from this grievous trial.

Readers tend to find the alternative—that Abraham acted with cold deliberation or with blind, unthinking obedience—intolerable. Abraham, it is felt, must have been feeling, must have been thinking, and there is no reader I know who has not read something into the character Abraham's heart and mind; indeed, most claim to know something of God's and Isaac's inner life as well.

Poets, like Amir Gilboa (1953), have given voice to the characters' emotions—Isaac's fear, Abraham's dissolution.[6] The composer Igor Stravinsky,

4. Pedersen (1940: 321) proposes a middle-of-the-road interpretation: God only demands a child sacrifice until it becomes clear that the worshiper possesses a 'disposition' to make such an offering; after that, 'God merely demands an animal sacrifice instead'. For a critique of the view that the narrative polemicizes against child sacrifice, see, e.g., Sarna 1989: 393-94; Levenson 1993: 111-24; Davis 1994: 31-32. For a comparative study of the *Akedah* in relation to other ancient stories of child sacrifice, arriving at an indecisive conclusion, see Prentiss 1990. My own understanding, from a historical perspective, is that the *Akedah* contains no signs of an etiology condemning child sacrifice in general; but that it does exhibit signs of an etiology establishing the site of the Akedah, Mt Moriah, as a cult site. Note that the patriarch Abraham himself constructs the altar that he uses (v. 9); cf. Abraham's construction of the altar near Shechem (Gen. 12.7) and that the name Abraham gives the site (22.14) is explained by the narrator to mean that Yhwh is worshipped ('is seen') there.

5. On Kierkegaard's gap-filling in reading the *Akedah*, see Robbins 1991: 74-76, 90-91.

6. For a convenient presentation with English translation, see Carmi 1981: 560; Burnshaw, Carmi and Spicehandler 1989: 136-37. For discussions of the poem, see, e.g., Aryeh Sachs in Burnshaw, Carmi and Spicehandler 1989: 136-38; Jacobson, 1987: 137-39; and Coffin 1987: 299-301. The *Akedah* theme of a parent sacrificing a child has been well

in his cantata *Abraham and Isaac* (1963), interrupts the narration and dialogue with musical interludes precisely where one would expect the audience to imagine the characters' responses. Ancient midrash, too, externalizes the characters' inner life through dialogue.[7] The Palestinian *Targum Neofiti*, for example, embellishes the drama of Isaac bound on the altar, as he tries to make it easier for Abraham. In the targumic reading, Isaac asks his father to tie him up tight, to prevent him from resisting the knife. 'The eyes of Abraham were (fixed) on the eyes of Isaac, and the eyes of Isaac were gazing on the angels on high' (Diez Macho 1968: 127 at v. 10; trans. McNamara 1992: 118).[8]

How does a reader know what a character is thinking, when the (implied) narrator appears reticent? One might suggest that readers simply read in what they will, when they want to, and leave it at that. Texts have meaning so far as we know, after all, only when they are read, and they will mean what readers take them to mean. That, however, is not how the making of meaning has been understood in literary theory by most critics and for most of the twentieth century; and that is not the theoretical understanding that is implied or made explicit in most literary interpretations of the *Akedah*.

A Critique of Text-Oriented Theory

Literary reading of biblical narrative is most often informed by the so-called 'close reading' practices of the New Criticism, an approach that locates meaning in neither the inaccessible process of composition (Wimsatt and Beardsley 1954a; cf., e.g., Frye 1963: 59) nor in the utterly subjective processes of reading (Wimsatt and Beardsley 1954b) but rather in the textual object (whatever that might be). Using Cleanth Brooks's (1947) analogy of a poem to a Grecian urn, the beauty of the urn/poem is not in the crafting of the artisan, nor in the aesthetic response of the observer, but in the thing itself.[9]

The New Criticism is not, as it is sometimes romantically idealized, simply a method of reading a text for its own sake and in its own right—a neutral, sensitive, meticulous analysis of textual phenomena with the goal of getting

worn in modern Hebrew literature; see, e.g., Brown 1982; Coffin 1987; Feldman 1998, with extensive bibliography; and esp. Feldman 2010.

7.   Cf., e.g., the dialogue made famous through Rashi's commentary in elaborating Gen. 22.2: *Gen. R.* 55.2, ed. Theodor-Albeck, p. 590. For a text-by-text survey of classical rabbinic treatment of the *Akedah*, see Saldarini 1982; for a thematic and exegetical analysis of ancient and early medieval Jewish interpretation of the *Akedah*, see Levenson 1993: 173-99 and further Agus 1988; Kalimi 2010 and the references there.

8.   For other ancient sources that develop a similar interpretation to that of Targum Neofiti here, see Kugel 1997: 174-75.

9.   See the discussion in Greenstein 1999: 212-13.

whatever meaning or meanings are embodied in the literary work. The New Criticism is a theory, or perhaps more accurately an ideology, laden with presuppositions (e.g. Leitch 1988: 24-59; Poirier 1992: 169-93; cf. Hartman 1980: 298).[10] It objectifies the text and transforms the experience of reading as a temporal process into the visualization of a static map of spatial relations—from a symphony into a diagram, so to speak (e.g. Eagleton 1983: 48; Leitch 1988: 29). Assuming ultimate coherence, it seeks to resolve all tensions and ambivalences by drawing a congeries of rhetorical features and semantic nuances into an integrated web of structures (e.g. Brooks 1992). Analysis of the structures and their patterning is meant to decode the meaning(s) of the work. Form is the key that unlocks the doors of understanding (e.g. Moulton 1915: 64-74). Brooks (1992: 964b), one of the leading exponents of the New Criticism, asserts that the literary work is an 'experience' in time, like watching a ballet or listening to a piece of music. But his rhetoric bespeaks a different understanding, as he refers to the 'pattern' and 'scheme' of the temporal experience and, in the same breath, compares 'the essential structure of a poem...[to] that of architecture or painting'.

The reader is understood not to be attributing meaning to the work but to be interpreting it in accordance with its forms. In one particularly telling image, the reader is said to interpret a text the way a builder follows a blueprint (Leibowitz 1990: 35, citing the poet and critic A.L. Strauss). The authority of the author as the arbiter of textual meaning, which the New Criticism arose to oppose, was replaced by the authority of the text, which controls or directs the interpreter.[11] The blatant personification of the text that is involved in saying that the text 'says', 'conveys', 'directs', 'compels', etc. (see, e.g., Frye 1963: 59), is rarely, if ever, acknowledged.

Of course, not everything is expressed in a text with the same degree of immediacy. Monroe C. Beardsley, a leading theoretician of the New Criticism, put it this way (1970: 36):

> Some things are definitely said in the poem and cannot be overlooked; others are suggested, as we find on careful reading; others are gently hinted, and whatever methods of literary interpretation we use, we can never establish them decisively as 'in' or 'out'.

Some meanings are here alleged to be indisputable, independent of readerly interpretation. Other meanings are admitted to be produced only by means of interpretation.

---

10. For a fine discussion of the New Criticism in relation to biblical studies, see Barton 1984: 140-57.

11. Cf., e.g., Booth 1961: 'Preface', where one finds the 'rhetoric of fiction' characterized as 'the author's means of controlling his reader'.

What this boils down to, however, is not an argument against the role of the reader in producing meaning, but rather an argument for it. For once one acknowledges the interpretative function of the reader, one becomes hard-pressed to discern when one is reading with interpretation and when one is reading without it. One can hardly read meaningfully with an empty head here and with a full apparatus there. It becomes clear that when Beardsley speaks of readers understanding what is 'definitely said', he is only intelligible if he means that the meaning is understood by any and all readers. But how can any one reader know, especially in the course of reading, what that meaning is (cf. Margolis 1986: 25-26)? (The notion that different close readers understand a text differently, suggesting the relativism of reading, 'haunted New Criticism' [Lentricchia 1980: 34].) Other meanings, says Beardsley, are found only by 'careful reading', while still other meanings are the product of somewhat freer interpretation. Read the whole excerpt, and one sees that the true locus of meaning, even for Beardsley, is the reader. The rhetoric that attributes meaning to the text (things are 'said' in it, things are 'hinted' by it) is designed to camouflage the role of the reader. Practitioners of the New Criticism and its allied approaches must, therefore, read 'as if' what they experience is a direct product of the inanimate text (Krieger 1976: 14-17; Leitch 1988: 48-52). They 'listen' to what the text has to 'say'. For example, Jan Fokkelman, a leading practitioner of 'close reading' in Hebrew Bible, asserts that the text 'really can speak', can really be 'heard', through the reading act (1989: 41). Fokkelman and all others who make similar claims repress all the while that they are the ventriloquists giving voice to the text (Greenstein 1989: x-xi).

Not only New Critics but some leading reader-oriented theorists have also endeavored to convince us that meaning is somehow inherent in the literary work. Consider the following excerpt from a landmark essay by Wolfgang Iser (1980: 50; for convenience I have numbered the sentences):

> [1] The phenomenological theory of art lays full stress on the idea that in considering a literary work, one must take into account not only the actual text but also, in equal measure, the actions involved in responding to that text…
> [2] The literary work has two poles, which we might call the artistic and the esthetic: the artistic refers to the text created by the author, and the esthetic to the realization accomplished by the reader. [3] From this polarity it follows that the literary work cannot be completely identical with the text, or with the realization of the text, but in fact must lie halfway between the two. [4] The work is more than the text, for the text only takes on life when it is realized, and furthermore the realization is by no means independent of the individual disposition of the reader—though this in turn is acted upon by the different patterns of the text. [5] The convergence of text and reader brings the literary work into existence…

Let us analyze the logic of, or deconstruct, Iser's argument (cf. Fish 1989). In sentence [1] Iser distinguishes between 'the actual text' and the responses of a reader to 'that text'. In sentence [2] 'the text' is a composition by an author. In sentences [2] and [3] the 'literary work' is distinguished from 'the text': the latter is the authorial contribution to the former; the full 'literary work' is composed of both the 'text' and the reader's 'realization of the text'. In sentence [4] it is maintained that 'the text' does not come into actual existence (see sentence [1]) until 'it is realized' by the reader who is affected 'by the different patterns of the text'. In sentence [5] it is summarized, that 'the literary work' is brought 'into existence' by the encounter of the reader with the 'text'.

The argument rests on a barely suppressed contradiction. The 'text' as well as the 'literary work' depend on the reader's reading of them in order to 'realize' or actualize them (note the term 'actual text' in sentences [1] and [4]). The reader, then, can hardly encounter a text, much less respond to one, that the reader has not yet brought to 'life' (sentence [4]). It is like the rhetorical quip of a speaker who insists on saying a few words before beginning to speak. It is a quip, and may evoke polite laughter, precisely because it is a bald self-contradiction. Iser's contradiction presupposes the point he is trying to make: the autonomous existence of the text. The fact that Iser can make his argument only by begging the question demonstrates the contrary point, which he also makes: the text is produced not before but in the act of reading. It follows that the meaning of a work is known to a reader only through an act of reading, by an act of interpretation (e.g. Barthes 1979).

The New Critics ascribe meaning to a text in the way that others ascribe textual meaning to the (absent) author. The devices of the text, which the critic claims to decipher, 'are', as Foucault (1979: 150) has said in regard to the author, 'only a projection, in more or less psychologizing terms, of the operations that we force texts to undergo, the connections that we make, the traits that we establish as pertinent, the continuities that we recognize, or the exclusions that we practice'.

The reasons that the New Critics, and most other critics, locate meaning in the inanimate textual object rather than in the human act of reading are evident. On the one hand, they want to establish, as was said above, an objective source of authority to which one can appeal in the event of disagreement, and, on the other, they want to turn the act of (proper) reading into a scientific procedure. Disparaging the role of the subjective reader, they invest their interpretations with validity or truth by ascribing them not to themselves but to some impersonal authority, albeit a personified text.[12]

---

12. Hirsch (1967: esp. 180-98), in a well-known attempt to make textual interpretation a quasi-scientific 'discipline', invokes the need to apply 'objective' criteria toward the evaluation of 'all relevant evidence', internal and external, for the explication of a text.

A Pragmatic Approach

The attribution to a text of some core meaning, some true interpretation, reflects a philosophical belief in the objectivity of truth. This is hardly the place to discuss and decide once and for all whether and in what way any assertion can be true. Modern philosophers have debated, and continue to debate, the merits and the difficulties of such views as: 'X is true because it corresponds to some otherwise known reality', or 'X is true because it conforms to the rules of a particular system'.[13]

For someone like me, who has been convinced that textual meaning is what a reader takes, or makes, it to mean, it makes no sense to attribute some core, true, meaning to a text. Texts, like the language of which they are made, mean what they mean only within a particular, and constantly shifting, set of contingencies (cf. Lecercle 1999). Each text, like every act of communication, has an occasion in which it is understood (see, e.g., Greenstein 1987). An entire area of linguistics and literary criticism, each called 'pragmatics', has been developed in order to study the pertinent aspects of the communicative situation (e.g. Green 1989; Mey 1993; cf. Sell 1991). Recalling Borges' use of Heraclitus' image of the ever-changing river—the reader, like the water flowing by in the river, does not remain in the same place—textual meaning is always and forever in flux (cf. Greenstein 1999: 211; Krieger 1976: 38). The conditions of making meaning are never the same.

In addition, meaning is, as is often noted, never an innocent activity, but always a (no less than partial) product of a reader. Wittgenstein asks us to 'imagine that human beings or animals were used as reading machines; assume that in order to become reading machines they need a particular training' (*The Brown Book*, p. 120; quoted in Monk 1991: 344). Wittgenstein is, of course, teasing us, inviting us to think about what it would mean for anyone to read.[14] Could an unprogrammed machine read? Could an animal that is not biologically equipped to perform the complex of processes used in reading, read? Could a human being uneducated to read, read? Can a reader

---

Hirsch does not come to grips with the role of the critic in construing the evidence itself and determining its relevance, both of which processes are preliminary to arriving at an understanding of a work.

13.   These are, of course, the views held earlier and later by Ludwig Wittgenstein in the *Tractatus Logico-Philosophicus* (1921) and *Philosophical Investigations* (1953), respectively; for a concise summary of leading theories of 'truth', see, e.g., Lowe 1995. The problem of defining 'truth' is very helpfully clarified in Putnam 1994. For a relatively recent effort to develop a not wholly relativistic yet pluralistic theory of truth, see Lynch 1998.

14.   Wittgenstein may well be referring only to the most mechanical form of reading by the rules; cf. Kripke 1982: 45-46.

without the benefit of certain experiences, unacquainted with certain subjects, etc. etc., read with any understanding?

Indeed, we read the way we do as a result of what we have been taught, what we have learned, and, not insignificantly, who we are. Our inclinations help determine *how* we read no less than they determine *what* we read. See the epigraph at the head of this essay from the writings of Charles Sanders Peirce, the late nineteenth-century founder of philosophical pragmatism (which he often preferred calling 'pragmaticism'), a line of thinking that appeals to people like me who would have us abandon the idea of an objective truth but would understand the notions of truth and knowledge in different ways. Our choices in reading as we do are also contingent upon our needs, desires, and interests at the time of reading (e.g. Margolis 1986: 44). The conditioning of behavior on a person's assessment of what is in one's best interests, along with the abandonment of a belief in any true essences, is a key element of pragmatic thought.

The focus of pragmatism in its somewhat diverse forms—in the work of such thinkers as Peirce, William James, John Dewey, and their more recent (and generally more technical) counterparts such as Donald Davidson, William V.O. Quine, Hilary Putnam, and Richard Rorty—is not, as it was for most philosophers, on the nature of the object but rather on the effect of the object on the subject (for surveys of pragmatism see Murphy 1990; Malachowski 2010).[15] The pragmatist claims to be unable to gain direct and true knowledge of the 'real', because all inquiry, like all observation, is contingent. Moreover, inquiry stems from a problem or irritant that we experience in one form or another (including cognition)—a shaking up of some belief we have held—and the result of inquiry is not objective knowledge but the resolution of the problem at hand by settling for this or another belief (see esp. Peirce 1966b; Dewey 1938: 7-9 and *passim*; cf. Putnam 1994b).[16] Seeking knowledge is a practical endeavor, using experimentation to test whether something does or does not work. What is true about something is tested not in the abstract, of which we have no experience, but in the differences in our behavior, of which we do have some awareness. For Peirce (1966b: 100 with n. 3), something is true for us if we actually act on it with circumspection and reflection.

---

15. For some clarifications of the history of pragmatism, such as the place of Kant and Wittgenstein in it, see Putnam 1995. On the problem of pragmatism's place in contemporary philosophy, see, e.g., Okrent 1989.

16. Rorty makes the important point that 'Dewey's description of moral and scientific progress is much more like somebody's description of how he or she managed to get from the age of twelve to the age of thirty…than like a series of choices between alternative theories on the basis of observational results' (1991: 69).

Meaning is found not in an idea but in a practical application (Peirce 1966c: 332). 'What a thing means', writes Peirce (1966d: 123), 'is simply what habits it involves'—what it does to you or what finds expression in what you do. For James (1955: 49), what is true is what works: 'truth in our ideas means their power to work' (cf. Rorty 1982: xxix). And we act on those beliefs we hold to be true because such action yields the results we desire (James 1955: 150). Knowledge, for Dewey (1938: 8), is not an integrated abstraction but the cumulative sum of practical results, the results that are variously reached in all inquiries. We choose the means of inquiry that, we think, will get us the consequences we would like (Dewey 1955: 10; Rorty 1982: xlii-iii), and we will prefer, in any endeavor, that plan of action that produces the more useful or more desirable result. That, for Dewey, is the truer path to take (Hook 1939: 75).

As Dewey explains, the pragmatist views the work of the scientist as of a kind with the life of the ordinary person. We all need 'constantly to inquire what it is better to do next'. We 'fram[e] and test [...] plans of action in their capacity as hypotheses: that is, as ideas' (Dewey 1955: 161).[17] We, like the scientist, decide what to do and 'what means to employ in doing it' (Dewey 1938: 161). Principles inform our practices, but our principles grow out of and are adjusted in consequence of our practices (Dewey 1938: 159-80).[18]

The implications for reading and interpretation are not difficult to extrapolate, and they have, in fact, been presented—though without explicit reference to pragmatism—by Ronald Crane in his prescient mid-twentieth-century lecture, 'The Multiplicity of Critical Languages' (1953: 3-38).[19] Like Dewey's scientist, the literary critic, Crane, adopts certain principles which are not understood to be descriptions of phenomena as they really are, but rather 'tools of inquiry and interpretation' (31) that are 'fitted to solve' particular problems (28) or are believed, on the basis of experience, to help the critic obtain 'the kind of knowledge' one would like to know (31). The application of the 'principles and methods' that the critic selects will produce results, the value of which can be assessed and verified (28). The critic will have a sense of having gotten the requisite results because the questions one

---

17.   Dewey early on underscores the importance of putting any 'truth' to repeated scrutiny; see Dewey 1977: 1-14, 31-49, 50-75, 78-90.

18.   Dewey (1925: 154) explains the relations of methods to consequences succinctly as follows: 'When things are defined as instruments, their value and validity reside in what proceeds from them; consequences not antecedents supply meaning and verity. Truths already possessed may have practical or moral certainty, but logically they never lose a hypothetical quality'; cf. Dewey 1977: 98-115; Rorty 1982: 160-75. For critical perspectives on Rorty, see Malachowski 1990; 2010: 33-59; Habermas 1999: 343-82.

19.   For an exemplary analysis of Crane's critical views, see Booth 1979: 37-97. Booth understands Crane to be somewhat more conventional than I do.

is seeking to answer or the problems one is seeking to solve are not superimposed from somewhere above but stem from one's own interests.

Each critical method works differently, not because it seeks to give a different answer to a common question, but rather because it seeks to answer a different question (16). Each approach is a different 'framework' or 'language' that is intended to deal with another question relating to a text (13).[20] Each language comprises its own discourse, which not only proves to be an instrument for analyzing and interpreting the textual data, but the discourse functions as 'an instrument of discovery and understanding' in the first place, helping to create the literary facts themselves (10-11). Different critical approaches will reflect not only the diversity of texts but, no less, the diversity of individuals who read them. For each critical stance is contingent upon the unique characteristics of the individual: 'We must all remain prejudiced by temperament or training with respect to what we want to do in criticism and, therefore, also, with respect to the kind of critical theory and method we prefer to use...' (xiii).

Crane (xv) shares with a growing number of recent critics the anti-foundationalist principle, that there is no way to ground any particular understanding and any particular way of getting an understanding in some principle that is objective and authoritative (for everyone). This does not mean, however, that there is no basis for making choices in what one seeks to do and in how one goes about doing it. While these choices rest, ultimately, on shifting and alterable grounds, we are all in the same boat—we must all make a case for our readings without recourse to a neutral arbiter. As Stanley Fish (1980a) has maintained, we all operate within finite communities of interpreters who play the 'game' of interpretation according to a shared set of rules.[21] And within the game, we use an arsenal of rhetorical means to argue for our own readings and to argue against others. 'We can [still]...argue that one interpretation is better than another, cite evidence in support of the interpretations we prefer; it is just that we do all those things within a set of institutional assumptions that [are not absolute and unchanging but] can themselves become the objects of dispute' (Fish 1980b: 367).

Such a critical view leads naturally, as in the case of Crane, to a rejection of totalizing explanations, on the one hand, and to an embrace of pluralism,

---

20. In relatively recent theory, 'frame' has been used to refer to the array of knowledge, experience, and social location that a subject brings to an act of understanding; cf., e.g., Lakoff 2000: 47-48. For a similar notion of shifting 'schemata' in a subject's understanding, see, e.g., Spiro 1980. For the use of 'context' in a similar fashion, see, e.g., Dascal 1989. See in general Gadamer 1982, esp. parts II and III.

21. Fish's ideas evolve from Wittgenstein's notions of the 'language-game', in which the meaning of language is the uses one makes of it; cf., e.g., Wittgenstein, *Philosophical Investigations*, excerpted in Brand 1979: 123-24.

on the other. Different methods ask different questions, explore different aspects, give different glimpses, produce different analyses, generate different understandings. One adopts a different approach for precisely these reasons. I know of no better illustration than the one adduced by Daniel Patte (1990: 7; cf. Greenstein 2009). If we want to get a view of what's beneath the skin—as well as other types of surfaces—we can use an X-ray, and see the skeleton, or ultra-sound, and see the organs. Both techniques provide a full view, but each view is of one type only. Textual meaning, too, can be construed in this way, or in that way; but there is no way to get more than one angle of vision by means of a single type of analysis. We will read one way to do one thing with a text, and another way to do something else.

Readings of the Akedah *Read Pragmatically*

In order to give weight and clarity to the theoretical notions I have expressed, let us consider the readings of primarily two interpreters of the *Akedah*, two interpreters who apparently share many of the same critical assumptions and who employ many of the same reading strategies. Their readings come out quite differently, however, because, as it quickly becomes clear, their theological agendas differ and their ultimate objectives are different. In the course of our review, we will compare several other readings as well. We will see that while the New Criticism and its allied approaches seek to assign specific meanings to particular features, the claims of this or that interpreter or narratologist are no more than assertions, to which exceptions can readily be invoked and to which exception can readily be made. Interpreters take this to mean this, and that to mean that, not on account of any characteristic that is inherent and evident to all, but because by interpreting this to mean this, interpreters get the meaning they want; and by interpreting that to mean that, other interpreters (or the same readers on other occasions) get the meaning they want. What, in the end, will lead us, as readers of the readings, to prefer one to another, may turn out to be not the way a reading was performed but rather the assumptions that this reading presupposes and the resultant interpretation that it ultimately proposes.

At the outset, I underscored the tendency of most interpreters to imagine the inner life of the leading characters, especially Abraham and Isaac. One exegete who has seemingly taken a different tack is Terence Fretheim, who makes protest against the literary tendency to 'overdramatiz[e] the story and [to] read [...] too much between the lines' (1994: 494). On principle, he objects to the exegetical externalization of Isaac's inner life, contending that 'Isaac's emotions are often overplayed' (1994: 496). Meir Sternberg, in his monumental *Poetics of Biblical Narrative*, agrees that fleshing out the inner life of a character 'enriches the drama', but he is not opposed to it; he only regards it as a 'secondary' activity (1985: 192). In the end it will come down to a reader's choice and interest.[22] Does the character interest you enough to imagine a full-bodied character, or would you rather leave the characters aside and move along in the action? While it would seem that on this principle Fretheim stands off against the majority of interpreters, in practice he reads no less than most others into the heads of the protagonists. It is just that for him the protagonists display a devout attitude more than they express various emotions.

The other interpreter on whom we will focus is Francis Landy, for whom the feelings of father and son, and especially the father, are the crux of the narrative (1990). While Landy spells out many of the reading strategies he will use (albeit in the form of textual devices), his reading as a whole is strikingly parallel to that of Fretheim. For what they share—in addition to similar methods of reading on a small scale, up close—is a penchant toward the symbolic and the allegorical, although they develop their allegorical readings in virtually opposite directions.[23]

Fretheim projects the allegorical meaning of the narrative outward, toward the situation of the historical Judean community that first knew the narrative in its canonical form, during or after the Babylonian exile in the sixth century BCE, and then further, typologically, toward the paradigm of the divine father sacrificing the divine son in the Christian scriptures (1994: 494, 498-501).[24] For Fretheim, both Abraham and Isaac in the biblical story symbolize the people Israel for the exilic community. Abraham represents the people with respect to the ordeal it has had to go through: 'God has put Israel to a test in which many children died, has called forth its continuing faith, has delivered it through the fires of judgment and renewed the promises' (Fretheim 1994: 494). Isaac symbolizes Israel in its roles as victim and survivor: 'As Isaac was saved from death, so was Israel delivered from the brink of annihilation' (499). The Christological interpretation of what Christians call the Sacrifice of Isaac, for Fretheim, 'constitutes an appropriate extension of the text' (499)— God as the father sacrifices Jesus as the son. Retrospectively, this reading also justifies God's demand of Abraham, since 'God does not expect of Abraham something God would be unwilling to do' (501). (The difficult fact that Isaac, unlike Jesus, was not sacrificed, is not addressed by Fretheim.)[25]

22. For a superb and richly worked out 'fleshing out' of character in biblical narrative, see Bach 1997: 1-33 and *passim*.

23. For a valuable discussion of the allegorical reading of biblical narrative, see Rosenberg 1986: 1-46. For an example of quasi-allegorical reading, see Greenstein 1981.

24. For a summary and discussion of the Christological interpretation, see, e.g., Levenson 1993: 200-219.

25. The sacrifice of Isaac was consummated, according to medieval Jewish exegesis, as Jews under mortal attack identified with their martyred ancestor; see Spiegel 1964; cf. also Agus 1988.

Fretheim's overall interpretation informs his hermeneutical moves and readings all along the way. Israel's faith is being tested in exile, in Fretheim's allegory, and so faith is the issue of the *Akedah*. In spite of his rhetorical objections to readerly 'dramatization' of the narrative, Fretheim claims to know what God intends, what Abraham believes, and what Isaac feels. While Fretheim, like most other critics, grounds his readings in various textual phenomena, these phenomena can be, and often are, taken to mean something else. Fretheim proceeds confidently, however, because somehow (typologically) he knows what the text is all about: the narrative, he asserts, was 'designed to demonstrate Abraham's trusting obedience' to God (496). (Design, one need hardly be reminded, is what the beholder abstracts or deduces from one's observations, as interpreted on the basis of experience, education, personal disposition and perceptual acuity, expectation, etc.).

Landy, by contrast, lays stress on the reader's role in filling out the motives and feelings of the characters. He removes a degree of responsibility from the reader, however, by defining the reader's moves as responses—and sometimes involuntary responses—to the text. The text, read 'closely', 'evoke[s] our imaginative sympathy' (1990: 10), operates by means of rhetorical devices that a reader like me would regard as reading strategies (Greenstein 1999), and may even compel a reader to (re)act in a certain way. Landy's own allegorical reading results, he maintains, from 'the narrative forc[ing] us to consider [Abraham's journey to a geographically unidentifiable place, Moriah] on a symbolic plane... Abraham's three-day journey is...to a part of himself that he most fears and is a symbol of that encounter' (Landy 1990: 29). Landy's allegorical interpretation will, therefore, delve into the inner life of Abraham, as well as the other characters, and will appeal to all manner of textual features to ground his thesis in his own announced 'close' reading.

In order to make the point felt that textual phenomena, even when they are similarly construed, do not simply convey meaning but may be interpreted altogether differently, we shall examine a number of moments in and features of the *Akedah* and consider the diverse meanings they have been taken to have, especially, but not exclusively, by Fretheim and Landy.

Gen. 22.1a: After these things, it happened that...

The opening of the *Akedah* is taken by many readers to place the present narrative in the context of the preceding ones. In view of the strong resemblance between the language and syntax of Gen. 22.2 and 12.1, where Abraham is commanded by God to leave his homeland and travel to Canaan, the *Akedah* is seen, as it was in classical rabbinic midrash, as the culmination of Abraham's education as a man in covenant with God (e.g. *Gen. R.* 55.2 [ed. Theodor-Albeck, p. 590]; see further Spiegel 1964; Kugel 1997: 165-68). Fretheim seizes upon this widely remarked parallel, which he defines as 'an overarching structure' that frames the Abraham stories: 'The former [Gen. 12] cuts Abraham off from his past; the latter threatens to cut him off from his future' (1994: 495; cf. von Rad 1961: 234). And what is the content of this framework? In a word, faith. Abraham from the start exhibits faith in God.

This means, of course, that for Fretheim, Abraham hardly matures as a character. Whereas Levenson (1993: 84-92) and certain other critics (e.g. Coats 1973: 396, 400; Gros Louis 1982a, 1982b; Gunn and Fewell 1993: 90-100; Miles 1995: 47-66) point to the doubts Abraham has displayed—his abandonment of Canaan almost immediately, as soon as food is scarce (Gen. 12.10-20), his adoption of his *major domo* as his heir (Gen. 15.1-6)—and delineate the stages in his evolution of trust, Fretheim finds Abraham to be Kierkegaard's 'knight of faith' from the get go. The two *lek-lekā*'s (Gen. 12.1; 22.2; the only two instances of precisely this phrase in the Bible; e.g., Sarna 1989: 150; Humphreys 2001: 139) are for Fretheim not the starting point and the end point but rather the 'framing' points of this story of faith.

For Landy the relation of the charge to Abraham in the *Akedah* and the experience of Abraham in Genesis 12 hinges, as we might expect, on the element of voice: Abraham 'only exists in the narrative as he responds to that voice'. Of course, the divine voice in the *Akedah* is for Landy an inner voice of Abraham, but it 'is experienced externally, as the voice of God', a voice familiar to him since he first experienced a calling (1990: 2).

The other narratives whose relation to the *Akedah* is frequently invoked are the stories of Hagar and Ishmael, in Genesis 16 and 21 (e.g. White 1979). While the latter has been found to have many linguistic and motivic features shared with the *Akedah* (e.g. Simon 1973: 164-65; Steinmetz 1991: 83; Levenson 1993: 104-105, 109; Deurloo 1994: 107-109; Wenham 1995: 99-100),[26] there is also a broader structural parallel. In each of the three stories— the flight of Hagar (Genesis 16), the banishment of Ishmael (Genesis 21), and the Binding of Isaac (Genesis 22)—a 'parent [is] driven into the wilderness with child', as Rosenberg puts it (1986: 74; cf. 1993: 32). For Fretheim (495), who focuses on Abraham's acts of faith, the Hagar stories are of little relevance; he finds the comparison of the banishment of Ishmael and the sacrifice of Isaac 'poignant'—but he does not develop the point. For Landy, whose interest lies in Abraham's inner journey throughout the *Akedah*, an intertextual reading would be a distraction, raising other kinds of issues, both theological and moral.

Returning to the phrase 'After these things, it happened...', we should note that while many commentators suggest that the phrase sends the reader back to a preceding narrative, for virtually no commentator does the phrase

26. Leiter (1979: 176) contrasts the 'trial by water' of Genesis 21 with the 'trial by fire' of Genesis 22.

send the reader back to what is arguably the most appropriate place, to the immediately preceding narrative—the treaty between Abraham and Abimelech the Philistine (Gen. 21.22-34).[27] Against the background of that episode, in which Abraham swears never to break faith with Abimelech's progeny (vv. 22-24), God's readiness to break faith with Abraham and Abraham's apparent readiness to sacrifice his son, may strike one as even more disturbing. Of course, the introductory phrase does not really send any reader anywhere. The reader will appeal to the phrase, or ignore it; the reader will look back at this episode or that. It is the reader who chooses what move to make and who judges whether that move was good or not on the basis of how satisfied one is with the results one has got.

22.1b: והאלהים נסה את אברהם
        when God tested Abraham…

Fretheim would not likely adopt the interpretation that I have raised as a result of setting the *Akedah* off against the show of trust between Abraham and Abimelech. In that interpretation one questions the fidelity of God to the promise of Isaac to Abraham and the devotion of Abraham to his son. In Fretheim's reading, Abraham's trust of God is assumed to be fully established at the beginning of the story. If so, then what is the point of the test?

Traditional commentators, like Abravanel, cannot believe that God would need to find out what Abraham would do—God, who knows everything, would know. Abravanel (1964: 267) goes so far as to remove the test from the narrative altogether by means of alternative philology. According to him, the verb *nissā* in this instance means not 'to test' or 'to try' but rather 'to set up as a *nēs*'—an 'exemplum' for everyone to see.[28] The *Akedah* is not for the benefit of God but for the benefit of Abraham and the audience.

Fretheim has no need of such an interpretation because he has no problem with the concept of God as a learner who needs to know how deep Abraham's trust is (497). This is not very different from Kierkegaard's claim, that Abraham must prove his faith to God. Landy, too, finds that in the course of the narrative, 'God acquires knowledge', as we read in v. 12: 'Now I know that you are God-fearing'. God learns, in Landy's reading, that Abraham possesses boundless obedience (1990: 4). Both Fretheim and Landy assume that the test was not to see how far Abraham would go—meaning he would actually sacrifice his son—but rather to see if Abraham would go to the limit on account of his faith or obedience.

27. Abravanel (1964: 267) relates 'After these things…' to this episode, but only along with others, as the last of a chain of episodes by which Abraham develops a covenantal relation with God.

28. Cf., e.g., Wenham 1995: 102: '[Abraham's] wholehearted devotion to God expressed through obedience and sacrifice is a model for every Israelite'; Coats, too, regards the story as 'an edifying example of obedience' (1983: 162).

They, like most commentators, assume that the test was not for real, that it was never meant to be completed (e.g. Landy 1985: 138; von Rad 1961: 234; Coats 1973: 393; Mazor 1986: 82; Sarna 1989: 151; Adar 1990: 83). Fretheim, who is critical of those who read into the mind of the characters, claims to know God's mind: 'God intends not to kill Isaac but to test Abraham's faithfulness' (497). Most readers take for granted that, because the test is ended by the angel calling out to Abraham from the sky (v. 11), the 'test' was not to see if Abraham would fulfill the command all the way. Such an interpretation is characterized by the critic Mieke Bal (1987: 108) as the 'retrospective fallacy'—the notion that a reader is justified in clarifying all earlier ambiguities on the basis of later developments. From a readerly perspective, reading in retrospect removes doubt and suspicion and, were it universally applied, would destroy any suspense, would ruin any story, by giving away the ending at the beginning.

Revealing to the reader that God is 'only' testing Abraham is most commonly understood to be a narrational strategy of relaxing the reader who is about to be confronted by a horrifying command (e.g. Coats 1973: 392; Licht 1973: 21 n. 23; Sternberg 1985: 268; Coffin 1987: 294; Adar 1990: 83). Some interpreters read the phrase differently; they take the command to sacrifice for real (e.g. White 1979: 13; Levenson 1993: 126; Amit 2000: 67-68; Humphreys 2001: 138; cf. Rouiller 1978: 15-16). 'The reader', argues White (1979: 13),

> has no reason to think that because this is a test, God does not intend for Abraham to actually go through with it to the bitter end. In fact, obeying the voice of God and keeping the law can also be referred to as a 'test' (Exod. 15.25), in which case literal fulfillment is clearly expected. The category of the 'test' serves not to lessen the suspense for the reader, but to provide an explanation for the command of God without which it would be totally dissociated from the narrative context.

The reader may think that God could not mean for Abraham to sacrifice his son on account of a belief that the Torah prohibits the sacrificial offering of a child. Without getting into the whole controversy, suffice it to say that Torah law is ambivalent on the point. Although Deuteronomy may forbid it, Exod. 22.28b demands it: 'The firstborn of your sons you shall give to me'. And if you would object that the verse refers to divine service and not sacrificial offering (e.g. Brin 1994: 209 and *passim*), you would face three serious difficulties. For one thing, the immediate context is one of sacrifices. The following verse (v. 29) commands the Israelite to give the firstborn of one's cattle to God—using the same Hebrew verb, תִּתֶּן. It makes sense to interpret that verse to refer to a sacrificial offering. Another difficulty is that the prophet Ezekiel cites Israelite human sacrifice, albeit critically (Ezek.

16.21; 23.39; cf., e.g., Fishbane 1985: 185).[29] Yet a third difficulty is presented by a case such as that of King Mesha of Moab, whose sacrifice of his firstborn son during an Israelite siege was not rejected but accepted by the divine powers, who afflicted the surrounding Israelite army with a plague and rescued the Moabites (2 Kgs 3.26-27). Rather, as Levenson (1993: 3-17) has convincingly argued, child sacrifice was both practiced and, at some stages, approved of in the biblical tradition.

In any event, there is no basis for believing that Abraham would not find the commandment to sacrifice his son illegitimate. What would understandably bother Abraham is the apparent contradiction between the divine promise to him that Isaac would inherit the covenant and the command to slaughter him on some mountain in the Land of Moriah (see the commentaries; cf. *Gen. R.* 56.11, ed. Theodor-Albeck, pp. 608-10). Fretheim (497) again follows Kierkegaard (1954: 31 and *passim*) in insisting that 'Abraham trusts that God's promise and command are not finally contradictory; whatever conflict there may be, it is up to God to resolve it, and God is up to it'. Fretheim, who, as has been said, objects to reading into a character's mind, here not only finds Abraham's trust, he even discovers Abraham's logic: God does not mean for Abraham to sacrifice his son; Abrahams knows this, and is only wondering how God will prevent the catastrophe from occurring.

> *Verse 3*: Abraham arose early in the morning, he saddled his he-ass, he took his two attendants with him, as well as Isaac, his son; he split wood for the sacrifice; he got up and went to the place of which God had told him.

How does Abraham react to the divine command? Fretheim (495), who finds Abraham to be faithful from the start, predictably finds in the sequence of Abraham's activities a sign of his 'unhesitating obedience'. He is supported by a number of biblical narratologists (e.g. Bar-Efrat 1989: 79-80; Berlin 1983: 39; Polak 1999: 284).[30] The Targum Neofiti reads similarly, adding the adverb בחדוה, 'in joy', in the first-person account of Abraham's own activities that we find there (Diez-Macho 1968: 129 at v. 14; McNamara 1992: 119). Perhaps the uninterrupted series of actions can be taken to indicate Abraham's eagerness to comply with the command—the fact that Abraham lost no sleep the night before, as Everett Fox (1995: 92) analyzes Abraham's silent compliance. But that is not the only exegetical option.

Some critics prefer to see in Abraham's silent actions a symptom of his psychic numbness, of his being stunned by the demand (e.g. Coats 1973: 397;

---

29. There may also be a reference to an ancient Israelite practice of firstborn sacrifice in Ezek. 20.25-26, but the interpretation of the passage is controversial; see Bodoff 2000.

30. Cf. Trible (1991: 173-75), who is primarily interested in the extent of the attachment between Abraham and Isaac that one can discern.

Humphreys 2001: 140).[31] In this vein the poet Delmore Schwartz (1967) has Abraham report on his reaction as follows: 'I said nothing, shocked and passive'. Mazor (1986: 85) reinforces such a reading by suggesting that in saving the cutting of the wood till last, Abraham was putting off the activity most directly connected with the sacrifice, reflecting his apprehension about what he felt he had to do. Abravanel wonders out loud why Abraham troubled himself to cut wood at home altogether—wouldn't there be wood in the Land of Moriah (1964: 263)? From this Bodoff (1993: 78) infers that Abraham was stalling—he did not really want to go through with it; he was conflicted. Walter Hertzberg (1997: 46), too, finds Abraham to be unsettled—that is why he puts off taking Isaac till last. Actually, however, as we have seen, the last thing Abraham does is to split the wood—only after taking his he-ass, his servants, and his son. Talmon (1965: 40) observes that the order of the delineated activities is illogical, and he interprets this to reflect the confused state of the patriarch.

As I read it, Abraham's immediate response is not this sequence of events, which is so variously interpreted, but his silence (cf. Polak 1999: 284). Many readers do not assume that the silence betokens a lack of feeling. 'It cannot be', writes Judith Elkan (1989–90: 29), a psychotherapist, 'that Abraham's mind is not teeming with thoughts'; 'our imagination is taken over by a tumult of thoughts and feelings which cannot be avoided'. Even Fretheim (495) admits that this silence 'may be designed to raise questions in the mind of the reader', but in line with his avowed policy of not 'dramatizing' the text, he does not (at this point) read into Abraham's soul. Restrospectively, as we have seen, Fretheim reconstructs the logic supporting Abraham's implicit trust in God.

Landy (1989: 12-13) is not so diffident about identifying Abraham's feelings:

> Abraham does not respond, despite our legitimate expectations... It is especially surprising given his fearlessness elsewhere [in the defense of Sodom in Gen. 18]... The test is only of interest because Abraham is not an obedient sheep. His puzzling acquiescence further suggests that it corresponds to an inner necessity.

In line with his overall reading of the *Akedah* as Abraham's journey into himself, Landy suspects that some inclination in Abraham to slay his son finds its justification in the divine command. Landy endeavors to buttress this interior reading of the narrative by calling our attention to the fact that Abraham, without being told the precise location of the mountain, proceeds 'intuitively' in the right direction (p. 13); and to the fact that we are led to see

---

31. Greenwood (1985: 127) reads the description of Abraham and Isaac's journey together as suggestive of a sleepwalk.

the destination through Abraham's eyes, as 'he sees the place from afar' (v. 4b; p. 14).

> *Verse 7*: Isaac said to Abraham, his father; he said, 'Father!' and he said, 'Here am I, my son!' He said, 'Here are the fire and the wood, but where is the lamb for the sacrificial offering?'

Isaac asks a question. What is Isaac's motivation and objective? For Landy it is the innocent question of a child (1989: 15-16; cf. Goitein 1957: 78):

> Every word shows us…that it is a child speaking. We project ourselves into that voice… He says אָבִי, 'father'…suggesting both a lack of communication and a connotative depth, everything a good father means to a son. There is a trust that Daddy is dependable and can answer all questions… It is a child's question, with no trace of foreboding. One may wonder why it has taken Isaac so long to notice that a requisite item [viz., the knife] is missing.

Uriel Simon (1981: 132 n. 15) takes the opposite view. He observes the all-too-close nexus between the knife and the sacrifice and proposes that Isaac is not so innocent after all. He is frightened of the knife and for that reason does not dare to mention it; he suspects what is about to happen and indirectly expresses his fear (cf. *Gen. R.* 56.8, ed. Theodor-Albeck, p. 599). What for Landy is a sign of 'curiosity' and 'guilelessness' is for Simon a token of fright and an appeal to his father, in whose hands are his life and death.

For Fretheim (496), Isaac's question threatens to rock his reading, whereby all relationships are suffused with trust. Accordingly, he advises us not to 'overplay' 'Isaac's emotions'. However, after Abraham has made his reply to Isaac (see immediately below) and 'the two of them walk on together' (v. 8b), Fretheim fails to follow his own advice. The repetition of this phrase he interprets as an 'explicit' indication that Isaac trusts his father: 'Isaac believes his father's trust to be well placed'.

> *Verse 8a*: Abraham said, 'God will himself see to[32] the lamb for the sacrificial offering, my son!'

What does Abraham mean by this answer? Kierkegaard understands it to be double-talk, but a favorable form of double-talk: Abraham says nothing untrue and expresses nothing. Kierkegaard says little himself, but saying anything about what Abraham means is for Fretheim more than what can be warranted by the text. Whatever Abraham says, Fretheim knows that he will express only a complete trust in God.

---

32. The verb רָאָה, ordinarily 'to see', here has the sense of 'to find' or 'select', as it does in Gen. 41.33; Deut. 12.13 (cf. v. 14 where ראה is replaced by בחר 'to choose'); 1 Sam. 16.1, 17, 18; and see Rashi's comment ad loc. I discuss this semantic development in my forthcoming article, 'On the Use of Akkadian in Biblical Hebrew Philology'.

To suggest that Abraham is equivocating or being ironic or deceptive or whistling in the dark finds no basis in the text; such ideas betray too much interest in dramatization. It would be strange for a narrative designed to demonstrate Abraham's trusting obedience to be punctuated with acts of deception (Fretheim 1994: 496).

You see, if you know what the text means, you can hardly abide anyone who would deign to interpret it. In a related vein, Westermann (1985: 359-60) finds the question of Abraham's veracity to be irrelevant. Abraham is not seeking to deceive anyone; he is in anguish and is leaving the matter up to God.

Most readers find Abraham's response to be problematic. Targum Neofiti removes the lie altogether by alternatively parsing the syntax: God will provide the lamb for the offering—(namely,) my son! (Diez-Macho 1968: 125 at v. 8; McNamara 1992: 117; cf. Rouiller 1978: 28). Among modern interpreters one encounters basically four different tacks, all of which, of course, make some effort to understand what lies behind Abraham's apparent lie. For some, Abraham is being evasive—he is not satisfying his son with the substance of an answer, only with the form of an answer (e.g. Coats 1973: 394; cf. Bar-Efrat 1989: 75-76). Elkan (1989-90: 33) suggests that Abraham is repressing the terrible truth from his own consciousness. For others, it is Abraham's wishful thinking, an expression of hope that somehow he will end up sacrificing an animal and not his son (e.g. Mazor 1986: 87; Humphreys 2001: 140). For still others, it is a lie, though a white one, meant to alleviate the anxieties of his son (e.g. White 1979: 15; Zakovitch 1985: 91). For Landy (1989: 18), the reply is enigmatic: 'Is it a lie or a residual hope?' (e.g. Prouser 1991: 96-97; Levenson 1993: 134). In the end, after all, both God's deception of Abraham—who, except in a reading such as Fretheim's, does not know that he will not have to go through with the horrific act—and Abraham's deception of Isaac—if it is that—turn out to be true (Landy 1989: 31)!

One should not, however, be too quick to let Abraham off the hook. For even though Abraham ends up sacrificing a ram in place of his son, even though the sacrifice of Isaac is called off from on high, still in Abraham's mind, the sacrifice must go on (e.g. Westermann 1985: 360). As Landy (p. 29) reminds us, it is Abraham who, on his own initiative, decides to make an offering of the ram (v. 13). God does not command it. One may infer that Abraham had all along sensed that God has demanded a sacrifice from him. Until he is interrupted in the act of offering up Isaac, Abraham seems convinced that Isaac is the sacrifice God wants.

The angel uses—and, one may infer, must use—powerful rhetoric to stop Abraham in the act: 'Do not extend your hand toward the boy, and do not do anything to him!' The twofold prohibition may be taken to indicate the importance of preventing a human sacrifice. But it may also indicate, as

Levenson suggests, that Abraham is so absorbed in sacrificing his son that to stop him requires a powerful rhetorical intervention (Levenson 1993: 137).

Similarly, the angel's double call to Abraham, while he is in the act of sacrifice, 'Abraham, Abraham!' (v. 11)—may, as some have proposed, indicate the urgency of the need to stop the patriarch (Ibn Ezra; R. David Qimḥi; Rappoport 1989 *ad loc.*; Westermann 1985: 361; Coffin 1987: 295; Levenson 1993: 137). Alternatively, it may be interpreted, with Uriel Simon (1981: 127, 131 n. 14), as the need to impress upon Abraham the fact that the voice that is calling is not, *pace* Landy, an internal voice, but rather an external one.[33] Simon compares the double address of Moses at the Burning Bush (Exod. 3.4) and of Samuel in the Shiloh shrine (1 Sam. 3.10), two other passages in which the divine voice would have to convince the subject that he is really being addressed. One should hesitate to convert this felicitous hermeneutic into a compositional convention. For one thing, the double call of Jacob in a nocturnal vision (Gen. 46.2) does not conform to the proposed semiotic pattern. For another, alternate interpretations are also plausible. For Polak (1999: 31), the reduplication of the addressee's name signifies that the dialogue is transpiring 'at a fateful moment'.[34] The repetition of a word or a name is understood by Bar-Efrat (1989: 211), in general, as an expression of 'strong emotion', and the repetition of a name is taken by Rashi (at Gen. 22.11; cf. *Gen. R.* 56.7; Ibn Ezra *ad loc.*) as a token of endearment. Considering the fact that inanimate objects can also be addressed in a double vocative (see the call to the altar in 1 Kgs 13.2), the doubling may be a rhetorical option that can be interpreted any way one wants or not at all.[35]

My point is simply that texts and the phenomena that we find in them do not have any predetermined meaning. Indeed they have no inherent meaning at all, except as a reader chooses to give that text or any part of it some meaning (see, e.g., Fish 1980c; Attridge 2004: 107-21). And a reader will perform the act of reading the way one performs any other activity—pragmatically, by making choices that reflect one's best understanding of what is best for one, whatever that may be. One may interpret a textual detail in order to conform to one's current hypothesis about a text's meaning; and a text in accord with one's current theory of what that text is about. We have seen examples of how this works in our examination of some readings of the *Akedah*.

33. My elaboration of Simon's interpretation is based on his presentation in class (Jewish Theological Seminary, New York, Fall 1969).

34. Of course, there are fateful moments in biblical dialogue in which no such reduplication occurs, so that, again, we are not dealing with a fixed convention but with a useful reading strategy—useful when it can be meaningfully applied.

35. The double vocative is also found in extra-biblical literature from the ancient Near East for both persons and objects; e.g., *ab ab* 'Father, father!', *um um* 'Mother, mother!' *CAT* 1.23 lines 32-33; Lewis 1997: 210; *kikkiš kikkiš igār igār* 'Reed mat, reed mat! Wall, wall!' Gilgamesh XI 21; Parpola 1997: 109.

In presenting a reading of a text, we will tend to find significance in some things more than in others, apply certain interpretive strategies rather than others, draw the meanings we have made into some larger, overarching understanding, because of where we are coming from and where we are going. The lesson here, from where I stand, is not to disparage what we, or others, do in the act of reading. That would be the response of a person who feels that one's bubble has been burst. I would take a more positive, constructive outlook. If in reading we have the power to make choices and to determine the outcome of our reading, then we can become more experienced and versatile readers so as to enhance the things we can do when we read, so that when there is something we might like to do, we will be in a better position to do it.

Our colleague and friend, Yairah Amit, has devoted her career to helping teachers teach better and readers read better. Her manifold contributions provide a stimulus to look again, read again, and consider a different interpretation. Our readings may not always agree, but they generally belong to the same 'game'—the effort to point to what we find significant, in order to make of that a meaningful sense.

Bibliography

Abravanel, Yitzhaq
    1964   פירוש על התורה ,1,בראשית (Jerusalem: Arbel).
Adar, Z.
    1990   *The Book of Genesis* (Jerusalem: Magnes Press).
Agus, A.R.E.
    1988   *The Binding of Isaac and the Messiah: Law, Martyrdom, and Deliverance in Early Rabbinic Religiosity* (Albany: State University of New York Press).
Amit, Y.
    2000   *Hidden Polemics in Biblical Narrative* (trans. J. Chipman; Biblical Interpretation Series, 25; Leiden: E.J. Brill).
Attridge, D.
    2004   *The Singularity of Literature* (London/New York: Routledge).
Auerbach, E.
    1953   'Odysseus' Scar', in *Mimesis: The Representation of Reality in Western Literature* (trans. W. Trask; Princeton, NJ: Princeton University Press): 3-23.
Bach, A.
    1997   *Women, Seduction, and Betrayal in Biblical Narrative* (Cambridge: Cambridge University Press).
Bal, M.
    1987   *Lethal Love: Feminist Literary Readings of Biblical Love Stories* (Bloomington: Indiana University Press).

Bar-Efrat, S.
    1989   *Narrative Art in the Bible* (trans. D. Shefer-Vanson; Sheffield: JSOT Press).
Barthes, R.
    1979   'From Work to Text', in J.V. Harari (ed.), *Textual Strategies: Perspectives in Post-Structuralist Criticism* (Ithaca, NY: Cornell University Press): 73-81.
Barton, J.
    1984   *Reading the Old Testament: Method in Biblical Study* (Philadelphia: Westminster Press).
Beardsley, M.C.
    1970   *The Possibility of Criticism* (Detroit: Wayne State University Press).
Berlin, A.
    1983   *Poetics and Interpretation of Biblical Narrative* (Sheffield: Almond Press).
Bodoff, L.
    1993   'The Real Test of the *Akedah*: Blind Obedience Versus Moral Choice', *Judaism* 42: 71-92.
    2000   'Ezekiel 20:25-26—Did God ever Command the Sacrifice of Israel's Firstborn Sons?', *B.D.D. Journal of Torah and Scholarship* 10: 23-36.
Booth, W.C.
    1961   *The Rhetoric of Fiction* (Chicago: University of Chicago Press).
    1979   *Critical Understanding: The Powers and Limits of Pluralism* (Chicago/London: University of Chicago Press).
Brand, G. (ed.)
    1979   *The Essential Wittgenstein* (trans. R.E. Innis; New York: Basic Books).
Brin, G.
    1994   *Studies in Biblical Law from the Hebrew Bible to the Dead Sea Scrolls* (JSOTSup, 176; Sheffield: JSOT Press).
Brooks, C.
    1947   *The Well-Wrought Urn: Studies in the Structure of Poetry* (New York: Harcourt Brace).
    1992   'The Heresy of Paraphrase', in H. Adams (ed.), *Critical Theory since Plato* (Fort Worth: Harcourt Brace Jovanovich, rev. edn): 961-68.
Brown, M.
    1982   'Biblical Myth and Contemporary Experience: The *Akedah* in Modern Jewish Literature', *Judaism* 31: 99-111.
Burnshaw, S., T. Carmi, and E. Spicehandler (eds.)
    1989   *The Modern Hebrew Poem Itself* (Cambridge, MA/London: Harvard University Press, 2nd edn).
Carmi, T. (ed.)
    1981   *The Penguin Book of Hebrew Verse* (New York: Penguin).
Coats, G.W.
    1973   'Abraham's Sacrifice of Faith: A Form-Critical Study of Genesis 22', *Interpretation* 27: 389-400.
    1983   *Genesis with an Introduction to Narrative Literature* (FOTL, 1; Grand Rapids: Eerdmans).

Coffin, E.A.

1987 'The Binding of Isaac in Modern Israeli Literature', in M.P. O'Connor and
D.N. Freedman (eds.), *Backgrounds for the Bible* (Winona Lake, IN:
Eisenbrauns): 293-308.

Conant, J. (ed.)

1994 *Words & Life* (Cambridge, MA/London: Harvard University Press).

Crane, R.S.

1953 *The Languages of Criticism and the Structure of Poetry* (Toronto: Toronto
University Press).

Dascal, M.

1989 'Hermeneutic Interpretation and Pragmatic Interpretation', *Philosophy and
Rhetoric* 22: 239-59.

Davis, E.F.

1991 'Self-Consciousness and Conversation: Reading Genesis 22', *Bulletin for
Biblical Research* 1: 27-40.

Deurloo, K.

1994 'The Way of Abraham: Routes and Localities as Narrative Data in Gen.
11:27-25:11', in *Voices from Amsterdam* (ed. and trans. M. Kessler;
SBLSemSt; Atlanta: Scholars Press): 95-112.

Dewey, J.

1925 *Experience and Nature* (Chicago/London: Open Court).

1938 *Logic: The Theory of Inquiry* (New York: Henry Holt).

1977 *Essays on Pragmatism and Truth 1907–1909* (ed. J.A. Boydston;
Carbondale/Edwardsville: Southern Illinois University Press).

Diez Macho, A.

1968 *Neophyti 1: Targum Palestinense Ms. de la Biblioteca Vaticana, Tomo I:
Genesis* (Madrid-Barcelona: Consejo Superior de Investigaciones
Científicas).

Eagleton, T.

1983 *Literary Theory: An Introduction* (Minneapolis: University of Minnesota
Press).

Elkan, J.

1989–90 'The Binding of Isaac: A Psycho-Analytic Perspective', *European
Judaism* 22: 26-35.

Exum, J.C., and J.W. Whedbee

1990 'Isaac, Samson, and Saul: Reflections on the Comic and Tragic Visions',
in Y.T. Radday and A. Brenner (eds.), *On Humour and the Comic in the
Hebrew Bible* (JSOTSup, 92; Sheffield: Almond Press): 117-59.

Feldman, Y.S.

1998 'Isaac or Oedipus? Jewish Tradition and the Israeli Aqedah', in J.C. Exum
and S.D. Moore (eds.), *Biblical Studies/Cultural Studies: The Third
Sheffield Colloquium* (JSOTSup, 266; Sheffield: Sheffield Academic
Press): 159-89.

2010 *Glory and Agony: Isaac's Sacrifice and National Narrative* (Stanford, CA:
Stanford University Press).

Fish, S.

1980 *Is There a Text in This Class?: The Authority of Interpretive Communities*
(Cambridge, MA: Harvard University Press).

1980a   'What Makes an Interpretation Acceptable?', in Fish 1980: 338-55.

1980b   'Demonstration vs. Persuasion: Two Models of Critical Activity', in Fish 1980: 356-71.

1980c   'Literature in the Reader: Affective Stylistics', in Fish 1980: 21-67.

1989   'Why No One's Afraid of Wolfgang Iser', in *Doing What Comes Naturally: Change, Rhetoric, and the Practice of Theory in Literary and Legal Studies* (Durham: Duke University Press): 68-86.

Fishbane, M.

1985   *Biblical Interpretation in Ancient Israel* (Oxford: Clarendon Press).

Fokkelman, J.P.

1989   '"On the Mountain of the Lord There Is Vision": A Response to Francis Landy Concerning the Akedah', in J.C. Exum (ed.), *Signs and Wonders: Biblical Texts in Literary Focus* (SBLSemSt; Atlanta: Scholars Press): 41-57.

Foucault, M.

1979   'What Is an Author?', in Josué V. Harari (ed.), *Textual Strategies: Perspectives in Post-Structuralist Criticism* (Ithaca, NY: Cornell University Press): 141-60.

Fox, E.

1995   *The Five Books of Moses* (Schocken Bible, 1; New York: Schocken Books).

Fretheim, T.E.

1994   *The Book of Genesis: Introduction, Commentary, and Reflections*, in L.E. Keck *et al.* (eds.), *The New Interpreter's Bible*, I (Nashville: Abingdon Press): 319-674.

Frye, N.

1963   'Literary Criticism', in J. Thorpe (ed.), *The Aims and Methods of Scholarship in Modern Languages and Literatures* (New York: Modern Language Association): 57-69.

Gadamer, H.-G.

1982   *Truth and Method* (New York: Crossroad).

Gilboa, A.

1953   'Isaac', in *Shirim ba-boqer ba-boqer* (Tel Aviv: Ha-Kibbutz Ha-Me'uhad [Hebrew]).

Goitein, S.D.

1957   *Bible Studies* (Tel Aviv: Yavneh; Hebrew).

Gottwald, N.K.

1959   *A Light to the Nations: An Introduction to the Old Testament* (New York: Harper).

Green, G.M.

1989   *Pragmatics and Natural Language Understanding* (Hillsdale, NJ: Lawrence Erlbaum Associates).

Greenstein, E.L.

1981   'The Riddle of Samson', *Prooftexts* 1: 237-60.

1987   'A Jewish Reading of Esther', in J. Neusner, B.A. Levine and E. Frerichs (eds.), *Judaic Perspectives on Ancient Israel* (Philadelphia: Fortress Press): 225-43.

1989   *Essays on Biblical Method and Translation* (Brown Judaic Studies, 92; Atlanta: Scholars Press).

1999   'Reading Strategies and the Story of Ruth', in A. Bach (ed.), *Women in the Hebrew Bible: A Reader* (New York/London: Routledge): 211-31

2009   'A Pragmatic Pedagogy of Bible', *Journal of Jewish Education* 75: 290-303.

forthcoming   'On the Use of Akkadian in Biblical Hebrew Philology', in K. Abraham and J. Fleishman (eds.), *Festschrift for Aaron Skaist* (Bethesda, MD: CDL Press).

Greenwood, D.

1985   *Structuralism and the Biblical Text* (Berlin/New York/Amsterdam: Mouton).

Gros Louis, K.R.R.

1982   'Abraham: I', 'Abraham: II', in K.R.R. Gros Louis with J.S. Ackerman (eds.), *Literary Interpretations of Biblical Narratives*, II (Nashville: Abingdon Press): 53-84.

Gunkel, H.

1964   *The Legends of Genesis* (trans. W.H. Carruth; New York: Schocken Books).

Gunn, D.M., and D.N. Fewell

1993   *Narrative in the Hebrew Bible* (Oxford: Oxford University Press).

Habermas, J.

1999   *On the Pragmatics of Communication* (ed. M. Cooke; Cambridge: Polity Press).

Hartman, G.

1980   *Criticism in the Wilderness* (New Haven: Yale University Press).

Hertzberg, W.

1997   'From the Intuitive to the Intentional', in *The Pardes Reader* (ed. F. K. Zisken; Jerusalem: Pardes Institute): 43-50.

Hirsch, E.D., Jr

1967   *Validity in Interpretation* (New Haven/London: Yale University Press).

Hook, S.

1939   *John Dewey: An Intellectual Portrait* (New York: John Day).

Humphreys, W.L.

1985   *The Tragic Vision and the Hebrew Tradition* (Philadelphia: Fortress Press).

2001   *The Character of God in the Book of Genesis: A Narrative Appraisal* (Louisville, KY: Westminster/John Knox Press).

Iser, W.

1980   'The Reading Process: A Phenomenological Approach', in J.P. Tompkins (ed.), *Reader-Response Criticism* (Baltimore/London: The Johns Hopkins University Press): 50-69.

Jacobson, D.C.

1987   *Modern Midrash: The Retelling of Traditional Jewish Narratives by Twentieth-Century Hebrew Writers* (Albany: State University of New York Press).

James, W.

1955   *Pragmatism and Four Essays on the Meaning of Truth* (Cleveland/New York: Meridian).

Kalimi, I.
  2010   '"Go, I Beg You, Take Your Beloved Son and Slay Him!": The Binding of
            Isaac in Rabbinic Literature and Thought', *Review of Rabbinic Judaism*
            13: 1-29.
Kaminsky, J.S.
  2000   'Humor and the Theology of Hope: Isaac as a Humorous Figure', *Interpre-
            tation* 54: 363-75.
Kaplan, K.J.
  1990   'Isaac and Oedipus: A Re-examination of the Father–Son Relationship',
            Judaism 39: 73-81.
Kierkegaard, S.
  1954   *Fear and Trembling and the Sickness unto Death* (trans. W. Lowie;
            Garden City, NY: Anchor Books).
Krieger, M.
  1976   *Theory of Criticism: A Tradition and Its System* (Baltimore/London: The
            Johns Hopkins University Press).
Kripke, S.A.
  1982   *Wittgenstein on Rules and Private Language* (Cambridge, MA: Harvard
            University Press).
Kugel, J.L.
  1997   *The Bible as It Was* (Cambridge, MA/London: Harvard University Press).
Lakoff, R.T.
  2000   *The Language War* (Berkeley/Los Angeles/London: University of
            California Press).
Landy, F.
  1985   'Are We in the Place of Averroes? Response to the Articles of Exum and
            Whedbee, Buss, Gottwald, and Good', in J.C. Exum (ed.), *Tragedy and
            Comedy in the Bible* (SBLSemSt; Decatur, GA: Scholars Press): 131-48.
  1989   'Narrative Techniques and Symbolic Transactions in the Akedah', in J.C.
            Exum (ed.), *Signs and Wonders* (SBLSemSt; Atlanta: Scholars Press):
            1-40.
Lecercle, J.-J.
  1999   *Interpretation as Pragmatics* (New York: St. Martin's Press).
Leibowitz, N.
  1990   'How to Read a Chapter of Tanakh', in H. Deitcher and A.J. Tannenbaum
            (eds.), *Studies in Jewish Education*, V (Jerusalem: Magnes Press): 35-47.
Leitch, V.B.
  1988   *American Literary Criticism from the Thirties to the Eighties* (New York:
            Columbia University Press).
Leiter, Sh.
  1979   'נס להתנוסס—נסיון בתוך נסיון', in U. Simon (ed.), *The Bible and Us* (Tel
            Aviv: Dvir): 172-78 (Hebrew).
Lentricchia, F.
  1980   *After the New Criticism* (Chicago: University of Chicago Press).
Levenson, J.D.
  1993   *The Death and Resurrection of the Beloved Son: The Transformation of
            Child Sacrifice in Judaism and Christianity* (New Haven: Yale University
            Press).

Lewis, T.J.
   1997   'The Birth of the Gracious Gods', in S.B. Parker (ed.), *Ugaritic Narrative Poetry* (SBLWAW; Atlanta: Scholars Press): 205-14.

Licht, J.
   1973   *Testing in the Hebrew Scriptures and in Post-Biblical Judaism* (Jerusalem: Magnes Press [Hebrew]).

Lowe, E.J.
   1995   'Truth', in T. Honderich (ed.), *The Oxford Companion to Philosophy* (Oxford/New York: Oxford University Press): 881-82.

Lynch, M.P.
   1998   *Truth in Context: An Essay in Pluralism and Objectivity* (Cambridge, MA/London: MIT Press).

Malachowski, A.
   2010   *The New Pragmatism* (Montreal/Kingston/Ithaca: McGill-Queen's University Press).

Malachowski, A.R. (ed.)
   1990   *Reading Rorty* (Oxford/Cambridge, MA: Blackwell).

Margolis, J.
   1986   *Pragmatism without Foundations* (Oxford: Basil Blackwell).

Mazor, Y.
   1986   'Genesis 22: The Ideological Rhetoric and the Psychological Composition', *Biblica* 67: 81-88.

McNamara, M.
   1992   *Targum Neofiti 1: Genesis* (Collegeville, MN: Liturgical Press).

Mey, J.L.
   1993   *Pragmatics: An Introduction* (Oxford/Cambridge, MA: Blackwell).

Miles, J.
   1995   *God: A Biography* (New York: Alfred A. Knopf).

Mleynek, S.
   1994   'Abraham, Aristotle, and God: The Poetics of Sacrifice', *Journal of the American Academy of Religion* 62: 107-21.

Monk, R.
   1991   *Ludwig Wittgenstein: The Duty of Genius* (New York: Penguin Books).

Moster, J. B.
   1988–89 'The Testing of Abraham', *Dor le-Dor* 17: 237-42.

Moulton, R.G.
   1915   *The Modern Study of Literature* (Chicago: University of Chicago Press).

Murphy, J.P.
   1990   *Pragmatism from Peirce to Davidson* (Boulder, CO: Westview Press).

Okrent, M.
   1989   'The Metaphilosophical Consequences of Pragmatism', in A. Cohen and M. Dascal (eds.), *The Institution of Philosophy: A Discipline in Crisis?* (LaSalle, IL: Open Court): 177-98.

Parpola, S.
   1997   *The Standard Babylonian Epic of Gilgamesh* (State Archives of Assyria Cuneiform Texts, 1; Helsinki: University of Helsinki).

Patte, D.
   1990   *The Religious Dimensions of Biblical Texts: Greimas' Structural Semiotics* (SBLSemSt; Atlanta: Scholars Press).

Pedersen, J.
    1940   *Israel: Its Life and Culture*, III–IV (London: Oxford University Press).
Peirce, C.S.
    1966   *Charles S. Peirce: Selected Writings* (ed. P.P. Weiner; New York: Dover).
    1966a   'What Pragmatism Is', in Peirce 1966: 180-202.
    1966b   'The Fixation of Belief', in Peirce 1966: 91-112.
    1966c   'Definition and Function of a University', in Peirce 1966: 331-35.
    1966d   'How To Make Our Ideas Clear', in Peirce 1966: 113-36.
Poirier, R.
    1992   *Poetry & Pragmatism* (Cambridge, MA: Harvard University Press).
Polak, F.H.
    1999   *Biblical Narrative: Aspects of Art and Design* (Jerusalem: Bialik Institute,
            2nd edn [Hebrew]).
Prentiss, J.J.
    1990   'The Sacrifice of Isaac: A Comparative View', in W.W. Hallo *et al.* (eds.),
            The Bible in the Light of Cuneiform Literature. Scripture in Context, III
            (Lewiston: Edwin Mellen Press): 203-30.
Prouser, O.H.
    1991   'The Phenomenology of the Lie in Biblical Narrative' (PhD dissertation,
            Jewish Theological Seminary, New York).
Putnam, H.
    1994a   'On Truth', in Conant 1994: 315-29.
    1994b   'Dewey's *Logic*: Epistemology as Hypothesis', in Conant 1994: 198-220.
    1995   *Pragmatism: An Open Question* (Oxford/Cambridge, MA: Basil Black-
            well).
Rad, G. von
    1961   *Genesis: A Commentary* (trans. J.H. Marks; OTL; Philadelphia: West-
            minster Press).
Rappoport, A.M.
    1989   *Minḥa belula* (repr., Bene Berak [Hebrew]).
Robbins, J.
    1991   *Prodigal Son/Elder Brother: Interpretation and Alterity in Augustine,
            Petrarch, Kafka, Levinas* (Chicago/London: University of Chicago Press).
Rorty, R.
    1982   *Consequences of Pragmatism (Essays: 1972–1980)* (Minneapolis: Uni-
            versity of Minnesota Press).
    1991   'Pragmatism without Method', in *Objectivity, Relativism, and Truth.
            Philosophical Papers*, I (Cambridge: Cambridge University Press): 63-77.
Rosenberg, J.
    1986   *King and Kin: Political Allegory in the Hebrew Bible* (Bloomington-
            Indianapolis: Indiana University Press).
    1993   'Genesis', in W.A. Meeks (ed.), *The HarperCollins Study Bible* (San
            Francisco: HarperCollins): 3-76.
Rouiller, G.
    1978   'The Sacrifice of Isaac (Genesis 22:1-29)', in *Exegesis: Problems of
            Method and Exercises in Reading (Genesis 22 and Luke 15)* (trans. D.G.
            Miller; Pittsburgh: Pickwick Press): 13-42.

Saldarini, A.J.
 1982   'Interpretation of the *Akedah* in Rabbinic Literature', in R. Polzin and
         E. Rothman (eds.), *The Biblical Mosaic: Changing Perspectives* (Phila-
         delphia: Fortress; Chico, CA: Scholars Press): 149-65.
Sarna, N.M.
 1989   *The JPS Torah Commentary: Genesis—*בראשית (Philadelphia: Jewish
         Publication Society).
Schwartz, D.
 1967   'Abraham', in *Selected Poems (1938–1958): Summer Knowledge* (New
         York: New Directions): 230-31.
Sell, R.D. (ed.)
 1991   *Literary Pragmatics* (London/New York: Routledge).
Simon, A.
 1973   'Remarks on the Binding of Isaac Episode', *Hagut ba-Miqra'* 1 (Tel Aviv:
         Am Oved): 163-70 (Hebrew).
Simon, U.
 1981   'Samuel's Call to Prophecy: Form Criticism with Close Reading',
         Prooftexts 1: 119-32.
Spiegel, Sh.
 1964   *The Last Trial* (trans. J. Goldin; New York: Schocken Books).
Spiro, R.J.
 1980   'Prior Knowledge and Story Processing: Integration, Selection, and
         Variation', *Poetics* 9: 313-27.
Steinmetz, D.
 1991   *From Father to Son: Kinship, Conflict and Continuity in Genesis* (Louis-
         ville, KY: Westminster/John Knox Press).
Sternberg, M.
 1985   *The Poetics of Biblical Narrative* (Bloomington: Indiana University Press).
Talmon, Sh.
 1964   *The Ways of Biblical Narrative* (ed. G. Gil; Jerusalem: Academon;
         Hebrew).
Theodor, Y., and H. Albeck
 1903   *Midrash Bereishit Rabba* (3 vols.; Berlin: Itzkowitz).
Trible, Ph.
 1991   'Genesis 22: The Sacrifice of Sarah', in J.P. Rosenblatt and J.C. Sitterson
         Jr (eds.), *'Not in Heaven': Coherence and Complexity in Biblical Narra-
         tive* (Bloomington: Indiana University Press): 170-91.
Wellisch, E.
 1954   *Isaac and Oedipus: A Study in Biblical Psychology of the Sacrifice of
         Isaac of Isaac—The Akedah* (London: Routledge & Kegan Paul).
Wenham, G.J.
 1995   'The Akedah: A Paradigm of Sacrifice', in D.P. Wright, D.N. Freedman
         and A. Hurvitz (eds.), *Pomegranates and Golden Bells: Studies in Biblical,
         Jewish, and Near Eastern Ritual, Law and Literature in Honor of Jacob
         Milgrom* (Winona Lake, IN: Eisenbrauns): 93-102.
Westermann, C.
 1985   *Genesis 12–36: A Commentary* (trans. J.J. Scullion; Hermeneia; Minnea-
         polis: Augsburg).

White, H.C.
    1979   'The Initiation Legend of Isaac', *ZAW* 91: 11-20.
Wiesel, E.
    1976   *Messengers of God* (trans. M. Wiesel; New York: Random House).
Wimsatt, W.K.
    1954   *The Verbal Icon: Studies in the Meaning of Poetry* (Louisville: University
                Press of Kentucky).
Wimsatt, W.K., and M.C. Beardsley
    1954a   'The Intentional Fallacy', in Wimsatt 1954: 3-18.
    1954b   'The Affective Fallacy', in Wimsatt 1954: 21-39.
Zakovitch, Y.
    1985   'On the Proleptic Allusion in Biblical Narrative', *Beer-sheva* 2: 85-105
                (Hebrew).

THE ART OF IRONY:
THE BOOK OF JUDGES

Lillian Klein Abensohn

Yairah Amit has established that the art of 'implied' editing in the book of Judges culminates in a newly historical perspective (Amit 1998: 9, 383). I suggest that the art of editing in Judges also shapes its message with an ironic tone that shifts and weaves its presentation so that the reader is repeatedly surprised both by the sophisticated expressions of irony and by the incremental irony which finally overwhelms the text. Amit shows the reader how history is conveyed through the text; I submit it is irony that structures the book and, implicitly, informs that history.[1]

Irony is introduced in the initial passages: the book opens with a two-pronged critical situation—the death of Joshua and the need to attack the Canaanites. The people inquire of God, 'Who shall go up against the Canaanites first, to fight against them?' (1.1). Responding to their question, God tells the people what to do: 'Judah will go up...I gave the land into his power'. Israel, however, only partially heeds that command: instead of the tribe of Judah going into battle alone, it establishes a battle-pact with Simeon. The resultant battles, some of which are elaborated upon in the following verses, uphold God's words, for Judah alone 'takes' cities and land; the battles of Simeon *and* Judah together merely 'destroy' the cities under attack. 'These verses may be regarded as introducing the ironic configuration of the book, the implicit difference in perception between God and Israel, and Israel's insistence on following human perception' (Klein 1988: 23).[2]

The first battle fought by Judah and Simeon involves Bezeq and Adoni-Bezek (1.4-7), who interprets his own fate in a note of irony: 'As I have done

---

1. For Cleanth Brooks, '...irony is considered the "principle of structure" in literary works, a reconciling power fusing ambiguity, paradox, multiplicity and variety of meaning in a work into the unity, wholeness, and identity which constitutes its modes of being' (Brooks 1993: 635b).

2. We will see that this initial irony—God's specific battle directive improperly heeded—is evoked again, at the conclusion of the book of Judges, forming an *inclusio* of this particular ironic motif.

to others, so has my God Lord repaid me'.[3] When Judah goes against Debir, the first narrative (1.12-15) emerges. Caleb promises his daughter in marriage to the man who will attack the city and conquer it. Othniel, a nephew of Caleb, succeeds in conquering Debir and, marriage subsumed, the narrative continues: Achsah 'provoked him to ask from her father a field'. The following verse is extremely dense, so that in few words, Achsah arrives, alights from her ass, and prostrates herself deferentially before her father—who asks what she wants. Achsah asks for a blessing and, since Caleb gave her husband land of the Negev, a source of water. Caleb responds by giving her two springs of water.

The brevity of this narrative belies its importance, for it can be read as an allegory of God's ideal relationship with his people. At the same time, this narrative establishes facets of an *interpersonal* focus for subsequent ironic contradiction: (1) Caleb promises his daughter as a reward for heroic action; (2) Othniel, a relative, fulfills the conditions; (3) Achsah, the bride, takes the initiative in moving her husband to act, to get a field; and (4) Achsah herself respectfully asks her father for a blessing and for a source of water. With 'field' and 'water' symbolizing fertility of the land and of Israel, this sparse narrative establishes an ideal of relations between generations and between marital partners. Achsah's request for 'blessings' implies the inclusion of God in daily life. Woman is introduced as clearly exercising power, albeit in specific ways: not seductive but provoking; her desires are not merely sensual-sexual but reproductive, not about the immediate moment but about time, about generations to come. Achsah, representing Israel as bride, provides an image of ideal covenantal womanhood. Each of these aspects serves as a separate focus for irony in later narratives.

Comparison of the four-verse tale of Adoni-bezek to that of Achsah-Othniel shows ironic oppositions between idol-worship and Lord-worship; death and marriage; foreign cities and their leaders, and individual Israelites. Following summaries of several more forays by Judah or Judah/Simeon, the narrative veers into subsequent battles involving other tribes as they attempt to take the lands promised to them, with varying success (1.21-36). Repeatedly, the Israelite tribes are unable to completely dispossess the Canaanites and must live among them. When the Israelites adopt the ways of their neighbors and forsake God, his anger grows and their fortunes decline. Thus begins the cycle of judges who lead Israel out of oppression by various means.

Through a flashback to the book of Joshua, Othniel is recalled, this time specifically in the role of a judge. In this second version (3.7-11), Othniel is presented as a model judge-leader, a standard for the judges that follow; and he establishes a paradigm for ironic reversal on a social level: (1) Othniel is

---

3. Adoni-Bezek's response is an example of 'horizontal irony' of the 'Speaker-ingenu' mode: naïve Adoni-bezek presenting himself as victim.

'raised up' by God; (2) God's spirit comes upon him; (3) the judge's singular characteristic is noted (Othniel is a younger kinsman, hence initially unexpected to dominate); (4) the judge takes action to deliver the people; and (5) the people have an extended period of social rest.

Like Othniel, Ehud (3.15-30) is raised up by God, and his unexpected quality is that Ehud, a Benjaminite, is described as 'impeded in his right hand' (3.15).[4] In addition to variations from the paradigm narrative, the reader is also called upon to be informed about ironic implications in cultural knowledge: here, the importance of the right hand in biblical literature,[5] the secondary nature of the left hand, and the presumed left-handedness of many Benjaminites (20.16, *pace* their name *ben-yāmīn*, 'son of the right [hand]'; another irony here). What follows is a clever and rather coarse depiction of how Ehud tricks the king of Moab. Ehud hides his double-edged sword on his right leg, tempts the king into a dangerous situation with double-edged words, and then stabs him—unexpectedly—with his left hand. Ehud is not a hero in the sense that Othniel is; he ironically conquers by treachery instead of bravery, but he does conquer the enemy and provides peace for Israel.

Despite the obvious potential for irony when a female is in leadership in biblical texts, the opening description of Deborah (4.4-16) as prophetess and judge leads the reader to expect the unexpected: a female who will lead Israel to victory. Instead, Deborah catalyzes *others* to acts of delivery, maintaining biblical restrictions on specific feminine roles. Even though Deborah has the God-given spirit to judge men, she needs Barak, a male, to fulfill her war prophecies. Barak agrees to lead the men into battle only if Deborah will agree to go with him—surely an ironic reversal of the Othniel hero paradigm. 'Deborah', which translates as 'bee', is constrained by two males: her husband, Lappidoth ('torches'), if we accept the traditional interpretation of 4.4a, see translations; and her general, Barak ('flash of lightning'), both of whose names in Hebrew convey two means of controlling bees by fire. A woman may be judge, may be prophetess, but warrior? Not a woman named Deborah.[6]

And if Deborah is ironically inverted from Queen Bee to God's background agent in war, Yael (4.17-24) achieves the crowning touch, killing the enemy leader, by being the *opposite* of Deborah. Whereas Deborah is a remarkable woman who leads men, Yael seems a stay-at-home biblical

---

4. Ehud is 'impeded' (BDB: 32 for אטר) in his right hand; the term is habitually translated as 'left handed'.

5. Blessings over favored descendants are given with the right hand (Gen. 48.13-14); the priest puts oil in his left palm to dip his right finger and sprinkle the oil before God (Lev. 14.9).

6. For fuller discussion of name symbolism in this episode see Klein 1988: 40-42 and especially nn. 8-11 thereof, and pp. 216-18.

woman. She is also a woman whose Kenite husband is an ally of Sisera, the enemy leader. These bits of information invite the reader's appreciation of irony when Yael does manage the kill that is denied both Deborah and Barak. In these interwoven stories, initial character description leads to surprising and ironic perception of that character's actions in the narratives' developments.

In the Song of Deborah (5.1-31), the opening verses exalt God; the oppression of the people leads to the appearance of Deborah, in this text as mother. No irony is suggested through all the poetic verses describing God's powers over nature and humans. Yael's section (vv. 24-27) is dramatic, but irony is introduced only in the poem's conclusion, when Sisera's mother is described. Deborah's wisdom, based on Israelite social values, contrasts ironically with the personal and selfish desires of Sisera's mother; and implied Israelite restraint contrasts ironically with her dreams of booty. This intimate scene affords further dramatic irony because the reader knows that Sisera has himself been 'plundered', and by a woman.

With the narrative of Gideon (6.1–8.32), ironic oppositions increase markedly. Instead of a deliverer, a judge, the sons of Israel are sent 'a man, a prophet' (6.8), which recalls the introduction of Deborah as 'a woman, a prophetess'. Later developments in the narrative recall the figure of Moses: both Moses and Gideon experience a true theophany, and Gideon's call observes the 'call pattern' of the Moses narrative (Exod. 3.10-12). But Gideon compares only ironically with both Deborah and Moses. Through these inter- and intra-textual allusions, irony is invested in the actions of the judge; and opposition between divine and human perspectives is integrated into the dynamics of the situation. God's satisfaction of Gideon's repeated requests for proof generates Gideon's willingness to act as God's agent, and eventually his successful action. Gideon's victories, then, serve as the basis for his reversal from belief in God to belief in himself, leading the people yet farther astray.

Smaller ironies permeate this narrative. Gideon is originally named a 'hewer, a hacker' of wheat, which he does in hiding (Judg. 6.11). He is later re-named Jerubbaal, 'let Baal contend' (6.32), but Gideon contends with God, not with Baal. Gideon becomes a literal (not ironic) hacker of the enemy, and finally, ironically, a hacker of Israel. It is Gideon who receives more support from God than any other judge, and ironically it is Gideon as judge who does most harm to Israel.

Recalling the ideal of the Achsah-Othniel marital relationship, Gideon's *many wives* suggest ironic contrast, but it is Gideon's Shechemite concubine and his one son by that concubine that make the irony more pointed. The Shechemite son, whose very name—Abimelech, 'my father is king'—poses irony, proves to be an anti-judge, anti-hero (9.1-57). Instead of a divine spirit,

God imposes an evil spirit upon Abimelech. Although Abimelech is made king in an un-holy, anti-holy ceremony,[7] he neither rules over nor judges Israel; he only 'contends', which evokes his father's second name, Jerubbaal. The son's name ironically invokes the father, and the son's actions evoke the father's ironic actions.

With Abimelech, the oppressor is ironically not a foreign enemy but within the people. Abimelech slaughters his seventy brothers born of legitimate wives in a perverted act of sacrifice, 'on one stone', in contempt of covenantal restrictions against human sacrifice. Although one of Gideon's sons escapes the slaughter, he manages only to briefly address the people with a parable, which accuses them of not behaving honorably toward his father's family, before he flees for his life. Gideon's diminished honor has been crushed by dishonor, and his lineage disappears into anonymity. No future generations of Israel here.

After a series of brutal scenes, Abimelech's surge of destruction leads to his own death, ironically in the most demeaning way possible: at the hands of a 'certain', unnamed (implicitly insignificant) woman who happens to be on the city Tower and in the position to drop a millstone on his head (9.53).[8] The judge-led occupation of the land, so bright in the opening narratives, has reached its antithesis in the totally ironic figure of Abimelech.

After the darkness of Abimelech's narrative, the book of Judges introduces two 'minor' judges—Tola and Jair (10.1-5)—and with them a new paradigm for subsequent judges. Both judges are characterized by their blood lines, but in opposite ways. Tola is identified by the unexpected details of his clan genealogy, his *past*; and he lives out of his Issachar territory, a fair sign of lack of prosperity. Jair the Gileadite is particularized by details of his descendants, his *future* generations, and they are characterized in ways that suggest power—rank or wealth. This polarized orientation—toward being a member of the social group or toward power—suggests shifting values among the Israelites, personified by their judges. Jair's brief (three-verse) narrative also involves word play with 'asses' (עירים) and 'towns' (ער[י]ם), which establishes a light tone. Repetition of the number 'thirty' seems to equalize all the nouns so identified: sons, wild ass-colts, towns, all with the

---

7. Abimelech is made king under a 'planted' tree, or 'by a terebinth and a pillar' (see translations; 9.6), in ironic contrast to the natural and holy trees associated with Deborah (4.5) and Gideon (6.11).

8. The irony at Abimelech's death is even more complex. He is killed by the 'upper' millstone, the רכב (Heb. *rekeb*, 'riding' stone), identified as the 'male' stone, in the conventional superior position, active, crushing, as against the female millstone lying underneath it, the שכב (Heb. *šekeb*, 'lying' stone, term not found in the Hebrew Bible but only in post-biblical language). Abimelech, then, is in the female position, beneath the upper millstone that landed on him, and propelled there by a female. See also Job 31.10 for a similar analogy of women 'grinding' under a man.

name of Jair. Even the geographical sites identified with these two judges are in opposition: Shamir of Ephraim and חות יאיר (Havvoth Jair, 'Jair's Farms, Settlements') are on opposite sides of the Jordan and in north–south opposition. The narratives use the paradigm elements to opposite ends, and the clever irony of the contrasting judges offers a moment of respite for the reader before the more bleakly ironic path of the narratives continues.

The story of Jephthah (11.1-40) invokes allusions to the earlier Abimelech narrative for ironic effect.[9] Both Abimelech and Jephthah are sons of extramarital liaisons, but whereas Abimelech is legally recognized as Gideon's son, Jephthah, as son of a harlot, has neither legal standing nor paternal inheritance. Both men interact, in opposite ways, with their half-brothers: Abimelech by murdering them (oppressor) and Jephthah initially by being driven out by them (victim). Both men associate with 'worthless men', but whereas Abimelech ignores God and uses others' power for personal gain, Jephthah has the inner power of a 'great warrior' and gains outward power legally and before God. Repeated ironic contrast with Abimelech leads the reader to hope for a judge who can honorably save Israel. However, the development of the narrative invites that hope to dissipate into irony. If Abimelech's narrative is the most brutal, Jephthah's is the most pitiable.

The Jephthah narrative is riddled with ironies. At the opening of the book of Judges, Israel has not yet occupied the land, but God is active and involved in Israel's life. By the time Jephthah is judge, Israel has succeeded in occupying some territories, but it has lost its spiritual domain. Even when the people cry for help, God does not initially respond. It is the people, not God, who offer Jephthah leadership of the very townspeople who had, ironically, formerly denied him even membership in their community. Notably, Jephthah agrees to lead the Gileadites only after proper ritual before God at Mizpah. The name of the historical site, Mizpah, 'place of outlook' anticipates the evolving irony; for Jephthah, in one important sense, fails to 'look out, watch' both when he makes a vow and when he fulfills it; and Mizpah is not mentioned again after the sacrifice of Jephthah's daughter.

Instead of responding to the Ammonite threat with military counter-threat, Jephthah first attempts diplomacy. Jephthah's tactics are admirable, but when he justifies Israel's occupation of the land, he gets all his facts wrong, conflating Ammonite and Amorite historical figures, events and even national gods. The reader grasps the irony.

Confronted with war, Jephthah makes a conditional vow to God, valid only if Jephthah were to succeed in battle. As victor, Jepthhah fulfills his

---

9.   The narrative of Jephthah combines both the major and the minor Judge paradigms, but these patterns do not influence the irony. See Amit's comments on the 'shaping of the information concerning each judge and the distribution of the judges throughout the text…as a rhetorical tactic'; Amit 1998: 84-85.

vow, even though it is altogether unsuitable as an offering to God. Both the vow and the fulfillment emphasize Jephthah's ignorance (for instance, traditionally, an appeal to a priest would have resulted in an appropriate price of redemption; and cf. Valler's essay in this volume) or inflexibility. Jephthah's lack of knowledge of Israelite history is shown to be compounded by his lack of spiritual knowledge. His overt acts of devout worship are shown to be ironically superficial. As a personification of Israel, Jephthah's ignorance, his inability to comprehend his errors, and his displacing them onto the victim, are subtle comments on Israel's condition. If Jephthah is ignorant, his daughter is innocent. The distinction is moot.

Jephthah's act of human sacrifice misses the point of the tale of Abraham's readiness to sacrifice his son Isaac (Gen. 22.2; and cf. Greenstein and Feldman's essays in this volume): eventually that sacrifice was averted, substituted with an animal. Allusion to the Abraham story is ironic and devastating. Subsequent to the human sacrifice, God becomes silent and remains inactive during the remainder of Jephthah's tale. Jephthah continues in what the reader now recognizes as pious ignorance. Son of a harlot, without a father to educate him in the covenant between Israel and God, Jephthah's many desirable qualities are rendered null by the one element transmitted from father to son in order that it be renewed through education in covenant and history. Jephthah's ignorance of Israelite history is central to this book.

Following Jephthah, several very brief tales of minor judges (12.8-15) afford relief from the foregoing oppressive tone.[10] The report of Ibzan of Bethlehem is singular in the marriage of Ibzan's thirty sons and daughters with spouses from 'abroad'. This probably alludes to distant tribes rather than to near relations. Elon the Zebulonite is distinguished by his tribal identification and by having no negative quality associated with his brief tale. The third in this series, Abdon the son of Hillel the Pirathonite, bears the name of his father, but the father has already lost his tribal identification; he is member of a clan named after a geographical area. Abdon has continuity one generation past and two generations in the future, but the future generations decrease in number. When his full name is repeated, it is ironically almost empty of meaning.

In none of the minor judges' narratives is there mention of God. These judges are the founders of wealthy clans which bear their names; and the covenantal attributes of the major judges are replaced by the time-, place-, and value-limited ones of people who cannot 'judge' themselves but are said to 'judge' Israel.

With the progression of the narratives, God has tended to be ever less present, less verbal, less participating. The reader is unprepared for another

---

10.   Amit (1998: 83-85) suggests that the minor judges are 'minor' because their tales were reduced by the editor to serve rhetorical purposes.

visit, this time from a divine messenger, and is probably as surprised as Manoah's barren wife at the message he brings (ch. 13). Biblical annunciation is a recurrent motif, and the son born is expected to be as remarkable as its announcement. The theophany Manoah's wife witnesses (13.2-25) recalls that of Sarah, but merely for ironic comparison. Sarah bore Isaac, one of the esteemed patriarchs of tradition. Manoah's wife will bear Samson.

With this theophany, God does not appoint or inspire a judge, as in earlier narratives; this time, he announces the birth of a savior-to-be, a son—and constrained by nazirite prohibitions even prior to conception. Once again, the reader anticipates that a hero will be forthcoming. If the hero's life is determined by 'heroic origins', then I suggest the principle is used in a manner patently ironic in the Samson narrative (Norhnberg 1981: 36).

Although Samson's mother, Manoah's wife, is unnamed, she ironically understands more than her husband, who *is* afforded a name. Unnamed, she nevertheless becomes a secondary model for ideal woman within this narrative as well as an ideal receptacle for wondrous conception—and an ironic foil for the other female characters in the Samson narrative. Manoah, however, is depicted as a weak, 'unmanly' character. It is his wife who stills his fears at having seen Elohim (13.22). This unexpected, inverted association of name and character emphasizes the ironic element.

Samson (14.1–16.31) is a *nāzīr* to God, and therefore dedicated to him. However, Samson's dedication, like that of Israel, is one of appearances. Both Samson and Israel are more concerned with personal gratification, including worldly values, than the less tangible covenant; and Samson's episodes are each an ironic inversion of dedication to Israel and to God.

Samson betrays the reader's expectations on the most demeaning grounds. Each of the 'major' judges has demonstrated a basic weakness, but Samson's 'surpasses' them all. Samson is not 'conniving', like Ehud; he is not a gender-limited female, like Deborah; not self-serving, like Gideon; not an unscrupulous enemy, like anti-judge Abimelech; not unknowledgeable, like Jephthah. Ironically, Samson, the strong-man of the book, reveals himself as essentially the weakest, weaker than any of his predecessor judges, for Samson is a slave, subject to physical passion: the lowest kind of subjugation. And because his passions demand women, Samson is at the mercy of womankind, a deplorable situation from the viewpoint of a patriarchal society. This last hope of Israel is a judge who chases women instead of enemies, and who avenges only personal grievances.

The potential for interpersonal irony established in the first narrative of a judge only begins to find its ironic complement in the last narrative of a major judge in the book, the story of Samson. Othniel's Israel-centric heroic actions are rendered ironic by Samson's ego-centric pranks, with no regard for Israel. Instead of an Israelite wife, ideally a relative, Samson repeatedly seeks foreign women. When he does involve his parents in his desire for a wife, he *demands* that they 'get her for him as a wife' (14.2), in ironic contrast with the inter-generational authority and respect in the earlier narrative. Samson does not acknowledge his parents' protests; instead, he shares his transgression by giving them impure food, the honey taken from the carcass of a dead animal. Samson has no concern for generation and dies without heirs, a bitterly ironic inversion of Achsah's concern for land and water and their symbolic generational component.

Other women in this narrative also contribute to the ironic element. Samson's Timnite wife cajoles him into disclosing the solution of his riddle to avoid retribution from her clansmen, and ironically brings upon herself the very fate she fears. But Samson's wife and his Gazan whore are mere foils for Delilah, whom Samson loves. Samson (שמשון) whose name derives from שמש, *sun,* becomes dependent on Delilah (דלילה), whose name—according to some folk etymologies, or following the sound similarity, may allude to לילה, '*night*'. In this reading, these two names—the only ones, apart from that of Manoah, the father, that are provided in the entire Samson narrative—buttress the focus on the ironic polarity of day and night, man and woman: Samson, the son/sun of Israel, and Delilah, the night of foreign womanhood.

In each of the earlier narratives, the judges are implicitly judged by God and the reader is an observer. In Samson's narrative, following all the expectations generated by the annunciation and nazirite consecration, the reader is fully drawn into the role of the ironist; it is the reader who must perceive the irony that Samson is blind to. As God is knowledgeable and Israel is victim, the reader is knowledgeable about Samson, and Samson is victim. Israel is reflected in Samson's foolish ways, and the reader must judge Samson as God has judged Israel.

With Samson, the period of judges has come to an end and the actions of the following narratives tend to evolve more from the actions taken within individual relationships than from leadership. The relationship between Micah and his mother (ch. 17) is immediately depicted as corrupt—not only by Micah's having stolen silver from his mother but also by her reaction: she blesses him for returning it and then 'consecrates' the returned silver to God—in the form of idols. Irony is piled on irony: Micah's 'house of gods' acquires a series of 'priests', and the idols are then stolen—complete with his Levite priest—by Danites, whom Micah has earlier hosted. Even the guest tradition has been subverted for personal purposes (ch. 18).[11] It is notable that

---

11. A coda paradigm, which appears between narrative shifts, adds to the irony: 'And there was no king in Israel; each man did [what was] right in his own eyes' offers an ironic opposition to the tribal, communal ethos described in the opening chapters.

the action generated by Micah's theft is the impetus for the sequence of narrative threads in the resolution: all the ensuing evil began with that theft, and it is theft between a son and his mother that leads to further theft.

The tribe of Dan conquers the peaceful city (irony here) of Laish and establishes there a house of god to house the graven image stolen from Micah. It is at this point that we learn the identity of the Levite priest: he is Jonathan, the son of Gershom, the son of Manasseh: 'he and his sons were priests to the tribe of the Danites...' (18.30). What bitter irony that a descendant of Joseph has come to this. And this is Israel.

With the coda phrase,[12] the narrative shifts once again (19.1-26), this time to another Levite, another member of the priestly tribe. This unnamed Levite pursues his concubine to her father's house, agrees to prolong his visit at his father-in-law's house, and overnights in Gibeah, a Benjaminite town, on his return. As an alien guest of an old man, the Levite is put in the position of Lot in the narrative of Sodom (Genesis 19). 'Sons of worthless men' come to the old man's house and demand to know the Levite guest for sexual purposes (Judg. 19.22). The outcome is ironic: instead of (1) behaving as a guest and (2) protecting his concubine, the Levite thrusts his concubine out the door to the men. The men rape the concubine all night; at dawn, she falls at the door of the old man's house. The mute echo of the Levite's original intention, 'to speak to her heart to bring her back', (19.3) is a cruelly ironic inversion of the Levite's actions.

The Levite is not moved by *her* pitiful image. He is, apparently, moved by the loss of *his* concubine: he brings her home, cuts her into twelve pieces and sends her parts to all Israel, to the twelve tribes, to protest the dastardly acts of the sons of Gibeah.

At his questioning by the heads of the tribes of Israel, the Levite offers his interpretation of the events, neglecting to mention his part in the woman's humiliation and death. In all of this, the reader is aware of distortions of the truth, of questions that should be asked, of hasty decisions by the Israelite tribes. The reader has become the ironist, the only party to the story—apart from the narrator—to know all the elements of the actions.

The social paradigm is evoked again, following the trial (20.1-14), at this development of the resolution. When the tribes of Israel unite to battle the tribe of Benjamin (20.12-21), the sons of Israel go up to Bethel and ask of God, 'Who shall go up for us at the beginning of the battle with Benjamin?' (20.18). As at the beginning of Judges, God once again tells them that Judah should go up—but the remainder of the phrase does not confirm victory here, as it did in the original response. Their asking seems irrelevant. As in the original Q and A between the Israelites and God (1.1), the Israelites ignore God's words: 'And the men of Israel went to battle with Benjamin' (20.20).

---

12. The phrase is shortened here. See Klein 1988: 143 for the coda pattern.

That war leads to some Benjaminites remaining without wives (21.1-25), as the other tribes had vowed not to give their daughters to the rebel tribe. The solution they find is to murder all the males of the town (Jabesh-Gilead) that had not assembled for the judgment, and to save the virgins. This is a massacre; the virgins are allotted as sexual objects and child-bearers. When even this solution fails to provide a wife for each of the remaining Benjaminites, the Israelites complain (instead of pray) to God, and they devise a loophole in their vows: they will not *give* their daughters but allow the Benjaminites to *take* them. Virgins, dancing at a festival, are seized and taken away. 'Instead of generosity between the generations, there is war; instead of fertility, there is murder of the men, women and children of a city; instead of a betrothal, there is kidnap and rape. The book has reversed its initial premises, its original focus has been ironically and brutally contradicted' (Klein 1988: 190).

The title given to this biblical book by its editors, simply שׁופטים (Judges), is more profound than a mere reference to a series of tales about some savior 'judges' (Driver 1913: 160). The sequence of narratives leads the reader to a position of knowledge with regard to these narratives, and to recognize the irony is to partake of judgment.

This summary has not even begun to exhaust the incidence of irony throughout the book of Judges. However, I shall refrain from recounting further details, and instead would like to recapitulate the ironic structure. The book opens with an exposition that provides two ideal models for Israel: individual (in interpersonal relationships) and social (in battle and subsequent Israelite behavior). The series of major judges dramatizes a variety of ironic deviations from the social paradigms and incorporates allusions to other biblical books, in what seems like ironic purposes. These narratives ironically refract the 'major judges' formula established in the exposition. Samson, the last 'judge' and in fact a minor[13] one despite the comparatively lengthy novella about him, adds an extreme level of irony on the social level, and introduces irony on the individual level.

The paradigm of individual relationships established in the exposition is evoked with increasing frequency in the post-Samson narratives of Judges. The honor and respect shown between Achsah and her father is ridiculed in the narrative of Micah, whose name (probably short for Micaiahu, 'Who is like God') is proven by his actions to be ironic. The honor with which Achsah is given as a bride to Othniel is rendered horrific when the Levite takes a distant (not related) woman as concubine (a secondary, not a chief wife), pursues her to her father's home, to which she has fled; then, having retrieved her, offers her to the Gibeaites for sexual abuse which proves

---

13. The minor judges' narratives likewise exhibit a characteristic formula.

to be deadly; and, finally, brutally dismembers her. Instead of intergenerational understanding and reproduction, this relationship leads to civil war and death.

The resolution focuses primarily on ironic reversal in relationships, familial and tribal, and the ethical morass at the conclusion of the book of Judges is emphasized by its ironic allusion to the ideals of the exposition. As Jephthah's narrative emphasizes, the irony which pervades the text informs the history '...which educates the people, especially the community of readers throughout the generations, to understand history as a chain of events reflecting the dialogue between God and his people, reality as a compromise between the divine will and human behavior, and the responsibility of man or the people in determining their destiny' (Amit 1998: 59).

Truly, the book of Judges is a remarkable example of the art of irony in a 'newly historical perspective'.

Bibliography

Amit, Y.
   1998   *The Book of Judges: The Art of Editing* (trans. Jonathan Chipman; Leiden: E.J. Brill).

Brooks, C.
   1993   'Irony', in Alex Preminger and T.V.F. Brogan (eds.), *The New Princeton Encyclopedia of Poetry and Poetics* (Princeton, NJ: Princeton University Press).

Driver, S.R.
   1913   *Introduction to the Literature of the Old Testament* (ITL; Edinburgh: T. & T. Clark, 9th edn).

Klein, L.R.
   1988   *The Triumph of Irony in the Book of Judges* (Sheffield: Almond Press).

Norhnberg, J.
   1981   'Moses', in Burke O. Long (ed.), *Images of Man and God: Old Testament Short Stories in Literary Focus* (Sheffield: Almond Press): 35-57.

GOD'S VICTORY OVER 'THE OLDEN GODS':
THEOLOGICAL CORRECTIONS IN DEUTERONOMY 33.12, 27

Israel Knohl

I offer this study as a token of appreciation and friendship to Professor Yairah Amit. Yairah is for me not only a colleague in biblical research and education, from whose scholarly methods I have learned much, but also an admirable and inspiring person in her way of life. Her joy in life, courage in coping with problems and impediments, capacity for friendship, and her ability to compliment and encourage—all these qualities and attitudes add up to a singular personality.

Deuteronomy 33.26-27, which is part of the 'Blessings of Moses', contains elements which are familiar to us from Ugaritic and Phoenician myth. In the first verse God is described as 'The Rider of the Heavens', רכב שׁמים, 'Riding through the heavens' (NJPSV), a title which reminds us of the title of Baal in the Ugaritic texts, *rkb 'rpt*, 'The Rider of the Clouds' (Weinfeld 1973). The next verse reads in the MT as follows: מעֹנָה אלהי קדם ומתחת זרעת עולם, 'The ancient God is a refuge, A support are the arms everlasting' (NJPSV).

There are some difficulties in this version: The form מעֹנָה is not known elsewhere and it is difficult to understand the meaning of the expression ומתחת זרעת עולם. Gaster (1947: 60) and Seeligmann (1964: 76, 87) have suggested to read מְעַנֵּה 'who humbles', instead of מעֹנָה and ומחתת זרעת עולם, 'and shatters all time-honored might' (Gaster 1947: 56), instead of ומתחת זרעת עולם. According to this reading, the verse describes the defeat of the gods of Canaan by Yahweh. Of course, קדם and עולם are designations of the old days in biblical Hebrew.

The picture of a younger god who struggles with the older generation is familiar to us from various myths in the ancient Near East and ancient Greece. The young god fights with an older god and castrates or kills him. After his victory, the younger god is declared as the king by the divine assembly (Cross 1998: 73-82). It seems that the 'Blessings of Moses' use this model and rework it: Yahweh, the God of Israel, battles and defeats the gods of Canaan and the earthly enemies of Israel (33.27, 29). The divine assembly is replaced here by the assembly of the tribes of Israel which proclaims Yahweh as their King (33.5; Seeligmann 1964: 83; Tigay 1996: 322).

Apparently the picture of the fight of Yahweh, the God of Israel, with the gods of Canaan, caused theological problems for later generations who wished to see Yahweh as the only existing god. This is probably the reason of the corrections which were made in v. 27.[1]

In my view, similar corrections are reflected in various versions of Deut. 33.12, the blessing of Benjamin. The MT reads:

ידיד יהוה ישכן לבטח עליו חפף עליו כל־היום ובין כתיפיו שכן

The version reflected in the Septuagint and partly attested in 4QDeut[h] (Duncan 1995a: 68; 1995b: 277-79) is:

ידיד יהוה ישכן לבטח אל[3] חפף[2] עליו כל היום ובין כתיפיו שכן

The Samaritan version is:[4]

יד יד יהוה ישכן לבטח וחופף עליו כל היום ובין כתפתיו שכן

I can see a reason for the change from the Masoretic version to the other versions but not for a change in the other way. Hence, it seems to me that the Masoretic version is the original one. The Masoretic version should be structured in the following way:

ידיד יהוה, ישכן לבטח עליו, חפף עליו כל־היום, ובין כתיפיו שכן

The verse sees Benjamin as God's beloved. It further states that God[5] dwells safely on[6] His beloved Benjamin. God hovers[7] over him all day as he (God)[8] dwells between his (Benjamin's)[9] shoulders.

1. Similar corrections were discussed by Goldstein 2004.
2. In the Qumran fragment we probably have here מחופף.
3. The discovery of the Qumran fragment with the reading אל refutes previous suggestions of various scholars who assumed that the Septuagint had here עלי or עליון. For a summary of previous discussions see Heck 1984: 524-25.
4. Tal and Florentin 1994: 617.
5. The word יהוה has here a dual function: it is part of the expression ידיד יהוה but it also serves as the subject of the phrase יהוה ישכן לבטח עליו.
6. This understanding fits with the plain and regular meaning of the word עליו. Those who want to understand the words ישכן לבטח עליו as referring to Benjamin's dwelling, are obliged to translate עליו as 'beside Him' or 'alongside Him'. However, as was correctly noted by Tigay (1996: 326) this goes against the usual meaning of עליו.
7. See Qimron 1979.
8. As was correctly noted by Avishur (1980: 131-32), the image here describes God as a bird who dwells between Benjamin shoulders and protects him. Avishur rightly pointed to the image of King Khafre who is protected by Horus symbolically represented as a hawk which stands between the King's shoulders. The argument of Korpel (1990: 95-96) that Benjamin is described here like a child who is carried between the shoulders of his mother, is not convincing: As shown by the image of King Khafre, one can be protected by a deity which stand between his shoulders.

There is a double use of the verb שכן here, both times with regard to God's dwelling on the territory of Benjamin. As customary in biblical poetry, the second mention gives more information: God dwells among the 'shoulders' of Benjamin, probably a reference to the mountain slopes[10] of the territory of Benjamin.

The theological difficulty in this verse is the use of the phrase ישכן לבטח, indicating God's dwelling on Benjamin. As was correctly pointed out by Tigay (1996: 408 n. 86), the other occurrences of this expression[11] always refer to humans and not to God. The very statement that God dwells safely is connected with the image of primeval times when he was insecure because of a threat from other Gods. This is an impossible image for most biblical sources. However, this goes very well with the image that is expressed in the concluding verses of this poem. As was noted above, the original version of Deut. 33.27 probably described the defeat of the gods of Canaan by Yahweh. It is only after this defeat that Yahweh can rest safely. In the same fashion, the tribes of Israel can rest safely only after the defeat of their enemies (vv. 27-29).

However, this image seemed difficult to late editors who have corrected it in two different ways:

1. In the version reflected in the Septuagint and partly attested in the Qumran fragment, the first occurrence of the word עליו was replaced by the word אל. This correction leads to a change of the syntactic structure of this verse:

ידיד יהוה ישכן לבטח, אל חפף עליו כל־היום, ובין כתיפיו שכן

According to this reading, it is Benjamin who dwells safely, not God.

2. The Samaritan version has a similar aim but it goes in a different way: The word ידיד is split up into יד יד. The first occurrence of the word עליו was dropped without any replacement. It seems that the expression, יד יד יהוה ישכן לבטח should be translated as: 'He (Benjamin) dwells safely in the place of God's hand'. The understanding of the first יד as a place,[12] is based on the evidence of an ancient Samaritan Dictionary.[13] This reading can be compared in my view to Isa. 49.2, בצל ידו החביאני ('He hid me in the shadow of His hand', NJPSV), and it fits in very well with the continuation of

---

9.   See Tigay 1996: 326.

10.   See the frequent mention of כתף in the description of Benjamin's territory in Josh. 18.12-19.

11.   See Deut. 33.28, Jer. 23.6; 33.16; Ps. 16.9; Prov. 1.33.

12.   Ben Hayyim (1957–77, III, 1: 162) has suggested to understand the whole expression as a reference to God's place. The interpretation 'God's hand place' was suggested to me by Professor M. Florentin.

13.   Ben Hayyim, 1957–77, II: 479.

the verse וחופף עליו כל היום.[14] Following this split of ידיד and the reading of
the first יד as a place description, there was no more room for the first עליו
which was dropped. Once again, the result is a change of the parsing of this
verse:

יד יד יהוה ישכן לבטח, וחופף עליו כל היום, ובין כתפתיו שכן

According to this version too, it is Benjamin who dwells safely, not God.

Yehezkel Kaufmann argued (1960: 62) that 'There is no biblical parallel to
pagan myths relating to the defeat of other gods by younger; no other gods
are presented in primordial times'. However, it seems that the original
version of the 'Blessing of Moses' was an exceptional case. According to this
version, Yahweh had to defeat the old generation of the Gods:

מענה אלהי קדם ומחתת זרעת עולם

Only after his victory over the olden gods could Yahweh dwell safely. Thus,
these corrections in Deut. 33.12, 27 were meant to bring the text of the
'Blessing of Moses', with its archaic theological conception, into harmony
with the main line of the Hebrew Bible.

Bibliography

Avishur, Yitshak
    1980   'Expressions of the Type *byn ydym* in the Bible and Semitic Languages',
            UF 12: 125-33.
Ben Hayyim, Zeev
    1957–77 *The Literary and Oral Tradition of Hebrew and Aramaic amongst the
             Samaritans* (5 vols.; Jerusalem: The Academy of the Hebrew Language).
Cross, Frank M.
    1998   *From Epic to Canon: History and Literature in Ancient Israel* (Baltimore:
            The Johns Hopkins University Press).
Duncan, Julie Ann
    1995a   '4QDeut^h^', in E. Ulrich c.s., *Qumran Cave 4, IX. Deuteronomy, Joshua,
            Judges, Kings* (DJD, XIV; Oxford: Clarendon Press): 61-70.
    1995b   'New Readings for the "Blessing of Moses" from Qumran', *JBL* 114:
            275-92.
Gaster, Theodor H.
    1947   'An Ancient Eulogy on Israel: Deuteronomy 33:3-5, 26-29', *JBL* 66
            53-62.
Goldstein, Ronnie
    2004   'From Gods to Idols', *Beer-Sheva* 18: 115-56 (Hebrew).
Heck, J.D.
    1984   'The Missing Sanctuary of Deut. 33:12', *JBL* 103: 523-29.

14.   It seems that the adding of the ו at the beginning of וחופף was meant to strength
the connection between the two parts of the verse.

Kaufmann, Yehezkel

1960   *The Religion of Israel, from its Beginnings to the Babylonian Exile* (trans. and abridged by Moshe Greenberg; Chicago: University of Chicago Press).

Korpel, Marjo C.A

1990   *A Rift in the Clouds: Ugarit and Hebrew Descriptions of the Divine* (Münster: Ugarit Verlag).

Qimron, Elisha

1979   '"חפף עליו כל־היום" (Deut. 33.12)', *BM* 24: 140-41 (Hebrew with English Summary).

Seeligmann, I.L.

1999   'A Psalm from Pre-Regal Times', *VT* 14: 75-92.

Tal, Avraham, and Moshe Florentin (eds.)

1994   *The Pentateuch: The Samaritan Version and the Masoretic Version* (Tel Aviv: Tel Aviv University, The Chaim Rosenberg School of Jewish Studies).

Tigay, Jeffrey H.

1996   *Deuteronomy* (JPS Torah Commentary, 5; Philadelphia: Jewish Publication Society).

Weinfeld, Moshe

1973   '"Rider of the Clouds" and "Gatherer of the Clouds"', *JANES* 5: 421-26.

ROADS THAT CONFIGURE THE SPACE
IN BIBLICAL NARRATIVES

Nadav Na'aman

Introduction

Topographical designations play a major role in the configuration of the space in biblical historiography. Many stories relate events that took place in areas well known to their intended readers. For these readers, clarifying the plot within the narrated area required the insertion of some topographical details. Thus, for example, the inhabitants of Jerusalem and Benjamin were acquainted with the areas in which many of the Saul and David story-cycles took place, and their authors inserted concrete topographical details for the readers' orientation. Similarly, the authors of north Israelite narratives, such as the pre-Deuteronomistic Judges story-cycle, included some environmental details, so that their intended readers could follow the plot and better understand the heroes' achievements.

Readers' orientation within a well-known narrated space is only one reason for including topographical details in biblical historiography. Equally important is that the topographical elements support the authenticity of the narrated events, thereby also the transmission of religious and theological messages they conveyed. The stories were part of the history of the people of Israel, and history represents the kind of writing designed—at least in theory—to record the events of the past 'as they really happened'. Biblical history is mainly transmitted by a chain of stories, which in combination amounts to the history of the people. Each story formed a link in the historical sequence, so its validity and coherence were important for the historical credibility of the whole, as well as the transmitted religious messages. We may conclude that the addition of topographical details was necessary both for understanding the plot in its setting, and as a means of creating the perception of authenticity for the story as a link in the story-cycle.

The role of topographical designations in biblical stories was studied in a programmatic article by Yairah Amit (1985). The focus of her study was literary and she examined the ways place-names defined the space in various genres and different kinds of historiographical compositions. Some scholars suggested that the aspect of space plays only a secondary or even marginal role in biblical narratives, but Amit demonstrated that the picture is more complex and diversified. Some authors included many topographical details in order to emphasize the historicity of the narrative, others put in few toponyms or left the physical background obscure, while still others deliberately blurred the geographical mapping to emphasize the fictive nature of their stories. Topographical indications might occupy a central place in the plot (e.g. the Naboth's vineyard story, 1 Kings 21), or even serve as a central element of the story (e.g. the story of the outrage of Gibeah, Judges 19). Amit's study presents a comprehensive map of the topographical indications and their literary functions in biblical historiography, but since it was published only in Hebrew it did not gain the attention it deserves.

The historical investigation of biblical stories necessarily involves a combination of literary analysis with the study of the topographical reality. Our ability to properly analyze the topographical details and understand the depicted reality depends (*inter alia*) on the integration of the topographical elements in the plot, the survival of the mentioned toponyms in modern toponymy and a good knowledge of the arena in which the story takes place. These issues will be illustrated in the study of several episodes in the following two parts of the article. Let me open by presenting a case-study that illustrates the importance of understanding the historical reality at the time when a story was written for understanding the narrated topographical details.

The Tribe of Benjamin in the Ehud Story

The literary quality, the messages and the possible historical background of the story of Ehud (Judg. 3.12-30) have been studied many times by commentators and scholars,[1] and its geographical details were recently discussed in detail by Gass (2005: 220-28, with earlier literature; 2008). The point that I would like to make is that the tribe of Benjamin referred to in the story encompassed only the inhabitants of that part of the district of Benjamin that was included in the Northern Kingdom. The historical situation reflected in the story is that of the time of writing, very likely in the eighth century BCE, when Moab governed the area called in biblical historiography 'the plains of Moab', east of the Jordan, and Jericho was located on Moab's border (Na'aman 2007: 168; Gass 2008: 43-44). Whether, following the conquest of 'the plains of Moab', Moabite troops crossed the Jordan and tried to expand westwards, is not known. In the exposition of the story, the author described a Moabite offensive from the east, in the course of which Israel was defeated

---

1. The literary quality and messages of the story of Ehud were studied in great detail by Yairah Amit (1999a: 171-98; 1999b: 71-79). See also Becker 1990: 107-22; Gunn 2005: 34-52; Gross 2009: 224-48, with earlier literature.

and Jericho ('the city of palm trees') was conquered (vv. 12-13). Eglon, the king of Moab, resided in the captured city and received tribute from the Israelites. The Benjaminite toponyms mentioned in the story are the city of Jericho and the cult place of Gilgal (vv. 19, 26). After killing Eglon, Ehud escaped to Seirah, a descriptive designation for the wooded, mountainous uninhabited area ('the shaggy mountain') of Mount Ephraim (Na'aman 1992: 288). He then assembled the inhabitants of Mount Ephraim (v. 27), north of the district of Benjamin, crossed the fords of the Jordan, smote the fleeing Moabites and seized the territory west of the Jordan (vv. 28-29). It is clear that the story was composed in the Kingdom of Israel and all the topographical elements included in the plot pertain to the territory of that kingdom. Ehud, although described as a Benjaminite of the family of Gera (v. 15), was a north-Israelite saviour, similar to all other saviours named in the pre-Deuteronomistic story-cycle of the book of Judges.

The Role of Roads for Configuring the Space in Biblical Narratives

The 'way of Beth-horon' was the most important road that rose from the northern Shephelah to the central hill country (Oelgarte 1918; Aharoni 1967: 55; Peterson 1992: 688-89). It passed from Gezer to Aijalon, climbed via the pass that connects Lower and Upper Beth-horon, and northwest of Gibeon split into two branches. One branch turned northeast, toward Mizpah (Tell en-Naṣbeh) and/or Zemaraim (Rās el-Ṭaḥûneh),[2] and continued southeast to Mount Bethel and Michmash, or north, along the longitudinal south-to-north road, toward Shechem. The other branch continued southeast, passed near Gibeon and reached Ramah (er-Ram), and turned south toward Jerusalem (Oelgarte 1918: 73-79 and Pl. 6).

The 'way of Beth-horon' is explicitly mentioned in 1 Sam. 13.18, a text that relates the march of a Philistine raiding force from Michmash westward. The ascent of Beth-horon is mentioned in Josh. 10.10, and the descent of Beth-horon in v. 11. The Gezer-Aijalon-Beth-horon road appears as Ephraim's southern border, running from Beth-horon westward to Gezer and the sea (Josh. 16.3, 5-6a). The topographical list of Shishak names the following group of four toponyms: Aijalon, Gittaim, Beth-horon and Gibeon (Nos. 23-26). The town of Zemaraim is mentioned in another column (No. 57). Shishak's list indicates that the Egyptians entered the hill country by the ascent of Beth-horon, reached Gibeon and continued to the highlands of Benjamin and the southernmost district of Mount Ephraim.

---

2. Zemaraim was probably the southernmost Israelite town, located over against Mizpah (Tell en-Naṣbeh), the northernmost Judahite town on the border with Israel. It was located near one of the crossroads of the Beth-horon road with the longitudinal south to north road that connected Jerusalem and Shechem.

The road that descends eastward from Zemaraim and Michmash to Jericho was detected in the excavations and surveys conducted in this area (Mazar, Amit and Ilan 1996: 193-211). Its westernmost section is mentioned in the description of Saul's struggle with the Philistines, according to which a Philistine raiding force 'took the border road overlooking the Valley of Hyenas toward the wilderness' (1 Sam. 13.18). The road is schematically delineated in the description of Benjamin's northern border (Josh. 18.12-13a) and the Josephites' southeastern border (Josh. 16.1). It is evident that the southern boundary of the biblical allotment of Ephraim (Josh. 16.1-5) follows the roads that led from the Jericho area to Mount Bethel and then descended along the way of Beth-horon to Gezer. The ascending and descending roads roughly correspond to the southern border of the Kingdom of Israel with Judah. Israel dominated the Jericho-Michmash-Zemaraim-Beth-horon-Gezer road, and the territory of the Kingdom of Judah extended south of it, with the towns of Mizpah and Geba located on Judah's northern and northeastern borders with Israel, Mizpah against Zemaraim and Geba against Michmash (see 1 Sam. 13.16).

Another road passed from Jerusalem to the northern end of the Dead Sea, along the route of the later Roman Road (see map in Mazar, Amit and Ilan 1996: 194). It passed through the 'ascent of Adummim' and roughly overlapped the tribe of Judah's northern border (Josh. 15.6-8) and Benjamin's southern border (18.16-19a). It is called 'the way of the Arabah' (Arabah = the plains of Jericho) in three biblical texts that describe the failed escape of Zedekiah after the fall of Jerusalem (2 Kgs 25.4; Jer. 39.4; 52.7).

The identity of biblical tribal boundaries with ancient roads is quite expected, remembering that the tribal allotments were artificial entities possibly drawn in the late monarchical period for historiographical purposes (see Lissovsky and Na'aman 2003, with earlier literature). The author of the boundary system was bound by his own decision where to draw the borders, and main routes were natural candidates for marking their outlines. The border between Ephraim and Manasseh (Josh. 16.6aβ-8a; 17.7-9), like the border between Benjamin and Ephraim, was probably drawn along the main latitudinal roads in this area. Also the boundaries of Zebulun's allotment (Josh. 19.10-14) and the border between the inheritances of Issachar and Naphtali (19.22, 33) passed along ancient roads (Lissovsky and Na'aman 2003: 306-309). The southern boundary of Judah's allotment (Josh. 15.1b-4) was possibly marked on desert routes that led from southern Judah to the region of Kadesh-barnea and hence to southern Philistia (Lissovsky and Na'aman 2003: 304). Once scholars abandon the old notion that the tribal inheritances reflect the reality of the pre-monarchical or early monarchical period, and the obsolete idea that the delineation of the borders was based on archival sources (still held by Wazana 2007: 249-65), the contribution of the tribal allotments to the reality of their author's time will become apparent.

Among the most important contributions of the tribal system is its reflection of the road system at the time of compilation, including the ascending and descending roads connecting the central hill country in the eighth-seventh centuries BCE.

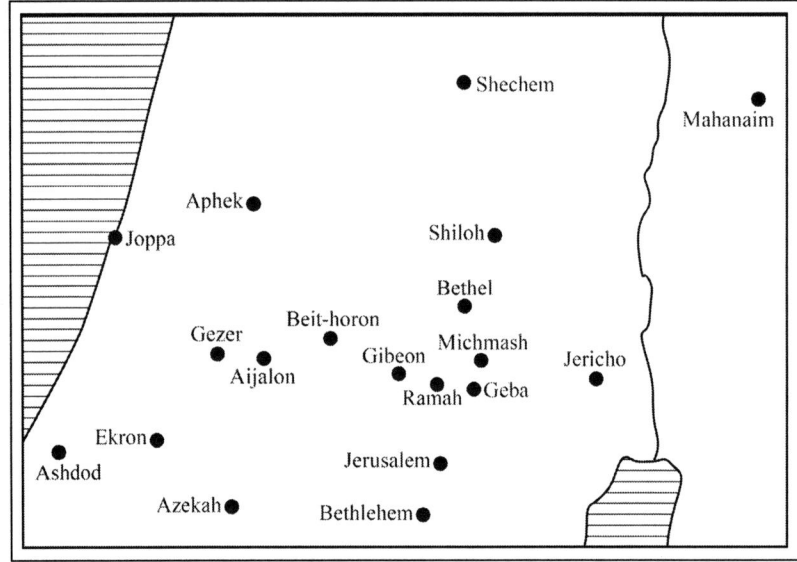

Figure 1. *Places mentioned*

I suggest that the familiarity of the intended readers with the road system in the area north of Jerusalem enabled the biblical narrators to mark the routes by only a few toponyms, and that the territorial picture the latter had in mind was clear to the readers. Let me illustrate this by some examples:

1. Following the Gibeonites' appeal to Joshua to come to their aid (Josh. 10.6), Joshua, 'having marched up all night from Gilgal' (v. 9), attacked and defeated the coalition of Amorite kings at Gibeon. He chased them all the way to the ascent of Beth-horon and as far as Azekah and Makkedah. He then addressed Yhwh with the famous words, 'Sun, stand thou still at Gibeon and thou Moon in the valley of Aijalon' (v. 12). It is clear that the author has in mind the roads that ascended from Jericho/Gilgal via Michmash to Gibeon and descended from Gibeon to the Aijalon-Gezer area. The mentioned toponyms were all it took for the readers to comprehend the course of the related battle.

2. The road that goes up from the northern Shephelah to the hill country is described several times in the story-cycles of Samuel, Saul and David. The city of Aphek, located on the border of the Kingdom of Israel with Philistia, and after the Assyrian conquest

and the annexation of Israel on the southwestern border of the Assyrian province of Samerīna,[3] was presented as the point of departure for the Philistine campaigns against Israel (1 Sam. 4.1; 29.1). The Israelites are described as marching by the way of Beth-horon and halting for battle in Eben-ezer, over against Aphek (4.1-4). After their second defeat, they escaped by ascending the Beth-horon road toward Benjamin (v. 12). Eli, anxiously waiting to hear the results of the battle, sat 'by the Mizpah [*sic*] road' (v. 13), the latter town being the point of departure for the south to north longitudinal road leading from Benjamin to Shiloh.

3. According to the story of the battle at Mizpah (1 Sam. 7.7-11), the Philistines marched along the Beth-horon road and attacked the Israelites at Mizpah. After their defeat, they must have escaped along the Beth-horon road, the Israelites chasing and smiting them 'as far as below Beth-car', a toponym that might be sought near the western end of the road.

4. In the battle of Michmash (1 Samuel 13–14) the Philistines marched along the Beth-horon way up to Michmash, located on the road that descends to Gilgal, where Saul's troops assembled for battle (13.4-5). After deploying for battle, Saul ascended by the Jericho-Ramah road and stopped in Geba (v. 15). The Israelite and Philistine troops encamped on the two sides of the Judahite-Israelite ninth–eighth-centuries' border, the former on the Judahite and the latter on the Israelite side. Having been defeated in the battle of Michmash, the Philistines retreated 'from Michmash to Aijalon' (14.31), a merism referring to the main road that connected the two places.

5. In the story of the contest at Flints' Field and the death of Asael (2 Sam. 2.12-32), Abner's troops marched along the Jordan rift from Mahanaim to Gilgal/Jericho and climbed the hill country up to Gibeon. Following their defeat in battle they retreated, reaching 'the hill of Ammah (*'mh*), which is opposite Giah (*gyh*), by the way of the wilderness of Gibeon' (v. 24). The identification of the last-mentioned toponym with Gibeon (el-Jîb) is problematic, as the latter is located in western Benjamin, far from the desert. Scholars noted that Hebrew *'ammâ* means 'water channel' and *gîah* means 'spring' (see McCarter 1984: 97). Elitzur (1994: 21-24) pointed out that 'the great waters which is at Gibeon' mentioned in Jer. 41.12 was located

---

3. Note its description in Esarhaddon's campaign to Egypt in 671 BCE: '...a distance of 30 double-hours from the town of Apqu (Aphek), which is in the district of Same<ri>na, as far as the town of Rapihu (Raphia)' (Borger 1967: 112 line 16). Aphek is also mentioned as the last station before Philistia in the late seventh-century Aramaic letter of Adon, probably the king of Ekron, to the Pharaoh: '[The force] of the king of Babylon has come (and) reached Aphek' (Porten 2003: 133 line 4).

on the escape route from Mizpah to the Kingdom of Ammon. Gibeon (el-Jîb) does not fit Ishmael's line of escape. He therefore suggested that there were two different places named Gibeon and that the Gibeon mentioned in 2 Sam. 2.12-13, 24 and Jer. 41.12 refers to a second city called by this name. He located it at Kh. el-Marjameh, in the southeastern highlands of Ephraim (for the site, see Mazar 1982: 171-73; 1992: 174-93).

Although the proposed identification of the Gibeon of 2 Samuel 2 and Jeremiah 41 as Kh. el-Marjameh is unlikely, the assumption that there was a second place called by this name, located on the main road from Michmash or Geba to Gilgal/Jericho, is possible. If this indeed is the case, I tentatively suggest the flowing stream of 'Ein el-Fara, located on the route that descends from Geba to Jericho, as the best candidate for the second Gibeon. From this place Abner and his troops descended to Jericho and proceeded through the 'Arabah', passing along the ravine' (*btrwn*), and arrived at Mahanaim (2 Sam. 2.29).

6. Following David's anointment as king of Israel, the Philistines marched to Jerusalem by the Beth-horon road and at Ramah advanced southward, toward Bethlehem. The battle took place in the valley of Rephaim and David won it by a frontal attack (2 Sam. 5.17-21; 1 Chron. 14.8-12). The second battle apparently took place near Gibeon and David launched a surprise night attack and smote the Philistines 'from Gibeon to Gezer' (1 Chron. 14.16; see 2 Sam. 5.25), a merism that refers to the way of Beth-horon (see Na'aman 1994: 253-54, with earlier literature).

7. The final example is that of David's escape from Jerusalem after Absalom's rebellion (2 Samuel 15–17). The author describes in great detail David's march in the district of Jerusalem, whereas the rest of the route before the arrival to Mahanaim is given only in general terms (17.16 'steps of the wilderness'; 17.22, the Jordan).

In sum, ancient roads had an important function in configuring the space in various biblical narratives. The road system was well known to the intended readers and the narrators could refer to them either by naming a few toponyms located along their course, or by using a merism, such as 'from Michmash to Aijalon' or 'from Gibeon to Gezer'. These short descriptions were sufficient for the readers to visualize the course of the narrated campaigns and to grasp the environmental reality of the stories. The economical use of the topographical elements need not indicate their secondary role in the plot, but rather the well-conceived presentation of the space by the authors, who were aware of the readers' acquaintance with the environmental reality and shaped their stories in accordance with the latter's perception of the space.

Bibliography

Aharoni, Y.
    1967   *The Land of the Bible: A Historical Geography* (Philadelphia: Westminster Press).

Amit, Yairah
    1985   'The Function of Topographical Indications in the Biblical Story', *Shnaton: An Annual for Biblical and Ancient Near Eastern Studies* 9: 15-30 (Hebrew with summary in English).
    1999a   *The Book of Judges: The Art of Editing* (trans. Jonathan Chipman; Biblical Interpretation Series, 38; Leiden: E.J. Brill).
    1999b   *Judges: Introduction and Commentary* (Mikra Leyisra'el; Jerusalem: Magnes Press [Hebrew]).

Becker, U.
    1990   *Richterzeit und Königtum: Redaktionsgeschichtliche Studien zum Richterbuch* (BZAW, 192; Berlin/New York: W. de Gruyter).

Borger, Rykle
    1967   *Die Inschriften Asarhaddons, Königs von Assyrien* (AfO Beiheft, 9; Osnabrück: Biblio-Verlag).

Elitzur, Y.
    1994   'A New Suggested Identification of the Israelite City at 'Ain es-Samiyeh', *Judea and Samaria Studies* 3: 17-28 (Hebrew).

Gass, E.
    2005   *Die Ortsnamen des Richterbuchs in historischer und redaktioneller Perspektive* (ADPV, 35; Wiesbaden: Harrassowitz).
    2008   'Zur Ehud-Tradition in historisch-topographischer Hinsicht', *ZDPV* 124: 38-50.

Gaster, Theodor H.
    1981   *Myth, Legend, and Custom in the Old Testament*, II (Gloucester, MA: Peter Smith).

Gross, W.
    2009   *Richter. Übersetzt und ausgelegt* (Herders Theologischer Kommentar zum Alten Testament; Freiburg: Herder).

Gunn, David M.
    2005   *Judges* (Blackwell Bible Commentaries; Malden, MA: Blackwell).

Lissovsky, N., and N. Na'aman
    2003   'A New Outlook at the Boundary System of the Twelve Tribes', *UF* 35: 291-332.

Mazar, A.
    1982   'Three Israelite Sites in the Hills of Judah and Ephraim', *BA* 45: 167-78.
    1992   'The Fortifications of the Israelite City at Kh. Marjameh in the Hills of Ephraim', *Eretz Israel* 23: 174-93 (Hebrew with summary in English).

Mazar, A., D. Amit, and Z. Ilan
    1996   'Hurvat Shilhah: An Iron Age Site in the Judean Desert', in J.D. Seger (ed.), *Retrieving the Past: Essays on Archaeological Research and Methodology in Honor of Gus W. Van Beek* (Winona Lake, IN: Eisenbrauns): 193-211.

McCarter, P.K.
   1984   *II Samuel: A New Translation with Introduction, Notes and Commentary* (AB, 9; Garden City, NY: Doubleday).

Na'aman, N.
   1992   'Canaanite Jerusalem and its Central Hill Country Neighbours in the Second Millennium BCE', *UF* 24: 257-91.
   1994   'The "Conquest of Canaan" in the Book of Joshua and in History', in I. Finkelstein and N. Na'aman (eds.), *From Nomadism to Monarchy. Archaeological and Historical Aspects of Early Israel* (Jerusalem: Yad Izhak Ben-Zvi and Israel Exploration Society): 218-81.
   2007   'Royal Inscription versus Prophetic Story: Mesha's Rebellion according to Biblical and Moabite Historiography', in L.L. Grabbe (ed.), *Ahab Agonistes: The Rise and Fall of the Omride Dynasty* (LHBOTS, 421; London and New York: T&T Clark): 145-83.

Oelgarte, T.
   1918   'Die Bethhoronstrasse', *Palästinajahrbuch* 14: 73-89.

Peterson, J.L.
   1992   'Beth-horon', in *The Anchor Bible Dictionary* (ed. D.N. Freedman; 6 vols.; New York: Doubleday): I, 688-89.

Porten, B.
   2003   'Appeal of Adon King of Ekron to Pharaoh (ca. 604 BCE)', in W.W. Hallo and K.L. Younger (eds.), *The Context of Scriptures. III. Archival Documents from the Biblical World* (Leiden/Boston: E.J. Brill): 132-33.

Wazana, N.
   2007   *All the Boundaries of the Land: The Territorial Land in Biblical Thought in Light of the Ancient Near East* (The Biblical Encyclopaedia Library, 24; Jerusalem: Bialik Institute [Hebrew]).

DIVINE NAMES, SOCIOLINGUISTICS AND THE PRAGMATICS OF PENTATEUCHAL NARRATIVE

Frank H. Polak

1. *Introduction: Proper Names in Discourse*

The distinction between the various divine names constitutes, since Astruc's analysis, one of the main pillars of the distinction between the 'sources' in the Pentateuch (Astruc 1753).[1] In this study I want to argue that this distinction counters all that is known about the impart of proper names in discourse, and makes the fundamental mistake of treating names mechanically as if they were passport numbers. Thus the time has come to subject the matter of the 'singular and bizarre variation' of divine names in the Pentateuch (Astruc 1753: 13) to literary scrutiny as well. It is a pleasure and a privilege to dedicate this study to Yairah with whom I share almost forty years of teaching at Tel Aviv University, struggling side by side for the face and content of our teaching, and though often at variance, likewise a common involvement in literary scrutiny of biblical narrative.

Although the personal name is meaningless in the vista of morphology and semantics, its use is highly meaningful in communication (Allerton 1987: 72-73; Allerton 1996).[2] Research in pragmatics, the branch of linguistics that deals with the communicative meaning imparted to spoken and written utterance by speaker and addressee, has established characteristic differences between various ways of addressing people: in many cultures, including the biblical world, the title has overtones of power, distance and authority, whereas the proper name connotes familiarity, solidarity and involvement

---

1.   Astruc (1753: 13) speaks of 'cette variation singulière et bizarre', but this view has been rejected by, e.g., Blum 1984: 471-77; Whybray 1987: 65-70.
2.   In biblical narrative the significance of naming is indicated by the etiological explanations of proper names (against Blum 1984: 472). Anthropological discussions include, for example, Aceto 2002; vom Bruck and Bodenhorn 2006; Hugh-Jones 2006; Benson 2006; Bloch 2006; Agyekum 2006. On name giving and name structure in classical, medieval and modern Europe see Wilson 1998.

(Ervin-Tripp 1972; Wardhaugh 2006: 267-83).[3] It is my purpose to show that in the large majority of cases a distinction of this type also explains the use of the appellation *'Elōhīm* (= AE, Appellation *'Elōhīm*) and the 'special' name, Yhwh (= SN, Special Name).[4] The use of these names is a matter of pragmatics, point of view and focalization, the status of speaker and addressee, and character representation. This view does not entail a different meaning in semantic terms. Since the title *'Elōhīm* and the special name share the same denotation,[5] the difference between them does not pertain to meaning, but to the way in which speaker or narrator addresses or mentions the deity, that is to say, attitude, point of view or ideational perspective. Contextual considerations can indicate part of these aspects, but do not cover them all. Hence for the theological-philological discussion context can form an important indication, although it is not decisive.

Before proceeding to discuss these issues I have to make a philological point: the co-occurrence of different names for one and the same deity is actually not exceptional in ancient Near Eastern literature. For instance, the opening of the Sumerian song of the Moon God's journey to Nippur uses no less than three terms: ᵈNanna, ᵈSuen and ᵈAš-im-babbar (Ferrara 1973: 4; Cohen 1981: 84, 90, 94). In Ugaritic texts the appellation *b'l* appears in one and the same line with the personal name *Hdd*, in parallelism (Blum 1984: 473; Whybray 1987: 68):

> *in. b'l. bbhth // il hdd. bqrb. hklh*
> Baal is not in his house// divine Hadad in his palace[6]

> *b'l yṯb kṯbt ġr // hd r[xxx] kmdb*
> Baal sat/sits like the sitting of a mountain // Haddu [...] like a flood[7]

And if that were not enough we also have the case of the divine craftsman *Koṯar-wa-ḥasis*, who has a second name, *Hyn*, which appears in the same context as the former appellation (Smith 1994: 170-72). By the same token,

---

3. I am quite aware of cultural differences, in particular with regard to name avoidance (Anchimbe 2010; Fleming 2011), but cross-cultural research indicates that the basic phenomena are found in many cultures, though with much variation (Fasold 1990: 29-36; Wardhaugh 2006: 260-76).

4. The Septuagint presents a number of cases of ὁ θεός, equalling *'Elōhīm*, for MT Yhwh, and of κύριος, the equivalent of Yhwh, for MT *'Elōhīm*. But in the large majority of cases the Greek reflects the same terms as the MT. Deviations need special study, in particular with regard to contextual harmonization—mostly in the Greek, but sometimes in the MT.

5. Of course, in some cases the term *'Elōhīm* is used to indicate other deities (Exod. 15.11; 2 Kgs 19.18; Ps. 82.1) or the dead.

6. *CAT* 1.10 II:4-5; see Parker 1997: 183.

7. *CAT* 1.101, lines 1-2.

in biblical poetry one bi-colon may include both SN and AE,[8] with or without suffix:[9]

Prov. 2.5:

אז תבין יראת ה' ודעת אלהים תמצא

Then you will understand the fear of Yhwh and attain knowledge of *God*

Deut. 32.3:

כי שם ה' אקרא הבו גדל לאלהינו

For the name of Yhwh I proclaim; Give glory to *our God*

Formally, then, the co-occurrence of divine name and appellation in one and the same context does not raise any problem. A major instance, the interchange of SN and AE in Jonah 4 (Segal 1967: 13; Whybray 1987: 67-68), will be discussed later.

2. *Power, Solidarity and the Pragmatics of Naming*

Thus, the interchange of divine names as in the Pentateuch needs reconsideration, in particular with regard to context in general, and especially in the book of Psalms. Segal (1967: 13-14) and Whybray (1987: 65-70) conclude that this interchange aims at stylistic variation. On the other hand, research in the beginning of the previous century, by Paul Vetter and Friedrich Baumgärtel (1914), points to a number of contextual conditions, and concludes, for instance, that non-Israelites mainly use AE; in Vetter's view *'Elōhīm* is the metaphysical and Yhwh the historical term (Baumgärtel 1914: 7-8; Cassuto 1934: 19-20, 33).

Cassuto (1934: 20-60) has extended these principles by his interpretation of AE as a generic term in universal use, thus an indication of universality and even transcendence, in particular in wisdom literature with its international cachet.[10] In this view, SN represents the intellectual property of Israelite believers, thus is indicative of the special qualities of the deity, in particular his moral rule of the world. But Cassuto also indicates that SN is used in the context of a personal and direct relationship with the deity, in prayer and in the traditions of Israel. Although Cassuto's distinctions are to a large extent aprioristic, the contrast between the personal aspect of the deity's special

8.   So also (with suffix, construct state or other attribute): 2 Sam. 22.7, 22, 32, 47 (with parallels in Ps. 18) and *passim* in prophetic prophecy. For the Psalms see nn. 23-24 below.

9.   Translations of biblical texts are based on the NJPSV, with slight variations. The dash indicates the clause boundary.

10.   To a large extent Cassuto follows Judah HaLevi's distinction between AE as an indication of a universal, supreme being and the *tetragrammaton* as special name used in personal communication; see Hirschfeld 1905: 198-201, 212-13, 223-24 (Part IV, 1-4, 16). Cassuto is followed by Engnell (1969: 55-56), and partly by Brichto (1998: 8-11).

name and the use of the appellation in a universal context squares with the sociolinguistic distinction between generic term or title, indicating power/ distance, and proper name, associated with personal contact/ familiarity/ solidarity.

a. *Name and Title in Social Interaction*

From the point of view of pragmatics, the significance of names and appellations is indicated by such studies as Paul Friedrich's famous essay on the rich variety of forms of address in Russian novels (Friedrich 1972: 284-98; Uspensky 1973: 23-27). In the Russian tradition the name by which one addresses a person is conditioned by a large number of considerations, from the status of speaker and addressee to personal attitude—which, to be sure, is to a certain extent true of all usage of names and titles in human interaction (Ervin-Tripp 1972: 218-31; Wardhaugh 2006: 267-83). A classical article by Brown and Gilman shows that many languages are characterized by the distinction between different kinds of pronouns, some of which connote distance and authority (as in French *vous* or German *Sie*); and others close familiarity, friendship and solidarity (as in French *tu*, or German *du*; Brown and Gilman 1960; Friedrich 1972: 276-86; Fasold 1990: 3-36; Scollon and Wong Scollon 2001: 43-57; Wardhaugh 2006: 260-76).

b. *Name and Title in Biblical Narrative*

In biblical Hebrew power and authority are indicated by the deferential forms of address, using the title: for instance, אדני המלך ('my lord, the king'), and the demeaning self reference, עבדך/עבדו ('your/his servant'), as in, 'Now therefore let *my lord the king* hear the words of *his servant*' (1 Sam. 26.19); or 'Today *your servant* knows that I have found favor in your sight, *my lord the king*, in that *the king* has granted the request of *his servant*' (2 Sam. 14.22).[11]

In narrative, differences in appellation may involve particular role descriptions or points of view (Uspensky 1973: 15-32, 81-134). Nechama Leibowitz points to differences in points of view/focalization between the various appellations of Isaac and Ishmael in the tale of Hagar's expulsion. Those are 'the son of Hagar the Egyptian' (Gen. 21.9, similarly v. 10), 'his son' (v. 11), 'the child' (vv. 14, 15-16), and 'the lad' in divine discourse (vv. 12, 17, 19; Leibowitz 1990; Weiss 1963: 465-70; Polak 1999: 327-30).

The same principle can be perceived in the Meriba'al (Mephiboshet) tale. In David's address to Ziba the narrator mentions the king by his title, המלך, 'the king' (2 Sam. 9.2b, 3a, b, 4a, b, 9, 11), highlighting royal authority.

---

11. Deferential address and self-reference appear together in 2 Sam. 14.19; 15.15, 21; 19.20, 21, 27-29, 36, 38; 24.21; 1 Kgs 1.27; 2.38; 20.9; *KAI* 200.1-2; 193.1. The epigraphic data show that these address forms do not represent just a literary conceit. The formal side of the issue is studied by Revell 1996.

David's personal name is used in contexts that relate to Meribaʻal (9.1, 9), indicating a personal relationship. The full address, המלך דוד, serves to introduce the official measure, 'So *King David* sent and had him brought from the house of Machir' (v. 5).[12] The sensitivity of the variation in the use of names is shown by the case of Meribaʻal himself, who is called 'son of Jonathan son of Saul' (v. 6), and who is promised benefits 'for the sake of Jonathan, your father' (v. 7); and further in David's instructions to Ziba. Meribaʻal is referred to as 'your master's (grand)son' (vv. 9-10). However, all changes in the tale of Absalom's rebellion. When Ziba appears before David, the king still speaks of 'your master's (grand)son' (16.3), but when David grants Meribaʻal's fields to the servant he speaks of 'all that belongs to Meribaʻal' (v. 4). In the episode of Meribaʻal's appearance before David after the rebellion the epithet applied is 'the (grand)son of Saul', suggesting rival claims rather than Jonathan's friendship (19.25).

These examples show that the use of different names is to be viewed in a literary, pragmatic perspective. In spite of the difference between divine and human names, a similar prism seems indicated for the use of Yhwh as against *'Elōhīm*.

c. *Divine Name and Appellation in the Jonah Narrative*

The co-occurrence of the special name and the appellation *'Elōhīm* in the concluding chapter of Jonah reveals a regularity that is close to the distinction between power and solidarity. Personal contact is indicated by the introduction to Jonah's prayer: 'He prayed to Yhwh, and said, 'Yhwh! Isn't this just what I said when I was still in my own country?' (Jon. 4.2; so also 4.3). The same terminology appears in the introduction to the divine answer: 'Yhwh said, "Are you that deeply grieved?"' (v. 4).

The second step presents both SN and AE: 'Then Yhwh *God* provided (וימן ה' אלהים) a Ricinus [castor oil] plant, which grew up over Jonah, to provide shade for his head'. But for the third step only AE is used: 'But the next day at dawn *God* (אלהים) provided a worm' (v. 7). The appellation returns when the east wind threatens to kill Jonah (v. 8) and in the opening of the ensuing divine address:

v. 9

ויאמר אלהים אל־יונה ההיטב חרה־לך על־הקיקיון

Then God said to Jonah, 'Are you so deeply grieved about the plant?'

---

12. The same terminology is found in passages in which David's status as king is explicitly at stake: 2 Sam. 5.3; 7.18; 19.12; where the status of the dynasty is threatened: 13.21; or where David's position is contrasted with the Saulides: 6.16 (ironical from Michal's point of view); 16.5. In the tale of Solomon's accession this nomenclature appears frequently in connection with dynastic concerns, in the narrator's domain (1 Kgs 1.1, 32, 38) and in character speech (vv. 13, 31, 43, 47).

This passage is extremely relevant for our issue. The bringing on of the Ricinus is presented as if it is related not only to Jonah personally, but also to the creation as a universal concern. This universal aspect is manifest again in the pericope on the appearance of the worm, the east wind. The use of the appellation to introduce the divine speech (v. 9) may imply a certain manifestation of power and, in particular, punishment. In any case it contrasts sharply with the use of the special name in the introduction of the final argument:[13]

vv. 10-11:

ויאמר ה' אתה חסת על־הקיקיון אשר לא־עמלת בו ולא גדלתו ...

ואני לא אחום על־נינוה העיר הגדולה אשר יש־בה הרבה משתים־עשרה רבו אדם

Then Yhwh said: 'You cared about the plant, which you did not work for and which you did not grow... And should not I care about Nineveh, that great city, in which there are more than a hundred and twenty thousand persons...'

The very use of the verbs חסת and אחום indicates an emotional concern, which tallies perfectly with the personal aspect of the special name, and maybe even foreshadows the midrashic 'mode of mercy'.[14]

In addition, one notes that the term *'Elōhīm* indicates the gods of the sailors (Jon. 1.5-6). The skipper even uses this term as a general appellation for any deity involved in the storm: 'Perhaps the god will think of us' (v. 6b, אולי יתעשת האלהים לנו).[15] The same term is used to indicate the deity invoked by the people of Nineveh (3.5, 8-9), as well as in the indication of the divine decision: *God* saw what they did, how they were turning back from their evil ways. And *God* renounced the punishment he had planned to bring upon them, and did not carry it out (3.10). This usage confirms Cassuto's intuition concerning the universality connotation of the term *'Elōhīm*.[16]

3. *Divine Names, Power and Solidarity in the Psalms*

a. *The Appellation 'Elōhīm in the Psalter: Power, Distance and Universal Authority*

In the book of Psalms we encounter numerous instances of AE in parallelism with SN, e.g.,[17]

13.   Simon (1994: 132-33) acknowledges only the universal/national use of AE/SN and, therefore, he is unable to recognize the use of SN for solidarity in this verse.

14.   In *Sifre Deut.* 26.24 and *Exod. Rab.* 3.6 the connection between the *tetragrammaton* and the 'mode of mercy' (*middat hārahămīm*) is motivated by reference to Exod. 34.6; see also Kadushin 1952: 215-17; Widmer 2004: 183-89.

15.   So with the Vulgate, *recogitet Deus de nobis.*

16.   So also Pss 82.6; 86.8. Cassuto (1934: 24) compares the general use of the Egyptian *pʔ nṯr* ('the god'); see Goelet and Levine 1998: 271-75.

17.   Boling 1960: 245-46. See also Pss 48.9; 69.14; 84.12.

Ps. 14.2:

ה' משמים השקיף על־בני־אדם לראות היש משכיל דרש את־אלהים

Yhwh looks down from heaven on mankind to find a man of understanding,
mindful of *God.*

The appellation can be used to express the place of man vis-à-vis the deity:[18]
'How precious is your faithful care, *God! Mankind* (ובני אדם) shelters in the
shadow of your wings' (36.8). In addition, it indicates distance, for instance
between the evildoers and the deity: 'Many say of me, there is no deliverance
for him through *God*' (3.3). Often the context suggests indifference and even
hostility: 'He does not call to account; *God* does not care' (Ps. 10.4); 'Fools
say in their hearts, There is no *God*' (14.1=53.1).[19]

On the other hand, the general appellation can indicate the power of the
divine overlord and, as such, the divine judge:[20] 'Condemn them, *God*; let
them fall by their own devices' (5.11). The connotation of divine majesty
may be indicated by the use of terms such as מלך, תרועה, עז, רום:

46.11:

הרפו ודעו כי־אנכי אלהים ארום בגוים ארום בארץ

Desist! Realize that I am *God!* I *dominate* the nations; I *dominate* the earth.

47.2:

כל־העמים תקעו־כף הריעו לאלהים בקול רנה

All you peoples, clap your hands, raise a joyous shout for *God.*

What complicates the situation is the well-known fact that in the so-called
'Elohistic Psalter' (=EP: Pss 42–83, with appendix, =AEP, in Pss 84–89)
the common designation of the deity is *'Elōhīm* rather than Yhwh, often
explained as the outcome of the redactorial replacement of SN by AE
(Whybray 1987: 69-70).[21] This small corpus contains many instances of AE

18. This dimension of the use of AE represents a hierarchy inherent in many forms of
politeness (Scollon and Wong Scollon 2001: 56-59; Wardhaugh 2006: 272). Similarly Ps.
8.6; and in EP, Pss 45.3, 7; 47.9, 10; 50.1; 53.3 (= 14.2); 55.20; 64.10; 67.4, 6, 8; 68.32.

19. See Hossfeld and Zenger 2003: 39, 43, 45-46, 50-51, and, e.g., Pss 14.5-6 (= 53.5-
6); 9.18; 10.13; 36.2; in EP: 42.4, 11; 49.8; 50.16; 52.9; 54.5; 60.3, 12; 68.2 (as against
Num. 10.35); Pss 71.11; 74.1, 10; 78.10, 19, 22, 59; 79.1; 80.5; 83.2-3, 13; in AEP:
86.14.

20. So also Ps. 7.10-12, and in EP: Pss 43.1; 44.22; 50.6; 58.12; 75.8; 76.10; 82.1, 8.
We note twelve passages in which the *tetragrammaton* connotes divine acts of justice:
Pss 7.9 (contrast v. 11); 9.8, 17, 20; 96.13; 98.9; 103.6; 105.7; 119.75, 137; 140.13; 146.7
(a personal relationship: 26.1; 35.24; 37.33; 139.1).

21. One notes the phrase אלהים צבאות (Pss 59.6; 80.5, 8, 15, 20) and the interchange
between Yhwh (14.2, 4, 7) and *'Elōhīm* (53.3, 5, 7) in two parallel chapters: Ps. 68.2, 5 as
against Num. 10.35; Judg. 5.4. See, e.g., Boling 1960: 253-55; Fohrer 1963: 294,
including Pss 84–89 as appendix (AEP), although this section includes 31 instances of the
tetragrammaton as against merely eight cases of *'Elōhīm* in the absolute state. One also

with no special overtones, such as, for example:[22] 'Like a hind crying for water, my soul cries for you, *God* (אֵלֶיךָ אֱלֹהִים); my soul thirsts for *God*, the living God (לְאֵל חָי); when will I come to appear before *God*!' (42.2-3).

However, when we take into account the exegetic categories mentioned above, we see that by far most instances of non-connotative usage appear in the near vicinity of usage with clear overtones of distance and divine power.[23] Moreover, in many Psalms in this small corpus we encounter SN in the vicinity of AE (e.g. Pss 46.8-9, 12; 47.3, 6; 48.2, 9; Hossfeld and Zenger 2003). Hossfeld and Zenger conclude that in EP the use of divine names largely reflects intentional choice in context. Accordingly we have to differentiate a number of categories:

- Psalms in which the use of Yhwh is the default, which is the large majority.[24]
- Psalms in which the terms AE and SN were used for stylistic and ideational purposes in context.
- Psalms in which the use of AE has been extended beyond the basic semantic conditions, possibly as the result of the substitution of AE for SN.

b. *The* Tetragrammaton, *Solidarity and Close Presence*

In the Psalms, the revealed name Yhwh is used to invoke the deity in prayer, and in this sense represents involvement and solidarity, for instance, in EP, 'Answer me, Yhwh, according to your great steadfastness; in accordance

---

notes AE in Ps. 25.22, the *peh*-verse secondarily added to the acrostic Psalm (cf. v. 16). On the other hand, the Elohistic Ps. 57.10 has אֲדֹנָי rather than *'Elōhīm* of the non-Elohistic parallel, Ps. 108.4.

22. So also Pss 42.5-6, 12; 45.8; 48.10; 49.16; 50.7, 14, 23; 51.3, 12, 16, 19; 52.10; 53.7; 54.3, 4; 55.2, 5, 17; 56.2, 5, 10 (with punishment in context), 11-14; 57.2, 8; 59.2, 11; 60.8, 14; 61.2, 6, 8; 62.2, 6, 8-9; 63.2, 12; 64.2; 65.2; 66.10, 16, 19; 67.2; 68.4, 6, 8 (as against Judg. 5.4), 10, 11, 18, 27; 69.2, 14; 69.30, 31, 33, 36; 70.2, 6; 71.12, 17, 18; 73.1, 26, 28; 77.2, 4, 17; 78.7, 35; 80.4, 8, 15, 20; and in AEP: 84.8, 10.

23. In Ps. 42 one notes the pivotal question אַיֵּה אֱלֹהֶיךָ (vv. 4, 11, 'where is your God'), and in Ps. 45 the opposition divine-human (vv. 3, 7; so also 73.1, 26, 28). The use of AE in Ps. 63.2 may be influenced by the indications of divine power in v. 3 (so also 61.4); in 63.12 the evildoers appear in the last colon (so also 60.14). In Ps. 51 the use of AE in a plea for mercy (v. 3) could relate to the profound sense of guilt, and the relationship to divine judgment (vv. 5-6).

24. Of course, SN is used in many passages of the Psalter where AE would tally well with the conditions sketched above. But regularity in stylistics does not have the same meaning as laws as phonology and morphology. Stylistic preference allows for and is based on the possibility of choice from a number of options. The hypothesis that one poet prefers a given option in a certain context does not entail that in such context every poet has to prefer this variant.

with your abundant mercy turn to me' (69.17); 'For You are my hope, my lord Yhwh[25] ('ה אדני), my trust from my youth' (71.5).[26] It would be difficult to construe a difference between those examples and well known instances from other parts of the Psalter, such as 'I lie down and sleep and wake again, for Yhwh sustains me' (3.6); 'Yhwh, you will not withhold your *compassion* from me; your steadfast love will always protect me' (40.12).[27] Here we note both solidarity and compassion (רחמיך, like in 69.17),[28] implying a close and as it were personal, relationship between the deity and the human worshipper.

4. *Power and Solidarity in Pentateuchal Narrative*

a. *The* Tetragrammaton *in Biblical Narrative according to the* MT

1. In Pentateuchal narrative we encounter the connotation of solidarity and compassion in the opening of Jacob's prayer: 'O God of my father Abraham…, Yhwh, who said to me, 'Return to your native land and I will deal bountifully with you' (Gen. 32.10).

2. A close personal relationship between the deity and the first human pair is entailed by the tale of the garden east of Eden, for instance, when Yhwh 'blew into his [the first human's] nostrils the breath of life' (Gen. 2.7). The wife was built out of a rib that was physically taken out of the man's body (vv. 21-22). The condemnation of Adam, wife and serpent was enunciated in a face to face conversation (3.9-19). By the same token, one notes the close relationship in Eve's declaration קניתי איש את ה' (4.1, 'I have gained a male [child] with [the help of] Yhwh'), and in the assertion of divine favour for Noah: ונח מצא חן בעיני ה' (6.8, 'But Noah found favor with Yhwh'). Divine favour is also involved in Lamech's hope that 'This one will provide us relief from our work and from the toil of our hands, out of the very soil which Yhwh placed under a curse' (5.29). This verse centers on relief (ינחמנו) rather than on the curse from the past. Pragmatically speaking, in this context the

---

25. In this pattern the *tetragrammaton* is vocalized by the vowel signs of *'Elōhīm*.

26. So also Pss 59.6, 9; 70.6; 71.1 (=31.2); in AEP: 86.17. The invocation אתה אלהים is found three times: 55.24; 60.1; 61.6. Once we find אליך אלהים (42.2).

27. See above, p. 164. Many passages in Pss 1–20 invoking Yhwh celebrate or presuppose a personal relationship between the deity, the supplicant or humanity: Pss 2.7; 3.1; and *passim*. The supplicant calls out, אליך ה' אקרא (Joel 1.19; Pss 28.1; 30.9; 88.14; 141.8; 142.6), or אתה ה'; similarly, e.g., Pss 22.20; 25.1; Num. 14.14; 2 Sam. 7.24,27; 1 Kgs 18.37; 2 Kgs 19.19; Jer. 3.22; 12.1, 3; 18.23; 31.18. In EP one notes Pss 42.9; 46.8-9, 12; 48.9; 54.8; 55.23; 64.11; 69.14, 17, 32, 34; 71.1; 74.18; 79.5; 80.5; 81.11; 83.17, 19.

28. So also, e.g., Pss 25.6; 86.17; Deut. 13.18; 2 Sam. 24.14. Similarly, with the verb רחם: Exod. 33.19; Deut. 13.18; 30.3; 2 Kgs 13.23; and *passim*. The verbal stem without SN is found in Hos. 2.25 (אלהי); Ps. 116.5; and the noun רחמים in EP: Ps. 51.3; and in late Dan. 1.9; 9.9, 18.

AE would indicate a different view of human fate (against Rofé 2009: 272). In the Moses tales SN indicates the contact between the deity and the chosen leader, with the divine self-presentation in the form of the 'Messenger of Yhwh' (Exod. 3.2), and with indications of visual perception (3.4, 7) and care for Israel (v. 15).[29]

3. The tale of Isaac's sacrifice, in which the systematic use of AE indicates divine distance and authority, uses SN to indicate divine involvement with Abraham and his son (Gen. 22.11, 14-16). In the Joseph narrative SN serves to indicate the personal care for Joseph (39.2-3, 5, 21-23).

4. The experience of close divine presence may involve immediate, almost physical numinous power such as in the tale of the bloody husband: At a night encampment on the way, Yhwh encountered him and sought to kill him (Exod. 4.24).[30] In the end, 'he let him alone', a clear sign of close presence in the preceding episode (v. 26). In Jacob's sleep the deity appears to the fugitive in a dream and stands near to him (Gen. 28.13).[31] The theophany makes Jacob recognize that, 'Surely Yhwh is present in this place', 'How awesome is this place' (vv. 16-17). His subsequent insight is expressed by two parallel clauses, in which the recognition of Yhwh's presence is followed by the understanding that 'this is none other than the abode of *God*' (בית אלהים).

b. *The Appellation* 'Elōhīm *in Biblical Narrative according to the* MT
In Pentateuchal narrative the conditions for the use of AE are largely similar to those prevalent in the Psalms.

1. The parallelism of the *tetragrammaton* and AE fits the norms of poetry, for instance, in Isaac's blessing:

Gen. 27.27-28:

רְאֵה רֵיחַ בְּנִי כְּרֵיחַ שָׂדֶה אֲשֶׁר בֵּרֲכוֹ ה'
וְיִתֶּן־לְךָ הָאֱלֹהִים מִטַּל הַשָּׁמַיִם וּמִשְׁמַנֵּי הָאָרֶץ

'See, the smell of my son is like the smell of the fields that Yhwh has blessed. May *God* give you of the dew of heaven and the fat of the earth'.

The appellation in the second line parallels the divine name in the first line, with connotations of heaven and earth, or nature is general.

A parallel structure is notable in many a narrative passage:[32]

Gen. 21.1-2:

וה' פָּקַד אֶת־שָׂרָה כַּאֲשֶׁר אָמַר וַיַּעַשׂ ה' לְשָׂרָה כַּאֲשֶׁר דִּבֵּר
וַתַּהַר וַתֵּלֶד שָׂרָה לְאַבְרָהָם בֵּן לִזְקֻנָיו לַמּוֹעֵד אֲשֶׁר־דִּבֶּר אֹתוֹ אֱלֹהִים

29. By contrast, Moses' fear of 'looking at God' is indicated by AE (3.6), as is the audial experience (3.4).

30. So also Gen. 38.7, 10; Num. 22.22-35.

31. So also Gen. 31.3.

32. So also Gen 26.24.

Yhwh took note of Sarah as he had promised, and Yhwh did for Sarah as he had spoken. Sarah conceived and bore a son to Abraham in his old age, at the set time of which *God* had spoken.

The first line is built on the parallelism of וה' פקד את שרה כאשר אמר (entailing personal care) and ויעש ה' לשרה כאשר דבר, with the repetition of SN. The second line continues with the specification of Sarah's pregnancy and childbirth, and concludes with an additional reference to the divine promise, אשר־דבר אתו אלהים. This phrase matches the closure of the first verse but uses AE.[33] The juxtaposition of SN and AE as an epithet, as found in the primeval Garden tale, demonstrates the possibility to combine lexical associates in one single noun phrase, an option studied by Melamed (1961) and Avishur (1984: 139-52).

2. The use of *'Elōhīm* as appellation of the universal divine sovereign obviously is present in the creation account in Gen. 1.1–2.4a, in which the human aspect of the creation (Gen. 1.26-30) is only part of the entire cosmos, 'the heaven and the earth…all their array' (1.31–2.1).[34]

3. The appellation *'Elōhīm* appears frequently in narratives concerning contacts with non-Israelites. In the Joseph narrative AE is used in connection with the Egyptian speakers and addressees (Rofé 2009: 272),[35] for instance when Joseph addresses Potiphar's wife (39.9).[36] By the same token, in the narrative about the dream of the king of Gerar, Abimelech describes how '*God* came to Abimelech in a dream by night' (20.3).[37] Abraham describes how '*God* made me wander from my father's house' (20.13). His prayer for Abimelech and his court is also viewed under the universal aspect (v. 17).[38]

---

33. This constellation is not explained by the assumption of secondary intrusion of Yhwh.

34. By contrast, the motivation for the Shabbat commandment (Exod. 20.11) uses SN, unlike the decalogue itself. In my view this usage could reflect particular care for the repose of the creatures, but could also indicate the quotation of an independent poetic source, as evidenced by the reference to physical divine rest (וינח ביום השביעי), also alluded to in the Shabbat commandment that closes the Tabernacle instructions (31.17, וינפש, not rendered in the Vulgate!), in contradistinction to the almost transcendent majesty of the creation account. Attribution of these different lines to one and the same 'document' (e.g. 'P' or 'H') is no more than *Systemzwang*/pseudo-critical apologetic.

35. Joseph's explanation of the divine providence behind his misfortunes and successes (Gen. 45.5-9) uses AE because of the implications of universal divine power. In the same way one understands the use of AE by the brothers (42.28), in the dream revelation to Jacob (46.2-3) and in the scenes of Jacob's blessing (48.9-21), and the brothers' supplication to Joseph (50.19-24).

36. So also when Pharaoh or his magicians speak (Exod. 5.8; 8.15, 21); but Pharaoh may use SN in derision (5.17, in comparison with the denial of Yhwh's authority, 5.2). On the brothers' use of AE see n. 35 above.

37. So also 20.6. Abimelech himself addresses the deity as 'my lord' (v. 4, אדני).

38. So also in Gen. 21.12, 17, 19, 20, 22-23.

But when the narrator explains how God defended Abraham and Sarah, he uses SN: 'for Yhwh had closed every womb of the household of Abimelech because of Sarah, Abraham's wife' (v. 18). Here it is the personal aspect that counts.[39]

4. AE also appears in the tale concerning the confrontation between Jacob and Laban (Genesis 31), to begin with Jacob's speech to his wives:[40] 'But your father has cheated me, changing my wages time and again. *God*, however, would not let him do me harm' (31.7); '*God* has taken away your father's livestock and given it to me' (v. 9). By the same token Jacob describes his dream, which the narrator introduced as an address by Yhwh (31.3), as a message from the 'messenger of *God*' and the God at Beth-el (v. 13, הָאֵל בֵּית אֵל).[41] Particularly notable is the introduction to the episode on Laban's dream, in which he is warned not to make any demands from Jacob (Gen. 31.24, like 20.3), in keeping with Laban's status as hostile foreigner. The term *'Elōhīm* also appears in Jacob's contacts with Esau (33.5, 10-11). The use of AE in the Jethro tale (Exodus 18) suits the non-Israelite context. However, in a few cases SN appears: 'Jethro...heard all that God had done for Moses and for his people Israel, how Yhwh had brought Israel out from Egypt' (Exod. 18.1). The appearance of both divine names in two consecutive clauses fits the conditions of parallelism, but in relation to 'the priest of Midian' precedence is given to AE. SN is used in Moses' account of what has happened (v. 8) and Jethro's praise of these divine acts (vv. 9-11). But the episodes of Jethro's sacrifice (v. 12) and his advice to Moses use AE throughout, even when Moses speaks (18.15-16). The use of the appellation squares with the dominant role of the Midianite priest.

5. The appellative *'Elōhīm* may also be used to indicate distance or lack of solidarity and involvement, for instance in the tale about the Israelites' fate in Egypt (Exod. 1.17, 20-21). The description of the divine attention to Israel (2.23-25) still preserves this distance, for what God 'saw' and 'knew' remains unsaid (Dozeman 2009: 93).

A perspective of distance is obvious in the opening of the tale of the sacrifice of Isaac: 'Some time afterward, God put Abraham to the test' (Gen. 22.1). The divine demand to sacrifice Isaac represents authority and power rather than solidarity. Another way in which this distance comes to the fore is

---

39. According to proponents of the documentary hypothesis this verse is a redactional adjustment in the wake of 12.10-20. However, without this retrospection Abraham's prayer (20.7, 17) does not make sense.

40. In 31.5 Jacob speaks of 'the God of my father'.

41. Jacob's dream account amalgamates the dream revelation that triggered his decision to leave (31.3) with other events in his life history, a freedom that is the privilege of character memory vis-à-vis the narrator's account, in particular when the speaking person has to persuade his addressees.

the lack of reference in Abraham's explanation, in which he does not say
whom they will worship: 'We will worship and we will return to you' (v. 5).
The tale continues along these lines (vv. 3, 8-9) until Yhwh's messenger
(מלאך ה') stops Abraham from proceeding with the cruel ceremony (v. 11).
Significantly, the attitude which gains the messenger's praise is the 'fear of
God' (v. 12, ירא אלהים). No less characteristic is the use of SN in the
explanation of the name of the place, 'Yhwh will provide' (v. 14, ה' יראה),
and in the repeated divine promise (v. 16).

6. Another aspect of distance is the fear of divine power, as evident in the
exchange between the people and Moses in the wake of the theophany on
mount Sinai: 'You will speak to us, and we will listen; but do not let God
speak to us, or we will die' (Exod. 20.19).[42] Viewed in this light, the introduction of the Decalogue connotes distance and authority as well (20.1).

A similar sentiment is suggested by the use of AE in the scene at the
burning bush, where it is used for Moses' fear to look at God (v. 6b) and for
auditory communication (v. 4, 11-15),[43] whereas SN is used for proximity and
visual contact (vv. 2, 4, 7). The perspective changes only when Moses starts
using the divine name (4.1), following the divine self-description (3.15-18).

7. The contrast of divine sovereignty and human humility, as in Psalms 8
and 36, is found in the opening of the record of Adam's descendants: 'When
God created man, He made him in the likeness of *God*' (Gen. 5.1). A similar
contrast presents itself in the note on Enoch's life, in which the human is
positioned vis-à-vis the divine sphere: 'Enoch walked with *God*; then he was
no more, for *God* took him' (5.24; compare 5.21).

Humility in view of divine sovereignty is also the point of the tale about
the revelation of divine identity to Abram and the circumcision command
(Genesis 17). This narrative is characterized by the use of three different
names. The opening of the tale mentions a divine revelation marked by SN
and attributed, by the divine speaker, to El Shaddai:[44]

Gen. 17.1:

וירא ה' אל־אברם ויאמר אליו אני־אל שדי התהלך לפני והיה תמים

Yhwh appeared to Abram and said to him, 'I am El Shaddai. Walk in My
ways and be blameless'.

The use of the personal name fits the idea of divine-human communication.
However, when Abraham reacts to the divine call, the narrator prefers the

---

42. Dozeman 2009: 499-500. Similarly in 19.3, 17, 19; 24.10-11 (see also LXX).

43. One notes the parallelism of Yhwh (Exod. 3.3a) and *'Elōhīm* (v. 3b).

44. Although this is not the place to discuss the term El Shaddai, it is to be noted that
its use is poetic (Gen. 49.25; Num. 24.4, 16; Isa. 13.6; Joel 1.15; Ps. 91.1 and frequently in
Job), and is not to be detached from the use of the term שדין, 'gods', in the Deir 'Alla
Balaam text.

appellation: 'Abram threw himself on his face; and *God* spoke to him further' (17.3).

Thus the narrative presents Abraham's point of view as a devoted servant who loyally accepts the commands of his overlord. AE is also used to indicate the position of the divine suzerain in the covenant between God and Israel:[45]

> v. 7:
>
> והקמתי את־בריתי ביני ובינך ובין זרעך אחריך ...
> להיות לך לאלהים ולזרעך אחריך
>
> I will establish my covenant between me and you, and your offspring to come…to be God to you and to your offspring to come.

8. An additional aspect of distance is hostility, as in the serpent's successful attempt to persuade the woman to eat from the forbidden tree (3.1b, 5),[46] and in the response which explains the divine interdiction (v. 3; Gunkel 1910: 16). This mode is similar to the use detected in Psalms 10 and 14, as noted above.

c. *Foreigners Using the Special Name*

In view of those considerations it is no small surprise to discover that SN is used by Laban in the discussion about the wages he is to pay his nephew:

> Gen. 30.27:
>
> ויאמר אליו לבן אם־נא מצאתי חן בעיניך נחשתי ויברכני ה' בגללך
>
> But Laban said to him, 'If you will indulge me, I have prospered and Yhwh has blessed me on your account'.

This name also appears in Abimelech's attempt to initiate an agreement with Isaac:

> 26.28:
>
> ויאמרו ראו ראינו כי־היה ה' עמך
> ונאמר תהי נא אלה בינותינו בינינו ובינך ונכרתה ברית עמך
>
> And they said, 'We now see plainly that Yhwh has been with you, and we thought: Let there be a sworn treaty between our two parties, between you and us. Let us make a pact with you'.

> v. 29:
>
> אתה עתה ברוך ה'
>
> 'From now on, be you blessed by Yhwh'.

---

45. Similarly Lev. 26.12 (as against 26.1); Jer. 7.23; 11.4; 24.7; 30.22; 31.1, 33; 32.28; Ezek. 11.20; 14.11; 36.28; 37.23, 25; Hos. 2.25 ('And I will say to Lō-'ammi, "You are My people", And he will say, "[You are] my God"'.).

46. According to Gunkel (1910: 26) this passage is to be attributed to a particular subsource of J, the so-called J^e.

Both Abimelech and Laban have to persuade their interlocutor to accept their proposal. Abimelech is in a tight situation since Isaac has received him with a scolding, 'Why have you come to me, seeing that you have been hostile to me and have driven me away from you?' (26.27). In this case, then, the use of SN can be viewed as a part of Abimelech's attempt to appease an impatient opponent by suggesting a personal connection.[47] Laban is in a similar position, for Jacob has requested to leave and to take his children with him (30.25b-26). Thus, Laban is seeking the favor of his nephew and son-in-law, and uses SN as an indication of solidarity in spite of his demands.[48]

Pharaoh starts using SN in the wake of the fourth plague (of the 'swarms of insects'), adopting Moses' terminology, when he begs Moses to remove the insects and to pray for him (Exod. 8.24). This could be a sign that the king is starting to give in, but also might be viewed as a negotiation ploy. After the plague of the hail, Pharaoh uses SN in his confession (9.27-28).[49]

d. *Psychological Perspective and Divine Names*

A significant distinction presents itself in the tales of Leah and Rachel. SN appears in the tale of the sons granted to Leah: 'Yhwh saw that Leah was unloved and he opened her womb' (Gen. 29.31). The explanation of Reuben's name states explicitly, 'Yhwh has seen my affliction' (29.32).[50] In these descriptions and utterances the personal aspect is obvious. On the other hand, the passage on Jacob's impatient response to Rachel's complaints uses the appellation *'Elōhīm*:

30.2:

התחת אלהים אנכי אשר־מנע ממך פרי־בטן

'Can I take the place of God, who has denied you fruit of the womb?'

Here the distance is palpable. However, in the sequel of the narrative the appellation is also used when personal closeness seems involved, such as Rachel's thanksgiving for the birth of Dan (30.6).[51] This is also the case in the account about the birth of Leah's youngest sons, Issachar (30.17-18) and Zebulun (30.20). Even the pericope on the birth of Rachel's first son, Joseph, uses AE (30.22-23), until Rachel explains the newborn baby's name: יסף ה' לי בן אחר (30.24, 'May Yhwh add to me another son'). Only after the

---

47. The negotiation tactics in the Isaac-Abimelech tale have been analyzed in Polak 2010: 173-75.

48. A similar explanation could be helpful in the case of Gen. 31.49, יצף ה' ביני ובינך, but it is unclear who is presented as speaker.

49. So also Pharaoh and his counselors before and after the plague of locusts (Exod. 10.7-8, 10-11, 16-17), and following the plague of darkness (10.24).

50. So also in the name explanations of vv. 33, 35.

51. In the explanation of Naphtali's name (30.8), the term *'Elōhīm* is used as an elative: 'enormous wrestlings'.

birth of Rachel's son does the narrator remove the cloud over the head of Jacob and his family. Until then, the narrative is coloured by Rachel's trauma. This psychological differentiation should not be neutralized by the mechanics of redaction criticism.

In the Balaam tale the interchange of *tetragrammaton* and the term *'Elōhīm* is to be viewed in a similar light. When Balaam addresses Balak's envoys, he highlights the intimate contact between him and the deity in whose name he speaks: 'I shall reply to you as Yhwh may instruct me' (Num. 22.8).[52] By contrast, the narrator from his viewpoint highlights divine sovereignty: '*God* came to Balaam' (v. 9).[53] When Balaam uses AE in his answer to Balak (22.38), the implication is the recognition of divine power, over against his personal wishes and, of course, the king's orders. But for the divine revelation itself the narrator prefers the special name (23.5, 8, 12 and *passim*), indicating the perfect communication between the prophet and his god and, equally, the divine protection of Israel.

5. *Preliminary Conclusions*

The conclusions of this study can only be preliminary. The biblical usage of divine name and appellation is too rich and varied to allow for unequivocal conclusions. The textual variation reflected by the Samaritan Pentateuch and the Septuagint is but an additional sign of the rich variety of the data. What can be asserted is that seemingly midrashic and apologetic notions, such as the intuitions of Judah HaLevi and Cassuto's detailed proposals, are not necessarily contrary to sound linguistic and literary methods. On the contrary: sociolinguistic study of the pragmatic implications of various address forms amply confirms the connotations of distance, power and authority of the term *'Elōhīm*, as against the overtones of solidarity, close personal contact, involvement and Israelite identity associated with the special name Yhwh.

Bibliography

Aceto, Michael
    2002   'Ethnic Personal Names and Multiple Identities in Anglophone Caribbean Speech Communities in Latin America', *Language in Society* 31: 577–608.
Agyekum, Kofi
    2006   'The Sociolinguistic of Akan Personal Names', *Nordic Journal of African Studies* 15: 206-35.

52. So also Num. 22.13, 18, 19; 23.3.
53. So also Num. 22.10, 12, 20, 22; 23.4. In 23.27 it is Balak who uses AE, properly presented as a foreign, polytheistic ruler.

Allerton, D.J.
1987 'The Linguistic and Sociolinguistic Status of Proper Names', *Journal of Pragmatics* 11: 61-92.
1996 'Proper Names and Definite Descriptions with the same Reference: A Pragmatic Choice for Language Users', *Journal of Pragmatics* 25: 621-33.

Anchimbe, Eric A.
2010 'On Not Calling People by their Names: Pragmatic Undertones of Sociocultural Relationships in a Postcolony', *Journal of Pragmatics* 43: 1472-83.

Astruc, Jean
1753 *Conjectures sur les mémoires originaux dont il paroit que Moyse s'est servi pour composer le livre de la Genèse* (Bruxelles: Fricx).

Avishur, Yitzhak
1984 *Stylistic Studies of Word Pairs in Biblical and Ancient Semitic Literatures* (AOAT, 210; Kevelaer: Butzon & Bercker; Neukirchen–Vluyn: Neukirchener Verlag).

Baumgärtel, Friedrich
1914 *Elohim ausserhalb des Pentateuch. Grundlegung zu einer Untersuchung über die Gottesnamen im Pentateuch* (BWAT, 19; Leipzig: Hinrichs).

Benson, Susan
2006 'Injurious Names: Naming, Disavowal, and Recuperation in Contexts of Slavery and Emancipation', in vom Bruck and Bodenhorn 2006: 177-99.

Bloch, Maurice
2006 'Teknonymy and the Evocation of the "Social" among the Zafimaniry of Madagascar', in vom Bruck and Bodenhorn 2006: 97-114.

Blum, Erhard
1984 *Die Komposition der Vätergeschichte* (WMANT, 57; Neukirchen–Vluyn: Neukirchener Verlag).

Boling, Robert G.
1960 '"Synonymous" Parallelism in the Psalms', *JSS* 5: 221-55.

Brichto, Herbert Chanan
1998 *The Names of God: Poetic Readings in Biblical Beginnings* (New York: Oxford University Press).

Brown, Roger, and Albert Gilman
1960 'The Pronouns of Power and Solidarity', in T.A. Sebeok (ed.), *Style in Language* (Cambridge, MA: MIT Press): 253-76.

Bruck, Gabriele vom, and Barbara Bodenhorn
2006 '"Entangled in Histories": An Introduction to the Anthropology of Names and Naming', in vom Bruck and Bodenhorn 2006: 1-30.

Bruck, Gabriele vom, and Barbara Bodenhorn (eds.)
2006 *The Anthropology of Names and Naming* (Cambridge: Cambridge University Press).

Burnett, Joel S.
2006 'Forty-Two Songs for Elohim: An Ancient Near Eastern Organizing Principle in the Shaping of the Elohistic Psalter', *JSOT* 31: 81-101.

Cassuto, M.D.
1990 ספר בראשית ומבנהו ('The Book of Genesis and its Structure') (trans. A. Hartum; Jerusalem: Magnes Press [Hebrew]).

Cassuto, U.
    1934   *La Questione della Genesi* (Firenze: Le Monnier).
Cohen, Mark E.
    1981   *Sumerian Hymnology: The Eršemma* (HUCA Supplements, 2; Cincinnati: Hebrew Union College-Jewish Institute of Religion).
Dozeman, Thomas
    2009   *Exodus* (Eerdmans Critical Commentary; Grand Rapids: Eerdmans).
Engnell, Ivan
    1969   *A Rigid Scrutiny: Critical Essays on the Old Testament* (ed. John T. Willis; Nashville: Vanderbilt University Press).
Ervin-Tripp, Susan
    1972   'On Sociolinguistic Rules: Alternation and Co-occurrence', in Gumperz and Hymes 1972: 213-50.
Fasold, Ralph
    1990   *The Sociolinguistics of Language* (Oxford: Basil Blackwell).
Ferrara, A.J.
    1973   *Nanna-Suen's Journey to Nippur* (Rome: Biblical Institute Press).
Fleming, Luke
    2011   'Name Taboos and Rigid Performativity', *Anthropological Quarterly* 84: 141-64.
Fohrer, Georg
    1963   *Introduction to the Old Testament* (trans. D. Green; Nashville: Abingdon Press).
Friedrich, Paul
    1972   'Social Context and Semantic Feature: The Russian Pronominal Usage', in Gumperz and Hymes 1972: 270-300.
Goelet, Ogden Jr, and Baruch Levine
    1998   'Making Peace in Heaven and on Earth: Religious and Legal Aspects of the Treaty between Ramesses II and Hattusili III', in Meir Lubetski, Claire Gottlieb and Sharon Keller (eds.), *Boundaries of the Ancient Near Eastern World: A Tribute to Cyrus H. Gordon* (JSOTSup, 273; Sheffield: Sheffield Academic Press): 252-99.
Gumperz, John J., and Dell Hymes (eds.)
    1972   *Directions in Sociolinguistics: The Ethnography of Communication* (New York: Holt, Rinehart & Winston).
Gunkel, Hermann
    1910   *Genesis übersetzt und erklärt* (HKAT, I/1; Göttingen: Vandenhoeck & Ruprecht, 3rd edn).
Hirschfeld, Hartwig (ed.)
    1905   *Judah Hallevi's Kitab Al Khazari Translated from the Arabic* (London: Routledge).
Hossfeld, Frank-Lothar, and Erich Zenger
    2003   'The So-Called Elohistic Psalter: A New Solution for an Old Problem', in Brent A. Strawn and Nancy R. Bowen (eds.), *A God So Near: Essays on Old Testament Theology in Honor of Patrick D. Miller* (Winona Lake, IN: Eisenbrauns): 35-51.
Hugh-Jones, Stephen
    2006   'The Substance of Northwest Amazonian Names', in vom Bruck and Bodenhorn 2006: 73-96.

Kadushin, Max
  1952   *The Rabbinic Mind* (New York: Jewish Theological Seminary).
Leibowitz, Nechama
  1990   'How to Read a Chapter in Tanakh', in H. Deitcher and A.J. Tannenbaum
          (eds.), *Studies in Jewish Education*, V (Jerusalem: Magnes Press): 35-47.
Melamed, Ezra Zion
  1961   'Break-Up of Stereotypic Phrases as an Artistic Device in Biblical Poetry',
          in C. Rabin (ed.), *Studies in the Bible* (Scripta Hierolymitana, 8; Jerusa-
          lem: Magnes Press): 115-53.
Parker, Simon B. (ed.)
  1997   *Ugaritic Narrative Poetry* (SBLWAW, 9; Atlanta: Scholars Press).
Polak, Frank H.
  1996   'Theophany and Mediator: The Unfolding of a Theme in the Book of
          Exodus', in Marc Vervenne (ed.), *Studies in the Book of Exodus:
          Redaction-Reception-Interpretation* (BETL, 126; Leuven: Leuven
          University Press): 117-47.
  1999   *Biblical Narrative: Aspects of Art and Design* (Jerusalem: Bialik Institute,
          2nd edn [Hebrew]).
  2010   'Forms of Talk in Hebrew Biblical Narrative: Negotiations, Interaction
          and Socio-cultural Context', in Hanna Liss and Manfred Oeming (eds.),
          Literary Construction of Identity in the Ancient World (Winona Lake, IN:
          Eisenbrauns): 167-98.
Revell, Ernst John
  1996   *The Designation of the Individual: Expressive Usage in Biblical Narrative*
          (Kampen: Kok Pharos).
Rofé, Alexander
  2009   *Introduction to the Literature of the Hebrew Bible* (Jerusalem: Simor).
Scollon, Ron, and Suzanne Wong Scollon
  2001   *Intercultural Communication: A Discourse Approach* (Oxford: Basil
          Blackwell, 2nd edn).
Segal, Moses Hirsch
  1967   *The Pentateuch: Its Composition and its Authorship, and Other Biblical
          Studies* (Jerusalem: Magnes Press).
Simon, Uriel
  1994   *Jona: Ein jüdischer Kommentar* (Stuttgart: Verlag Katholisches Bibel-
          werk).
Smith, Mark S.
  1994   *The Ugaritic Baal Cycle.* I. *Introduction with Text, Translation and
          Commentary of KTU I.1–I.2* (VTSup, 55; Leiden: E.J. Brill).
Uspensky, Boris
  1973   *A Poetics of Composition: The Structure of the Artistic Text and Typology
          of a Compositional Form* (trans. Valentina Zavarin and Susan Wittig;
          Berkeley: University of California Press).
Wardhaugh, Ronald
  2006   *An Introduction to Sociolinguistics* (Oxford: Basil Blackwell, 5th edn).
Weiss, Meir
  1963   'Einiges über die Bauformen des Erzählens in der Bibel', *VT* 13: 456-75.

Whybray, R.N.
1987   *The Making of the Pentateuch: A Methodological Study* (JSOTSup, 53; Sheffield: Sheffield Academic Press).

Widmer, Michael
2004   *Moses, God and the Dynamics of Intercessory Prayer* (FAT, 8; Tübingen: Mohr Siebeck).

Wilson, Stephen
1998   *The Means of Naming: A Social and Cultural History of Personal Naming in Western Europe* (London: UCL Press).

'THE UNSEEN JOINTS OF THE TEXT': ON THE MEDIEVAL JUDAEO-ARABIC CONCEPT OF ELISION (*IḤTIṢĀR*) AND ITS GAP-FILLING FUNCTIONS IN BIBLICAL INTERPRETATION*

Meira Polliack

> It is only when the schemata of the text are related to one another that the imaginary object can begin to be formed, and it is the blanks that get this connecting operation under way. They indicate that the different segments of the text are to be connected, even though the text itself does not say so. They are *the unseen joints of the text*, and as they mark off schemata and textual perspectives from one another, they simultaneously trigger acts of ideation on the reader's part. Consequently, when the schemata and perspectives have been linked together, the blanks 'disappear' (Iser 1980: 182-83).

Preface

In the history of biblical interpretation gaps have had their share, or shall we say 'place'. As modernists we can hardly fathom approaching the Bible (e.g. through structuralism, feminism, canonical or redaction criticism) without conceding 'missing' bits of 'information' that have been 'left out' of its text, whether by design or a haphazard historical process, to which we 'respond', in the act of reading and exegesis, by 'filling in' the gaps, thus making real a 'connectedness' necessary for the text's forming as an 'imaginary object'. This essay focuses on *how* medieval Bible interpreters, a millennium prior to reader-response theory, recognized significant parts of this process in the text's forming as a 'sanctified object'.

In her pioneering work on the book of Judges Yairah Amit attempted a synthesis between literary and redaction criticism, so as to interpret the biblical text within a new ideational framework, which emphasized its integrative compositional and editorial aspects (Amit 1992: 3-10). Her work resulted from the understanding that in the long historical and collective process through which a biblical composition finally became canonized, it is often

* This research was supported by the Israel Science Foundation (grant no. 410/10).

impossible to differentiate between author and editor or such 'implied' entities (Amit 1992: 16-17). This essay suggests that a not altogether dissimilar
understanding of the complex collective history underlying the formation of
the biblical text, including the inevitable blurring of compositional and
editorial functions, was reached by medieval Jewish Bible exegetes who
belonged to the Karaite school in tenth-century Jerusalem.[1] Their innovative
theory was formulated partly as the result of their structural analysis of
biblical language and discourse, including its usage of 'gaps', and partly as
the result of their radical revision of rabbinic notions. It is important to
integrate these exegetes' contribution into the history of biblical interpretation as leading up to (and to a certain extent anticipating) Spinoza's rejection
of rabbinic notions of biblical authorship, which inaugurated modern biblical
science (Spinoza 1670: chs. VIII–X).

Over the years in which I have known Yairah I have often been surprised
by her enduring encouragement of my work on medieval hermeneutics, and
by her openness to a field of research which tends to be unjustifiably tagged
as esoteric or marginal to 'mainstream' biblical scholarship. It is the same
kind of openness which I recognize in her intriguing analysis of biblical
passages, themes or wider issues, and in her nourishing ability to bring about
cognition in the more complex sphere of human relations through her candid
personality, her supportiveness and loyalty as a colleague and friend. It is my
pleasure, therefore, to offer her this tribute on the occasion of her retirement,
and so to wish her many more fruitful years of 'filling in the gaps'.

As already mentioned, contemporary biblical scholarship rarely gives
serious consideration to pre-modern developments in the understanding of
biblical literature that foreshadowed, in many respects, the modernist focus
on this literature's functions. The New Critics that transfigured my generation's understanding of the Bible as literature sometimes tapped into and
celebrated the literary sensibilities of ancient Jewish Midrash; yet the distinctively 'medieval' Jewish (and Christian) exegetical sources, ranging from the
tenth to the fifteenth centuries, were rarely mentioned in their works (Alter
1981; Frye 1982; Ricoeur 1975; Sternberg 1985). Paradoxically, however,
one can safely apply Iser's observation on the New Criticism to a large

---

1. Karaite Judaism emerged in the ninth century as a scriptural religious movement
that rejected the validity of Jewish oral law, and continues its existence to the present day.
In the Middle Ages it thrived in Jerusalem, Cairo, parts of Spain and Byzantium. In the
pre-modern period it spread to communities in the Crimea and Eastern Europe as well.
From the nineteenth century the Karaites under the jurisdiction of the Russian Empire
ceased to define themselves ethnically as Jews, whereas those of Egypt retained their
strong Jewish identity. The latter subsequently emigrated to modern Israel in the 1950s,
where they continue to lead a community life, running their own synagogues, in the
centers of Jerusalem, Ashdod, Maṣliaḥ and Ramle. For further reading on their history and
literature, see Polliack 2003.

portion of Jewish medieval exegesis, namely, that it 'changed the direction of literary perception in so far as it has turned attention away from representative meanings and onto functions operating within a work'. Indeed if Iser is correct in continuing to point out that,

> Where it (i.e. New Criticism) has fallen down is in its attempt to define these functions through the same norms of interpretation that were used in uncovering representative meanings. A function is not a meaning—it brings about an effect, and this effect cannot be measured by the same criteria as are used in evaluating the appearance of truth (Iser 1980: 15-16),

then it would not be far-fetched to claim that several of the great medieval exegetes avoided this pitfall, and were rather careful, as we shall see in the following, to separate their functional analysis from any claim on the Bible's universal meaning or representative truth.

It is an enigma to me why the fascinating and sophisticated corpus of medieval Jewish exegesis, and especially that written in Arabic within the Islamic domain, has remained for so long an un-integrated corpus within biblical study and hermeneutics even though a fair portion of exegetical works is now available in translation and in critical editions. Apart from the objective difficulties represented by their language and complex manuscript and transmission history, my sense is that these sources' marginalization results from tenuous pre-conceptions which often mar the study of culture and religion, to wit the assumptions that the medieval exegetes were mostly engaged in re-hashing 'classical' ancient Jewish exegesis (especially Midrash), while lacking the same creative or subversive edge of the Sages; that they were over-occupied with 'theological systems' slavishly adopted from their Christian or Muslim host cultures; and that their rationalistic mindset is akin to the dogmatic positivism of nineteenth-century Bible critics, who were engaged in uncovering the Bible's 'representative' or 'original' meaning. Nonetheless, while the latter critics are duly upheld as the founders of modern biblical *Wissenschaft*, the medieval exegetes are perceived as sharing a 'religious' (often a euphemism for 'un-scientific') outlook on the Bible. Hence they have been described as 'traditional' (*masorti* in modern Hebrew), an innocuous yet senseless term, since several of the greatest medieval Jewish exegetes conceived of their work as quite removed from tradition, certainly as farthest as was possible for Jews in their day and time. In point of fact, major Rabbanite[2] exegetes that come to mind, such as Sa'adya Gaon, Abraham Ibn Ezra and Rashbam (Rashi's grandson), not to mention the

---

2.   This term is used in Jewish Studies to distinguish the medieval Jews who continued to uphold the 'rabbinic' notion of the dual Torah from the Karaite Jews, who rejected it. The name Karaite (Hebrew: *qārā/qārā 'īm*) is derived from their association with the Bible (Hebrew: *miqrā).*

Karaite exegetes, were engaged in challenging Jewish tradition, skirting on its edges or discarding it.

Growing research in the field of medieval Jewish exegesis underlines the depth of its literary and functional analysis of the Bible, while attempting to integrate its teaching and understanding into the larger intellectual and historical milieus of the Christian and Islamic cultural domains in which it thrived.[3] This effort has borne partial fruits among biblical scholars, yet many remain resistant to it. Some may reject it as a 'reductionist' harping back, while others may concede its limited value as a quaint and un-harmful pastime for those who find 'hard core' biblical study too difficult or too mind-numbing. These flimsy reactions are a troubling reflection, in my view, of the sad state of current biblical study, which in many respects is unable or unwilling to re-invent itself as a discipline relevant to the twenty-first century and informed, as such, by wider developments in the Humanities and Social Sciences. While the analysis of the state of biblical studies is not the topic of this essay, I know it to be a burning concern of Yairah's, and by way of a dialogue with her, I end this preface with some degree of observation on the matter. Scholarly preconceptions and preoccupations with what *is* or *is not* to be construed as 'proper' biblical study have contributed to a sense of stagnation which alienates many a keen mind of upcoming students and researches from a field that was, not so long ago, a cutting edge of exciting and experimental thought on literature, religion and culture. The Bible, however, still offers that unique cross-cultural nexus of a wondrous, multi-layered and vastly complex oeuvre, from which so much can be gleaned about human nature, society and history. The Middle Ages are a rich terrain and vantage point from which to view this crossroad of Bible and culture. The re-invention of the Bible's significance and the all-encompassing grasp of its literary corpus during 'la longue durée' (Braudel 1958) can teach us much about comparative questions and the engendering of the relevance that appears to have been lost.

Karaite Jews and their Exegesis: An Entryway

Among the various exegetical schools that sought to re-cast the study of the Bible in the tenth and eleventh century were the Karaite Jews, who espoused a radical scriptural ideology (Ben-Shammai 1993) that resulted in a surge of innovative exegetical writing.[4] Effectively, they engaged in two interlocking

---

3. See, for example, Ben-Shammai 2003; Cohen 2003, 2011, 2012; Drory 1988; Polliack 2012b; Wechsler 2010; Wiesel and Yefet 2011.

4. For recent discussions of their exegetical output and methodology see, for example, Frank 2004; Polliack 2003b, 2011; Wechsler 2008: 13-135; Zawanowska 2012 (Introduction).

(and sometimes incompatible) moves. On the one hand, they attempted to disentangle Jewish 'written Torah' from 'oral Torah' by systematically dissociating the former's exegesis from the midrashic system which dominated rabbinic hermeneutic at large. In this they were dismantling, in effect, their rabbinic heritage as medieval Jews. On the other hand, they strove to base biblical study on a new exegetical system in which the analysis of biblical Hebrew, partly informed by Arabic linguistics and the comparison with known Semitic tongues (Aramaic, and especially Arabic), informed the contextual and structural analysis of wider sentence and discourse units. The Karaites recognized, nonetheless, that their semantic and thematic understanding of the Bible was at times paralleled by the potential meanings uncovered in various midrashim. The content matter of rabbinic Midrash, as distinguished from its system of interpretation, formed a legitimate springboard, at times, for contemplating a biblical text; and midrashic solutions to exegetical cruxes could be found sound, provided they accorded with the Karaites' linguistic and contextual criteria. Hence, from the inception of their movement there was a certain ambiguity in the Karaites' attitude to Midrash, a creative tension that brought about their fruitful dialectic with it (Polliack 2012a).

In the following I offer a preliminary attempt to chart out the Karaite perception of gaps and its diachronic development within this wider hermeneutic context. Firstly, a conceptual shift is traced from grammatical 'ellipsis' to a discourse 'gap' (both features are equally designated by the Arabic term *iḥtiṣār*). Later, the basic methods of Karaite gap-filling are illustrated and divided into contextual, canonical and extra-canonical categories. These are based on the work of the towering tenth-century exegete, Yefet ben 'Eli (Wechsler 2009), whose analysis of gaps is generally representative of the achievements of the Jerusalem school of Karaite exegesis. It will be shown how the Karaite Jews fashioned their understanding of gap deployment in a distinctively functional direction, as a means for analyzing discourse units and exploring the connectedness of biblical materials. In their basic understanding that gaps operate in the text (and upon its reader) as generators of semantic and thematic linkage, the medieval Karaites came close, in phenomenological terms, to the understanding of the connecting function of 'blanks' in modern reader-response theory.[5] The possible cross-cultural background of this medieval discovery is addressed in the Conclusions.[6]

5.   I refer here especially to Iser's fundamental work on the specific ways the *text* draws in the reader, including, most notably, the connective function of blanks, which formed an enhancement and critique (1978: 17-179) of Ingarden's pioneering notions on 'places of indeterminacy' and their role in the process of concretization through the reader (1973: 24-43). Further on these aspects of reader response theory see Eco 1979. Reader response theory has been widely applied to the Bible (Sternberg 1985: 201-213; Polak 1994: 331-44) and even more so to Rabbinic Midrash (see Stern 1991: 74-82; Boyarin

Iḥtiṣār: *From Grammatical 'Elision' to Narrative 'Gap' Employment*

The Arabic noun *iḥtiṣār* (verbal form *iḥtiṣara*, اختصر, namely: to shorten, elide, omit) is found in Judaeo-Arabic grammatical and exegetical works from the tenth century onwards. The Jews appear to have adopted it from Qur'ānic exegesis where it designates a syntactic ellipsis, such as the omission of an expected subject or object from the verse, which is promptly 'supplied' in its interpretation (Wansbrough 1968, 1970). The great Karaite grammarian of the late ninth century, Yūsuf ibn Nūn, who was among the founders of the Karaite school of Jerusalem, was the first to apply it to the Bible in his *Kitāb al-Diqdūq* (= Book of [biblical] Grammar), referring to the 'elision of letters in the morphological derivation of a word and the elision of words from a verse' (Khan 2000: 147; and see also 48-49, 128-31).

Ibn Nūn's terminology appears in some way related to the ninth herme-neutical principle attributed to Rabbi Eliezer ben Yosé Ha-Gelili, known as *derekh qeṣarah*, (קצרה דרך, a condensed, shortened style of Scripture). Arabic خصر and Hebrew קצר ('short') are similar in sound (and may possi-bly constitute cognate root forms).[7] This principle is enumerated within the thirty-two exegetical principles (מדות, *middōt*) of the *midrash aggadah* (the mostly narrative Midrash) found in the introductory part of the medieval work known as *Midrash ha-Gadol*, yet is not included in the seven *middōt* of

1990: x-xi, 41-56 and more recently Levinson 2005: 29-59; and cf. Rubenstein's review of the latter's book, Rubenstein 2009: 94-96). Levinson suggests differentiating between the concept of a 'gap' and a 'blank' on the basis of artistic intent (46-47). I prefer herein to use these terms interchangeably since (as acknowledged) they have the same formal function in triggering acts of ideation on the reader's part. In addition, Levinson suggests differentiating between inter-textual and intra-textual gaps (48-59; cf. Boyarin 1990: 17 and Rubenstein 2009: 94-96)—the former are distinguished through the text's poetic conventions, while the latter by the reader/exegete's cultural world. Though this differ-entiation is fruitful in the study of midrashic gap exegesis, it is less relevant to the medieval hermeneutic discussed below since its ultimate measure lies in the *formal features* of the biblical text that medieval Jewish culture, indeed, and especially its Karaite contingent came to view as central. See further in n. 16 and in the Conclusions.

6. My earlier work contains short discussions of Yefet's approach to gaps (see Polliack 2003b: 403-409; 2005: 366-68) in which some of the following examples have also been utilized. Below, however, I attempt a more comprehensive analysis of this feature in Karaite exegesis.

7. In medieval Arabic exegetical works ellipsis is also denoted by the term *ḥadaf* while in poetic manuals it is further subsumed within the technique of *al-iktifā'* (condensed /compressed expression), based on the understanding that the poet relies on the reader's ability to complete missing elements in the poem. The Hebrew poets of medieval Spain used this technique, identifying for it a biblical precedent of the kind encapsulated in the hermeneutic principle of קצרה דרך ('short[ened] way'); see Yellin 1978: 206-16.

the *midrash halakhah* (legal Midrash) attributed to Rabbi Hillel (preserved in the Babylonian Talmud) or in the thirteen *middōt* attributed to Rabbi Ishmael (preserved in the introductory part of the *Sifra*, a tannaitic legal Midrash on Leviticus). For this reason, among others, it has been plausibly suggested that the thirty-two *middōt* are a distinctive medieval composition that expanded the ancient rabbinic listings of *middōt* in an attempt to systematize the principles of Jewish narrative Bible exegesis, in addition to those already established in relation to its legal exegesis (Zucker 1954). Lists of hermeneutical principles were common in Qur'ānic exegesis, and in the medieval Arabic milieu we know of further Jewish attempts to systematize biblical exegesis from the tenth century, including the Gaon Rabbi Shemuel ben Ḥofni's forty-nine principles for aggadic exegesis (in the introductory part of his Pentateuch commentary); or the work of his earlier contemporary, the Karaite philosopher and exegete Abū Yūsuf Ya'aqūb al-Qirqisānī, who enumerates thirty-seven such principles in the introduction to his commentary on the Pentateuch. Several of Qirqisānī's principles (nos. 7-10; 20-21) are in fact concerned with semantic gaps (Drory 1988: 115-17; Hirschfeld 1918; Sklare 1996: 44-6; Khan 2000: 137).

Nevertheless, Ibn Nūn also used the phrase *iḥtiṣār al-tadwīn* in defining the elision of certain words within a wider grammatical structure. The term *tadwīn* in these contexts means: 'the text', and more precisely: 'the *form* of the text that is actually expressed in language as opposed to elements of the *meaning* that are not directly expressed' (Khan 2000: 150; my emphasis). In such cases, Ibn Nūn's Arabic translation of the biblical Hebrew verse includes the words that have been elided from the text:

> The concept is that these words exist *implicitly* in the *structure* of the text, but have been omitted in the *explicit written form*: *'uḥtuṣira fī al-tadwīn*. The *implicit* presence of such words in the structure of the text is posited only if some structural feature in the text requires this. Such features include, for instance, conjoined forms that occur without being followed by an item to which they are conjoined, problematic use of grammatical gender (Khan 2000: 133; my emphasis, MP).

Ibn Nūn also uses a related technique in calling attention to a syntactic gap in the second half a verse, which he does not explain as a form of 'elision' of words but by the principle of משך עצמו משך אחרים, namely, that something may include in its scope both itself and other things. This Hebrew principle is also attested in the works of other Karaite exegetes and was subsequently applied by Abraham ibn Ezra, who is likely to have adopted it from them (Khan 2000: 130-31).

The distinctive medieval concept of elision within a sentence structure was informed, as it appears, by a common Judaeo-Arabic milieu. It is certainly possible that, alongside Arabic influence, terms such as *iḥtiṣār*/דרך קצרה were affected also by ancient midrashic norms and ancient translation practices (especially those of the Aramaic Targum) that sometimes employ grammatical complements in response to ellipsis, even though they appear to lack a theoretical formulation of this feature. Nevertheless, it is only in the Judaeo-Arabic and primarily Karaite milieu that the very same term— *iḥtiṣār*—is employed in identifying 'gaps' within larger biblical discourse units. As a textual phenomenon 'ellipsis' should be differentiated from 'gap filling' of discourse and narrative spans that extend the sentence unit (Polak 1994: 30, 331-38). The Karaite exegetes' innovative understanding of narrative flowed and followed from their grammatical thinking. Both grammatical and narrative exegesis became dependent on their theoretical discovery that there exists a connection between the *explicit written form* of the text and its *implicit structure*, and by extension, between the text's 'form' and its 'meaning'.[8] This connection, first formulated in their grammatical work, was later developed in their exegesis, most notably by that of the great commentator of the second half of the tenth century, Yefet ben 'Eli, whose magnum opus—a highly innovative and voluminous Arabic translation and commentary on all the twenty-four books of the Hebrew Bible, spanning thousands of pages and also rendered into abridged medieval Hebrew versions—has survived in more than 700 manuscript copies. This work, whose immense scale and importance can be grasped by analogy to Aquinas's *Summa*, was in many ways a summation and perfection of the achievements of the Karaite Jerusalem school, and was duly recognized as canonical by the medieval Karaites, while leading Rabbanite exegetes (Abraham Ibn Ezra, Tanḥum ben Yosef ha-Yerushalmi, Isaac al-Kinzi and others) clearly saw in it one of the greatest works of their era in the field of Bible exegesis (see Wechsler 2009, and further references therein).

Yefet used three distinctive strategies in the 'filling in' of discourse gaps. These are illustrated and divided below into *contextual, canonical* and *extra-canonical*.

a. *The gap is 'filled in' contextually, relying on the verses in the immediate proximity in the narrative span.*
In his commentary on Gen. 31.7 Yefet ben 'Eli interprets the dialogue between Jacob and his wives as containing information that was not reported earlier in the plot: in his words, the information was 'elided/shortened' from its sequential place in the narrative's timeline. In this, as in other examples, we come across another idiosyncratic Arabic concept of Karaite exegesis, that of the biblical authorial-narrator-editor (*mudawwin*), who is usually described as implementing the gap (*iḥtiṣār*).

---

8. Khan's above-cited illuminating definition is applied throughout this article in elaborating the Karaites' theoretical understanding of the process of 'gapping' in larger units of discourse narrative.

The *mudawwin* concept is the focus of several recent studies. It generally designates the various functions of the anonymous/collective body of authors/ narrators and/or editors/compilers who formulated individual biblical books, and the biblical collection (*diwān*) as a whole.[9] It is mentioned here by way of emphasizing the intrinsic connection that the Karaites perceived between the activity of these *mudawwin*s and the employment of gaps in the biblical composition (*iḥtiṣār al-tadwīn*). The two terms usually appear hand in hand in Yefet's exegetical works, whose structural analysis leads him to finger an anonymous *mudawwin* as the figure responsible for the 'enactment' of *iḥtiṣār* in the organization and ordering of narrative (and other) materials:

> And his (Jacob's) words (to his wives): '(yet your father has cheated me) and changed my wages ten times' inform (us) that he (i.e, Laban) changed his salary ten times. We do not come across this information except here, and it is possible that the *narrator-editor omitted it* (*wa-'in kāna al-mudawwin iḥtaṣarahu*), yet Jacob is obviously correct without doubt, for he stated this (again) in Laban's face, as he says (Gen. 31.41) 'and you have changed my wages ten times'.[10]

Yefet is concerned with the 'displacement' of information concerning Laban's alleged cheating of Jacob outside its expected place within the chronological sequence of the story ('we do not come across *this information except here*'). In his reconstructed timeline of the plot, the event of the changing of wages should have been reported by the *mudawwin* when it 'actually' occurred in the history of the relationship between the two characters of Jacob and Laban. Yet for some reason it is only related 'post-factum', and then too in the first person voice of the character, Jacob, and not in the third person (omniscient) voice of the narrator.[11] Yefet's further unease results from the implications of this narrative strategy for the characterization of Jacob, in that it casts doubt on the veracity of his accusation that Laban has changed his wages. Did this event 'actually' take place if the *mudawwin* did not take the trouble to report it? Yefet's solution is to construe a deliberate 'gap' (in his words, a 'shortening/elision') in the *mudawwin*'s record of the event in its due place in the narrative span. The *mudawwin*'s motivation

9. The *mudawwin* theory was central to the exegesis of the Karaite schools of Jerusalem and Byzantium (tenth century onwards). It was later adopted by Rabbanite exegetes within the Judaeo-Arabic milieu (of the eleventh–thirteenth centuries), such as Isaac ibn al-Kinzi, 'Eli ben Israel, and Tanḥum ben Yosef ha-Yerushalmi; see recently Ben-Shammai 2009; Polliack 2005, 2008; and Wechsler 2010: 40-54.

10. According to MS B221, Russian Institute of Oriental Studies, Saint Petersburg Branch (fols. 136b-137a).

11. Although the change of voice is not discussed here by Yefet, he certainly refers to such changes many a time in his commentaries, and so it is likely he was also conscious of it here (see Polliack 2008).

for the creation of this gap in his readers' knowledge of the story (*'we do not come across* this information except here') is not explored by Yefet, nor are its possible narrative effects (such as an upping of the narrative pace or the creation of irony, both undoubtedly explored in modern readings). Nevertheless, the gapping itself is recognized by Yefet as a *function* of the narrative, a device employed (here and in many other relays of biblical data) by the *mudawwin*. Yefet's solution to the ambiguity that arises as the result of this gap regarding the credibility of Jacob's accusation of Laban is partly apologetic, in that he appears defensive of Jacob's stance. Nevertheless, it does have narrative consistency: Jacob is not lying, at least not in this case, for his accusation of Laban is reported twice in the narrative—first in his outpouring to his wives, which can, as such, be suspected by the reader for various reasons; and secondly, when it is re-iterated, verbatim, in Laban's face. The repetition confirms the accusation as genuine, since from a narrative perspective it is unlikely that Jacob would be leveling unfounded accusations at Laban after having been described as conducting himself so as to avoid as much as possible any direct confrontation with his father-in-law. Here and in other narratives Yefet perceives a mechanism: a certain matter that was gapped in the third-person report (or indirect speech) of the *mudawwin* is subsequently mentioned twice, and in different situations, in the first-person report (or direct speech) of the same character/s. In Yefet's view this mechanism acts to confirm, for the reader, the authenticity of the information provided by the character/s. Furthermore, in Yefet's eyes, it is actually the *mudawwin* who chooses to 'provide' this 'raw' data through the mouth of the character rather than through his own mouth, in his capacity as narrator, and so the gap is filled in by the immediate context. This mechanism serves two purposes (and we can say, in effect, that it creates two forms of reader-response): it 'fills in' the sequential gap in the 'original' reportage of the events through the immediate context of the story, and it establishes the veracity of the words of an otherwise suspect or dubious character. Yefet's insights into Jacob's character elsewhere in his commentary on Genesis suggest he was not unaware of a literary tension in this Patriarch's portrayal. For Yefet, the identification of a gap (*iḥtiṣār*) and its 'completion' via the immediate narrative context is primarily an *exegetical* method; yet his method *traces out*, on the formal level, the same narrative features which modernists would describe as *literary devices*, namely, upheld/delayed information, narrative tension and characterization; or, in a reader-response emphasis, the 'blanks' that induce the reader to acts of 'connectedness' and so enable the formation of an 'imaginary object'. By comparison, midrashic gap-filling, which often also relies on the immediate or wider context of the interpreted verse, rarely leads to any recognition of narrative build-up or reader-effect. For such a conception to enter the history of biblical exegesis one must have a well-formed notion of the role of the author as the creator or fashioner of a written text; to wit: a 'narratology'.

The persona of the author was highly celebrated in medieval Arabic literature, as was narrative in general. Various historical and other sources suggest the intellectual Jewish elites of the Islamic world keenly adopted these sensibilities from around the tenth century, as the result of their growing literacy and acculturation in the Arabic urban milieu (Drory 1988: 101-106; Frenkel 2010). The Karaites' innovative understanding of biblical narrative features and the process of narration was clearly affected by this wider cultural milieu and mentality.

Another fine example of Yefet's gap theory is found in his comment on the dialogue between Joseph and his brothers in Gen. 42.12-13:[12]

> He said to them: 'No, it is the weakness of the land that you have come to see', and they said: 'We, your servants, are twelve brothers, the sons of one man in the land of Canaan; and behold, the youngest is this day with our father, and one is no more'—And he (i.e. Joseph) said to them, following this (v. 12), something further which the narrator did not narrate here (*wa-lam yudawwinuhu hā-hahūnā al-mudawwin*) and we know this from the continuation (of the narrative) as we shall explain when we get there, God willing.

The information which the narrator omitted, and which led to the brothers' volunteering information about their father and brothers was not disclosed at this point in the narrative; rather, it was 'delayed' or 'gapped', to be provided in retrospect, according to Yefet, in Gen. 43.6-7:

> (Israel said, 'Why did you treat me so ill as to tell the man that you had another brother?' They replied, 'The man questioned us carefully about ourselves and our kindred, saying, "Is your father still alive?" "Have you another brother?"') What we told him was in answer to these questions; could we in any way know that he would say, "Bring your brother down?"' And from their saying 'he questioned us' we know that he had asked them this matter (if they have a brother) but he (i.e. the *mudawwin*) did not narrate this earlier (*lam yakun dawwanahā fī mā taqaddama*), and they are speaking the truth in saying this, and so Judah said in the presence of Joseph, 'My lord asked his servants, saying, "Have you a father, or a brother?"' (Gen. 44.19), and this is the way/ style of scripture (*ṭarīq lil-kitāb*) which it uses in many places, namely, it elides (*yaḥtaṣir*) in some places and it does not supply the words in full/properly (*ḥaqqatan*) and it relies on what it explains concerning this in a different place (*'ali mā yašruḥuhu fī mawḍa' 'āḥar*).

As in the case of Jacob's accusation of Laban, the brothers' divulging of what appears in its place as uncalled for information to the Ruler of Egypt should not be construed, as suggested by Jacob [*sic*], as an unguarded or

---

12.   MS B217, Russian Institute of Oriental Studies, Saint Petersburg Branch (fols. 89 and following.).

malicious statement on their part. The narrative confirms that they did so in answer to a 'real' question posed to them by Joseph, yet omitted from its 'proper' narrative place. This is so through the same mechanism of retrospective double repetition in the mouth of the same characters, firstly in their justification to their father, which may be circumspect for various reasons, and secondly in the words voiced by Judah in the Ruler's very face. This clearly confirms their authenticity, for the last thing Judah wishes in his speech is to antagonize this Ruler by making false accusations.

In this structural analysis Yefet uncovers, in fact, the same narrative patterning behind the ordeal of Jacob and his father-in-law, as behind that of Joseph's brothers and their father Jacob (and, by extension, of Joseph). Here too the filling in of the gap serves two purposes: it 'fills in' the sequential gap in the 'original' reportage of the events through the immediate context of the story, and it establishes the veracity of the words of an otherwise suspect or dubious character. Though Yefet himself does not point out the analogy between both ordeals (which has wider thematic implications, casting the characters of Laban, Jacob, Joseph and his brothers in interchanging roles) he does, in this instance, point out a general rule, which is clearly perceived throughout biblical literature. This rule echoes the Rabbinic phrase, דברי תורה עניים במקומן ועשירים במקום אחר ('the words of Scripture are poor in their place and rich in another place'), especially in its use of Arabic *mawḍaʻ* ('place'). Nevertheless, Yefet's formulation reflects a developed narrative consciousness that springs from a distinctive theoretical milieu. It transforms the Sages' notion of the inner unity and connectedness of Scripture into a *structural* and *time-bound* notion of biblical narration, one which postulates a connection between the *progression* of the text and its *meaning*. Biblical narrative is thus understood as a medium that operates through time, and the explicit (gapped) sequencing of events in the text's *written form* is structurally related to its *implicit* (full) sequencing in the text's abstracted storyline.[13] This 'fuller' sequencing is actually 'reconstructed' through Yefet's contextual completion of the gaps in the narrative. In this sense he views these gaps as 'the unseen joints of the text' because they induce the reader to search for the missing data further along the story, and so effectively trigger acts of ideation on the reader's part. The *mudawwin*, or the book/text (*al-kitāb*) creates meaning by withholding data that is subsequently revealed elsewhere. Whenever Yefet discusses this feature the revealed data comes *later* in the time sequence

---

13. In Polliack (2005: 373) I compared this notion to the formalist narrative distinction between *sujet*/plot as the 'finished product' and *fabula*/story as the 'raw material' (see Sternberg 1978: 8-14 and further references therein). In my current discussion, however, the grammatical grounding of the Karaite perception of narrative gaps is more pronounced, and so it is best captured, I believe, in Khan's distinction between *explicit written form* and *implicit* structure/meaning (see in the above).

of the narrative. That is, it is revealed retrospectively, mostly by the characters. It is therefore bound to the particular sequencing of the plot from beginning to end. Gapping is calculated and planned, an integral feature of biblical narration. This notion is actually opposed to the expanse which the ancient Sages refer to in their above-cited maxim on the richness and poverty of the biblical text, for in their formulation data may be gleaned from any place in the Bible, in a 'multi-directional' fashion that is not bound to any conventional form of time bound (and space bound) sequencing from A to Z. According to this maxim, the *explicit form* of the biblical text does not teach us anything about its *meaning*. It is not reflective of an *implicit structure* and there is no need to posit such a connection between form and meaning; rather, it is a *timeless* entity, of the kind captured in yet another of the Sages' famous maxims, אין מוקדם ומאוחר בתורה ('there is nothing early or late in Scripture'). In this respect Yefet's reasoning comes full circle in its dialectic with the Midrash. In his medieval mind-set there is indeed an abstracted timeline of early and late to Scripture which, when reconstructed, can explain its explicit (gapped) written form. Moreover, such a reconstruction through the filling in of the gaps turns the written form into an ideal of writing, a carefully worked out medium of expression whose blanks disappear once they have played their role of forming ideational acts. The Bible's apparent contradictions are hence smoothed out and perfected as part of a textual system that has textual and narrative logic of the kind befitting a divinely revealed text. In the Islamic system of philosophy known as *Mu'tazilite kalām* which was adopted by the Karaites, God's reason was upheld and worked out in exegetical terms, in that the commentator strove to demonstrate an inner logic in the Bible, its stories and other genres, which distinguishes it as a divinely inspired/originated text.[14] Once this logic is revealed to the reader the Bible's 'perfection' and 'flawlessness' as a literary text is also illuminated, and its knots and bolts are construed as a sign of literary acumen and masterfulness rather than as a springboard to an endless deconstruction of its meanings (Midrash). This inner logic accords with yet another Islamic principle, known as *'i'jāz al-qur'ān*, namely, the 'inimitability' (in the sense of literary uniqueness and perfection) of Muslim scripture (Drory 1988: 84-85; von Grunebaum 1971). An inner logic that leads to recognition of the Bible's literary perfection naturally suited the medieval milieu of Judeo-Arabic culture in which the Karaite Jews formed a formidable intellectual force. Hence, the Karaites' narrative theory is not only reflective of their ambivalent dialectic with rabbinic Midrash, or of their linguistic and structural discoveries, or of the rise of literacy and the concept of the author in their intellectual setting; it also resulted from an interreligious dialogue and

---

14.   On the principles of *Mu'tazilite kalām* as adopted in medieval Jewish sources see, for instance, Sklare 1996: 143-65; Adang 2007: 11-20; Wechsler 2008: 40-58.

polemic with contemporary Islamic scriptural culture (see further in the conclusions).

Other 'contextual' examples illustrate the same exegetical method in Yefet's gap analysis, and accentuate the difference between his reading and midrashic parallels. Yefet's commentary on the Joseph narrative, which he interprets as a cohesive literary unit, is most fruitful in this regard, no doubt since this biblical narrative reaches utter perfection in its artistic employment of delayed information for the buildup of narrative tension. Here are two of Yefet's salient comments, on Gen. 37.28, and 42.21:[15]

> ('The Midianites traders passed by; and they drew Joseph up and lifted him out of the pit, and sold him to the Ishmaelites for twenty shekels of silver; and they took Joseph to Egypt')— Note that the book/text omitted mentioning here (*al-kitāb iḥtaṣara an yaḏkur hā-hunā*) the words which Joseph said to them, but we know he cried before them and screamed to them and begged them that they don't kill him and that they don't sell him, and that they didn't act (according to his pleas), but were cruel towards him from what they say at the time of their regret (Gen. 42.21): 'but we are guilty over our brother for we saw the distress of his soul, when he besought us and we would not listen; therefore is this distress come upon us'.

In commenting on Gen. 42.21, on the basis of which Yefet 'completed' the missing data on Joseph's pleas in Gen. 37.28, he further 'reconstructs' Joseph's missing words:

> Twice he appealed to them, when they threw him into the pit and when they took him out—he screamed to them asking them not to kill him and not to sell him to the nations and he tried to soften their hearts by saying to them: 'I am your brother, your flesh and blood, please have mercy over me and if you don't pity me, pity the old man who is attached to me and won't be able to be comforted over me', and he said such things and the like but they did not accept (them).

As indicated in his last comment, 'and he said such things and the like', Yefet's gap-filling is a self-conscious attempt to reconstruct, in this case, the *possible* words Joseph may have said to his brothers, on the basis of their wording: *when he besought us and we would not listen* (בהתחננו אלינו ולא שמענו). Yefet focuses on the auditory aspect of their reminiscence in forming a connectedness between what was 'left out' and what is later 'reported', indirectly, of Joseph's words, yet never quoted directly, and hence may only be construed as *such things and the like*.

By comparison, in the ancient rabbinic Midrash *aggadah* known as *Genesis Rabbah* (whose compilation is dated sometime in the fourth–fifth

---

15. MS B217, Institute of Oriental Studies, Saint Petersburg Branch (folios not numbered).

centuries), a gap-fillling midrash reflects upon 'missing information' in the brothers' reminiscence as follows:

> Rabbi Levi in the name of Rabbi Johanan son of Sheila: Is it possible that Joseph, seventeen years of age, *saw* his brothers sell him and was silent? Rather this (verse) teaches us that he threw himself at the feet of each and every one of them in order that they become filled with mercy for him, but they were not filled with mercy (*Gen. Rab.* 91:10; emphasis is mine).

This midrash describes Joseph's dramatic and wordless act of groveling at the feet of each of his brothers in turn, in response to the verse's specific wording '*for we <u>saw</u> the distress of his soul*' (Gen. 42.21). Characteristically disconnecting this phrase from the auditory elements in the continuation of the verse ('*when he besought us and we would not listen*'), this midrash takes it to indicate no words were uttered on Joseph's or his brothers' part while he was thrown into the pit and later pulled out of it and sold (Genesis 37), thus accentuating these scenes' horrific significance through forming an imaginary object of the protagonists' actions as undertaken in an unnerving, isolating, almost voyeuristic silence. In this manner the midrash also highlights the brothers' act of memory as primarily visual and, as such, a typically traumatic reminiscence of their unspeakable act of brotherly abuse and betrayal. It focuses on the visual rather than the auditory aspect of the verse in construing an 'untold tale'[16] beneath their memory. This narrative exegesis completes the 'gap' as to *what* the brothers saw, dramatically dissociating sight from sound, in highlighting the connectedness of the underlying theme, one of enacted cruelty and its long denial (silencing), which is now coming to the fore in the re-encounter of Joseph and his brothers. In this respect the midrashic gap-filling response is no less 'contextual' than Yefet's, and arguably more sensitive to the psychological nuances and overall themes of the Joseph narrative. What concerns us here, however, is the Sages' respective recognition of narration as an operating *medium* through which the biblical text can be unraveled and interpreted. It is in this respect that Yefet's conception is far removed from that of the midrash in *Genesis Rabbah*, whose authors and/or redactors do not appear to connect in any *linear narrative time frame* to the earlier scenes of Joseph's casting into the pit and selling (Genesis 37). The brothers' memory of *what* happened is thus disengaged from the issue of *when* it happened and from the time line and sequencing of the Joseph narrative as a whole. Yefet, on the other hand, is very much engaged in this question, since he understands biblical narrative as a medium that is

---

16.   On the 'twice told' or 'double' narrative of biblical text and exegetical narrative in ancient Rabbinic hermeneutic and its relationship to narrative gapping see Levinson 2005: 102-49, and cf. Rubenstein (2009: 94), who underlines the influence of Foucault's model of interpretation as that of the 'nevertheless never said' (Foucault 1972: 221). See also n. 5 above and further in the Conclusions.

primarily worked out through its relationship with time. Hence, in his eyes, the question of *what* happened *when* is essential. In this case, *what* actually happened represents a piece of data that in the *abstracted* time line of the story could have been recorded *when* it actually happened. By contrast, the sequencing of the narrative and its pacing as a narrative is of little interest to the Rabbinic Sages. Hence their gap-filling is not reflective of a gap theory of the kind Yefet is putting into work in his understanding of the *unraveling* of the plot. Although it is always possible that this individual midrash may have been used to elucidate more than one context of the Joseph saga, its literary formulation as it has come down to us appears as a 'filling in' of the brothers' retrospective (and awakened) glance back at past (repressed) experiences. In Yefet's view, however, the missing data—alluded to in the brothers' confession—was not provided in its place, but elided, by the 'book/text'. Consequently, one can only imagine what Joseph might have said and how many times he might have done so ('twice he appealed to them') in the description of his casting into and pulling out of the pit. 'Such things and the like' is an indication of what may be construed by the reader when reading this story (and any other story) as a *time-bound* medium, on the basis of the brothers' retrospective report. Nevertheless, what he *truly* said at the time of the chronological (and only 'real') occurrence will never be properly known, since for some reason it was elided from the *explicit written form* of the book/text, and can only be reconstructed through recourse to the *implicit structure* of the story. The *explicit written form*, moreover, is to be analyzed accurately and fully, in accordance with the rules of biblical syntax, and cannot be truncated. The brothers remember what Joseph 'besought' of them and what they refused, at the time, to 'listen' to. Semantically, the text refers to 'words' that Joseph must have said at the time and which remained locked in their memory. That this is also what the brothers mean by the evocative idiom 'we saw the plight of his soul' is evident to Yefet, since in the narratives linear unfolding one phrase follows upon the other and is bound to it consecutively in the build-up of meaning. It is on the basis, therefore, of the second part of Gen. 42.21 that we are given to understand its metaphorical beginning.

Though the focus on sound rather than sight may appear as a slight difference in the 'gap-filling' process of this midrash and Yefet's comment, it reflects a different hermeneutic. Essentially, Yefet does not attempt to create a new story or tell an 'untold tale' which in some way lies behind the explicit one and yet is very different from it. Yefet's interpretation is motivated by the need to explain what the narrator/text omitted or delayed in its place and revealed in the form of condensed information in the brothers' retrospective admission; and to suggest, carefully and conscientiously, the kind of words Joseph *could have* said under such circumstances, for the purpose of illuminating the mechanism and structure of the plot. This is why, unlike the midrash in *Genesis Rabbah*, he places the gap in, or pinpoints its narrative occurrence to, Genesis 37, only then connecting between it and its subsequent 'completion' in Genesis 42. Unraveling the workings of the gap is thus more significant to him than providing his interpretive reader-response to the brothers' allusion, although some of his suggestions as to Joseph's possible wording, such as 'if you don't pity me, pity the old man who is attached to me' reveal his acute sensibility towards psychological nuance in biblical characterization, manifested in his commentary on the Joseph narrative in general as well as in his exegesis of other biblical narratives (Wechsler 2008: 26-28; Zawanowska 2008).

b. *The gap is 'filled in' canonically, beyond the immediate context, on the basis of other biblical sources.*
There are instances in which Yefet 'fills in a gap' on the basis of wider canonical sources, which I provide here in exemplifying yet again through his commentary on the Joseph narrative, as in his comment on Gen. 39.20:[17]

> 'And Joseph's master took him and put him into the prison, the place where the king's prisoners where confined'—And he (i.e. the mudawwin) omitted recounting for us (*wa-iḥtaṣara an yudawwin lanā hā-hunā*) that he tied him and constrained him, and he explains this in the poem (*al-šiʿr*), as it is said (Ps. 105.18) of Joseph who was sold as a slave. ('His feet were hurt with fetters, his neck was put in a collar of iron')—he fastened a fetter to his foot and one to his neck and he imprisoned him with prisoners that are not let out of jail until the day of death.

Yefet continues his completion of this 'gap' in Gen. 41.14[18]

> 'And they did not release him before opening his fetter by the order of the king'—and if this was omitted (*wa- ʾin kāna ʾiḥtaṣarahu*) then it was explained in the poem, as it is said: (Ps. 105.20): 'The king sent and released him, the ruler of the peoples set him free'.

c. *The gap 'filled in' by postulating the existence of extra-canonical narrative materials that were, historically, at the disposal of the biblical narrator.*
Lastly, it is illuminating to consider but one instance where Yefet notes a gap whose completion lies outside the canon, yet again referring to the *mudawwin*'s general purpose in the technique of *'iḥtiṣār*, as in his commentary on Gen. 25.19.[19]

17. MS B217 (folios not numbered).
18. MS B217 (folios not numbered).
19. MS B221, fol. 40b.

After he (i.e. the *mudawwin*) completed the stories of Abraham, he connected to them the stories of Isaac, and for this reason he narrated them by (use of) the connective *waw* (= *'and* these are the stories of Isaac son of Abraham'). And he omitted (*'ihtaṣara*) recording the stories of the sons of Qeturah and Ishmael since the purpose of the narrator was to connect the stories of our forbears (*wa-kāna gardֹ al-mudawwin yansuq 'ahֹbār 'uṣūlinā*). Furthermore, he did not want to preoccupy us with the stories of those (i.e. other descendants) who are like the stories of the rest of the world. Rather he mentioned for us the stories of the forefathers which are of benefit to us (i.e. as Jews), and for this reason he omitted (*'ihtaṣara*) mentioning (the stories of) those (others) and he mentioned (only) the stories of Isaac.

In this remark Yefet refers to gapping in the editorial/redactional sense. The reason behind the *mudawwin's* omission of relevant data at this point in the narrative, where we could have expected lengthier tales concerning Abraham's other sons (for only the genealogies of the sons of Keturah and Ishmael/Hagar are condensed in Gen. 25.1-18) is related to his overall purpose in the structuring of Genesis. The full stories of Abraham's other descendants, who became the forefathers of other nations, existed at the time of the *mudawwin,* and he could have included them in his collection (yet made do with their genealogies alone). According to Yefet, these fuller stories were consciously omitted or gapped since they were not deemed relevant to the *mudawwin's* 'objective' (in effect, his thematic purpose, ideology), namely, the recounting of the history of the Israelites, who descend from Abraham via Isaac's line ('he mentioned for us the stories of the forefathers which are of benefit to us' [i.e. as Jews]). In this case the gapping (also referred to by the verb *'ihtaṣara*) is not an aspect of the buildup of the narrative plot, of its *explicit written form* in relation to its *implicit (abstracted) structure*, as would be the gapping of the event of Jacob's cheating of Laban and its retrospective disclosure. Rather, the gapping is a *procedure* in the editing of the wider book of Genesis (and possibly the whole Bible), and an expression of its overall 'purpose'; or in other words, of its redactors' intents and motivations. As a general rule, in his discussion of the gapping of larger pieces of data Yefet often points out an overall thematic consideration on the part of the *mudawwin*, whereas in his discussion of the gapping of smaller pieces of information, vital to the plot, which may be 'successfully' completed through the immediate or wider canonical context (see sections a–b above), he refrains from a direct discussion of the *mudawwin's* objectives, and concentrates on uncovering the *mechanism* behind the gap, as one of deliberate delay and retrospective completion. We have seen how this mechanism serves Yefet in highlighting the connectedness of the plot and the authentication of the characters' wording. It is possible that Yefet refrained from emphasizing the rhetoric and/or aesthetic objective behind this mechanism for fear of coming too close to a perception of Jewish Scripture as a humanly formed text. As it is, the notion of an active human agent, the *mudawwin*, so dominant in his work, comes close to such a perception. It raises disturbing questions which remain unvoiced in his work yet undoubtedly reflect an inner-polemic, an insoluble tension on his part as an exegete, as to the nature of the relationship between this human agent and 'divinely revealed' Scripture. Such tensions may have been recognized and/or echoed by Yefet's contemporary and subsequent readers, and ultimately may have led to the suppression of his innovative theory of biblical composition and redaction in later medieval and pre-modern Jewish circles.

Further Analysis and Conclusions

In the spirit of their era, the Karaite Jewish exegetes' perception of gaps was a 'middle' one, in between the ancient and the modern. Theirs is not yet a formulated concept of the 'blank' as an intrinsic connecting feature to any text and an ideational trigger to any act of reading; yet, they do conceive of elision as a cohesion-building feature of the biblical text, a *function* operating within sentences as well as larger discourse unites, even within whole books and smaller collections of the Bible. The Karaites' reading of gaps is radically removed from the various forms of midrashic responses to it, despite their appropriation of some of the Rabbinic Sages' formations and interpretive solutions. Essentially, midrashic gap-filling is a form of 'stepping into' the gap, as one would step into a vacant (yet existing) space (not a 'blank'), into an unseen room (an attic, or cellar), as it were, which lies hidden (and full of mysteries) behind the apparent vista of the text. As alluded to above, the Midrash often fills in an existing or imaginary grammatical elision or narrative gap by telling an 'untold tale' behind the given tale and in a more limited sense, by 'realizing' a different/surprising meaning *alongside* the given/ explicit meaning. The Karaite exegetes tend to relate in a generalizing (and negative) fashion to this typified midrashic 'filling in', referring to it by the Arabic term *ta'wīl*, namely, 'non-literal' (sometimes in the sense of 'far-fetched' or 'unreasonable') interpretation (Polliack 2003b: 373; 2011). Their method of gap-filling is focused, by contrast, on the 'told' story (that is, on the *explicit written form* of the text), and it is highly dependent on the *immediate* and more rarely on the wider contexts of the interpreted span. In this respect 'context' does not serve the Karaites as a source for semantic or thematic interpretive reasoning in the way claimed for 'intertext' in Midrash (Boyarin 1990: 16-17; Rubenstein 2009: 90). Rather, context, as the syntactic and lexical as well as wider discourse fabric of the interpreted text, becomes the *criterion* for gap-filling, its ultimate measure and purpose. The explicit written form provides the *texture* into which the interpretive solution is spun, through which the gap is 'filled' and consequently 'disappears'. The gaps identified by the Karaites through the terminology of *'iḥtiṣār* come close, in this sense, to Iser's 'blanks', since they cannot be artificially construed, as they may be in Midrash. Exegetically, they are identified and traced through some 'ungrammaticality' (Rifatterre 1987) in the biblical text, which the Karaites recognize as an intrinsic feature of the biblical (and especially narrative) style of writing.[20] Hence gaps are intentionally deployed by the Bible's authorial-narrators in structuring the narrative data at their disposal into an *explicit written form*. In completing these gaps the reader-exegete is compelled to address the *implicit structure* of these narrative materials on the basis of what he uncovers *in* the Bible, as a sanctified literary corpus, so forming a meaningful connection between its parts, primarily on the basis of the immediate narrative, and when unable to do so, on the basis of the Bible's wider themes, schemata, and genres. The Karaites clearly recognized truncation and delay of data in the narrative span as *functions* of this gapping mechanism that served in the narrational and editorial build-up of the biblical plot. They also understood the semantic function of gaps in the creation of meaning, not in the theoretical (and universal) sense that they 'trigger acts of ideation on the reader's part', but rather in the sense that they compel the reader-exegete to synthesize different parts of the biblical text.

In addition, the inter-cultural and inter-religious implications of the Karaites' conception should also be highlighted, in that it may serve to counter Islamic polemical arguments against the Bible. These hinged on the 'gaps' (irregularities, inconsistencies and other such 'ungrammatical' features) in the Bible as proofs that it was falsified in some way, as a *text*, by the Jews (and Christians), who thus own an impaired version of God's message to humankind, in contrast to its true version that has come down in the form of the Qur'ān, thus abrogating Jewish and Christian scriptures.[21] The Karaite theory of gaps could have constituted a textual and literary answer to this effective undermining of Jewish Scripture, in that it turned the Bible's explicit written form into a sublimely devised and intentionally gap-prolife-rated text. The Bible's explicit written structures were shown to intricately correspond to its divinely instilled and inspired meanings, which could, when unclear, be clarified through recourse to its implicit (unwritten) structure. Hence, the 'uneven' 'deficient' places in the text cannot, indeed must not be construed as a sign of the Hebrew Bible's deficiency, inconsistency, incom-pleteness of expression or weakness of transmission. On the contrary, they are the ultimate signs of the Bible's refined textual encoding. The gaps are primarily to be interpreted as conscious measures, intricate techniques

---

20.   See as an example Yefet's reference to the unusual appearance of the connective *waw* in Gen. 25.19, above.

21.   On the detailed medieval Muslim arguments of falsification (*taḥrīf*) and abro-gation (*nasḥ*) see Lazarus-Yafeh 1992: 19-74; Adang 1996: 110-38, 192-255.

through which the Bible's ancient authors/editors (the *mudawwin*/s) inspirationally worked out how to tell its divinely revealed content in the most adequate and befitting *explicit written form*. On the other hand, there was an inherent danger in undertaking this course of explanation too far, for ultimately it affords too much freedom, self-will and choice to the anonymous and collective body of authors and editors of ancient times, and leads Scripture to an all too human domain. Hence there was an inherent ambivalence in the Karaites' approach to their discovery of the functions of gaps and the entity of the *mudawwin*/s, which is reflected in their reticence to elaborate his or their historical identity and wider literary and historical functions. Ambivalence, in general, marks the attitudes of radical and reformist scriptural movements, especially those exposed to an erosion of their oral culture as the result of an upsurge in literacy (Stock 1983), as the Karaites undoubtedly had been (Polliack 2012c).

The notion of gapped narrative materials also enabled the Karaite Jewish exegetes to offer a 'reconstruction' of the type of materials 'elided' from the Canon. These were classified above as 'extra-canonical', for example the 'fuller' (and subsequently elided) materials on Ishmael. Whereas gaps that may be filled in contextually or canonically form part of the buildup of plot and narrative meaning, gaps that can only be filled in by positing the existence of extra-canonical materials act as vestiges of the historical process underlying the formation of the biblical collection (*diwān*) and as indicators of its overall significance, as perceived by its ancient collectors. Their function is editorial rather than narrational, although at times these two functions may converge or overlap. Nevertheless, such editorial elisions are not devoid of meaning, since they too enable the understanding of the wider 'purpose' that the biblical authors and editors had in mind for their collection. One such purpose was to tell the story of the nation of the children of Israel, and not that of the children of Abraham as a whole (see above). In this respect such editorial gaps, like the narrative ones, are conceived by the Karaites as triggering acts of ideation on the part of the Bible's readers.

The Karaite Jewish exegetes' editorial gap theory may also have had inter-religious significance, for it effectively explains the concurrence of biblical and Qur'ānic 'materials' on the same families and biblical personae as the result of a natural historical and literary development. In positing this theory it helps counter Muslim polemic on the Bible's alleged falsification (*taḥrīf*) by the Jews. By the same token this explanation retrieves the Qur'ān from being alternatively blemished as a defective form of borrowing or copying from the Hebrew Bible. It has a 'neutralizing' effect on both sides. Accordingly, the overall 'purpose' of the narrative materials in the Torah (and the Hebrew Bible) was to relate the history of the Jewish people and to be of perpetual relevance to them. Its editing was directed primarily at this purpose and so entailed the elision of materials regarding those sons (and wives) of the shared Patriarchs that did not become the forefathers of the Jews but of other nations in world history, who also had their part in God's ultimate and universal design. Similarly, the stories of various Israelite Kings and Prophets were also omitted from the finalized form of the Canon, and possibly other generic materials, for they too were found in some way unfitting of the Bible's overall ideational and editorial designs (Polliack 2005: 356-57).

In addition, this type of explanation could also have served effectively in quailing surmounting doubts as to the Hebrew Bible's lack of reliable transmission (*tawātur*) and textual authenticity as a revealed scripture, a notion which gained force from the tenth century not only among Muslim polemicists but also among educated Jewish circles who internalized the new Arabic modes of the literate and rationalistically orientated religious culture ushered in by Islam (Frenkel 2010; Polliack 2012c).

In sum: The Karaites' editorial-gapping theory is ultimately suggestive of a relatively tolerant inter-religious framework for regulating and working out the perplexing interconnectedness of the Bible and the Qur'ān, and in reflecting upon their common materials, matters which were most conspicuous to the medieval Judeo-Arabic mentality. This may effectively signify that these Scriptures neither rely on one another directly, nor constitute, from whatever side, an impaired (secondary) borrowing. Alternatively, this theory implies that both religious traditions contain authentic narrative materials that were deemed relevant by their respective authors and collators for their separate religious communities, taking into account their overall purpose as religious histories. This type of reasoning concurs with Yefet's unusually positive exegesis of the stories of Hagar and Ishmael, and also concords with his relative openness and mellow tone towards non-Israelite (including female) characters in the Bible as a whole (Wechsler 2008: 26-28; Zawanowska 2008). If my tentative suggestion is correct then it leaves much to be desired in the future research of the inter-cultural and inter-religious dimension of the Karaites' functional exploration of biblical gapping.

Finally, some preliminary words should be devoted to the medieval Rabbanite reckoning with gapping, which by comparison, and only on the basis of the limited materials I examined so far, is mostly absent or non-innovative. Despite their intellectual acumen and engagement with novel genres and inner and inter-religious debate in other fields, Sa'adya Gaon and the Rabbanite exegetes of the tenth century generally ignored the narrational and editorial discoveries of the Karaites, including their understanding of the functions of gaps. One reason for this silence maybe the Rabbanite reliance and ideational indebtedness to the Midrash which, in the case of Sa'adya at least, was worked through by an all-encompassing harmonistic attempt to enfold detailed midrashic readings into his exegetical system (Ben-Shammai

2003). This ideological (pro-traditional and anti-reformation, anti-Karaite) stance in itself would have prevented a structural breakthrough in Sa'adya's understanding of gaps. Rabbanites would be encouraged to uphold midrashic gap-filling, including its 'telling' of the untold tale, as dimensions of the sanctified and divinely inaugurated 'oral Torah'. In many respects, for Sa'adya's generation at least, upholding oral law meant in some way uphold- ing the Midrash as an exegetical system. By and by, however, the Midrash lost some of its intrinsically sanctified and binding religious value in Rabbanite eyes as well. As the Karaite exegetical achievements became known and recognized, and the strained social relations with them eased somewhat, Rabbanite exegetes of the Islamic world engaged more and more with their theories; and the Karaite concept of the *mudawwin* as the imple- menter of gaps entered Rabbanite Judeo-Arabic works throughout the eleventh to the thirteenth centuries. In the tenth century, however, it was still necessary for Rabbanite Jews to validate oral law and, by implication, the midrashic-type treatment of gaps had to be upheld alongside the Bible in some way and could not yet be partially dismissed as an 'illogical', 'counter- linguistic', 'a-historical' or just intuitively as a 'far-fetched' stepping into the gap. In respect of the wider Muslim-Jewish polemic, Sa'adya Gaon does not seem to suggest that an 'elision mechanism' took place in the formation of biblical narrative spans, books or the biblical canon at large[22]—even though such a mechanism, which may have effected materials on certain characters common to the Bible and to the Qur'ān, would have served Sa'adya's gener- ally positive attitude towards the diasporic model of Jewish life quite well (Wechsler 2012). In my view Sa'adya probably did not have or was not able to sustain an outreaching theory about biblical gapping of the kind distinc- tively developed by his younger Karaite co-religionists of the tenth century, one which was so effectively carried through from their grammatical thinking into their narratology. Hence neither he nor his contemporaries among the Rabbanite exegetes could engage in this unique and fruitful hermeneutic of inner and cross-cultural exploration of the unseen joints of Scripture/s.

Bibliography

Adang, Camilla
   1996   *Muslim Writers on Judaism and the Hebrew Bible: From Ibn Rabban to Ibn Hazm* (Leiden: E.J. Brill).
Adang, Camilla *et al.* (eds.)
   2007   *A Common Rationality: Mu'tazilism in Islam and Judaism* (Würzburg: Ergon Verlag).

22.   I have found no clear-cut instances of this type in his commentary on Genesis (Zucker 1984).

Amit, Yairah
    1992   *The Book of Judges: The Art of Editing* (Jerusalem: Bialik Institute
            [Hebrew]).
Alter, Robert
    1981   *The Art of Biblical Narrative* (New York: Basic Books).
Ben Shammai, Haggai
    1993   'Return to Scriptures in Ancient and Medieval Jewish Sectarianism and in
            Early Islam', in E. Patlagean and A. Le Boulluec (eds.), *Les Retours aux
            Écritures, Fondamentalismes Présents et Passés* (Louvain/Paris: Peeters):
            319-39.
    2003   'The Tension between Literal Interpretation and Exegetical Freedom:
            Comparative Observations on Saadia's Method', in A. D. McAuliffe *et al.*
            (eds.), *With Reverence for the Word: Medieval Scriptural Exegesis in
            Judaism, Christianity, and Islam* (Oxford: Oxford University Press):
            33-50.
    2009   'On *mudawwin*—the Editor of the Books of the Bible in Judaeo-Arabic
            Exegesis', in Joseph Hacker *et al.* (eds.), *Rishonim ve-Achronim: Studies
            in Jewish History Presented to Avraham Grossman* (Jerusalem: Shazar
            Center for Jewish History [Hebrew]): 73-110.
Boyarin, Daniel
    1990   *Intertextuality and the Reading of Midrash* (Bloomington/Indianapolis:
            Indiana University Press).
Braudel, Fernand
    1958   'Histoire et sciences sociales: La longue durée', *Annales, Histoire,
            Sciences Sociales* 13.4: 725-53.
Cohen, Mordechai Z.
    2003   *Three Approaches to Biblical Metaphor, From Abraham Ibn Ezra and
            Maimonides to David Kimhi* (Leiden: E.J. Brill).
    2011   'Reflections on the Concept of Peshuto Shel Miqra at the Beginning of
            the Twenty-First Century', in E. Wiesel and S. Japhet (eds.), *'But I Have
            Come to Resolve the Plain Sense of Scriptures [peshuto shel mikra]':
            Studies in Biblical Exegesis* (Jerusalem: Bialik Institute [Hebrew]): 5-58.
    2012   *Opening the Gates of Interpretation: Maimonides' Biblical Hermeneutics
            in light of His Gaonic-Andalusian Heritage and Muslim Milieu* (Leiden:
            E.J. Brill, in press).
Grunebaum, G.E. von
    1971   'I'djāz', in *The Encyclopaedia of Islam* (Leiden: E.J. Brill, 2nd edn): III,
            1018-20.
Drory, Rina
    1988   *The Emergence of Jewish-Arabic Literary Contacts at the Beginning of the
            Tenth Century* (Tel-Aviv: Publications of Porter Institute of Poetics and
            Semiotics, Tel-Aviv University [Hebrew]).
Eco, Umberto
    1979   *The Role of the Reader: Explorations in the Semiotics of Texts* (Bloom-
            ington/Indianapolis: Indiana University Press).
Foucault, Michel
    1972 (2002) 'The Discourse on Language', in *The Archeology of Knowledge* (trans.
            A.M. Sheridan Smith; New York: Routledge): 215-37.

Frank, Daniel
    2004   *Search Scripture Well: Karaite Exegesis and the Origins of the Jewish Bible Commentary in the Islamic East* (Leiden: E.J. Brill).

Frenkel, Miriam
    2010   'Literary Canon and Social Elite in the Genizah Society', in M. Ben-Sasson *et al.* (eds.), *Uncovering the Canon: Studies in Canonicity and the Genizah* (Jerusalem: Magnes Press [Hebrew]): 88-110.

Frye, Northrop
    1983   *The Great Code: The Bible and Literature* (London: Ark Paperbacks).

Hirschfeld, Hartwig
    1918   *Qirqisāni Studies* (London: Jews' College Publication).

Ingarden, Roman
    1973   *The Cognition of the Literary Work of Art* (trans. Ruth Ann Crowley and Kenneth R. Olson; Evanston, IL: Northwestern University Press).

Iser, Wolfgang
    1980   *The Act of Reading: A Theory of Aesthetic Response* (Baltimore/London: The Johns Hopkins University Press).

Khan, Geoffrey
    2000   *The Early Karaite Tradition of Hebrew Grammatical Thought* (Leiden: E.J. Brill).

Kraemer, J.L., and Michael G. Wechsler (eds.)
    2012   *Pesher Nahum: Texts and Studies in Jewish History and Literature from Antiquity through the Middle Ages Presented to Norman Golb* (Chicago: The Oriental Institute of the Chicago University).

Lazarus-Yafeh, Hava
    1992   *Intertwined Worlds: Medieval Islam and Bible Criticism* (Princeton, NJ: Princeton University Press).

Levinson, Joshua
    2005   *The Twice-Told Tale: A Poetics of the Exegetical Narrative in Rabbinic Midrash* (Jerusalem: Magnes Press [Hebrew]).

Polak, Frank
    1999   *Biblical Narrative: Aspects of Art and Design* (Jerusalem: Bialik Institute [Hebrew]).

Polliack, Meira
    2000   'The Spanish Legacy in the Hebrew Bible Commentaries of Abraham Ibn Ezra and Profayt Duran', in C.C. Parrondo *et al.* (eds.), *Encuentros and Desencuentros: Spanish Jewish Cultural Interaction* (Tel-Aviv: Tel-Aviv University Press): 82-103.

    2003b   'Major Trends in Karaite Biblical Exegesis in the Tenth and Eleventh Centuries', in Polliack 2003a: 363-413.

    2005   'Karaite Conceptions of the Biblical Narrator (Mudawwin)', in J. Neusner and A.J. Avery-Peck (eds.), *Encyclopaedia of Midrash: Biblical Interpretation in Formative Judaism* (Leiden: E.J. Brill): I, 350-73.

    2008   'The "Voice" of the Narrator and the "Voice" of the Characters in the Bible Commentaries of Yefet ben 'Eli', in C. Cohen *et al.* (eds.), *Birkat Shalom* (Winona Lake, IN: Eisenbrauns): II, 891-916.

    2012a   'Historicizing Prophetic Literature: Yefet's Commentary on Hosea and its Relationship to al-Qūmisī's *Pitron*', in Kraemer and Wechsler 2012: 149-86.

2012b   'Scripture in the Judaeo-Arabic Sphere: The Karaite and Rabbanite Interpreters', in B. Sommer (ed.), *Jewish Conceptions of Scripture* (New York: New York University Press [in press]).

2012c   'Karaism, Literacy and Ambivalence: On the Disintegration of the "Dual Torah" Among the Medieval Jews of the Islamic World' (in press).

Polliack, Meira (ed.)

2003a   *Karaite Judaism: A Guide to Its History and Literary Sources* (Leiden: E.J. Brill).

Ricoeur, Paul

1975   'Biblical Hermeneutics', *Semeia* 4: 29-148.

Rifatterre, Michael

1987   'The Intertextual Unconscious' *Critical Inquiry* 13: 371-85.

Rubenstein, Jeffrey L.

2009   'The Exegetical Narrative: New Directions' (review of J. Levinson), *JQR* 99: 88-106.

Sklare, David, E.

1996   *Samuel Ben Ḥofni Gaon and his Cultural World* (Leiden: E.J. Brill).

Spinoza, Benedict de

2007 (originally published anonymously, 1670)

        Theological-Political Treatise (ed. J. Israel and M. Silverstone; Cambridge: Cambridge University Press): 97-154 (= chs. VIII–X).

Stern, David

1991   *Parables in Midrash, Narrative and Exegesis in Rabbinic Literature* (Cambridge, MA: Harvard University Press).

Sternberg, Meir

1978   *Expositional Modes and Temporal Ordering in Fiction* (Bloomington/Indianapolis: Indiana University Press).

1985   *The Poetics of Biblical Narrative: Ideological Literature and the Drama of Reading* (Bloomington/Indianapolis: Indiana University Press).

Stock, Brian

1983   *The Implications of Literacy: Written Language and Models of Interpretation in the Eleventh and Twelfth Centuries* (New Haven: Yale University Press).

Wansbrough, John

1968   'Arabic rhetoric and Qur'anic Exegesis', *Bulletin of the School of Oriental and African Studies* 31: 469-85.

1970   '*Majāz al-Qur'ān*: Periphrastic Exegesis', *Bulletin of the School of Oriental and African Studies* 33: 237-66.

Wechsler, Michael G.

2008   *The Arabic Translation and Commentary of Yefet ben 'Eli the Karaite on the Book of Esther* (Leiden: E.J. Brill).

2009   'Japheth (Abū 'Alī Ḥasan) ben Eli', in N.A. Stillman (ed.), *Encyclopedia of Jews in the Islamic World* (5 vols.; Leiden: E.J. Brill): III, 11-13.

2010   *Strangers in the Land: The Judaeo-Arabic Exegesis of Tanhum ha-Yerushalmi on the Books of Ruth and Esther* (Jerusalem: Magnes Press).

2012   'Ten Newly Identified Fragments of Saadia's Commentary on Esther: Introduction and Translation', in Kraemer and Wechsler 2012: 237-91.

Yellin, David
  1978   *Introduction to the Hebrew Poetry of the Spanish Period* (Jerusalem: Magnes Press [Hebrew]).
Zawanowska, Marzena
  2008   'The Literary Approach to the Bible and its Characters—Yefet ben 'Eli and his Commentary on the Book of Genesis: An Example of Competing Females in the Story of Abraham', in *Proceedings of the Fourteenth World Congress of Jewish Studies* (Jerusalem: Magnes Press): 69–84.
  2012   *The Arabic Translation and Commentary of Yefet ben 'Eli on the Abraham Narratives (Genesis 11:10–25:18)* (Leiden: E.J. Brill).
Zucker, Moshe
  1954   'Towards Solving the Problem of the Thirty-two Middot and the "Mishnah" of Rabbi *Eliezer*', *Proceedings of the American Academy of Jewish Research* 23: 1-39 (Hebrew).
  1984   *Saadya's Commentary on Genesis* (New York: Jewish Theological Seminary of America [Hebrew]).

WHEN AN EXPLICIT POLEMIC INITIATES A HIDDEN ONE: JACOB'S ARAMAEAN IDENTITY[*]

Dalit Rom-Shiloni

1. Introduction

Jacob's parting from Laban the Aramaean in Genesis 31 is at face value the last segment that completes the Jacob-Laban cycle. However, the story re-examines Jacob's long stay in Haran, and in its fifty-five verses (31.1–32.1) it actually revises earlier stories and suggests an alternative description of events.[1] This essay examines the literary evidence presented in Genesis 31: first, in comparison to its place within the earlier Haran chapters (Genesis 29–30); and second, as part of a larger controversy regarding the national identity of Jacob, who is designated as 'a wandering Aramaean' in Deut. 26.5,

אֲרַמִּי אֹבֵד אָבִי וַיֵּרֶד מִצְרַיְמָה
וַיָּגָר שָׁם בִּמְתֵי מְעָט וַיְהִי שָׁם לְגוֹי גָּדוֹל עָצוּם וָרָב

'My father was a fugitive Aramean. He went down to Egypt with meager numbers and sojourned there; but there he became a great and very populous nation',[2]

and whose 'Aramaean' genealogy is transparent in Genesis (24; 25.19-20; 27.46–28.9). Thus, following Yairah Amit's contributions to the study of

* I am grateful to Dr Ruth Clements for her reading and improving my language as well as my arguments, and to the editors of this volume for their important and con-structive suggestions. This study was written with the support of the Israel Science Foundation.

1. Genesis 31 was recognized mostly as Elohistic, with verses or parts of verses that scholars felt were duplicates, and thus were designated as Yahwistic (vv. 1, 3, 19a, 21-23, 25b, 27, 31, 36a, 38-40, 44, 46, 48, 51-53a). Verse 18a2-b was classified as Priestly, along with additional glosses within vv. 10, 12, 24, 29b, 42, 47, 48b-49, 51-53a. See Gunkel 1997: 331-42 and compare to Westermann (1995: 489-99), who accentuated the special position and unity of Genesis 31 in the context of the Haran stories. Westermann found the chapter to be Yahwistic, with no Elohistic level at all, but with necessary non-Yahwistic additions. On the function of ch. 31 as a completion of the previous Haran chapters, see Fokkelman 1975: 157-62; Fishbane 1975: 30-31. I will argue below that the chapter has been written by one single author, different from that of chs. 28–29; and see also n. 6.

2. The translation of biblical verses follows the NJPS Tanakh.

biblical polemics, and using sociological methods to explore the dynamics of group identity, I wish to add another example to the long list of hidden polemics in biblical literature, on the topic of Jacob's debated Aramaean origin; in fact, I will suggest that this hidden polemic arises from another, explicit one.

2. *Genesis 31 as a 'Composition Variant'*

In his studies of the Abraham stories, John Van Seters designated an essential feature of the 'composition variant' as the literary dependence of one literary work on another. Van Seters thus explained doublets in the Abraham stories as the result of an oral, and later written, process of transformation of the traditions, wherein later authors borrowed and revised earlier stories (1975: 162-64, 167-83). Applying these observations to the Jacob cycle, I propose that we view Genesis 31 as such a 'composition variant', for while it is completely dependent upon chs. 29–30, it counters many of the fundamental perceptions of those earlier chapters.

An important feature of these stories is their characterization of the main figures. Jacob's figure is constructed in reference to two spheres: his intrapersonal relationship with Laban, and his relationship with God. In Genesis 25–28, Jacob's relationship with Esau is governed by the themes of cheating and deception; the Haran stories of chs. 29–30 add to this portrait further elements of trickery and deception, though here practiced by both Laban and Jacob.[3] Genesis 31, by contrast, suggests a very different portrait of Jacob. The Jacob of this chapter is faultless; no trace of any deceitful action or trickery on his part mars his relationship with Laban. Jacob's speech to his wives summarizing his stay with Laban (vv. 6-7), the alternative version of the story of the increase in the flocks (vv. 8-13), and Jacob's tough counteraccusation of Laban (vv. 38-42), put Jacob's stay in Haran in a completely different light than do chs. 29–30.[4] We meet Jacob here as the devoted and loyal worker, the one who has taken pains beyond the call of duty to preserve and increase his employer father-in-law's herds (31.38-40). Laban, on the contrary, has acted consistently as a ruthless employer, deceiving Jacob throughout the entire period and changing his wages time and again (vv. 41-42).[5]

---

3. Nahum M. Sarna says: 'The perpetrator of deception is now the victim, hoist with his own petard' (Sarna 1989: 398).

4. Westermann (1995: 491) explained the differences between the stories as the result of Jacob's distinctive goal in addressing his wives. Based on similar arguments, however, Hamilton (1995: 288-289) harmonized the two descriptions. In the following discussion, I find the stories to be significantly different; this difference is the result of a purposeful revision made by a later author.

5. The Jacob–Laban relationship is set out in vv. 38-42 by means of terms known from Ancient Near Eastern herdsmen contracts, concerning the commitments of herdsmen

Moreover, Genesis 31 suggests a different assessment of the power relations between the two main figures. Genesis 29–30 illustrates the transfer of
power from Laban, who at first governs Jacob's life in all respects (29.15-30),
to Jacob who controls their second set of working terms and initiates his
eventual departure (30.25-43). Genesis 31.5-9, however, rules out Jacob's
active role in his relationship with Laban. Instead, God enters the Laban–
Jacob relationship. In Genesis 31 Jacob is passive in the face of the divine
direction of every step in his life. Jacob indeed has been the devoted worker,
but he does not initiate the departure (contra 30.25): it is a divine command
(31.3, 13) given immediately after the description of the explicit hostility
manifested towards Jacob by Laban and his sons (31.1-2).[6] In similar fashion,
the increase of the herds is depicted in ch. 30 as the result of interventions by
Jacob, the highly trained herdsman, aided by magic (30.31-43); the alternative description in ch. 31 features God as the agent who acted to circumvent
Laban's attempt to cheat Jacob (31.7), thus effecting a miracle subsequently
revealed to Jacob in a dream (vv. 10-13).[7]

In the sphere of Jacob's relationship with God, Jacob of ch. 31 is the pious
obedient person who constantly recognizes God's favorable involvement
with him (Fokkelman 1975: 159-62). Chapter 31 accentuates God's role in
saving Jacob from Laban (31.7, 24, 29, 42), a point not mentioned in the
Jacob–Laban relationship of chs. 29–30, where divine assistance is related
only to the economic wealth Laban has acquired (30:27, 30).[8] Chapter 31
illustrates recognition on the part of the narrator (v. 24), and even Laban
(v. 29), of divine involvement on Jacob's behalf; but this is most explicitly
acknowledged by Jacob himself in his speech to his wives (vv. 5-13) and
in his counteraccusation of Laban (v. 42). This recognition indicates an
important difference between ch. 31 and the preceding chapters. This is the
point where ch. 31 looks back and revises/corrects the trilateral relationship
between God, Jacob and Laban, emphasizing, on the one hand, Jacob's
devotion to Laban over the years, and on the other hand, the constant guid-
ance by divine providence that time and again has saved Jacob from Laban

towards herd owners; see Finkelstein 1968: 30-36. Accordingly, Jacob's speech distinguishes between his commitments (vv. 38-39) and those of Laban (vv. 40-42), emphasizing the exceptions to the norm; thus there is no reason to divide these verses between
diverse literary sources.

6. In vv. 2-3 the author depicts the opposition between Laban's negative attitude
toward Jacob (והנה איננו עמו) and God's support of him (ואהיה עמך; Hamilton 1995: 289).

7. In 30.39 and 31.10, 12 the circumstances (the time of the mating of the flocks) and
the results are similar (except for the difference in detail between טלאים and ברדים). The
major difference is the implement: Jacob's placement of the rods in the troughs (30.39)
versus a divine act that thwarts Laban's deception (31.8). Thus, in the second telling,
human magic is transformed into a divine miracle.

8. On references to God in the birth stories of Jacob's sons, see below.

(v. 42). Moreover, in comparison to other stories within the Jacob cycle, Genesis 31 is exceptional in that the divine involvement on his behalf is not connected to any cultic action taken by Jacob.[9] According to ch. 31 Jacob has merited unrestricted divine protection.

Finally, Jacob's pious portrayal gains further force from the allusions to Abraham.[10] Like Abraham, Jacob receives a divine command to go to Canaan, which in his case means to return to the land of his forefathers (31.3); but instead of Abraham's immediate and unhesitating emigration, the description of Jacob's departure from Haran features an elaborate account of Jacob's consultation with Rachel and Leah (vv. 4-16). This elaboration in Genesis 31 serves a central role in the departure story, as it contains four components that stand in clear distinction from chs. 29–30: (1) an alternative description of the Jacob–Laban relationship (vv. 5-9, contrast 30.25-31); (2) an alternative description of the increase in the herds (vv. 5-13, as against 30.31-43); (3) the dream revelation (vv. 1-13); (4) the wives' response (vv. 14-16). These components are brought together in a significantly different account of the Haran episode: Jacob's character is redrawn and purified in relationship to both Laban and God, even as these verses put a stain on Laban's character. The dialogue with the women is highly apologetic, answering the unspoken protest against the sources of Jacob's wealth (31.1); at the same time, it aims to smooth the offense against family laws caused by Jacob's flight from Haran. This leads to a different assessment of divine involvement on Jacob's behalf: according to ch. 31 the actual struggle is between God and Laban, while Jacob is only a passive onlooker (vv. 7b-12). Rachel and Leah's

9. Compare to descriptions of Jacob as a pious person who receives a divine revelation in Beth El (28.10-22; 35.1, 9-12); at the time of his prayer before his meeting with Esau (32.9-12); and at the time of God's revelation to him in Beer Sheva, prior to his descent to Egypt (46.1-4). In these stories, either before or after the revelation, Jacob establishes cultic sites (28.18; 35.7, 14); offers sacrifices (46.1); rids his camp of alien gods (35.1); and prays. Chapter 31 does not belong to this pattern.

10. This schematization of the direction of the literary borrowing, from the earlier Abraham stories to Genesis 31, is based on two arguments. First, the two major components of לך לך—the initial contact between God and Abraham and the first immigration to Canaan—do not match the story of Jacob's return from Haran, because God had already revealed Himself to him (28.10-20) and Canaan was his homeland (31.3). This borrowing, therefore, represents Van Seters' 'blind motive', a feature that characterizes the composition variant. Jacob's long stay in Haran enables the author of Gen. 31 to present Jacob's return as an event as important as Abraham's first immigration to Canaan. Second, phraseological connections occur in the departure descriptions and the taking along of family members and possessions. Gen. 31.18 integrates shorter formulae from other immigration stories (Gen. 12.5; 36.6; 46.6), and thus alludes to the immigration stories of Abraham, Esau, and even Jacob and his household's descent to Egypt, which it puts last. Finally, the target phrase ללכת/לבוא ארצה כנען (set out for the land of Canaan / arrive in the land of Canaan) brings together Abraham's and Jacob's migration stories (12.5; 31.18).

response becomes the initiating step in the familial-legal and economic separation between Jacob and Laban. This combination of divergences from the Abraham story of לך לך, together with the similarities to and differences from the Haran stories (chs. 29–30), highlights the initial reason why the author of Genesis 31 has thus revised the Abraham story: in this way he indicates that Jacob's return from Haran is as important a foundational story as Abraham's previous immigration from that place.

This intention to portray Jacob in Abraham's likeness in their trek to Canaan stands also behind another resemblance between the two forefathers. God's appearance to Laban in a night dream to warn him not to offend Jacob (31.24) resembles God's appearance to Abimelech king of Gerar, in which God warns him not to offend Abraham (20.3-7). Through this allusion, Genesis 31 portrays Laban altogether differently from the earlier portrait. He is referred to here—for the first time in the Haran stories—as Laban the Aramaean (לבן הארמי), appearing as a foreign king who plots against Jacob.

The unique role of Genesis 31 as a later revision of the Haran stories is further emphasized by the addition of a national element to the family story that governs chs. 29–30. This element denotes the story of Jacob's departure as a story of familial (legal)-economic, national, religious, linguistic, and geographic separation.

1. *The familial (legal)-economic separation* from Laban's household is expressed by the daughters/wives. In their clear answer to Jacob (31.14-16) the two wives proclaim their justification for such a break, saying העוד לנו חלק ונחלה בבית אבינו ('Have we still a share in the inheritance of our father's house?');[11] they explain their position as a reaction to Laban's attitude towards them, הלוא נכריות נחשבנו לו ('Surely, he regards us as outsiders'),[12] and they add two further legal arguments from the laws of marriage (v. 16). By this reasoning, the wealth Jacob has gained from their father indeed belongs legally to them and to their children. Thus, they declare their independence from their father Laban by virtue of their marriage to Jacob.

2. *The national separation.* The national character of the departure story is made explicit as of the second scene (vv. 19-25):

11. The declaration העוד לנו חלק ונחלה בבית אבינו is not taken from the family laws, and does not refer to a protest against deprivation of the daughters/wives from Laban's inheritance (contra Rashi; and see 30.35). It seems that the wives' proclamation is borrowed in this chapter from political discourse (2 Sam. 20.1; 1 Kgs 12.16).

12. Explaining the extremity of their action in the words, הלוא נכריות נחשבנו לו (v. 15), Laban's daughters compare their status in the eyes of their father to the deprived status of foreign women detached from their families in Israel and throughout the Ancient Near East, thus opening an ironic conflict that runs through the story (vv. 26, 28, 50). See also Ruth 2.10; and the comparative discussions of Gordon 1936: 156-57; 1937; Speiser and Pfeiffer 1935-1936: 95-96; Speiser 1964: 244-45, although this comparative direction has later been challenged by Greengus (1975: 5-31) and Eichler (1977: 45-59).

a) For the first time in the Haran stories, Laban is designated Laban the Aramaean, לבן הארמי (vv. 20, 24), and his family lineage is not given (as it was in 29.5, 10 [2×], 11, 12).

b) Laban's pursuit of Jacob (31.22-25) evokes Pharaoh's pursuit of the Israelites (Exod. 14.5-9), in both literary structure and phraseology.[13]

c) Laban's words, ותנהג את בנתי כשביות חרב ('and carrying off my daughters like captives of the sword', Gen. 31.26), borrows the language of war between nations. In fact, Gen. 31.26 is the only passage where this phrase is transferred from the international battlefield to the family domain.[14]

d) The treaty at Gilead (the fourth scene, 31.44–32.1) represents a two-phase treaty. The first phase focuses upon the status of the daughters, the second on the Laban–Jacob relationship. The former is portrayed as a one-sided treaty initiated by the women's father, Laban, who is interested in assuring their status within Jacob's household (vv. 48-50, following Laban's accusation in v. 26); the latter is a two-sided treaty initiated by Laban (vv. 51-53a). The difference between the two aspects of the agreement seems to reflect the two spheres of the departure story as a whole, as told in ch. 31, which is rooted in the family story of chs. 29–30, yet adds a national-etiological sphere to it.[15] This two-sided treaty, which shows clear connections to the ancient Near Eastern parity treaty, expresses the mutual commitment of two parties not to cross into one another's territory, with each evoking his god as witness to the treaty's validity (v. 53a). This designates the tendency to portray the end of the hostile relationship between Jacob and Laban with a declaration of peace based on clear geographical distinctions between them.[16]

---

13. Rabbinic sources continued this line and treated Laban as an earlier equivalent to Pharaoh. Daube (1963: 62-72) points out similarities between the Jacob-Laban stories and the Israel-Pharaoh relationship in the Exodus tradition.

14. Qimhi felt the tension between the family sphere of the Jacob–Laban relationship and the national sphere. The phrase כשביות חרב (as captives of the sword) is taken from the latter; see 2 Chron. 29.9; stories about the capture of Israelite women by non-Israelites (1 Sam. 30.2; 2 Kgs 5.2) and vice versa (Gen. 34.29; Num. 31.9); and the law regarding foreign female captives (Deut. 21.10-14). In all these passages the foreign woman is defenseless and has the lowest social status in her place of captivity.

15. This option seems more reasonable than the scholarly attempts to allot the two treaties to the supposed literary sources J and E (Westermann 1995: 497-98).

16. The prohibition of the transit of one party to the territory of the other is known from international political equity treaties, as in the treaty between Raamses II and Hattushili III (c. 1280 BCE), see *ANET*: 201-203; McCarthy 1978: 48. Von Rad (1972: 312) opines that the international covenant is much earlier than the family covenant.

3. *The religious separation.* Jacob's God is distinguished from Laban's gods. This distinction is developed throughout the chapter, as the *teraphim* are repeatedly designated as Laban's gods, התרפים אשר לאביה ('her father's household idols', vv. 19, 30, 32).[17] By contrast, Jacob refers to his God as אלהי אבי אלהי אברהם ופחד יצחק ('the God of my father, the God of Abraham and the Fear of Isaac', v. 42).[18] Following this, in the treaty oath the two distinct gods are called אלהי אברהם ואלהי נחור ('the God of Abraham and the god of Nahor', v. 53a), and each party swears by his own god, וישבע יעקב בפחד אביו יצחק ('And Jacob swore by the Fear of his father Isaac', v. 53b). Genesis 31 expresses an exceptional position within the stories of the fathers: Jacob and Laban each has a distinct 'father's god' (so also vv. 5, 29; see below). After twenty years in Haran within his Aramaean family, Jacob is heading back to his father, thus returning to his religious and cultural Israelite identity.[19]

4. *The linguistic separation.* Laban speaks Aramaic, Jacob Hebrew. The mound Jacob establishes is given two names: Laban gives it an Aramaic name, יגר שהדותא and Jacob calls it by the Hebrew name גלעד (v. 47).[20] The Aramaic phrase, the only two Aramaic words in the entire Pentateuch, reflects the understanding of גלעד as a construct phrase: 'a mound of witness'. This is the only explicit testimony to a linguistic difference between the descendants of Nahor and those of Abraham (Ibn Ezra; Nachmanides).[21]

17.   Genesis 31, the only passage that identifies the *teraphim* as Laban's gods, suggests a threefold denigration: they are easily stolen; they are profaned by Rachel who sits upon them in her menstruation; and their believer has to helplessly search for them. Genesis 31 accuses Rachel harshly: the worship of the *teraphim* is Aramaean in origin, brought by Rachel to Canaan against Jacob's will (and see Ibn Ezra). Compare to Gen. 35.1-7, where אלהי הנכר are referred to as part of Jacob's camp, with no specific connection to Rachel. In other places תרפים are but a mantic device, either Yahwistic (Judg. 17–18; 1 Sam. 15.23; Hos. 3.4), or one of the foreign (and thus denigrated) divination devices, Canaanite or Babylonian (2 Kgs 23.24; Ezek. 21.26; Zech. 10.2).

18.   The *hapax legomenon* פחד יצחק (vv. 42, 53a) may be understood as an Aramaism, reflecting דחלתא/דחלא as a divine epithet (by metonymy); see Hillers 1972 as against Malul 1985; Westermann 1995: 497.

19.   Gen. 31.53a refers to the gods of Abraham and Nahor and not to the gods of the biological parents of Jacob and Laban (Isaac and Bethuel), although here and also in v. 42 Isaac is also mentioned as in the *hapax* פחד יצחק (previous note). Cf. Josh. 24.2.

20.   The tension between vv. 47 and 48 led to the identification of v. 47 as a later gloss (Gunkel 1997: 339). While v. 47 is indeed alien to the form of the family treaty, it fits in with a separatist interpretation of Jacob's departure from Laban the Aramaean.

21.   See Skinner 1930: 401; Hamilton 1995: 314. Besides these two Aramaic words, there is a fairly large amount of Aramaisms in Gen. 31. Greenfield (1981) enumerates the following phrases: ויצל...ויתן לי ('God has taken away your father's livestock and given it to me', v. 9, Jacob speaking), ולא נטשתני לנשק ('You did not even let me kiss my sons and daughters good-by!' v. 28, Laban speaking), וידבק אתו ('catching up with him', v. 23, the

5. *The geographical separation.* The border established in Gilead (v. 48), or at Mitzpah (v. 49), designates the line northeast of which is the territory of Laban, and west of which is the area of Jacob.[22] This geographical note merits a comment on the historical location of the Aramaeans and the Israelites. The struggles between Israel and Aram over the control of the trans-Jordan area, reported as occurring from the tenth to the eighth centuries BCE (as for instance in 1 Kings 22), do not seem to be reflected in Genesis 31, since this story expropriates territory from both sides. Gilead appears here as territory that formerly belonged to neither party. Laban resides in the Haran area of North Mesopotamia, Jacob returns to the western side of the Jordan, the Gilead is the area into which none of them will ever again cross.[23]

These five dimensions of Jacob's departure from Laban the Aramaean illustrate Jacob's meaningful separation from the Aramaean world he was forced to reside in for more than twenty years, before he could return to his father's household. Even more emphatically, the story portrays this departure as a sheer new beginning—this is Jacob's emigration story, following his great forefather, Abraham. If we analyze this story from the perspective of national group identity, it becomes clear that Genesis 31 adds to the family story dimensions that create a national separation, as each of the two ethnic groups is seen to have distinctive culture, religion, language, group heritage, memories, and territory.[24]

3. *Genesis 31 as a Polemical Story*

a. *Biblical Polemic: Overt, Indirect and Hidden*

In both her English (2000) and Hebrew (2003) books on biblical polemics, Yairah Amit called attention to the ideological positions embedded overtly or—as is often the case—covertly within biblical literature, and to the literary

narrator's voice); he poses the question of whether they reflect the linguistic sensitivity of the early author, or the final revision of the text, conducted at a time when Aramaic was well known in Judah. I would add other phrases to this list: ברדים ('speckled', v. 12), פחד יצחק ('the Fear of Isaac', v. 42), וירימה מצבה ('and set it up as a pillar', v. 45), המצבה אשר יריתי ('the pillar which I have set up', v. 51). On אחטנה ('I myself made good the loss', v. 39) as a borrowing from Akkadian, see Finkelstein 1968: 30-36.

22. The double toponyms have been considered as evidence for the intertwining of two literary sources (Skinner 1930: 399).

23. The Gilead area was not part of the Aramaean residential territories; see Dion 1995: 1281-94; Pitard 1994: 207-30. This ethno-genealogical connection to the Aramaeans is only one of four different traditions of origin in the Bible (see Gen. 10.22; 22.21; Amos 9.7). This plethora of traditions attests to the obscurity of the 'true' origin and genealogy of the Aramaeans among biblical authors.

24. In its perspective on ethnic identity, Gen. 31 illustrates all six elements delineated by Smith 1986: 6-46; Hutchinson and Smith 1996: 4-16.

devices used to convey those positions. Amit argues that biblical literature demonstrates a profound 'polemical tendency', illustrating diverse internal ideological struggles that occupied Israelites and Judaeans time and again over centuries, throughout the biblical era (Amit 2000: 3-6).

The great challenge Amit faces concerns the arguments used to define a biblical text as a polemical text, and all the more as a hidden polemic. According to Amit (7), a text may be designated polemical if it raises an ideological issue towards which several different stances may be located in the Bible (though not necessarily in similar contexts). This requirement is not free of difficulties, which Amit addresses one by one. First, polemical arguments in biblical literature must be distinguished from textual or literary variants that often occur alongside each other with no traces of conflict (7-11). Second, Amit searches for 'convincing arguments' to validate the ideological conflict. The text has to present 'an issue for polemic' (10), and demonstrate this issue's position within existing 'polemical tension' (14).

This leads to a third point, the relationship between polemical positions and historical realities. A polemical text addresses an issue that was being debated in ancient Israelite society and reflects 'the pluralistic and complex nature of reality' (12-15). Accordingly, the scholarly task is to supply 'proof' to validate the presence of antagonistic positions within biblical literature (15). This may be done by clarifying and sharpening the 'polemic situation(s)' through analysis of the historical reality depicted in the text.[25] A fourth element is the cross-biblical interest in polemics. Amit points out that instances of ideological struggle occur within various genres: in historiography, law, prophecy, wisdom, and psalmodic literature. This diversity demonstrates that no polemical issue is ever discussed systematically. Hence, the scholar needs to assemble the relevant texts in a kind of pastiche, which often does not produce a unified (or closed) statement (24-26).[26]

25. Amit herself (2000: 16-22) makes the distinction between a literary-ideological picture and reality (or even 'depicted [fictional] reality', p. 16 n. 26). She uses the example of Pentateuchal slavery laws and their concrete contexts in Jer. 34 and Neh. 5 to show how one might reconstruct an ongoing polemic within Israelite society. The latter two writings provide the description of the concrete reality which, according to Amit, informed the Pentateuchal laws themselves. This is one of the points at which circular arguments may develop, thus great caution is required. See Amit's conclusion regarding the polemic over 'the place of the Sabbath in everyday life' (22-24): 'Thus, knowledge of a polemic, based upon reconstruction of the world following from other texts, may shed light upon a text as representing a stance' (24).

26. Amit adds a fifth point, a methodological comment for scholars to bear in mind when studying polemical texts: 'in many cases the reader is unable to free himself from his own world-view or from the exegetical tradition in which he was trained and interprets the text accordingly' (2000: 26).

Amit praises the editorial processes that left antagonistic positions side by side within biblical literature (32-33), and suggests that the editors intentionally left those conflicts intact, exemplifying the complexity and the multifacetedness of reality. At the same time, she demonstrates the diverse ways through which editors give room to their own stances (as for instance in Chronicles), deliberately hint at a polemic (e.g. concerning David as the killer of Goliath), or seek to shape the reader's perspective on the a given polemical issue (as in the monotheistic proclamation of Deuteronomy 4; or via the closing motto of Judges, with its pro-monarchic position). She finds that these diverse editorial tactics reflect the editors' consciousness of and sensitivity to changing stands and to pluralism of thought (33-39).

Focusing on biblical stories, Amit distinguishes three kinds of polemic—open, indirect, and hidden—judging by their degree of explicitness in presenting the subject matter and their stance toward it (44). While she calls attention to the lack of systematic (modern) 'abstract terms' by which polemical issues may be identified within a specific story, she does maintain that a direct or open polemic presents its subject and its position explicitly (56). Hence, locating them may require a more attentive reading of the text (49). Open polemics present their polemical issue through both explicit and implicit literary devices (44-49), and readers are expected to realize them both.[27]

Indirect (or implicit) polemics do present an explicit subject (as for instance the polemic against human sacrifice that is explicitly mounted in Genesis 22), but the story masks its specific stance (the divine command is only a test, and the child sacrifice was prevented through the substitution of a ram, 66-70). Therefore, readers need to figure out the text's polemical position by looking at the implicit literary devices utilized, such as plot, sequence of occurrences, shaping of characters, analogies, viewpoint or perspective, and style (57). Amit finds in implicit polemic a tendency to draw the readers into greater involvement with the story, as they are expected to uncover the concealed position themselves.[28] In addition, at times, the implicit polemic stands for the author's uneasiness with the story's anticipated position. With regard to both explicit and implicit polemics, Amit points out 'an essential condition'; that is, advocating the particular polemical position through a reliable figure within the story, i.e., the narrator; a respected character; or even, and preferably, God (50-56).

27. An explicit polemic is for instance Elijah's trial by fire at Mt. Carmel (1 Kgs 18.16), where the issue is explicitly specified in v. 21, and in addition the author's position governs the whole story through both explicit and implicit devices (Amit 2000: 58-61).

28. In connection with the issue of child sacrifice Amit also discusses two other texts, 2 Kgs 3.27 and Judg. 11.31 (2000: 70-72).

Hidden polemic, according to Amit, involves a subject that is not explicitly mentioned; or to put it positively, the polemical issue has been purposely concealed, although hints within the text lead the reader to tease out the hidden subject. Amit notes special efforts to hide the polemic through 'techniques of avoidance and camouflage' (93-94). This tactic of concealment guarantees that the story stands on its own, even without revealing its polemical nature; but once this element is revealed, the story gains further depth.

Uncovering a hidden polemic is thus the most difficult challenge of all. Amit spells out four characteristics that identify a hidden polemic. First (and a given), the polemical subject is concealed. Second, and a controlling criterion, other overtly or indirectly polemical texts on the same topic should be located to assure that the subject is indeed one of conflict within the biblical literature (94, 96-97), and 'a concrete problem of the authors' world' (95). Third, the author will have left specific 'landmarks' to lead the reader to the polemical subject. Thus readers need to discover the 'accumulative evidence...a series of signs that converge at one point: the hidden subject of the polemic' (96). Fourth (and another controlling criterion)—it should be possible to locate the subject of the hidden polemic within postbiblical exegetical tradition, in order 'to assure that the polemic is not only the idea of a commentator with an imagination or relevant needs' (97).

These guidelines for detecting biblical polemical texts substantiate my reading of Genesis 31 in two ways. First, as a 'composition variant', Genesis 31 illustrates an explicit polemic that responds to several issues raised by the Haran stories (chs. 29–30). Genesis 31 wrestles with the earlier portrayal of Jacob in reference to his working relationship with Laban, his wealth, and the issue of his legal status in parting from Laban, who is still recognized as the head of the household. It wrestles, further, with the length of Jacob's sojourn in Haran, portraying his journey back home as a divinely commanded emigration (following the model of Abraham); furthermore, it wrestles with the not-pious-enough portrayal of the relationship between Jacob and his God, adding 'corrective' markers.

I would like to suggest that in its insistence on Jacob's non-Aramaean *origin* in spite of the family connection, in its presentation of the legal, religious, linguistic, national, and geographical distinctions between Jacob and Laban at their parting, Genesis 31 reveals a hidden polemic and establishes its own position within the polemics concerning Jacob's identity. To validate this point, I shall address other texts that demonstrate both 'the issue for polemic' and 'polemical tension(s)'. As is typical for hidden biblical polemics, these texts are scattered and function independently, each in its own context; but, as will be suggested further on, each expresses a clear (though covert) stance on Jacob's identity. The texts are mostly within the Abraham and Jacob cycles that refer to the family connections maintained with descendants of Terah in Haran; added to these is Deut. 26.5, which explicitly refers to Jacob as Aramaean.[29] I will analyze these texts in order to tease out their ethnic/group identity perspectives, using the following criteria of identity definition: kinship (i.e. common ancestry, lineage, familial relationships), cultural heritage (including religion and language), territory, and solidarity.[30]

b. *Family Lineage in the Fathers' Stories: The House of Abraham and the House of Nahor*

The stories of the fathers in Genesis emphasize that the fathers kept in contact with their family in Haran. Thus Abraham in his later years sends his servant to Haran to find a wife for Isaac (Genesis 24). These family connections again play a major role in Jacob's life, when his parents send him to Rebecca's family, to Laban (Gen. 27.46–28.9). There he finds his wives, there his children are born, and from there he sets out to return to Canaan (chs. 28–35).[31]

1. *Genesis 24*. The story of the winning of Rebecca in Genesis 24 is the first text we will consider. The story, the longest novella of Genesis, opens with Abraham's command to his servant (vv. 1-9), and concludes with the servant's recognition that Isaac is his lord (vv. 65-66). This story relates the transition from Abraham–Sarah to Isaac–Rebecca. Moreover, Rebecca's departure from Haran resembles Abraham's emigration to Canaan: in Abraham's command כי אל ארצי ואל מולדתי תלך ולקחת אשה לבני ליצחק ('but you will go to the land of my birth and get a wife for my son Isaac', v. 4; cf. 12.1); in the servant's words to Laban, where he repeats his master's command, and adds 'the household' to this construction, to make the choice even more inclusive: אל בית אבי תלך ואל משפחתי ולקחת אשה לבני ('but you shall go to my father's house, to my kindred, and get a wife for my son', v. 38; so also v. 40); in Rebecca's immediate readiness to leave—ותאמר אלך ('And she said, "I will go"', v. 58); and in the servant's diligence at executing his master's command without delay (v. 61), thus fully completing his

29. These texts are presumably of different literary sources and dates. The following discussion places them only in a relative chronology.

30. The following discussion utilizes some of the six characteristics of ethnic identity suggested by Smith 1986: 6-46; Hutchinson and Smith 1996: 4-16. The first two characteristics mentioned by Smith (name and shared memories) do not seem to be of relevance to the biblical family stories.

31. The present view on the group identity of the forefathers rests on the understanding of each literary composition in Genesis as an independent tradition that could have been developed over a long period of time and by different authors. The rich literary materials in Genesis do not seem to add up to continuous literary sources, but comprise a rich and diverse anthology. In this judgment I therefore follow Cassuto 1961: 6; Rofé 1990: 27-39; and Westermann 1995: 33, among others.

assignment.[32] While Isaac is forbidden to return to Aram (vv. 5-9), ch. 24 is well-contextualized within the general picture that describes Abraham as the first to emigrate from Haran to Canaan; through Rebecca, his wife and the mother of his children, Isaac's place within this family pattern is maintained.[33] Although born in Canaan, Isaac's ongoing family and marriage connections guarantee that the foreign/non-Canaanite character of the fathers' family is continuously acknowledged.

Amit (2000: 78) views Genesis 24 as an explicit polemic regarding marriage to Canaanite women, a suggestion further substantiated by Isaac and Rebecca's displeasure with Esau's Hittite wives (26.34; 27.46; 28.1-9). On the basis of this observation, I will highlight some of the major features that construct this chapter's perspectives on Isaac's marriage within the family.

First, the story's primary interest is the divine providence that accompanies the servant throughout his journey and leads him to the successful completion of his mission (vv. 1-9 and 61-67).[34] This accompanying providence is acknowledged in the second scene (vv. 10-27), when the servant's prayer (vv. 12-14) is immediately answered by way of his meeting with Rebecca (vv. 15-25, and 45), for which the servant is grateful (vv. 26-27). It is further stressed in the servant's words to Laban and his household concerning his master's command (vv. 35, 37-41, cf. vv. 1-9); in his retelling of the meeting with Rebecca (vv. 42-48); and finally in Laban and Bethuel's reactions, in which they recognize that human actions are all directed by God (vv. 50-51).[35]

Second, emphasis is laid on Rebecca's lineage. Her descent from Nahor, Abraham's brother, and Milcah, Nahor's wife, is spelled out three times in the course of the narrative (רבקה...אשר ילדה לבתואל בן מלכה אשת נחור אחי אברהם, 'Rebekah, who was born to Bethuel, the son of Milcah the wife of Abraham's brother Nahor', vv. 15, 24, 47).[36] In addition, the servant

32: לקח ('take') and הלך ('go') serve as leading words in this story, see Hamilton 1995: 159.

33. Sternberg (1987: 138-39) pointed out the similarity between Rebecca's deeds (24.14, 18-20) to Abraham's hospitality in 18.2-7, and found that the goal of this allusion was to illustrate Rebecca as the proper wife for Abraham's son. Sternberg did not discuss the above-mentioned similarities between the characters of Rebecca and Abraham in regard to the emigration to Canaan.

34. Scholars have highlighted the idea of divine providence from diverse literary viewpoints, see Skinner 1930: 340; von Rad 1972: 259-60; Van Seters 1975: 241-48; Westermann 1995: 382-83; and finally, Sternberg 1987: 131-52.

35. Sternberg (1987: 138) accentuated the dramatic role of the repetitions in Genesis 24 and called it 'the fireworks of repetition'; see Savran 1988: 46-48.

36. Also note the strategically placed foreshadowing of this family relationship at Gen. 22.20-23, immediately following the *Akedah*, when Abraham is told of his brother Nahor's growing family.

emphasizes the close family connection when he mentions that he has arrived at the house of his master's brothers (בית אחי אדני, 'to the house of my master's kinsmen', v. 27),[37] and when he repeats Abraham's directive to find a wife for Isaac within בית אבי and משפחתי (vv. 38-40). All these family details underscore Rebecca's ties to Isaac on both sides of the family; not only is Nahor Abraham's brother, but Milcah is the sister of Lot and the daughter of Haran (11.29). Isaac's marriage thus proceeds according to the Nahor–Milcah pattern: the father or his son marries the brother's daughter (or granddaughter; this pattern recurs again in Jacob's marriage to the daughters of Laban).

Third, Laban's character is of great interest in this chapter. It is Laban who runs to welcome the servant, as soon as he sees Rebecca approaching the house with new jewelry and upon hearing her report (24.29). Does Laban welcome foreign guests just as do his uncles (Abraham and Lot) and his sister, Rebecca (v. 20)? Or is he perhaps merely hoping for monetary gain from this stranger? As Christopher Heard has shown, the narrative leaves these questions unanswered, calling the reader to perceive Laban's motives in one of these two antagonistic ways.[38] But could we do that in ch. 24, and free our minds from Laban's characterization in other episodes within the Jacob stories? It is important to note that unlike the characterization of Laban in chs. 29–30 and 31, ch. 24 does not identify Laban as Aramaean, and does not connect him with cheating and deception.

Fourth, the Nahorite family in Haran appears in this story to accept Yahweh, the God who had earlier revealed himself to Abraham and commanded him to leave his country with his family and his household (12.1-3). In addition to Laban's welcoming formula, בוא ברוך יהוה ('Come in, O blessed of the LORD', v. 31),[39] Laban and Bethuel agree to give Rebecca to

---

37. The plural form אחי (v. 27) is difficult. The Versions read the term as singular here, as in v. 48, see Westermann 1995: 381.

38. Heard 2001: 139-45. Among the interpreters who judge Laban critically in this story and connect his first appearance here to the development of his character in the Jacob–Laban stories, see Rashi and Qimhi; and among the moderns, Skinner 1930: 344; Speiser 1964: 184. By contrast, Westermann (1995: 388) and Hamilton (1995: 152) find his haste to welcome the servant as hospitable as Rebecca's. It should be emphasized that 'running' (v. 29) also appears in reference to the servant (v. 17) and Rebecca (vv. 20, 28), as also in vv. 18, 20, 46; and note the use of the same term in the quintessential hospitality narrative of Abraham welcoming the three angels (Genesis 18.).

39. Hamilton (1995: 152-53) neglects the proclamation of Laban's connection with Yahweh in this formula. As for vv. 50-51, Hamilton aptly notes the theological argument and the lack of any mention of the family connections by Laban or Bethuel as support for their consent to give Rebecca to Abraham's son. Sternberg finds this reaction to express that 'the Mesopotamians have passed a process in which they had discovered Yahweh as the "Lord of the universe"' (1987: 151-52).

Isaac, *because* (it seems) they are able to acknowledge that Yahweh is the actor behind the scenes:

מיהוה יצא הדבר לא נוכל דבר אליך רע או טוב
הנה רבקה לפניך קח ולך ותהי אשה לבן אדניך כאשר דבר יהוה

'The matter was decreed by the LORD; we cannot speak to you bad or good. Here is Rebekah before you; take her and go, and let her be a wife to your master's son, as the LORD has spoken' (vv. 50-51).

Or, should we consider the possibility that Laban and Bethuel's words are but a fawning formula for opening the negotiations concerning the marriage agreement?

Genesis 24 is narrowly focused on the family story and family ties between the Abrahamic and Nahorite branches of Terah's descendants, so much so that the narrative contains no indication of any linguistic or cultural-religious difference between the two families. This position stands in clear contrast to Josh. 24.2, and to the midrashic traditions depicting Abraham as the destroyer of his father's idols, the idols of Ur (e.g. *Jubilees* 12). Genesis 24 does not understand Abraham's emigration story as one of cultural-religious separation from his family's polytheism.[40]

Hence, while Genesis 24 should indeed be considered a late story and part of the explicit polemic against marriage to Canaanite women, its silence on Laban's Aramaic identity points to another polemical content as well. In its positive presentation of family relationships, this novella presents an altogether different stance toward Laban than does the negative presentation of Laban the Aramaean in Genesis 31. Neither does it accord with the identification of Laban as Aramaean in Priestly sources (to be discussed below). Thus, I would accentuate the chapter's independent status on the issue of Jacob's identity and family lineage.[41]

2. *Genesis 29–30.* When analyzed according to their conceptions of kinship, chs. 29–30 of the Jacob-Laban cycle portray tight family bonds between Jacob and Laban, his mother's brother. Beginning with Jacob's initial question to the herdsmen, הידעתם את לבן בן נחור ('Do you know Laban the son of Nahor?' 29.5), where the family lineage jumps over Bethuel and reaches back to Nahor,[42] Genesis 29–30 treats Laban as the head of the

---

40. Applying Laban's characterization in ch. 31 to ch. 24 and the Haran stories, commentators argue that, as an Aramaean, Laban is a polytheist by definition (Hamilton 1995: 140).

41. Rofé 1990: 27-39. Suggestions to date the chapter late within the cycle of forefathers' stories have been made from very early in studies of Genesis. Commentators have usually considered Gen. 24 a late stratum in J (Westermann 1995: 383); and see below.

42. Inaccurate familial information is also present in Jacob's words to Rachel (29.12), and there is no reason to suppose an interchangeable tradition. Compare to Westermann 1995: 463 and note the harmonistic efforts of Nachmanides and Qimhi on Gen. 29.5.

household. Thus, Jacob is Laban's nephew (29.10), and Laban indeed recognizes the close relationship when he says: אך עצמי ובשרי אתה ('You are truly my bone and flesh', v. 14). In marrying Laban's daughters Jacob *enters* Laban's household, from which he eventually initiates departure in order to set up his own independent household (30.25). Throughout these two chapters Laban is never tagged as Aramaean.

As for cultural–religious identity, the birth stories focus on Jacob's sons and the names given and explained by their mothers. These stories show no difference between Jacob and his wives in reference to their recognition of Yahweh. He is invoked by Laban's daughters in the naming of Reuben, Simeon, Judah, Dan, Naphtali, Asher, Issachar, Zebulun and Joseph.[43] Moreover, Laban himself recognizes God's involvement in his life when he acknowledges that his wealth stems from Yahweh's blessing upon him, given for the sake of Jacob, ויברכני יהוה בגללך ('the LORD has blessed me on your account', 30.27, and see Jacob's response, v. 30).[44]

Within this framework of the closed familial bond of Jacob's marriage relationship, these chapters construct the animosity between Laban and Jacob. These are the stories that continue the stamp of cheating that clung to Jacob from his encounters with Esau. For the first time, though (and one might say, in retribution), deceit is not committed only by Jacob. But while, in accordance with the midrash, Jacob and Laban may be seen as 'brothers in cheating', it is important to realize that the stories distinguish clearly between them. On the overt level the narrative avoids denigrating Jacob. He is not labeled as a cheater; in fact, throughout the Jacob cycle only once is the root רמה Pi. ('cheat') applied to his actions (by Isaac; 27.35).[45] A direct accusation of cheating appears once in the Jacob stories, and not-surprisingly it is leveled by Jacob against Laban: ולמה רמיתני ('Why did you deceive me?', 29.25). But the covert level of the Jacob stories (revealed by the general structure of the cycle and the episodes that it contains) does not clear Jacob of this accusation (see for instance Esau's accusation, 27.36). Jacob of chs. 29–30 is not only a victim of deceit, but also one who through his wisdom (and tricks) succeeds in overturning long term exploitation. Thus, as Buber and Cassuto show, Jacob was punished and suffered for his

43. Gen. 29.32, 33, 35; 30:5, 6, 17, 20, 23-24. Westermann (1995: 472) regards the name explanations where God is invoked as a late elaboration in the birth stories.

44. In contradistinction to Hamilton (1995: 278, 282) who argues that Laban is a non-Yahwistic foreigner, one may notice that Laban's words do not pose a distinction between Jacob's God and his. It seems that here (as in his reading of Genesis 24), Hamilton is swayed by his perspective on the portrait of Laban in Genesis 31, and he unjustifiably harmonizes the stories as regards their attitudes towards Laban.

45. The prophets add this exegetical layer to Jacob's character when they appropriate this term to admonish the people for their sins (Jer. 9.3; Hos. 12).

trickery throughout his life, and the Haran stories occupy a central role in that thematic complex.[46] Yet, this animosity between Jacob and Laban in chs. 29–30 has nothing to do with Laban's ethnic identity, which is completely framed within the familial relationship of the uncle turned father-in-law, who exploits his son-in-law's powers to enrich himself.

3. *Laban the Aramaean.* In addition to Gen. 31.20, 24, only two Priestly passages in the Jacob stories call Laban 'the Aramaean' (Gen. 25.19-20; 27.46–28.9). The two have a bridging role in the stories, and thus appear to be editorial.

In Gen. 25.19-20 we read:

> This is the story of Isaac, son of Abraham. Abraham begot Isaac. Isaac was forty years old when he took to wife Rebekah, daughter of Bethuel the Aramean of Paddan-aram, sister of Laban the Aramean (בקחתו את רבקה
> בת בתואל הארמי מפדן ארם אחות לבן הארמי לו לאשה).

As in its other occurrences in Genesis, this *toledot*-formula mentions the father (Isaac) in order to introduce the stories of his descendants, Jacob and Esau (25.19–35.29; 36). The *toledot*-formula focuses on procreation and marriage; accordingly it first mentions Isaac's lineage and then jumps immediately to his marriage with Rebecca, so as to introduce the birth of their twin sons (25.21-26). The atypical designation of Bethuel and Laban as 'the Aramaean', and the reference to their territory as Paddan-Aram, are emphasized by the proximity of this formulation to Genesis 24. The formula in 25.19-20 is interested in Rebecca's lineage too, but the designations differ. In this *toledot*-formula two comments are brought together: the first referring to Rebecca's father, the second to her brother. Unlike Genesis 24, where the lineage reference goes back two generations to Milcah and Nahor (24.15, 24, 47), in 25.19-20 it goes only as far as Rebecca's father and brother, and each is separately tagged as Aramaean.

Genesis 27.46–28.9 is the second bridging passage, coming between the close of the story about the theft of Isaac's blessing and the opening of the story of Jacob's escape to Haran. It contains two subunits, vv. 41-45 and 27.46–28.9. As Claus Westermann has shown, vv. 41-45 are connected to the previous story through v. 41, which refers again to Esau's hatred toward Jacob (mentioned already in v. 36); to this the passage adds Rebecca's new plan, which introduces the following unit—Jacob's escape and return (chs. 28, and even more so, chs. 29–33). After the failure of her first plan,

---

Rebecca's new plot aims at securing Jacob's life, now under threat from Esau (vv. 43-45). In Rebecca's effort to convince Jacob to leave she minimizes the length of the proposed separation; promises that she will send for him to return as soon as possible; and does not mention marriage. Like in the other family stories, the family bonds are tightly maintained, thus Laban is designated as 'my brother' residing in Haran (v. 43).[47]

Genesis 27.46–28.9 presents yet a different connection to a previous passage, as well as an opening to the one that follows. This time the connection is made to the concluding comment (Gen. 26.34-35), which precedes the story of the theft of the blessing (ch. 27).[48] Rebecca's complaint, אם לקח יעקב אשה מבנות חת כאלה ('If Jacob marries a Hittite woman like these, from among the native women', 27.46), corresponds with the report of Esau's marrying Hittite women (26.34-35). The following verses (28.1-9) elaborate further on those women, using the general designation בנות כנען ('daughters of Canaan', 28.1, 6, 8).[49]

Genesis 28.1-5 is easily marked as Priestly. The passage opens with Jacob's prohibition to his son (לא תקח אשה מבנות כנען 'You shall not take a wife from among the Canaanite women', v. 1), and continues with a positive command, קום לך פדנה ארם ביתה בתואל אבי אמך וקח לך משם אשה מבנות לבן אחי אמך ('Up, go to Paddan-aram, to the house of Bethuel, your mother's father, and take a wife there from among the daughters of Laban, your mother's brother', v. 2), and closes with a blessing (vv. 3-4) that promises reward for obedience. This blessing is very different from Isaac's blessings to Jacob and Esau in ch. 27 (Westermann 1995: 447-48). Genesis 28.3-4 portrays no physical contact between father and son, nor any sign of a ceremonial act; in fact, the blessing is closer to the promises in the forefathers' stories including procreation, political greatness, and the land (as in Gen. 17.1-8).[50] In its emphasis on marriage within the family, Gen. 27.46–28.9 contributes another example to the explicit polemic against marriage with Canaanite women (and see the discussion on Genesis 24 above). This literary opposition between the Canaanite women and the daughters of Laban highlights the differences between the two brothers, Jacob and Esau. Genesis 28.2 accentuates the closeness of the family bond: Bethuel is the father

47. Westermann (1995: 443) found these verses to be J's bridging verses, like Gen. 25.27-28. For distinctions between Gen. 27.46–28.9 and the previous narrative in Gen. 27, see Speiser 1964: 215-16.

48. Gen. 26.34-35 is Priestly as well (Speiser 1964: 202; Hamilton 1995: 210).

49. Interchanges between החתי and הכנעני are not uncommon in Genesis and in the lists of the nations (Ishida 1979: 464-65, 470-74).

50. According to Westermann (1995: 446-48), this ideological content is of major importance to the Priestly source that wished to add what are considered to be more significant blessings to the earlier ones, and likewise to connect Jacob with Abraham.

of Jacob's mother, and the potential wives will be the daughters of Laban, his mother's brother. Genesis 28.5 describes Jacob's full execution of his father's command, and repeats Laban's lineage in a combined description as both the son of Bethuel and the brother of Rebecca (similar to 25.20). Rebecca, in her turn, is recognized as the mother of Jacob and Esau. In addition to his characterization by family lineage, Laban is also tagged as 'the Aramaean'.

The traditions concerning Esau and Jacob's marriages (26.34-35; 27.46–28.9) close the first round of the struggle between Jacob and Esau (chs. 25–28).[51] The author uses these traditions to suggest Esau's perspective on Jacob's obedience to his father's instructions (28.6-9). Within the *Wiederauf-nahme*, וירא עשו כי ('When Esau saw that', vv. 6, 8), Esau's wish to appease his father is brought forth. But it seems that Esau's corrective actions only bring additional mockery upon him, since in an effort to rectify his earlier mistake he now takes Mahalat, Ishmael's daughter, as his wife. Mahalat is indeed a family relative, but in marrying her Esau perpetuates his 'outsider' status in the family as he ties himself to one of the rejected descendants of Abraham-Isaac. This episode thus designates Jacob as the chosen son who is in consequence ordered to leave for Paddan Aram.[52] The passage (28.6-9) ends with Esau's clear recognition of Jacob's advantage over him—Jacob has gained the birthright, his father's blessing, and both his parents' pleasure in his proposed marriage. With this passage, the Priestly author/editor suggests that the family in Paddan Aram is the only legitimate marriage option.

This last comment is of great importance for understanding the Priestly attitude to Bethuel and Laban's designation as 'the Aramaean'. In both Priestly passages this tagging is set in the same context with the mention of the close family bonds to the family in Aram, preferable probably because of its physical distance from the Canaanite women/peoples of the land. In this context, the tagging as 'Aramaean' does not offend or denigrate Bethuel and Laban ethnically; and the text clearly does not find fault with Jacob's marriage connections.[53] The reinforcement of close family connections alongside of the Aramaean tagging suggests that for the Priestly writer, 'Aramaean' is but a geographical and spatial term, which indicates a region as far as possible from Canaan.

---

51. Fokkelman (1975: 115-21) pointed out the overt and the covert literary progression of chs. 25–28.

52. Fokkelman (1975: 105-106) noted the way these verses denigrate Esau. Although Westermann (1995: 448) found this text sympathetic to Esau, I find it very disparaging.

53. Compare Rashi (on Gen. 25.20): 'Bethuel of Paddan Aram's daughter, Laban's sister. Was not it already written that she was Bethuel's daughter and Laban of Paddan Aram's sister? But to give her praise: although she was the daughter of a villain and the sister of one, and her place was that of evil men, she did not learn from their deeds'.

4. *'A Wandering Aramaean was my Father': Deuteronomy 26.5.*
Deuteronomy 26.1-11 features one of two liturgical declarations delivered
annually by every Israelite before God, as part of the first-fruits ceremony
(v. 5; and see v. 13). The theological importance of this proclamation has
been widely recognized since Gerhard von Rad's designation of this passage
as the Israelite *credo* (1966: 3-13, originally 1938).[54] It may be so designated,
insofar as this declaration constructs the religious identity of each member of
the Israelite people as a follower of Yahweh by narrating in capsule form, in
the first person,[55] the story of the divine salvation of Israel: from the bondage
in Egypt; through the journey through the desert; and through the gift of the
land, of which the first-fruits are now brought as a thanksgiving gift to God
(v. 10).[56] In addition, this *credo* also serves to construct the national-religious
identity of Israel by anchoring the story of the Exodus within the history of
the forefathers.[57] Opening with the statement, 'A wandering Aramaean was
my father', this retrospective tells of Jacob, who goes down to Egypt and
becomes there a great nation, which is then enslaved by the Egyptians, saved
and freed by God, and brought to the land.[58] This limited historical retrospection accentuates the national narrative of the common ancestor(s) who
came from the outside to the land that God had given them.[59] However אבד is

54.   On the Christian origin of *credo* as a genre see Speight 1987: 138-40.
55.   In the singular, at vv. 5 and 10; and in the plural, at v. 6.
56.   The declaration itself mounts an explicit polemic against syncretistic perceptions
connecting agriculture and fertility to worship of the Canaanite gods Baal and Astarte.
This passage introduces the monotheistic conception that God, the Lord of History and
Savior, is also the One responsible for those ecological spheres of life (Rofé 1988: 49-55,
esp. p. 53). On instruction in monotheism through liturgical speeches, see Weinfeld 1972:
32-42; Tigay 1996: 237-42. Martin Buber (1964: 82-88) called attention to the movement
from the individual to the community in this text, and between the historical event of
giving the land and its annual liturgical repetition.
57.   Deut. 26.3 prefaces the longer speech of vv. 5-9 with a thankful proclamation,
emphasizing the bond by which every person is connected to the Israelite narrative. On the
importance of both proclamations, see Tigay 1996: 238.
58.   Ibn Ezra, Hizquni and Sforno identified 'my father' with Jacob, whereas Rashbam
and Bechor Shor argued it was Abraham, and that ארמי אבד refers to his wandering or to
his status as an emigrant. But Abraham, while he did descend to Egypt, did not become
there a great nation. Traditional and critical exegetes diverge on the question of whether
Abraham and Isaac are included in the proclamation. It is also possible that the singular
form refers to the entire family, as in Num. 20.15 (Steiner 1997). Nelson (2002: 309)
argues that phrases that usually function in the Abraham stories (ירד and גור Qal, Gen.
12.10; 18.18) were connected to Jacob, and thus configure Jacob as the collective
representative of all the forefathers.
59.   Important chapters in the people's history are not included in this short summary.
Von Rad (1966: 5-8; 1966a: 159) has already called attention to the lack of any hint concerning the Sinai traditions, as is also the case in Josh. 24; Num. 20.15-16; Deut. 6.20-25.

to be interpreted, the opening phrase emphasizes the opposition between the nameless, homeless, landless father and the permanent residence of the Israelites in the land.[60]

The phrase ארמי אבד אבי has challenged interpreters throughout the ages. Its main difficulty seems to be the tension between its syntactical construction and its contents. Syntactically, it is a nominal clause that suggests the identical construction where 'my father' is the subject and 'wandering Aramaean' is the predicate. Hence, 'my father', Jacob, is identified as an Aramaean. The reception history of the phrase shows two lines of interpretation, the one geographical the other ethnic. On the geographical side, the Septuagint reads: Συρίαν ἀπέβαλεν ὁ πατήρ μου, 'my father has abandoned Syria/Aram',[61] while the Peshitta suggests the opposite direction: *'by 'tdbr l'rm*, 'my father was taken to Aram'. Both versions suggest the same interpretive procedure, whereby the ethnic adjective ארמי was understood to refer to the name of the place, to which Jacob had been taken or from which he had departed (so also Ibn Ezra and Hizkuni; and Tigay, among present-day critical scholars).

The option of understanding the phrase at stake as a nominal identity clause that identifies Jacob ethnically as an Aramaean puzzled the Aramaic Targums and postbiblical interpreters (the Midrash, followed by medieval exegetes). Therefore, they syntactically distinguished ארמי from אבי. The nominal clause was transformed into a verbal one where the attribute ארמי takes the place of the *subject*, that is, Laban; and where אבי-Jacob is the

Accordingly he opines (1966: 13) that the Sinai tradition was not part of 'the basic stock of the historical facts recorded in those summaries', but was added in a fairly late stage.

60. So Driver (1901: 321-22) and others. אבד was interpreted in diverse ways according to this verb's principal meanings: (1) 'become lost', 'go astray', 'wander' (as in Ps. 119.176; in the parallelism אבד/נדח, of Isa. 27.17; and in reference to Abraham, Gen. 20.13; Ps. 105.13). Deriving from this sense, ארמי אבד may designate a fugitive, and this accords with Jacob's flight from Esau (Gen. 27.43). On the suggestion to see ארמי אבד as a phrase borrowed from Akkadian, see Tigay 1996: 240. (2) אבד means 'be destroyed', 'be carried off' (as in the parallelisms נכחד/אבד, Job 4.7; כלה/אבד, Job 4.9; Ps. 37.20). Furthermore, (3) אבד (participle) occurs in parallelism with יתום, אלמנה, אביון, עני and thus designates the weak within society (Job 29.11-14; 31.19). Accordingly, Tigay suggested that the phrase refers to the danger forecast for Jacob because of the famine in Canaan, that caused the fathers to descend to Egypt. See Millard 1980: 153-5; and Steiner's suggestion (1997: 136-8) that אבד should not only be interpreted as Qal participle, describing the Aramaean's condition, but also as an Aramaic form of the perfect causative Af'el, thus as the predicate of the subject ארמי as in the Midrash.

61. For ἀπέβαλεν (LXX-B) 'throw off, reject', LXX-A reads ἀπέλαβεν 'take away', 'cut off'. Wevers (1995: 404) suggests a phonological switch between λ and β that led to morphological changes in the two verbs. I am grateful to Michal Crystal for checking the version.

object affected by Laban's deeds against him.[62] According to this analysis, Jacob is not Aramaean at all!

Critical interpreters added another option to this ethnic line of thought. ארמי is indeed an ethnic marker, but within this syntactical context allows for the possibility that this is a term meant to denigrate Jacob (so S.R. Driver).[63] Dweit Daniels and Jeffery H. Tigay, however, did not find any evaluative nuance, negative or positive, in the use of ארמי. Therefore, they each interpreted this statement as crucial evidence for the historical background of the passage, assigning the entire passage to an early pre-Deuteronomistic provenance.[64]

This exegetical polemics (extending from early postbiblical times to the present) on ארמי אבד אבי, that is, on Jacob's Aramaean identity, seems to be well-contextualized within biblical literature itself. The liturgical declaration of Deut. 26.5 suggests two options for understanding the focus of this polemic: spatial (Aram as the place where Jacob came from) or ethnic (Jacob as the son of Rebecca, the sister of Laban, and the daughter of Bethuel, both Aramaean). The significance of these two possibilities may be further clarified through a look at the potential circumstances to which the polemic is responding.

4. *Summary: Polemics and Reality(/ies), a Relative Chronology*

The Abraham story (Genesis 24) and the Jacob stories (chs. 29–30; and 27.46–28.9) reveal a unanimous position on the matter of family bonds and proper marriage partners for the sons, Isaac and Jacob. From the early layers (chs. 29–30) to the later traditions (27.46–28.9; 24), these stories accentuate the familial–ethnic bond of the father(s) with the Nahorite family in Haran, representing the descendants of Terah as the only legitimate family to marry (see 24.3, 37; 27.36; 28.1; 29.10-30). But family bonds go beyond marriage to the common cultural–religious bond that unites the two branches of this family. The family stories of Genesis 29–30, as well as Genesis 24, depict no

---

62. See Targum Onqelos, and the double translation presented by Pseudo-Jonathan; the Passover Haggadah; and following those Sa'adiah, Rashi and Rashbam among others.

63. See Driver 1901: 289. Craigie (1976: 321) explained the term as likely referring to Jacob's marriage to Rachel and Leah, two Aramaean women; and he does not add a further word on such a problematic tagging.

64. Daniels (1990) searches for a time when the relationship with Aram was not hostile, thus suggesting the period of the Judges, or even of the forefathers themselves; whereas Tigay (1996: 240) points to a time earlier then the ninth century BCE, prior to the rise of political tensions between Israel/Judah and the Aramaean states (Nelson 2002: 308). But is it correct to relate this tagging to the political relationship between Israel/Judah and Aram?

differences in the recognition of Yahweh as God, nor any sign of linguistic distinctions.

The Priestly editorial passages (25.19-20; 27.46–28.9) retain the element of close family connections, and add the attribute 'Aramaean' to both Bethuel and Laban, without any delegitimization of the marriage relationship. Therefore, the attribute 'Aramaean' seems here to serve an exclusivizing function, by which the Priestly author/editor accentuates the forefathers' non-Canaanite origin. Through their marriages (and thus their descendants) both Isaac and Jacob continue the genealogy of the Haran/Aramaean, indisputably non-Canaanite, 'outsider' lineage. The common denominator of this consensus among the literary traditions seems, then, to be territorial—the region whence the forefathers had come, the region known as 'Aram'.

This line of thought seems to be taken a step further by Deut. 26.5, when the latter is compared with these Priestly comments. While ארמי אבד אבי clearly follows the exclusivizing tendency of the other passages, it identifies *Jacob* as Aramaean. This is the 'innovation' of Deut. 26.5; the Priestly sources, which have no problem tagging Bethuel and Laban with this label, never so designate Rebecca or Jacob. Deuteronomy 26.5 borrows the 'Aramaean' tagging as it appears in those Priestly passages, without any denigrating meaning. Jacob's 'Aramaean' identity tag emphasizes the outsider, non-Canaanite status of Israel. This historical exposition reflects on the common ancestor who came first from the territory of Aram and then went down to Egypt, before his descendants were brought to the land of Canaan.

The thesis that 'Aramaean' designates a territory, remote from the land of the Canaanites, rather than an ethnic–cultural distinction between Jacob and Laban, brings me to Peter Machinist's discussions of Israelite identity. Machinist holds that a central aspect of this identity is that the Israelites are outsiders to the land and to its ethnic inhabitants (Machinist 1991: 196-212; 1994: 35-60). Machinist pointed out the numerous occurrences of this concept within diverse genres and literary compositions spread over different times and places across the biblical corpus. This allochthonous conception of Israel is understood to emerge out of the ideological necessity to distinguish Israel from the autochthonous peoples of the land of Canaan. Israel has come from the outside, from the desert, where it was formed as a unique social–cultural unit, as a nation, distinct in its religious–cultural–cultic characteristics from the peoples of the land.

While Machinist differentiated between two groups of Gentile peoples—the autochthonous peoples of Canaan and those considered non-Canaanitic (Philistines, Aramaeans, Egyptians, etc.)—there are in fact three central circles of peoples surrounding Israel that dominate the stories in Genesis (and are reflected in Deuteronomy 2 as well). The first group is that of the peoples who are descendants of Terah; they might be called 'the cognate peoples'. Yet these are also the peoples who were excluded from the principal lineage, and also from the land. They either reside in the desert (Ishmael), or in trans-Jordan (Ammon and Moab, the descendants of Lot, Edom-Esau).[65] The Canaanite peoples, on the other hand, are those who reside on the western side of the Jordan, in the territories of Israel. They are 'the proximate others' of the Israelite social and cultural context during the first centuries of the first millennium. Israel is commanded not to be in any contact with them (Exod. 34.16; Deut. 7.3-4), since Israel is supposed to maintain its ethnic (religious-cultural) uniqueness and its 'foreign' nature even in its land. The Aramaean connection designates a third circle of related peoples, and geographically the most distant one, the one on which the allochthonous conception of Israel is in fact constructed.[66] The marriage connections with the Nahorite family in Haran guarantee the ongoing relevance of this concept.[67] The patriarchal traditions, *especially* under their Priestly redaction, all report how each of the first three generations of the ancestors had maintained their identity as 'outsiders' by marrying women of that distant, foreign family from Haran/Aram.[68]

In light of the foregoing, it is possible to recognize that the explicit polemic in these passages operates not only as against marriage with Canaanite women (which unfortunately is usually connected to Ezra–Nehemiah's argument against intermarriage among the repatriates of the Persian period), but as part of a larger polemic against any contact with Canaanites. This polemic is part of the struggle over Israelite national-religious-cultic identity, which may be dated to the eighth or seventh centuries BCE. This thread of controversy runs through the Pentateuch and the Deuteronomistic historiography, and among other restrictions excludes marriage with Canaanite women (as in Exod. 34.11-16; Deut. 7.1-6).

65. Machinist (1994: 49-51) discusses this 'outsiders' concept of origin among other peoples within the Ancient Near East (and the Greco-Roman world). He finds that it comes into play among relatively new groups, all of which emerged in the transitional period from the end of the Late Bronze through the Early Iron ages. While the archaeological evidence points to a continuity of settlement from within in both the Levant and Greco-Roman regions, this self-perception styles these 'young' peoples as coming into these areas from outside.

66. The Aramaeans had already been settled in their own territory, long before the 'young' people settled between Beer-Sheva and Gerar and the southern coast. On the Philistines that arrived from the Aegean area by the twelfth century BCE, see Howard 1994 and the rich literature cited there.

67. Hamilton (1995: 150) claims that the preference for Aramaeans comes from the prohibition to marry the local peoples in order to prevent them from possessing the land.

68. This tendency was subverted already by Abraham (in his marriage to Keturah), and more so in the generation of Jacob's sons, though details are known only about three of them: Judah, Joseph and Simeon (Gen. 38.2; 41.45; 46.10, 20).

Genesis 31 stands last in the sequence of sources referring to Jacob's Aramaean origin and marriage connections, and it takes a special position in it. The author of Genesis 31 knows not only the Haran stories, but some of the Abraham and Isaac stories as well. More interesting is the fact that the author of Genesis 31 polemicizes against Deut. 26.5, where Jacob is clearly identified as Aramaean, refuting this option through every possible avenue. Genesis 31 closes the Haran chapters by adding a hidden polemic that rests precisely on the explicit connection of Jacob with Laban, with Haran. The author of this revision seems to have understood ארמי אבד אבי according to its ethnic meaning and could not make peace with this identification. In his hidden polemic he wrestles with the implications of Jacob's presentation as an outsider. Neither by ancestors nor by religion, language, or geographical territory is Jacob the least bit Aramaean!

Nevertheless, Genesis 31 follows the consensus on Jacob's foreign origin; in fact, it further augments the account of Jacob's departure by framing it within the literary pattern of Abraham's לך לך emigration. Although actually born in the land of Canaan, Jacob is styled as another outsider commanded by God to return/emigrate back to Canaan following more than twenty years abroad; and he brings with him his wives and children, themselves born and raised outside of Canaan, in far away Haran.

The relative order of the discussed texts, thus, may be seen as follows: (1) The Haran stories (Genesis 29–30); (2) the priestly passages (25.19-20; 27.46–28.9); (3) Deut. 26.5; (4) Jacob's departure from Laban the Aramaean (ch. 31). Of course, it is most difficult and speculative to turn the relative chronology of these texts into a definitive chronology.

The explicit polemics on the question of Israelite identity versus the Canaanites seem to date to the eighth and seventh centuries BCE, and this may be the time and context whence the Deuteronomic *credo* evolved.

The choice of the Aramaeans as the forefathers' family-ethnic background seems to be based on their special history. While the Aramaeans had not established a unified powerful political entity in any of the regions they had settled in during the second and the first millennia BCE, excepting perhaps the kingdom of Damascus, they did attain a growing cultural influence (through the spread of their language and script) in the ancient Near East, especially after they had ceased to have an independent kingdom and became an Assyrian province (after 732 BCE). Aramaic became the *lingua franca* of the Assyrian empire from about the second half of the eighth century BCE, and this linguistic hegemony lasted throughout the Babylonian and Persian periods as well.[69] Hence, this Aramaic context suggests several possible

---

69. The identity of the Aramaeans and the period that may suit the description of family connections with them have intrigued both traditional and critical exegetes (Dion 1995). Of the diverse options, I find convincing the period when the Aramaean kingdoms

historical points at which an Aramaean identity could have been considered a
prestigious 'outsider' status (Machinist 1994: 51-60). Genesis 31, while it
must be dated after the Priestly passages and after Deut. 26.5, nevertheless
tries to validate a national Israelite identity within the land, eschewing the
'outsider' dynamic; thus, it may be quite close in time to the texts it
polemicizes against and may also be dated to the time of Josiah, i.e., the end
of the seventh century BCE.

This leaves us with Genesis 24, which has been dated to the Persian period
based on linguistic, literary, and ideological arguments.[70] When it comes to
the question of ethnic identity, however, this chapter shows great conservatism, espousing the traditional lineage that connects the forefathers with the
Nahorite family in Haran. The evidence for the relative lateness of this
passage allows for the possibility that Genesis 24 *purposely* avoids any
mention of this lineage as Aramaean. This avoidance may thus be taken as
another stance in the hidden polemic over Jacob's Aramaean identity—that
is, Genesis 24 takes a stand against the positive construal of that characteristic in the Priestly passages (and Deut. 26.5), just as it implicitly refutes
the negative construal thereof in Genesis 31. In contradistinction to Genesis
31, Genesis 24 joins the earliest stories (chs. 29–30) in focusing only on the
family connections of Abraham (and Isaac) to Rebecca, Nahor, and Milcah.[71]

These last observations point to several possible historical contexts for
both the explicit and the hidden polemics. Contextualizing them all as of the
eighth, and more probably the seventh centuries BCE, these explicit polemics

---

ceased to exist politically, after they were subjugated by the Assyrians in the 30's of the
eighth century BCE.

70. But see Rendsburg (2002: 23-46, especially, 23-35), who challenges Rofé's
reliance on the linguistic data for dating the story as late. Rendsburg finds Genesis 24's
unique language (mostly Aramaisms and MH equivalents) to be an intentional Aramaic
flavor given to the story to validate its geographical setting in Haran (pp. 24, 31-32).
Furthermore, Rendsburg brings evidence for its pre-exilic (SBH) origin which, following
Polak (1998: 59-105), he suggests to even be dated in the early monarchic period (pp. 32-
35). Following this line of thought, Genesis 24's avoidance of mentioning Laban (and the
Nahorite family) as Aramaean, is even more outstanding.

71. The late dating of ch. 24 may rest on a variety of arguments. In reference to the
issue of separation from the women of the land, as well as in the matter of the 'outsider'
conception of origins, ch. 24 does not accord with the polemics of Ezra–Nehemiah. The
only possible connection may be that the story adds a hitherto unknown position to this
debate, since ch. 24 might be seen as legitimizing marriage connections between the
Repatriates and their parent-community in Babylon, distanced physically from their
repatriates-relatives that are now settled in Yehud. Were there such marriages being
attempted? Would this have seemed like an attractive solution to the problem posed by the
ban on local intermarriage? These questions are unanswered in the sources at hand.
Nevertheless, the differences between Genesis 24 and Ezra–Nehemiah should not be
disregarded.

touch upon the crucial issue of Israelite identity in the Canaanite arena. The implicit polemic over Jacob's Aramaic identity arose out of that explicit encounter, which called forth attempts to refute the identification of Jacob as 'a wandering Aramaean'. This discussion leaves open the option that these explicit and hidden polemics were reevaluated and nuanced time and again even through the Persian period. However, there is no need to designate the Persian period as specifically the time when they came into being.

Bibliography

Amit, Yairah
    2000   *Hidden Polemics in Biblical Narrative* (trans. Jonathan Chipman; Biblical Interpretation Series, 25; Leiden: E.J. Brill).
    2003   *Hidden Polemics in Biblical Narrative* (Tel Aviv: Yediot Aharonot and Hemed [Hebrew]).
Buber, Martin
    1964   *Darko shel Mikra* (Jerusalem: Bialik Institute [Hebrew]).
Cassuto, Umberto
    1961   *The Documentary Hypothesis and the Composition of the Pentateuch: Eight Lectures* (trans. I. Abrahams; Jerusalem: Magnes Press).
Cohn, Robert L.
    1983   'Narrative Structure and Canonical Perspective in Genesis', *JSOT* 25: 3-16.
Craigie, Peter C.
    1976   *Deuteronomy* (NICOT; Grand Rapids: Eerdmans).
Daube, David
    1963   *The Exodus Pattern in the Bible* (London: Faber & Faber).
Dion, Paul E.
    1995   'Aramaean Tribes and Nations of First Millennium Western Asia', *CANE* II: 1281-94.
Driver, Samuel R.
    1901   *Deuteronomy* (ICC; Edinburgh: T. & T. Clark, 3rd edn).
Daniels, Dwight R.
    1990   'The Creed of Deuteronomy XXVI Revisited', in J.A. Emerton (ed.), *Studies in the Pentateuch* (VTSup, 41; Leiden: E.J. Brill): 231-42.
Eichler, Barry L.
    1977   'Another Look at the Nuzi Sistership Contracts', in M. de Jong Ellis (ed.), *Essays on the Ancient Near East in the Memory of Jacob Joel Finkelstein* (Hamden, CT: Academy by Archon, 1977): 45-59.
Fishbane, Michael
    1975   'Composition and Structure in the Jacob Cycle', *JJS* 26: 15-38.
Finkelstein, Jacob J.
    1968   'An Old Babylonian Herding Contract and Gen. 31:38f.', *JAOS* 88: 30-36.
Fokkelman, Jan P.
    1975   *Narrative Art in Genesis* (Assen: Van Gorcum).

Gordon, Cyrus H.
    1936   'The Status of Women in the Nuzi Tablets', *ZA*: 147-69.
    1937   'The Story of Jacob and Laban in Light of the Nuzi Tablets', *BASOR* 66: 25-27.
Greenberg, Moshe
    1962   'Another Look at Rachel's Theft of the Teraphim', *JBL* 81: 239-48.
Greenfield, Jonas C.
    1981   'Aramaic Studies and the Bible', in J.A. Emerton (ed.), *Congress Volume: Vienna 1980* (VTSup, 32; Leiden: E.J. Brill): 110-30.
Gunkel, Hermann
    1997   *Genesis* (trans. M.E. Biddle; Macon, GA: Mercer University Press).
Hamilton, Victor P.
    1995   *Genesis 18–50* (NICOT; Grand Rapids: Eerdmans).
Heard, Christopher
    2001   *Dynamics of Diselection: Ambiguity in Genesis 12–36 and Ethnic Boundaries in Post-Exilic Judah* (SBLSemSt, 39; Atlanta: Society of Biblical Literature).
Hillers, Delbert R.
    1972   'Pahad Yishaq', *JBL* 91: 90-92.
Hoerth, A.J., G.L. Mattingly and E.M. Yamauchi (eds.)
    1994   *Peoples of the Old Testament World* (Cambridge: Lutterworth Press).
Howard, David M.
    1994   'Philistines', in Hoerth, Mattingly and Yamauchi 1994: 231-50.
Hutchinson, John, and Anthony D. Smith
    1996   'Introduction', in John Hutchison and Anthony D. Smith (eds.), *Ethnicity* (Oxford: Oxford University Press): 4-16.
Ishida, Tomoo
    1979   'The Structure and Historical Implications of the Lists of Pre-Israelite Nations', *Biblica* 60: 461-69.
Machinist, Peter
    1991   'The Question of Distinctiveness in Ancient Israel: An Essay', in M. Cogan and I. Eph'al (eds.), *Ah, Assyria...: Studies in Assyrian History and Ancient Near Eastern Historiography Presented to Hayim Tadmor* (Eretz Israel, 33; Jerusalem: Magnes Press): 196-212.
    1994   'Outsiders or Insiders: The Biblical View of Emergent Israel and Its Contexts', in L.J. Silberstein and R.L. Cohn (ed.), *The Other in Jewish Thought and History: Constructions of Jewish Culture and Identity* (New York: New York University Press): 35-60.
Malul, Meir
    1985   'More on PAHAD YISHAQ (Genesis XXXI 42, 53) and the Oath by the Thigh', *VT* 35: 192-200.
McCarthy, Dennis J.
    1978   *Treaty and Covenant* (Analecta Biblica, 21a; Rome: Biblical Institute Press, 2nd edn).
Millard, Alan R.
    1980   'A Wandering Aramaean', *JNES* 39: 153-55.
Nelson, Richard D.
    2002   *Deuteronomy* (OTL; Louisville, KY: Westminster/John Knox Press).

Pitard, Wayne T.
    1994   'Aramaeans', in Hoerth, Mattingly and Yamauchi 1994: 207-30.
Polak, Frank
    1998   'The Oral and the Written: Syntax, Stylistics, and the Development of Biblical Prose Narratives', *JANES* 26: 59-105.
Rad, Gerhard von
    1966   *The Problem of the Hexateuch and Other Essays* (trans. E.W. Trueman Dicken; Edinburgh: Oliver & Boyd).
    1966a   *Deuteronomy* (trans. D. Barton; OTL; London: SCM Press).
    1972   *Genesis* (trans. J.H. Marks; OTL; Philadelphia: Westminster Press).
Rendsburg, Gary A.
    2002   'Some False Leads in the Identification of Late Biblical Hebrew Texts: The Cases of Genesis 24 and 1 Samuel 2:27-36', *JBL* 121:23-46.
Rofé, Alexander
    1988   'The Ceremony of the 'First' (26:1-11)', in *Introduction to Deuteronomy* (Jerusalem: Akademon, 1988): 49-55.
    1990   'An Enquiry into the Betrothal of Rebekah', in Erhard Blum, Ch. Macholz and E. W. Stegemann (eds.), *Die Hebräische Bibel und ihre zweifache Nachgeschichte: Festschrift für Rolf Rendtorff zum 65. Geburtstag* (Neukirchen–Vluyn: Neukirchener Verlag): 27-39.
Sarna, Nahum M.
    1989   *Genesis* (JPS Torah Commentary; Philadelphia: Jewish Publication Society).
Savran, George W.
    1988   *Telling and Retelling: Quotation in Biblical Narrative* (Bloomington: Indiana University Press).
Skinner, John
    1930   *Genesis* (ICC; Edinburgh: T. & T. Clark, 2nd edn).
Smith, Anthony D.
    1986   *The Ethnic Origins of Nations* (Oxford: Basil Blackwell).
Speight, R. Marston
    1987   'Creeds', in M. Eliade (ed.), *The Encyclopedia of Religion* (New York: Macmillan): 138-40.
Speiser, Ephraim A.
    1964   *Genesis* (AB, 1; Garden City, NY: Doubleday).
Speiser, Ephraim A., and Robert H. Pfeiffer (eds.)
    1935–1936 *One Hundred New Selected Nuzi Texts* (AASOR, 16; New Haven: AASOR).
Steiner, Richard C.
    1997   '"Aramaean" of Deuteronomy 26.5 "*Peshat*" and "*Derash*"', in M. Cogan, B.L. Eichler and J.H. Tigay (eds.), *Tehillah le-Moshe: Biblical and Judaic Studies in Honor of Moshe Greenberg* (Winona Lake: Eisenbrauns): 127-38.
Sternberg, Meir
    1987   *Poetics of Biblical Narrative: Ideological Literature and the Drama of Reading* (Bloomington: Indiana University Press, 2nd edn).

Tigay, Jeffrey H.
    1996   *Deuteronomy* (JPS Torah Commentary; Philadelphia: Jewish Publication
           Society).
Van Seters, John
    1975   *Abraham in History and Tradition* (New Haven/London: Yale University
           Press).
Westermann, Claus
    1995   *Genesis 12–36* (trans. J.J Scullion; Minneapolis: Augsburg).
Wevers, John W.
    1995   *Notes on the Greek Text of Deuteronomy* (SBLSCS, 39; Atlanta: Scholars
           Press).

STRONG WOMEN CONFRONT HELPLESS MEN:
DEBORAH AND JEPHTHAH'S DAUGHTER IN THE MIDRASH

Shulamit Valler

This article discusses the midrashim that evolved around Deborah and Jephthah's daughter, two women involved in the war stories of the book of Judges.

In the Hebrew Bible the roles and the images of these two women are entirely different than in the midrashim. The midrashic commentators, however, structure those images in a way that shows their similarities. In so doing, they express an interesting worldview concerning everything connected with the female image and role, as against those of the male. I shall try to show the differences between the Hebrew Bible and the Midrash in the midrashists' perceptions of Deborah and Jephthah's daughter, beginning with the Bible.

Deborah

Deborah's story in Judges 4 calls her both 'prophetess' and 'woman of Lappidoth'. Some commentators interpreted Lappidoth as the name of Deborah's husband. According to Radak, Lappidoth is said to be Barak son of Abinoam, as 'barak' and 'lappidoth' are close in meaning. Ralbag also writes that she is called wife of Lappidoth because her husband's name was Barak and ברק ('lightning') and לפיד ('torch') have similar meanings. He writes also that another meaning of Deborah's name is: woman of valor. *Metzudat David*'s interpretation is that woman of Lappidoth 'means that she is a valorous woman quick in action as a flaming torch, which is a figure of speech that people use'.

The first two explanations, those that make Deborah the wife of Barak, are midrashic explanations, while the literal meaning of 'woman of Lappidoth' is in fact 'woman of valor'. Deborah is thus presented as a valorous woman so famous that the place where she sat in judgment was called the Palm of Deborah, after her. She is described as a leader active outside her home, in the public domain at the Palm of Deborah, to which the Israelites would come to seek judgment. The main point of the story is her initiative in the war against Jabin king of Canaan. According to the Hebrew Bible, in her time God 'surrendered' Israel into the hands of Jabin the Canaanite king at Hazor and into the hands of Sisera his commander whose base was at Harosheth-goiim: 'The Israelites cried out to the Lord for he had nine hundred iron chariots, and he had oppressed Israel ruthlessly for twenty years' (Judg. 4.3).[1] The Bible does not relate how Deborah arrived at the decision to go forth to war against Jabin. We learn of it indirectly through what she says to Barak:

> She summoned Barak son of Abinoam of Kadesh Naphtali and said to him, '…Go march up to Mount Tabor and take with you ten thousand men of Naphtali and Zebulun. And I will draw Sisera, Jabin's army commander, with his chariots and his troops towards you up to the Wadi Kishon, and I will deliver them into your hands' (Judg. 4.6-7).

This shows that the will to go to war came from her as a prophetic vision and divine command, leading to the initiative to summon Barak and plan the battle strategy.

In apposition to the figure of Deborah the prophetess and heroic leader stands the pale figure of Barak son of Abinoam, who feebly answers her:

> If you go with me, I will go; if not, I will not go (4.8).[2]

The contrast between them is evident also from Deborah's answer:

> I will go with you. However there will be no glory for you in the course you are taking, for then the Lord will deliver Sisera into the hands of a woman (4.9).

Cohen thinks that the gender role reversal expressed by Deborah's initiative in summoning Barak to go forth to war led him to respond with, 'If you will go with me…' According to Cohen, Barak perceived that the conventional gender role division did not apply in Deborah's special case, so he did not feel threatened by her warning, '…there will be no glory for you…', and because he misunderstood '…the Lord will deliver Sisera into the hands of a woman' to refer to herself (2000: 179-88).

---

1. Throughout this essay, Bible quotations are from the JPS.

2. Gil'ad (1989: 292-301) assesses Barak favorably. He writes: 'Barak's response did not stem from false modesty and not from fear of failure. The main reason appears to have been related to the tribe of Issachar. Deborah's conscription program included Naphtali, Zebulun and the northern area of Issachar. Regarding Naphtali (his own tribe) and Zebulun, Barak had no doubts. He had misgivings about Issachar, known as "one who liked to rest", that they might refuse him. Here a venerated and generally accepted leader was needed and most importantly, one of the tribe' (Deborah was from Issachar).

Indeed, the central figures in the war against Jabin king of Canaan are women: Deborah, who goes with Barak to Kadesh to summon the warriors and strengthens him with her prophecies:

> Up! This is the day on which the lord will deliver Sisera into your hand: the Lord is marching before you (4.14);

and Jael wife of Heber the Kenite, into whose hand the Lord delivered Sisera. Despite Barak's secondary place in the story, he is the central hero in the war itself. At the head of his ten thousand soldiers he pursued Sisera's army and defeated it. Even though the slaying of Sisera signaled the total defeat of that army, the outcome of the war had been determined earlier when all Sisera's chariots fled before Barak and Sisera himself abandoned his chariot to flee on foot.

The story as a whole shows that while Deborah is an exceptional woman, the division of roles between her and Barak is gender based. She spreads the message to the warriors, encourages the commander ahead of the battle and celebrates the victory in a stirring song afterwards, while Barak takes charge of the battle itself. At the same time, Deborah is shown as a strong and dominant figure who acts by herself or with a man in two areas of the public domain that are considered male—the judgment seat, and the war.

According to Cohen, Deborah's leadership is expressed in 'three principal areas of male leadership: the religious (as a prophetess), the social (as a judge) and in the military area (leadership in the battle against Sisera)'. Cohen adds that Deborah did not act as women were expected to in patriarchal society: she is not shown as an erotic object, her external appearance is not described, and she acts solely in the public domain.[3]

It was by no means easy for the Sages of the Talmud and the Midrash to accept this image of Deborah. Several midrashim show that they did not easily accede to the biblical story about her.[4] In *b. Meg.* 14a, Deborah is mentioned among the seven prophetesses of the Israelites: Sarah, Miriam, Deborah, Hannah, Abigail, Huldah and Esther. However, the proof that Deborah had the role of prophetess— 'As it is written (Judg. 4.4) "Now Deborah a prophetess"'—is followed immediately by an explanation for her other designation, אשת לפידות, 'woman of flames'.

> Why 'a woman of flames'? She used to make wicks for the Sanctuary'.

---

3. Cohen maintains that Deborah's identification with the public-national-male domain is highlighted in her song of victory. In her opinion, it resembles Moses' male victory song of the sea, not Miriam's female victory song (2000: 179-88). On the typology of the war of God in the song of Deborah see M. Weinfeld 1978: 23-30.

4. Rozen cites several midrashim of later collections in which Deborah and Barak function together as judges (1994: 31-47).

This firmly places Deborah, although a prophetess, in the feminine sphere by giving her a female role, for according to the Babylonian *Amora* Samuel, women worked at various crafts connected with the Temple:

> Samuel said [that] the women who wove the curtain received their payment from the funds of the Assembly Hall' (*Lev. Rab.* [Warsaw], portion 11).

The Sages' need to put back biblical women who deviated from their gender role and from what the Sages regarded as women's proper place, is seen in another midrash, this time from the late collection *Yalkut Shimoni*, on Jael:

> And what was the nature of Jael from whose hand came great deliverance? It is said that she was a proper woman and did her husband's will, for it is said that there is no proper woman among women save she who does her husband's will (*Yalkut Shimoni* 247.42).

This midrash not only attributes to Jael what it considers positive female behavior—doing her husband's will—but also derives from this attribution a principle concerning proper female behavior in general.

Some Sages were highly ambivalent about Deborah, the biblical prophetess and leader, because of the contradiction she posed to their image of a woman, and this led them to criticize her. Thus the second generation *Amora* Rav Judah in the name of Rav, his teacher:

> Rav Judah said in Rav's name, Whoever is boastful, if he is a Sage, his wisdom departs from him; if he is a prophet, his prophecy departs from him. If he is a Sage, his wisdom departs from him: [we learn this] from Hillel. For the Master said, 'He began by rebuking them with words', and [then] he said to them, 'I have heard this *halakhah*, but have forgotten it'. If he is a prophet, his prophecy departs from him. [We learn this] from Deborah. For it is written, 'The rulers ceased in Israel, they ceased, until I arose, Deborah, I arose a mother in Israel', and it is written, 'Awake, awake, Deborah, awake, utter a song' (*b. Pes.* 66b).

These words, attributed to Rav, simultaneously empower and rebuke Deborah. On the one hand she is given the same status as Hillel; but on the other hand, her self-praise in her song is perceived as arrogance. That the people urge her to prophesy, 'Awake, awake Deborah...' (Judg. 4.12), is seen as evidence that the prophetic gift was taken away from her as punishment for her arrogance.

Opposition in principle to female leadership, with Deborah as a negative example, is attributed to R. Berekiah, a great Sage of the *aggadah* of the fourth Eretz Israel generation:

> R. Berekiah said four things, three of a man and one of a woman: 'Woe to the living who needs the dead, woe to the hero who needs the weak, woe to him who sees and needs the blind, woe to the generation led by a woman, and Deborah is a woman and a prophetess (*Midrash Tehillim* [Buber] on Ps. 22.2).

Differently from the midrashim above, there are several midrashic passages in later collections that praise Deborah's qualities and performance. For instance in *Midrash Tanhuma* she is shown as one who understood what Barak failed to understand, that the war against Jabin and Sisera was not their war but God's:

> ...and so Debora told Barak, 'arise for this is the day on which the Lord will deliver Sisera into your hands: the Lord is marching before you' (Judg. 4.14), and Barak said to her, 'if you go with me I will go' (4.9), and she said to him: do you need me when the Lord is marching before you? (*Tanhuma* [Warsaw], *Shoftim* §17).

Thus she is portrayed also in another commentary, on the Psalms, where she is placed beside none other than Moses, greatest of all the prophets:

> 'To the Lord of victories: [A Psalm] of David, the servant of the Lord' (Ps. 36.1). The phrase 'Lord of victories' is to be considered in the light of the verse, 'Happy art thou O Israel; who is like unto thee? a people saved by the Lord' (Deut. 33.29). The Holy One, blessed be He wages Israel's wars, but the victory is ascribed to Israel. Thus Scripture says, 'in all the signs and wonders...and all the mighty hand...which Moses wrought' (Deut. 34.11-12). Here it is not written 'which the Lord wrought' but which Moses wrought. The Holy one, blessed be He, empowered Moses to perform wonders, but the victory was ascribed to Moses. So too Deborah said, 'Arise, Barak and lead thy captivity captive, thou son of Abinoam' (Judg.5.12) as if it were really his captivity? What could Deborah have meant by 'Arise' except Arise, but you will not do battle, for the battle is the Lord's'... And yet instead of saying: 'The victory is the Lord's', Deborah said: 'Lead thy captivity captive...' (*Midrash Tehillim* [Buber] on Ps. 36).

And just as this midrash praises Deborah and sets her beside Moses, elsewhere in this collection of midrashim she is compared to Joshua.

> 'Day unto day utters knowledge'. Said R. Zeira, the day of Joshua presents the condition of the day of Deborah. As it is said, 'in the day of Joshua the sun stood still and the moon halted' (Josh. 10.13), and it is written of the day of Deborah, 'the stars from heaven, from their courses they fought against Sisera' (Judg. 5.20); and the day of Deborah tells of several miracles and wonders performed on that day (*Midrash Tehillim* [Buber] on Ps. 19).

The most extreme midrash in praise of Deborah is included in an early collection, *Bereshit (Genesis) Rabbah,* and tells of a confrontation between Deborah and Barak. Here I will discuss the midrash itself in detail and later, at the end of this essay, confront it with the midrash on another biblical heroine—Jephthah's daughter.

The midrash on Deborah and Barak in *Bereshit Rabbah* is attributed to R. Phinehas in the name of R. Reuben,[5] who said:

> Two men had the main role but treated themselves as subordinates, Abraham and Barak.
>
> Barak: 'And she sent and called Barak…and Barak said to her, "If you go with me, then I will go, but if you will not go with me, then I will not go" (Judg. 4.6 ff)'. R. Judah said, 'If you will go with me to Kadesh, I will go with you against Hazor, but if you will not go with me to Kadesh, I will not go with you against Hazor'. R. Nehemiah said, 'If you will go with me in song, I shall go with you in battle, and if you will not go with me in song, I will not go with you in battle'. 'And she said, "I will surely go with you, notwithstanding [Heb. אֶפֶס] the journey that you take shall not be for your honor" (Judg. 4.9)'. Said R. Reuben, 'The word for 'notwithstanding' is a Greek word that stands for 'let alone'. So the sense of what she said to him is this: 'What are you now supposing? Is it that the glory of the song will be handed over to you for a blessing?' [Reverting to Barak]. So he turned out to be subordinated: 'Then sang Deborah and Barak the son of Abinoam'… (Judg. 5.1).
>
> Abraham held the principal role but treated himself as secondary: 'Say you are my sister' (Gen. 12.13), and as a result he was made subordinate: 'And he dealt well with Abram on her account [בעבורה] (12.16)' (*Bereshit Rabbah* [Theodor-Albeck], 40.11-13).

The story of Abram who when he was about to enter Egypt told Sarai, 'Say you are my sister, that it may go well with me because of you' (Gen. 12.13), raises astonishing moral and theological issues that the midrash addresses at length.

First, there was astonishment as to how Abram, chosen by God for His covenant and thus expected to be a model of morality, initiated such a lie about his wife. Because of it, in the best case his wife could be exposed to adultery and in a worse case fall victim to rape and abuse. Further astonishment arises from 'that it may go well with me because of you' (12.13). There, on top of his fear of being killed he adds the desire for material gain, making him appear to be soliciting for his wife! Besides the bewilderment created by Abram's behavior there are two difficult questions about divine justice: Pharaoh, who does not 'know' Sarai is already married when he takes her into his household, is nevertheless severely punished: 'But the Lord afflicted Pharaoh and his household with mighty plagues on account of Sarai, the wife of Abram' (12.17). Moreover, Abram, the guilty party, is rewarded: 'And because of her it went well with Abram; he acquired sheep, oxen, asses, male and female slaves, she-asses and camels' (12.16). Since, according to the authors of the midrashim, both reward and punishment come from God, there

---

5. R. Phinehas is an Eretz Israel *Amora* of the fourth generation (first half of the fourth century CE); R. Reuben is an Eretz Israel *Amora* of the third generation (end of the third century CE).

is a serious theological problem here. Another unanswered question is, what did happen to Sarai in Pharaoh's house? A parallel story in which Abraham faces Abimelech king of Gerar states explicitly, 'Now Abimelech had not approached her' (20.4).[6] In yet another parallel story whose protagonists are Isaac, Rebekah and Abimelech, physical intimacy is a calamity averted: 'One of our people might have lain with your wife' (26.11).

Some midrashim on this subject, particularly those centered around Abram, are apologetic. Others, especially those addressing the theological issue of Pharaoh's punishment, show him as a man whose evil intentions God thwarted, and relate what happened by night in Pharaoh's house.

The midrash deals with Abram's desire to profit from delivering his wife to Pharaoh: 'that it may go well with me because of you' (12.13), to which God responds so positively.

The use of the same phrase, בעבור—'because of you' and 'because of her'—in Abram's request and in the reward from Pharaoh indicate the biblical author's intention to link the two and to indicate that Pharaoh's gifts were without doubt the will of God in response to Abram's request to Sarai. But the very request, 'Say you are my sister, that it may go well with me because of you', shows Abram as a man of dubious morality. God's response to such a request is even harder to comprehend from a moral standpoint. The midrash from *Bereshit Rabbah* quoted above is based on the linguistic link between the request and the response, using it to rebuke Abram and exalt Sarai. In so doing the comparison between these two female and male figures, in the encounter with Pharaoh, is also compared to the relationship between the figures of Deborah and Barak in the story of the war against Jabin king of Canaan.

Let us have another look. The biblical connective בעבור may carry one of two meanings: (1) 'because', as in '*because* of what the Lord did for me when I went out of Egypt' (Exod. 13.8), and (2) 'for the sake of [for my sake]', as in 'Prepare a dish *for* me…that I may give you my innermost blessing' (Gen. 27.4).[7] R. Phinehas in the name of R. Reuben reads Gen. 12.13 as '*because* of you', and 12.16 as '*for* her sake'. Thus he concluded that giving Sarai to Pharaoh placed Abram in a subordinate position as one wishing to become rich because of her. For this base intention the Lord distanced Abram and brought Sarai closer, and all He did, even enriching Abram, was for Sarai's sake. R. Reuben's midrash serves two purposes. (a) It rebukes Abram by depicting what he told Sarai as reprehensible and

---

6.   Later Abimelech protests to God on the undeserved punishment that would have befallen him. God's answer in a dream was 'I knew that you did this with a blameless heart and so I kept you from sinning against me. That is why I did not let you touch her' (Gen. 20.6).

7.   See Even Shoshan's *Dictionary* (1964) for בעבור.

(b) 'justifies' the Lord who enriched Abram by explaining that it was all done for Sarai's sake. The midrash is sarcastically critical of Abram as one divinely chosen for chief and leader who even acts as such in the beginning: 'And Abram took his wife Sarai…and they set out for the land of Canaan' (Gen. 12.5). However, when he encounters a difficulty he evades leadership and hides behind his wife. The midrash justifies God's act as a sort of punishment for Abram with an element of retribution [for Pharaoh], and by showing Sarai as the main beneficiary of the increased material wealth.

We shall now focus on the central part of the homily that relates to Deborah and Barak, which is introduced solely as support for the Abram-Sarai theme. The homilist begins with the statement:

> Two men had the main roles but [humbled themselves and] treated themselves as subordinates.

The three stages as regards Abram are relevant for Barak as well. In the first stage God designates him to deliver Israel, at least according to what Deborah tells him. In the second stage the difficulty frightens him, he refuses leadership and chooses to be second to Deborah, while in the third stage the choice boomerangs as Deborah reaps the laurels in her victory song. According to the biblical text, there is no literal connection whatever between the feats of Deborah and Barak son of Abinoam on the one hand, and what is related about Abram, Sarai and Pharaoh on the other hand. The Judges 4 story raises no moral and theological doubts and even if Barak's conduct does not arouse admiration, it is not immoral. The common factor according to the midrashic author is the weakness of the central male figure, although open confrontation over leadership exists only in the story of Deborah and Barak: in the story of Abram, Sarai and Pharaoh Sarai keeps silent and her position remains unknown. Just because of the open confrontation and the reversal of traditional gender roles between Deborah and Barak, the author brought it into play in criticizing Abram's hesitation and in showing him to have failed as a man, husband and leader. In a kind of parenthetical remark the midrash editor cited the explanations of the *Amoraim* R. Judah and R. Nehemiah for the biblical text, 'If you will go with me, I will go with you, but if you will not go with me, I will not go with you'. The repetition in the biblical text is expounded in a way that divides it into two parts related to two different situations.

> R. Judah said: 'If you will go with me to Kadesh, I will go with you against Hazor, but if you will not go with me to Kadesh, I will not go with you against Hazor'.

He asked her to go with him, that is, to be second to him in the gatherings to raise an army, promising that if she did that he would go with her, as second to her, in the war.

> R. Nehemiah said, 'If you will go with me in song, I shall go with you to battle, and if you do not go with me in song, I will not go with you to battle'.

He asked her to be second to him in raising the warriors' spirit, promising that if she did that he would go with her, as second to her in the war.

Both Sages thus present Barak as rejecting his principal role and giving it to a woman and, worse yet, on the battlefield, the ultimate male domain. They rely on the biblical story that sets forth the initiative for the war, its outcome and the victory song all as the work of women. They go even further and wrest from Barak the leadership in battle that according to the Bible was his.

The homilists pounced on Barak's weakness first by explicating his demand that Deborah share leadership with him as an agreement to be second to her, even if not in every respect. Secondly, they link what they see as his agreement to take second place in conducting the war to his secondary role in Deborah's victory song.

Showing Barak in this way enhances Deborah. She is even further enhanced by the midrashic explanation for her agreement to Barak's request: her prophetic knowledge of its results.

In the revealed stratum, the midrash expresses no surprise over the prophetic gifts, courage and leadership that placed Deborah high above her male partner.

In a midrash from a late collection, סדר אליהו רבה (*Seder Eliyahu Rabbah*), a specific question is given a liberal answer:

> 'And Deborah was a prophetess...' (Judg. 4.4). And what is the nature of Deborah who judged Israel and prophesied for them? Did not Phinehas son of Eleazar testify before heaven and earth, between Gentile and Israel, between man and woman, between slave and handmaid [he judged] according to the fact and according to the holy spirit within him (*Seder Eliahu Rabbah*, Ish Shalom edn, 10).

Later the midrash shows that Deborah became a judge and prophetess because of her high moral quality in dealing with her husband, who was an ignorant man:

> It is said that Deborah's husband was an ignorant man. His wife said to him, 'go make wicks', and he went to the sanctuary at Shiloh, so that your portion will be among decent people and you will inherit the world to come. And he made heavy wicks that gave off much light, so he was called Lappidot. And it is said that he had three names, Barak, Lappidot and Michael, Barak because his face was like lightning, Lappidot because he made wicks and went to the sanctuary at Shiloh, and Michael because the Lord examines heart and conscience.
>
> ...And who caused Lappidot to be among decent people and inherit the world to come? They said Deborah his wife, of whom, and of whose like, and of those who resemble her and of those who emulate her deeds it is said, 'The wisest of women builds her house...' (Prov. 14.1; *Seder Eliyahu Rabbah*, Ish Shalom edn, 10).

At any rate, the rebuke of Barak, relegated to second place in the song (Judg. 5.1) as punishment for his refusal to be the sole leader, presents his behavior and hence Deborah's as extraordinary and as such are rooted in the patriarchal concept that women's abilities are by nature inferior to men's.

The Daughter of Jephthah

In contrast to the close correspondence in the images of Deborah and Barak between the biblical story and this midrash, the situation is quite different in the second pair that this article discusses, Jephthah and his daughter. Here the midrash moves far away from the biblical tale and creates quite different characters.

Anyone who reads the story in Judg. 11.29-40 cannot fail to be moved by its double tragedy. The story form, a dialogue accompanied by a kind of evil chorus, together with its content of a father sacrificing his daughter to appease a deity, brings to mind the Greek tragedies from the sixth and fifth centuries BCE, like the tale of Iphigenia sacrificed by Agamemnon to placate the gods.

The ideological perception in this story resembles that of the Greek tragedies, where human heroes are trapped in crises and calamities not because they have done ill but because it was so decreed by higher forces beyond their control and understanding. In the biblical story both Jephthah and his daughter are victims of their beliefs. His vow to sacrifice to God 'whatever comes out of the door of my house' (Judg. 11.31a) to meet him on his victorious return from the war against the Ammonites may be stupid or hasty but is not cruel, is not designed to destroy his daughter. Differently from the dedication vows of Samson's mother (13.3-6) or Hannah (1 Sam. 1.11-25) Jephthah, after he says 'shall be the Lord's', explicitly declares that whatever comes out 'shall be offered up by me *as a burnt offering*' (Judg. 11.31). He may have been affected by Canaanite custom that did not recoil from human sacrifice. However, the thought of sacrificing his only daughter could not have crossed his mind, for his agonized cry,

> Alas, daughter, you have brought me low and you have become my troubler!
> (v. 35)

sounds entirely credible. Moreover, in his heart of hearts Jephthah may have feared that his daughter would come out to meet him, given the custom of girls coming out in joyful dancing to greet victors (for instance Exod. 15.21; 1 Sam. 18.6-7), so he phrased 'whatever/whoever comes out'[8] in the grammatical masculine gender.

---

8. Walfish suggests: 'Jephthah knew what he intended but avoided an exact formulation so as not to commit to the full price in advance' (1991: 283-92).

The author's addition, too—'She was an only child; he had no other son or daughter' (Judg. 11.34)—shows Jephthah as an unfortunate man who fell victim to himself, not a cruel and heartless one.[9] Moreover, the daughter herself is convinced that he has to make good his vow. She fears the price of breaking it just as her father does. He says:

> For I have uttered a vow to the Lord and cannot retract (v. 35).

She uses the identical words:

> You have vowed a vow to the Lord; do to me as you have vowed, seeing that the Lord has vindicated you against your enemies the Ammonites (v. 36).

Father and daughter are therefore victims of a tragedy they encounter through no fault of their own, for 'the spirit of the Lord' was upon Jephthah when he went to war, and even his vow is 'a vow to the Lord'. It seems as if only the Lord could have prevented the tragedy, but God did not stop the daughter from going out to meet her father, and did not prevent her from coming back to her father at the end of the story, so that he could do to her 'as he had vowed' (v. 39).

The story of Jephthah's vow and its results were totally unacceptable to a number of Sages for whom the principle of divine justice was an unquestionable guiding light. Elsewhere in the Hebrew Bible where questions arise as to the way God rules the world, it is hinted or stated that His ways are hidden and His justice beyond human understanding. Such an answer, found also in Greek philosophy, could not satisfy the commentators in the case of so serious a flaw in the way the Divinity functioned. They made tremendous efforts to explain Jephthah's tragic case in a way that would erase any thought of a possible divine connection with the terrible deed of sacrificing a daughter. With this end in view, several midrashim effected a metamorphosis of Jephthah's biblical image, and textual data were enlisted to construct a new image of ultimate evil. Thus was created a new story in which Jephthah is the sole cause that sets off the tragic train of events.

There are several facets to the biblical image of Jephthah. In the beginning he is a ruffian without family ties who gathers around him men of low character (Judg. 11.1-4). Later this mighty man is seen as a leader to be reckoned with, who coldly plans his career (vv. 6-12), and as one thoroughly familiar with his people's history and a believer in the God of Israel (vv. 15-28).[10]

---

9. On the daughter as an only child, see the moving discussion in Ben-Dov 1993: 7-16.

10. His answer to the Ammonite king seems to express a pagan view: 'Do you not hold what Chemosh your god gave you to possess? So we will hold on to everything that the Lord our God has given us to possess' (v. 24). With that, the statement may be regarded as a diplomatic one in which Jephthah addresses the king in a language he will understand.

The encounter of Jephthah with his daughter after he has returned from the war marks the beginning of his fall. He leaves the meeting spiritually stricken and battered, and then faces an unexpected threat from the men of Ephraim: 'We'll burn your house down over you' (12.1). His first response is not violent. He explains to them the circumstances for not involving them in the Ammonite war and expresses amazement that they should want revenge on him for that. But his next response is violent indeed. He embarks on a bloody civil war and treats its refugees with cynical cruelty. In his last phase he becomes once again the ruffian he was at the outset; however, now he is no longer a local bully who gathers like men around him but a ruler who commands brutal murder of the weak and innocent.

In contrast to the fuller biography and image of Jephthah that the Bible offers us, the life and image of his daughter are shown but sketchily. She appears in two situations, the first when Jephthah returns from the war and she joyfully goes out to meet him, her joy shattered at once when she hears her father's vow. She accepts her fate and asks to go out upon the mountains with her companions and mourn her virginity. The second time is when she returns from the mountains after two months' time (11.39), and her father 'did to her as he had vowed'. All that we learn about her is that she is a loving, devoted and obedient daughter who humbly endures the blow inflicted on her by her father's hand.

Most of the midrashim,[11] like the Bible, deal extensively with Jephthah's character. In the midrashim the end of his life colors his entire image, and in their efforts to explain the terrible story of sacrificing a daughter without undermining the principles of faith, they take away from Jephthah's image the few bright spots that grace it in the biblical story.

Only one midrash, *Tanhuma* in *Behukotai* 5, shows the daughter and her father in confrontation, reinforcing the father's negative image while extending the positive one of the daughter. This unique midrash will be quoted in translation now.[12]

> Another interpretation: When anyone explicitly vows to the Lord the value of human beings... This text is related (to Prov. 11.30). If a man is righteous and although he is righteous he does not study Torah, he is nothing, but 'the fruit of the righteous is a tree of life' refers to the Torah, because when one is a Torah scholar he learns how one acquires lives, as it is stated. And so you find in the case of Jephthah the Gileadite, because he was not a Torah scholar, he forfeited his daughter. When? In the time that he fought with the children of Ammon and made a vow, as stated (Judg. 11.30-31): 'Then Jephthah made a

11. E.g. *Ber. (Gen.) Rab.* 60.3 and *Vayikra (Lev.) Rab.* 37.3.
12 The midrash presented here is quoted from the *Tanhuma, Behukotai* 5. Similar fragments are found in the late collections, such as the *Midrash Aggadah on Leviticus* (Buber) 27, and *Bereshit Rabati Vayetze*, p. 3.

vow to the Lord and said: If you indeed give the children of Ammon into my hand, then it shall be that whatever comes forth…shall belong to the Lord, and I will offer it up as a burnt offering'. At that time the Holy One was angry with him. The Holy one said: 'If there had come out from his house a dog, a pig or a camel, he would have offered it to me?' The Holy One summoned his daughter to him. Why? To teach all those who make vows the laws of oaths and vows not to err in this matter. And there was his daughter coming out to meet him… 'And it came to pass when he saw her, that he rent his clothes and said Alas daughter, I vowed a vow to the Lord and I cannot retract…' (11.36). But was not Phinehas there? Still he said (in v. 35): and I cannot retract. However, Phinehas had said, I am a high priest and the son of a high priest, shall I humble myself and go to an ignoramus? But Jephthah said: I am head of the tribes of Israel and head of the magistrates. Shall I humble myself and go to a commoner? Between the two of them that poor woman perished; so the two were liable for her blood. In the case of Phinehas, the holy spirit left him. In the case of Jephthah, his bones were scattered as stated (Judg. 12.7) and he was buried in the *cities* [my italics; plural, SV] of Gilead.

Since he sought to sacrifice her, his daughter wept before him and said to him, I went out to you in joy and you slaughter me! Is it ever written in the Torah that they offer the lives of their sons upon the altar? And is it not written (Lev. 1.2) 'you shall present your offering from the herd or from the flock and not from the children of Adam'? He said to her: my daughter, I made a vow that it shall be whatever comes forth… [She said to him] When our father Jacob made a vow (Gen. 28.22) that 'of all you give me I will surely set aside a tithe for you', and when the Holy One gave him twelve tribes did he ever offer up one of them as a sacrifice? Moreover, does not Hannah do likewise when she makes a vow and says (1 Sam. 1.11), 'Then I will give him to the Lord all the days of his life'? Did she ever offer up her son as a sacrifice to the Holy One? All these things she said to him but he did not heed her. She said to him: Let me go to a court of law. Perhaps one of them will find a loophole for your words. Thus it is stated (Judg. 11.37): 'Let me be for two months [so that I may go down to the mountains]'… R. Levi ben Berekhyah said: Is there anyone who comes down to the mountains? Does not one go up to the mountains? So what is the meaning of 'come down' to the mountains? These represent the Sanhedrin, as it is said (Mic. 6.4): 'Hear O mountains the lawsuit of the Lord'. She went to them and they did not find a loophole for undoing Jephthah's vow for the sin of the slaughter in Ephraim, and of him it is said (Prov. 28.3), 'A poor man who exploits the indigent is a torrential rain which leaves no bread'. A poor man, this is Jephthah since he was poor in Torah; who exploits the indigent, since he exploited the indigent when he said (Judg. 12.6) 'say shibboleth and he said sibboleth. Then he slaughtered him'; 'torrential rain and there is no bread', in that he had no one who would undo his vow, however there is no bread in that the Holy One had taken the *halakhah* away from them, so they would not find a loophole for undoing his vow. When they did not find [a loophole] for undoing his vow, he went up and slaughtered her before the Holy One. Then the Holy Spirit shouted: 'Did I desire you to sacrifice lives to me' (Jer. 19.5), which I never commanded, never spoke for, and which never entered my mind?' ([and cf. also] Jer. 7.31), which I never commanded Abraham that he slaughter his son. Instead I said to him (Gen. 22.12): 'Do not raise your hand against the lad…', to make known to the nations of the world why the Holy One loved Abraham so much for he did not withhold his only son from me, to do the will of his creator…never spoke for Jephthah to offer up his daughter.

'…and which never entered my mind' that the king of Moab would fall into the hand of the king of Israel and offer up his firstborn son, as it is stated (2 Kings 3.27) 'so he took his firstborn son, who would be king after him, and offered him up as a burnt offering upon the wall'. Who caused Mesha to sacrifice his son? Because he was not a Torah scholar, for if he read the Torah he would not have lost his son, as it is written, 'When anyone explicitly makes a vow the value of a male, and if it be female…', for a wise person acquires life. (*Tanhuma, behukotai* 5, on Lev. 27.1 and the following verses).

The dialogue between father and daughter proceeds in a three-stage hierarchic format that is based on the biblical passages. The first stage is based on Jephthah's monologue in the biblical story, which the midrash presents as a dialogue in which the daughter makes an emotional appeal. In the Bible Jephthah declares: 'whatever comes out of my house to meet me on my safe return…' The midrashic author constructs a verbal parallel as the daughter says: 'My Father, I went out to meet you in joy and you would slaughter me?' The use of 'slaughter' emphasizes the contrast between the daughter's joy and the terrible thing her father is about to do to her. In the second stage the daughter's arguments come from the domain of faith, based on Jephthah's words in the biblical text: 'whatever comes out of the door of my house to meet me on my safe return from the Ammonites shall be the Lord's and shall be offered by me as a burnt offering'. Echoing his own words, the daughter shows him as an ignorant believer who fails to understand God's will: 'My Father, is it ever written in the Torah they offer the lives of their sons on the altar?' The third stage shows the daughter as one who makes legal arguments based on knowledge and the ability to draw conclusions from it. In the Bible Jephthah says, 'I have uttered a vow to the Lord and I cannot retract', and she answers 'You have uttered a vow to the Lord, do to me as you have vowed'. In the midrash, however, she defends her position in a quasi-legal argument, with a series of examples to show her father how completely he has misunderstood God's law. Friedland-Ben Arza sums up the daughter's arguments thus: 'Jephthah's daughter of the midrash used all the learned means that the Sages themselves used in such circumstances' (1992: 74-81). In this author's view, the daughter speaks for the Sages.

Possibly, in attributing textual and 'historical' examples (one of them anachronistic—the Sanhedrin!) to the daughter, the Sage reverts to the argument with the king of Ammon in which Jephthah displays broad knowledge of the history of Israel and of the greatness of its God (Judg. 11.15-27), making the daughter's argument an ironic accusation of her father. She suggests that her father does not know how to interpret his store of historical knowledge in order to derive conclusions as to God's nature and the divine will.

In all three stages of the dialogue, the daughter's statements show the absurdity of the idea that God should desire human sacrifices. In the first statement the word 'slaughter' is used, with its associations of a revolting crime, indicating what Jephthah intended to do.[13] In her second statement she says, 'Is it ever written in the Torah they offer the lives of their sons upon the altar?' Her third statement presents a broad if indirect view of the 'historical' arguments. At the end of the dialogue, with her father clinging to his foolish position, the daughter in her desperation turns to the voice of wisdom and sanity, the highest instance in religious law, the Sanhedrin:

> But he did not heed her, so she said to him: Let me go to a court of law, perhaps they may find a loophole for your vow. As it is said, 'leave me alone for two months' [so that I may go and come down to the mountains] (Judg. 11.37). R. Levi ben Berekhyah said: Is there anyone who comes down to the mountains? Does not one go up to the mountains? So what is the meaning of come down to the mountains? These represent the Sanhedrin, as it is said, 'Hear O mountains the lawsuit of the Lord' (Mic. 6.4).

These lines show the daughter as a diplomat who chooses her words to her father carefully: '*Perhaps* they may find a loophole for your vow'. She is also a Torah scholar who knows about the procedure for release from vows, and about the authority of the Sanhedrin Sages. This distances her from her father who is no Torah scholar, fails to understand the importance of the Sages and their institutions and would not swallow his pride and ask Phinehas the priest to free him from his vow.

At this point, as the daughter takes the reins into her own hands, one would expect a dramatic change in the course of events, but nothing happens, for the Lord took away the *halakhah* from the Sages because of Jephthah's wickedness. 'A poor man who exploits the indigent' he is called as it is said (Judg. 12.6), "They would say to him, say shibboleth and he would say sibboleth", not being able to pronounce it correctly. Thereupon they would slay him'. Thus 'the torrential rain that leaves no bread': Jephthah could have been released from his vow except that 'there is no bread'. The Holy One had taken the *halakhah* from the Sages who therefore did not find the loophole through which to undo Jephthah's vow. And so 'He went up and slaughtered her'.

---

13. The verb and noun for slaughter, from the root שחט (*šḥṭ*) in the Qal formation, are used only in connection with Jephthah. In the daughter's examples and in the attributions to God at the end of the midrash, the writer uses the root *qrb in the Hif.*, meaning 'to sacrifice'. *šḥṭ* is also used in 'I never commanded Abraham that he slaughter his son', possibly because that is the Hebrew verb used in Gen. 22.10, in the story of the *Akedah*.

Like the dialogue, the story of the lost *halakhah* has its roots in the biblical text. There the daughter's words are divided into two parts: (Judg. 11.36)

...Father, she said, you have uttered a vow to the Lord...

and (v. 37):

And she said to her father. Let this be done for me, let me be for two months...

While the homilist quotes only the second statement, he makes the tacit assumption that between it and the first statement there occurred the horrible murder of the Ephraimites. On this he bases the cruel story that the *halakhah* lost to the Sages of the Sanhedrin was Jephthah's punishment for the bloodshed he inflicted.

According to the first passage of the midrash, the coming out of Jephthah's daughter to meet him was punishment for the effrontery of his vow before God. But had he not been such an ignoramus he would have known that vows may be annulled. Here too the homilist attempts to say that depriving the Sanhedrin of *halakhah* was a punishment for Jephthah. But here too the midrash insists that the punishment was to shock Jephthah into understanding the horror of shedding blood through the peril of losing a loved one. Never was there any intention that he should carry out the ghastly plan of sacrificing his daughter, but rather to make him seek a way out of the situation.

Other midrashim as well contain the motif of the *halakhah* lost or forgotten as punishment, in order both to teach the culprit a lesson and to motivate him to resolve his predicament. For example, in *b. Tem.* 16a, a midrash relates that Joshua sinned through pride and his punishment was to forget *halakhot*. Joshua refuses to respond to Moses' request, 'Ask me about all the doubts you have', because he thinks he has already acquired all Moses' knowledge, for he has never left Moses' tent. As punishment,

At once Joshua's strength failed, he forgot three hundred *halakhot*, there arose in him seven hundred doubts and all Israel was about to kill him.

The solution found for Joshua was, 'Go busy them with a war'.

Tanhuma, Va-Ethannan 6 tells that Moses refused to die, and the Holy One caused him to forget *halakhah*. Moses sat among the last of the scholars and '*did not understand what Joshua was teaching*'. Then he accepted his approaching death and said, 'Lord of the worlds, until now I sought to live and now my soul is given over to you'.[14]

14.   There is a similar midrash in *Dev. (Deut.) Rab.* 9.5: 'And when the cloud lifted Moses went to Joshua and said, "What did the Word tell you?" Joshua said to him, "When the Word was revealed to you, did I ask you what it said to you?" Then Moses cried out and said: "To die a hundred deaths and not envy once".'

We now turn back to *Tanhuma Behukotai* 5. The homilist creates symmetry between the first and last parts of the midrash, between the story of the daughter going out to meet Jephthah as punishment for his vow, and the story of her 'going down' to the mountains, to the Sanhedrin, and the *halakhah* concealed from its Sages as punishment for the bloodshed wrought by the father.[15] The symmetry shows Jephthah as a cruel man who does not spare human life (in his vow he is willing to destroy one life, and in his war against the Ephraimites he kills thousands.) God is depicted as trying in vain to cause Jephthah to change his nature and perception, first by having his only daughter come out to meet him and ultimately by the failure of her plea to the Sanhedrin. The symmetry, then, is the means the homilist uses to create a hierarchy among factors, deeds and outcomes to show Jephthah's sins growing ever greater, as consequently do his punishments and the difficulty of freeing himself from them. Gradually Jephthah's character flaws are revealed until it becomes absolutely clear why this man—a combination of a closed mind, ignorance, pride, lust for power and lust for blood—fails to extricate himself from the self-imposed tragedy despite the lifelines flung out to him.

The story of the *halakhah* taken away from the Sages of the Sanhedrin ends with the verbal expression 'he went up and slaughtered her', stressing Jephthah's sole responsibility for the horrible act. It is as if the homilist is trying once again to persuade us that sacrificing the daughter was a foregone conclusion with a man of Jephthah's character, having nothing whatever to do with the will of God.

Earlier it was noted that the biblical story of Jephthah and his daughter has elements in common with Greek tragedy. It seems to me that the author of *Tanhuma* indeed structured the story according to the tragic formula, complicating the protagonist's predicament within the web he himself has created, up until the bitter end. In the beginning Jephthah is seen as failing to understand the fine points of the law, and later as not understanding the details of historical events, so unable to learn from history. His inability to learn from either history or the Torah closes his mind completely to principles and to people—and finally turns him into a mass murderer.

Jephthah's daughter is very different from her father. He is ignorant and she is learned. He is a foolish believer who overlooks the moral foundations of the Torah, whereas she understands God's will and brings him proofs from the Torah and from Israelite history. Differently from the gender centered midrash on Deborah and Barak, the present midrash is entirely theological. The midrash on Deborah and Barak takes a gender position according to which the man is more important and may become secondary to a woman

---

15. A quasi-inverted symmetry exists between Jephthah's ignorance of *halakhah*, the sin in the first story, and the Sages' ignorance of *halakhah* as punishment for Jephthah in the second story.

only if he puts himself at that level. Not so in the midrash about Jephthah's daughter, for the female figure seems to have been developed only because she appears in the Bible. The formulation of the father-daughter dialogue in the midrash has one purpose only: to remove any possibility of attributing to God a desire for human sacrifice.

Friedland-Ben Arza finds in the outcry of the Holy Spirit, 'Did I desire you to sacrifice lives to me', a female voice parallel to the female voice of the daughter and quite different from that of the Holy One who concealed the *halakhah* from the Sages of the Sanhedrin, which she sees as parallel to the male voice of Jephthah (1992: 74-81). Nonetheless, in my opinion not gender but theology lies at the ideological center of the midrash in the *Tanhuma*. The homilist could not countenance the idea that God failed to prevent Jephthah from making a human sacrifice, so put the arguments against it into the daughter's mouth not because she was a woman, but because she was the victim.

* * *

I wish to thank my friend Athalya Brenner, the initiator and one of the editors of this book, for the opportunity to honor our friend and colleague Yairah Amit with an article of mine. I hope Yairah will find value and interest in this essay about the writings of the Sages on biblical themes so dear to her—the book of Judges and the female figures in it.

Bibliography

Ben Dov, N.
    1993   '"And She Had Never Known a Man": On the Conclusion the Story of Jephthah's Daughter, the Conclusion of the Book of Judges, and on the Conclusion of the Story of Michal Daughter of Saul and on Other Conclusions', *'Alei Siah* 48: 7-18 (Hebrew).
Cohen, T.
    2000   '"Most Blessed of Women in Tents"—Indeed? Miriam, Deborah and Esther as Leaders in a Patriarchal Society', in Hannah Amit (ed.), *Follow Him: Leadership and Leaders* (Jerusalem: Ministry of Defense): 178-79 (Hebrew).
Even Shoshan, A.
    1964   *New Hebrew Dictionary* (Jerusalem: Qiryat Sefer) (Hebrew).
Friedland-Ben Arza, S.
    1994   'Openings of Revolt: the Sages' Protest through the Mouths of Biblical Women', *Dimui* 20: 31-47 (Hebrew).
Gil'ad, H.
    1989   'The Literal Story of the War of Deborah and Barak against Sisera', *BM* 34: 292-301 (Hebrew).
Ish Shalom, M.
    1902   *Seder Eliyahu Rabbah* (Vienna: Verlag der Israel.-Theol. Lehranstalt).

Rozen, Y.
    1994   'Deborah and Barak: A Controversial Pair of Judges', *Megadim* 40: 31-47
            (Hebrew).
Theodor, Y., and H. Albeck
    1903   *Midrash Bereshit Rabba* (3 vols.; Berlin: Itkkowitz).
Walfish, R.
    1991   'Textual and Cinematic Interpretation of the Story of Jephthah's
            Daughter', *Derech Efrata* 9–10: 283-92 (Hebrew).
Weinfeld, M.
    1978   'The Stars Fought from Heaven', *Eretz Israel* 14 (in honor of H.L.
            Ginzberg): 31-47 (Hebrew).

Rabbinic Sources Discussed

B. *Megilla* 14a, *Pesachim* 66b
Bereshit (Gen.) Rabbah (Theodor-Albeck) 40.4; 40.11-13; 60.3
Vayikra (Lev.) Rabbah 37.3
Devarim (Deut.) Rabbah 9.5
Midrash Tehillim (Buber) on Ps. 19; 22; 36
Yalkut Shimoni, Judges, 247.42
Tanhuma (Warsaw), *Shoftim* 17; *Behukotai* 5
Seder Eliyahu Rabbah (Ish Shalom) 10.

INDEX OF REFERENCES

INDEX OF AUTHORS